COMPUTING
AN INTRODUCTION TO PROCEDURES AND PROCEDURE-FOLLOWERS

**McGRAW-HILL
COMPUTER SCIENCE SERIES**

RICHARD W. HAMMING
Bell Telephone Laboratories

EDWARD A. FEIGENBAUM
Stanford University

BELL and NEWELL Computer structures: readings and examples
COLE Introduction to computing
DONOVAN Systems programming
GEAR Computer organization and programming
GIVONE Introduction to switching circuit theory
HAMMING Computers and society
HAMMING Introduction to applied numerical analysis
HELLERMAN Digital computer system principles
HELLERMAN and CONROY Computer system performance
KAIN Automata theory: machines and languages
KOHAVI Switching and finite automata theory
LIU Introduction to combinatorial mathematics
MADNICK and DONOVAN Operating systems
MANNA Mathematical theory of computation
NEWMAN and SPROULL Principles of interactive computer graphics
NILSSON Artificial intelligence
RALSTON Introduction to programming and computer science
ROSEN Programming systems and languages
SALTON Automatic information organization and retrieval
STONE Introduction to computer organization and data structures
STONE and SIEWIOREK Introduction to computer organization and data structures:
                     PDP-11 edition
TONGE and FELDMAN Computing: an introduction to procedures and
                     procedure-followers
TREMBLAY and MANOHAR Discrete mathematical structures with
                     applications to computer science
WATSON Timesharing system design concepts
WEGNER Programming languages, information structures, and machine
    organization

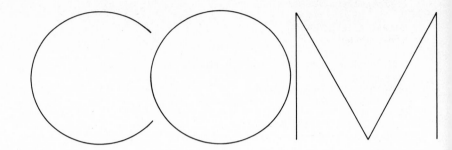

McGraw-Hill Book Company

NEW YORK ST. LOUIS SAN FRANCISCO AUCKLAND DÜSSELDORF JOHANNESBURG KUALA LUMPUR LONDON

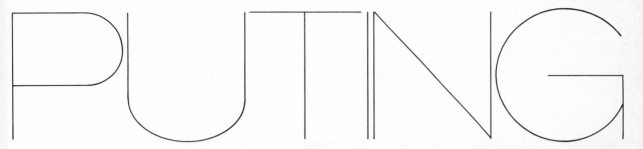

AN INTRODUCTION TO PROCEDURES AND PROCEDURE-FOLLOWERS

FRED M. TONGE
JULIAN FELDMAN
UNIVERSITY OF CALIFORNIA, IRVINE

MEXICO MONTREAL NEW DELHI PANAMA PARIS SÃO PAULO SINGAPORE SYDNEY TOKYO TORONTO

Library of Congress Cataloging in Publication Data

Tonge, Frederic M
    Computing: an introduction to procedures and
procedure-followers.

    (McGraw-Hill computer science series)
    1.   Electronic digital computers—Programming.
I.   Feldman, Julian, joint author.   II.   Title.
QA76.6.T66   001.6'42   74-18466
ISBN 0-07-064947-2

COMPUTING

AN INTRODUCTION TO PROCEDURES AND PROCEDURE-FOLLOWERS

1234567890 VHVH 798765

This book was set in Trade Gothic Light by Progressive Typographers.
The editors were Kenneth J. Bowman and Matthew Cahill;
the designer was Barbara Ellwood;
the production supervisor was Leroy A. Young.
The drawings were done by J & R Services, Inc.
Von Hoffmann Press, Inc., was printer and binder.

CONTENTS

PREFACE

Many of the ideas in this book come from our experience and the experience of our colleagues in teaching a one-quarter introduction to computing to more than 5,000 students during the past 10 years. Most of these students were freshmen with no previous experience in computing, majoring in a variety of disciplines, and having studied perhaps 2 years of high school mathematics but no college level mathematics. Many of them took the course as a prerequisite to introductory physics. Some took the course as the first step in an information and computer science degree program. Others took the course as part of a degree requirement in social sciences or biological sciences. And still others took the course "just" to learn something about computing.

This book (and the course mentioned above) is an introduction to computing—to the use of computers as an aid to problem solving. It is not intended as a formal introduction to computer science, the scientific study of phenomena associated with the computer as information processor. However, the first exposure to computing provided in our course has infected some enthusiastic students with the computer science bug. The Department of Information and Computer Science at the University of California, Irvine, began in part as a result of the demand generated by these infected students.

For us the most important aspects of computing are encompassed in a broad view of the activity called programming. In this view the computer is a procedure-follower, and its behavior is determined jointly by the procedures which it executes and the input sensations (data) which it receives. The problem-solving activity of developing those procedures, and thus determining the behavior of the computer in the face of a particular set of data, is programming.

Within this broader view, four major themes occur throughout the text. One is an emphasis on problem solving. A procedure is a method for producing the solution to a problem. Usually the human problem solver is required only to produce a solution to the given problem. He need not understand nor be able to explain in detail how he arrived at that solution. The development of an explicit procedure for solving a problem is a more difficult task. And further, a computer program is typically a general procedure, i.e., a procedure to solve a class of problems rather than a particular case.

The second theme is a stress on the role of data representation in programming and on the interrelationship of data structures and procedures. Implicit in any problem-solving procedure is information about the problem data and the nature of a solution. In choosing a data representation the programmer is also choosing how and where to represent much of that information and is determining the time and space efficiency and the logical complexity of the resulting program.

Third is a twofold emphasis on the use of procedures. Many important intellectual issues in the study of programming can be approached by way of procedures—notions of functional notation, variable scope and binding, recursion, the use of procedures in subdividing and structuring large tasks, and so forth. Related to this is the use of procedures as a means of presenting new material throughout the book. For example, the discussion of computer organization and machine language combines a model of data flow within the computer and also the development of procedures for simulating that flow. We believe that the understanding of new concepts is greatly enhanced by involving the learner in the construction of procedures for simulating and applying those concepts.

The fourth theme is a stress on the real practice of computing. For example, numbers as represented within the computer do not behave the same as abstract mathematical entities. The order in which operations are performed may completely change the computed result. Or, virtually all implementations of programming languages contain subtle restrictions that occasionally surprise even the experienced programmer, and implementations on different computers of the same "standard" language are never quite compatible. Experience repeatly shows that, even for the best programmers, the first draft of a program rarely is entirely correct. One mark of a competent programmer is the set of tools ("debugging" techniques) he uses for finding and correcting mistakes. Good programs, like good essays, require several drafts and careful polishing to become objects of pride. Even "correct" programs fail when presented with unexpected pieces of misinformation or with erroneous or meaningless data. And so forth. Throughout the text we have attempted to place abstract concepts and exercises in this context of reality.

The book has four parts and several appendixes. Part One sets a context for the study of computing, discussing the general notion of procedures and procedure-followers, the history and current use of computing, and the nature of problem solving. Part Two, the heart of the introductory material, presents specific techniques for developing procedures and their associated data representation, and for ensuring that those procedures do indeed compute. In this part a notation for describing procedures is introduced; the appendixes relate this notation to several existing programming languages. Part Three examines how computer systems work, ranging in level of detail from machine-level organization and operation, and the underlying logical components, through the workings of language translators to the hardware and software combinations making up today's large computer systems. Part Four presents some common problem situations and related problem-solving procedures, specifically, searching and sorting, some commonly used numerical methods, and simulation techniques.

In our own one-quarter introductory course, we concentrate on the material in Part Two using Part One as an introduction, making minor excursions into some of the concepts in Parts Three and Four as examples. The material in Parts Three and Four provides the instructor with some freedom in designing the course and gives the student some reference material to topics which may be raised only in passing in a one-quarter course. More of the material from Parts Three and Four could be used to make a comprehensive one-semester introduction to computing.

Chapters 11 to 16 (number representations and approximations and all of Part Three) can be used as the basis for a second one-quarter course in computing, focusing on computer organization and assembly language programming. These chapters could be supplemented by programming experience in a "real" assembly language. The use of procedures to illustrate and represent the important topics in Part Three should ease the transition into this second course. We have found that an abrupt break is often introduced unnecessarily between the first and second course when the higher-level language and programming style of the first course are dropped and the student is dumped into the abyss of assembly language programming.

In terms of the courses described in Curriculum '68 (*CACM,* March, 1968, *3,* 151–197), this book covers the topics of course B1, Introduction to Computing, in Parts One and Two, most of the material of course B2, Computers and Programming, in Part Three, and important elements of course I1, Data Structures, in Chapters 8 and 17.

We believe that a first course in computing should be a laboratory course. Perhaps even more than in most science courses, the laboratory experience provides the student with an exposure to the phenomena which he or she is trying to understand. No amount of the most poetic description available can replace the student's first experience with the literal nature of programming systems, nor his first thrill when a complicated program "works." Gradually the student develops the attention to detail and skill in debugging necessary to master the degree of precision required by programming systems.

We start our laboratory activity at the beginning of the quarter. The student explores the local (interactive) programming system with a "10-finger" exercise designed to expose him to the rudiments of the language he will be using. After this experience, he proceeds to a more formal introduction to the programming system along with an introduction to the notation and language concepts in Chapter 5.

The example procedures in this book are written in TL—a notation or publication language closely related to such programming languages as BASIC, FORTRAN, PL/1, and ALGOL. We have chosen to use this notation to free ourselves, teachers, and students from limitations in most versions of most popular programming languages. Many of these limitations derived initially from implementation problems and have been retained to provide compatibility. Because it is a descriptive notation for publication use, TL suffers less from such constraints than most languages. It is sufficiently close in all important concepts to most algebraic programming languages so that learning to use it is far simpler than learning a new programming language. This situation is clearly demonstrated in the appendixes, which provide transliterations of the example procedures in Chapters 5, 6, and 7 into ALGOL, APL, BASIC, FORTRAN, and PL/1. These transliterations serve as a basis from which the student can learn to move back and forth freely between the TL notation and his local programming language.

ACKNOWLEDGMENTS   To the many, many colleagues, both teachers and students, from whom we have learned in writing this book. Without slighting others, especially to Alfred Bork, Robert Gordon, Marsha Hopwood, Greg Hopwood, David Feign, and Don Loomis.

To the many patient friends who have somehow unscrambled our scribbled madness into unsuspected order on the printed page. Most particularly to Christine Turbitt, Virginia Brakeley, Barbara Ingerfill, Marion Kaufman, and Jeannie Waddell.

To those in the administration of the University of California, Irvine, who have consistently supported the efforts of ourselves and others to make computing a worthwhile part of the educational experience. Among these, and with a very special intellectual debt, to the late Ralph Waldo Gerard.

To the Carnegie Corporation of New York, whose generous support of developments in computer-assisted instruction in the social sciences nourished many of the early activities from which work grew.

And finally, to Mary Jane and Rita, to whom this work is dedicated.

FRED M. TONGE
JULIAN FELDMAN

COMPUTING
AN INTRODUCTION TO PROCEDURES AND PROCEDURE-FOLLOWERS

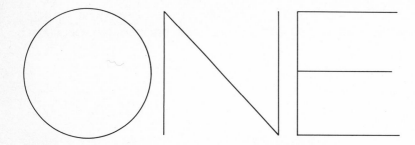

INTRODUCTION

Since a primary aim of this book is to help the reader learn how to use computers in problem solving, we might begin by teaching the relevant techniques directly. Indeed, much of this book is devoted to presenting such direct knowledge.

But there is another way of presenting a subject, the less direct method of discussing it by presenting what it is not, of indicating its form by the space it leaves in that which surrounds it. This approach is more characteristic of Eastern than of Western cultures. As R. G. H. Siu says in *The Tao of Science,* "The scientific West adopts the positive method and the Taoist East the negative. In the positive method the item under question is intentionally pointed out and described. In the negative method, it is specifically not discussed. By not dissecting the ineffable *x* in question but merely restricting discourse to objects that it is not, the features of the *x* are revealed in our dim consciousness." This negative method is particularly appropriate here because the form of our subject is not completely defined. We do not know the complete solution to the problem of how to use computers in problem solving.

The three chapters of Part One that follow are something of a mixture of these two approaches. The programming of computers is not discussed directly, but the situation surrounding programming is considered. Thus Part One should convey, in a manner different from direct description, just what programming must be. In Chap. 1, the general characteristics of procedures and procedure-followers are discussed, for a computer program is one kind of procedure and a computer is one kind of procedure-follower. In Chap. 2, some aspects of the impact of computers on our society are examined. Chapter 3 considers the specific role of computers in problem solving. Thus we begin by surrounding the question of how to program, yet we do not touch it.

1

PROCEDURES AND PROCEDURE-FOLLOWERS

**WHAT IS
A COMPUTER?**

Questions such as "What is a man" or "What is a computer" can be answered at many levels. A man is a member of a particular species of mammal. A man is an elaborate mechanism of muscles, bones, nerves, etc. A man is an upright animal with a soul. A man is a device for transforming free oxygen in the atmosphere into carbon dioxide. And so forth. Each of these descriptions is both accurate and incomplete.

Similarly, a computer is a collection of wires, transistors, resistors, etc. Or, at a more aggregate level, a computer is made up of a memory for storing data, an arithmetic unit for executing computations, and input-output devices such as electric typewriters. A computer is a device for computing and printing paychecks, for verifying the credit of purchasers, and for keeping track of available seats on airplanes. A computer is the ultimate in automation: the monster who at best will replace the honest workingman and possibly may amplify some human error of judgment and plunge the world into conflict.

Each of these statements has some truth to it, some reflection of reality from a certain perspective. Some look to the structure of an object, others to its function. Some look to detail, others take a more global view. In describing the working of computers, we shall adopt each of these viewpoints at various times since each is useful in its own way. To begin with, however, and as an underlying theme for the book, computers will be viewed as one of a class of devices with which you are quite familiar—procedure-followers.

The gestalt suggested by this point of view has been a rich and rewarding one in the study of computers and computing.

**THE NATURE
OF PROCEDURES**

A *procedure* is a set of instructions to a procedure-follower describing how to do some task. We are all accustomed to *following procedures* for carrying out certain tasks. The recipe from a child's cookbook, given as the first example in Fig. 1-1 is such a procedure. We expect 10-year-old children, with some help from their mothers, to be able to follow such procedures.

Heat oven to 350 degrees.
Grease and flour 13-inch oblong pan.

Sift together into mixing bowl: 1¾ cups sifted flour
                                 1⅓ cups sugar
                                 1 teaspoon soda
                                 1 teaspoon salt
                                 6 tablespoons cocoa

                        Add: ½ cup soft shortening
                              2 cups buttermilk
                              1 teaspoon vanilla

Beat vigorously for 2 minutes (300 strokes). You can use an electric beater if you scrape the sides down often. (Use medium speed.)

                        Add: 2 eggs.
                        Beat 2 more minutes.

Scrape batter together and be sure it is all blended.
Pour into prepared pan.
Bake 40 to 45 minutes.
Cool on rack.
Ice, in or out of pan, with your favorite icing.

DIRECTIONS FOR GETTING TO JIM'S HOUSE

Drive south on Coast Highway through Corona del Mar to Poppy Street (a signal). Turn left on Poppy and drive one block to Second. Turn right on Second. It's the second house on the right.

HOW TO KEEP YOUR OVEN CLEAN

Use only clear water and a cloth or sponge to wipe away any spillovers. Never use a scraper or any abrasive material on the oven lining, as you might scratch and damage the special finish. In positioning, removing, and/or replacing linings, be careful not to scratch the specially treated surfaces.

FIGURE 1-1
Examples of procedures.

We are also accustomed to *stating procedures* for others (or ourselves, at a later time) to follow. The second example in Fig. 1-1 could well be our answer to the question, "How do I get to your house tonight, Jim?"

In this chapter we examine the properties of procedures and the kinds of assumptions often made in stating and in following them. The study of procedures can be interesting because the world is full of procedure-followers: people, white mice, dogs, birds, and even some types of machinery—in particular, computers. All of these procedure-followers can execute a set of instructions leading to the accomplishment of a task. These different procedure-followers, and the procedures that they follow, have many elements in common. It is these common elements, independent of form of presentation, which we examine.

PROCEDURES AND
PROCEDURE-FOLLOWERS

3

FIGURE 1-2
Directions rewritten with step labels.

1 Drive south on Coast Highway through Corona del Mar to Poppy Street.
2 Turn left on Poppy.
3 Drive one block to Second.
4 Turn right on Second.
5 Stop at the second house on the right.

A procedure is composed of a *sequence* of *steps*. Each step specifies an *action* to be taken by the procedure-follower. The sequence specifies the *order* in which the actions are to be taken.

Often the order of execution of the steps of a procedure is indicated by the order in which the steps are written or spoken. Sometimes the order can be made clearer by attaching to each step a name or *label*. If these labels are numbers, then their numerical order can indicate the sequence in which steps are to be carried out. For example, the directions from the second example of Fig. 1-1 are rewritten in Fig. 1-2 with numbers as step labels.

Like all names, these labels are also a compact way of referring to the things they name (here, steps in a procedure). With step labels, we can speak of "step 2" rather than "the part where you sift all the ingredients together in the mixing bowl."

We can distinguish two types of actions in our example procedures: *operations* (as, "Drive south on Coast Highway through Corona del Mar") and *tests* (as "to Poppy Street," or said another way, "until you reach Poppy Street"). An *operation* is an action that changes the state of the world. A *test* is an action that checks to see what is the state of the world. Very often in stating procedures we intermix and combine operations and tests.

If a procedure is composed only of operations without any tests, then the procedure-writer must know in advance exactly how many times an operation must be executed to attain the desired result. In step 1 of Fig. 1-2 the procedure-follower is instructed to "Drive south on Coast Highway . . . to Poppy Street." The operation of "driving south" is continued (repeated one block at a time) until Poppy Street is reached. If the test "to Poppy Street" were not used, the procedure would have to contain exactly the number of blocks that the procedure-follower would have to drive. Stating this procedure without the test requires that the procedure-writer know the layout of Corona del Mar and also know exactly from where the procedure-follower is starting. The use of a test allows a more general and less rigid (but still precise) procedure.

Note that the test determines the order in which the steps of the procedure are executed. If the test is not satisfied, that is, the cross street is not Poppy, the operation part of step 1, "drive south," is repeated. If the test is satisfied, then step 2 is executed.

DATA In carrying out the directions on how to get to Jim's house, the procedure-follower must examine each cross street to see if it is

Poppy Street. (The first step of the procedure could be written as "drive south on Coast Highway through Corona del Mar until the cross street is Poppy Street.")

The names of the cross streets and "Poppy Street" are the data on which the procedure operates. We can distinguish *constants* such as "Poppy Street" and *variables* such as "cross street." Constants are specified in the statement of the procedure and do not change as the procedure is being carried out. They remain constant. Variables have *values,* such as "Marigold Street" or "Narcissus Street," which do change as the procedure-follower proceeds.

Directions to someone's house are procedures which operate on street names and similar information. Payroll programs are procedures which operate on hours worked, pay rates, and tax schedules. The *data* are the information used by the procedure. They are the "states of the world" referred to earlier.

CREATING NEW ACTIONS

In a mathematics course, we might state procedures including such steps as "Take the square root of . . . ." If the student did not know how to take square roots, we could teach him any of several procedures for that purpose (such as looking them up in a table or repeated approximation). We could then proceed to use the term *square root* without repeating the details of the square-root procedure each time. (This assumes, of course, that the new procedure can be expressed using a set of actions already known to the procedure-follower.)

This example illustrates how our ability to create such procedures enables us to add to our repertoire of actions. By naming a frequently used procedure, we simplify the task of writing other procedures. We incorporate previously written procedures into the procedure we are currently preparing by using them as actions. In programming, these previously written, frequently used procedures are called *functions, subroutines,* or simply *procedures.*

PROCEDURAL LANGUAGES

In order for a procedure-follower to comprehend and follow them, procedures must be expressed in a language known both to the procedure-writer and to the procedure-follower. This language includes a *vocabulary* (words for labels, actions, and data), a *grammar* (rules for putting together words to form legal steps and legal procedures), and *sequencing rules* (rules for determining the order in which the steps are executed). For most adult American procedure-followers, this language includes English as well as writing from left to right on the page and sequentially from top to bottom.

You may have noticed that our examples are primarily of written rather than verbal procedures. Of course, many procedures are spoken rather than written, and most adult American procedure-followers deal quite well with an oral procedure language. But since most procedures for computers presently are expressed in a linear, written form, we shall use that mode in our presentation.

SYMBOLS AND SYMBOL MANIPULATIONS

In following directions as in our example, the procedure-follower does more than just manipulate physical objects such as the car or motorbike he is driving. He also manipulates information—symbols representing physical objects. In checking for the right place to turn, he does not compare the actual cross street—paving, curbs, and all—with the actual Poppy Street. Rather, he compares the symbols on a street sign with symbols for Poppy Street written on a note or stored away in his memory.

Many of the procedures we follow in our daily activities are symbol-manipulating procedures. The payroll clerk deals mostly with dollar figures not dollar bills. The launch control officer monitors information giving the status of rocket components not the components themselves. And computers which assist with these and a multitude of other tasks deal *only* with information representing physical reality. Even the process control computer controlling a steel mill takes as data the information from metering devices not from the steel itself.

Notice that the procedures themselves are expressed in symbols. One major symbol-manipulation task for the procedure-follower is to take in and process procedures so that he can carry out the actions they prescribe.

COMPONENTS OF PROCEDURE-FOLLOWERS

In this discussion of procedures, we have been making certain assumptions about procedure-followers. If procedures like those in the preceding examples are to work (to be "followable"), the procedure-follower itself must have certain properties.

The procedure-follower must have devices for communicating with the world, such as eyes, ears, card readers, printers, or photosensitive cells. In human beings, we call these sensory organs; in computers, *input-output (I/O) devices.*

The procedure-follower must have some internal storage within which data may be kept. There the input data is recorded, intermediate results are developed, and answers stored. In some procedure-followers, this internal storage may also hold some or all of the procedures to be executed; for example, computer procedures are stored within the machine in this manner. In human beings, this internal storage is called *memory.* This storage is also called memory in computers, but that should not suggest that either the physical mechanism of storage or its capabilities are identical for human beings and computers.

There must be a set of actions that the procedure-follower can carry out. These actions are referred to in the procedure language. In computers, this set of actions is often called the *instruction set* or *operation set,* and the electronic circuitry that executes these actions is called the *arithmetic and logical unit.*

Finally, the procedure-follower must have a means of determining the sequence in which the steps of a procedure are to be interpreted. In computers, the electronic unit performing this function is called the *control unit.*

THE NEED TO SAY WHAT YOU MEAN

One important characteristic of a procedural language, and of a procedure-follower's ability to comprehend, is the *precision* required in stating procedures. In preparing procedures in non-technical areas for adult human procedure-followers, we generally can be quite imprecise, loose, and suggestive. We can use pronouns whose referents are vague. We expect that any instructions we give will be checked for general reasonableness. We expect that most gaps in detail will be filled in "in the usual manner."

With children, we often must be more precise, depending on their age and their mood. ("Put your dirty clothes in the washer!" "All of them?" "Yes, all of them." "Even my shoes?") Literal-minded procedure-followers can be quite vexing.

One of the annoying attributes of computers as procedure-followers is that their procedures must be stated in a very exact and precise manner. The computer will do exactly what you tell it to do, no more, no less. Obviously, this is the way that we would want computer designers to design computers. It is better that computers do exactly what their instructions dictate, every time, rather than something less regular and predictable. However, this also means that the procedure-writer must figure out exactly what is to be done for all possible types of data and exactly how it is to be expressed in the computer's language.

While the computer will do only what it is told to do, that does not close the door (conceptually) to having a literal-minded procedure-follower deal with imprecise procedures in some reasonable (and possibly surprising) manner.

Suppose we wrote the cocoa fudge cake recipe with the first step at the bottom of the page, the second step just above that, and so on up the page. Now, if we told a 10-year-old child to read the recipe from bottom to top and follow it, we would most likely end up with an edible cake.

Note that there are two procedures involved in this example: one for baking a cake (the recipe), and one for reading from the bottom of the page to the top. The "read from the bottom" procedure replaces one which we assumed the child already had for reading from the top.

The interesting point is that, in some cases and for some procedure-followers, we can state a *procedure whose data are other procedures*. The data on which the "read from the bottom" procedure operates are the steps of the procedure for baking a cake. Another example of a procedure operating on another procedure would be a procedure for copying the recipe. Loosely speaking, the requirements for this to occur are that: (1) the procedure language include means for "talking about" procedures; (2) the procedure be available like other data, that is, in explicit form in the procedure-follower's memory; and (3) the procedure-follower include among its instruction set appropriate actions for carrying out procedures whose data are other procedures.

The general purpose digital computer is a procedure-follower that meets these requirements in that procedures are stored in memory with and in the same general form as data. Therefore, again conceptually, one could conceive of a procedure for instructing the computer how to interpret imprecise procedures. The catch is that one must first be able to state exactly and precisely what is to be done with imprecise procedures. This is an interesting unsolved problem that is the focus of much current research in that part of computer science called *artificial intelligence* (see Chap. 3).

EXERCISES

1 Write out in detail a procedure for some everyday task, such as making a peanut butter sandwich or paying for your lunch in the cafeteria. Follow the procedure yourself to check it out. Notice what assumptions you have made in writing the procedure. Now have another person carry out the written procedure. What other assumptions and errors in the procedure now come to light? What assumptions did the other person make in following the procedure?

2 Learn how to perform some simple action that you cannot now do, for example, finding the square root of a number, or threading a sewing machine, or shifting a 10-speed bicycle. While learning, notice how the new procedure is presented, and what procedure you are following in learning. Write out the new procedure that you have learned. Also write out as best you can the procedure you followed in acquiring a new procedure.

3 Several examples of common procedures are given in the chapter, such as recipes or directions for getting from one place to another. Find another common instance of a procedure (for example, the directions in the front on the Post Office ZIP code directory on how to find a ZIP code). Analyze that procedure in terms of the components of procedures discussed in this chapter.

4 We can view a work of music as a procedure to be followed by the performer, in which case musical notation is a procedural language. Analyze musical notation in terms of the characteristics of procedural languages given in this chapter.

5 Obtain a "programmed instruction" textbook. What is the procedure that the text uses for teaching? What are the characteristics of the procedural language in which that procedure is expressed?

REFERENCES

Gear, C. W.: *Introduction to Computer Science,* Science Research Associates, Chicago, 1973.

H.E.L.P. Home Emergency Ladies' Pal, Xyzyx, Canoga Park, Calif., 1972, 154 p.

Moursund, David G.: *How Computers Do It,* Wadsworth, Belmont, Calif., 1969, 124 p.

Siu, Ralph G. H.: *Tao of Science: An Essay on Western Knowledge and Eastern Wisdom,* MIT Press, Cambridge, 1958.

Wilde, Daniel U.: *An Introduction to Computing: Problem Solving, Algorithms, and Data Structure,* Prentice-Hall, Englewood Cliffs, N.J., 1973, 418 p.

COMPUTERS IN CONTEXT

In 1948 the high-speed, general purpose, electronic digital computer did not exist. Today that device affects the life of every citizen. So completely has the computer become a part of the "standard operating procedure" of business, government, and science that the average citizen accepts the computer without a second thought. He accepts the computer, respects it, possibly fears it, but rarely understands it. Yet the very pervasiveness of these information processing machines calls their existence and value into question. Citizens must have sufficient understanding of the power and potential of computers to participate intelligently in current economic and political decisions as to how computers shall be used.

In this chapter we examine the ways in which computers enter into our lives today, the characteristics of the computer as procedure-follower which determine its usefulness, and the developments in information processing technology that have led to the present uses of computers.

Perhaps the most visible uses of computers in everyday life are in business. Each of us handles computer-produced bills, checks, statements of account, etc. Much of the vast stream of accounting paperwork produced in the daily transaction of business is now produced and processed by computer. For some firms, because their basic product is symbols, the computer has a deeper impact, possibly leading to a revised way of doing business. As an example, the market for over-the-counter trading in securities has been greatly changed by the introduction of computers. And even for some industries with more tangible output, pressures such as product perishability have made quick-reacting computer-based control systems a competitive necessity. Airline reservation systems are an example.

The financial sector of business has become heavily dependent on the computer. Credit information is now kept routinely in computer-maintained data banks. Transfers of funds and of stocks are accounted for by computer. Computerized corporate

CURRENT USES OF COMPUTERS

planning models are used to help predict possible futures of the firm and the economy as a basis for investment decisions. Banks use data processing systems for internal operations, and often have expanded into the business of providing data processing service for their customers. Indeed, it has been said that given the choice of losing their vaults or their data center, most banks today would give up the vaults. The flow of money and credit capital in our economy is now inexorably tied to the use of computers.

The uses of computers in government are no less pervasive. There are many accounting-like applications, both within agencies and between agencies and their constituents. Social security files are maintained by computer as are those of the Internal Revenue Service. Indeed, the IRS uses computerized procedures to screen tax returns for more detailed checking by human agents.

A different aspect of the use of computers can be found in the more technologically based branches of government, such as the Department of Defense and the National Aeronautics and Space Agency. Each space shot, for example, requires extensive engineering and scientific computations in the many months of design and test activities that precede the shot, and during the mission, computers are used to monitor and control flight activities. The corporate planning models of business are analogous to the computer-based war games played as part of the military planning process. But even in such organizations as the Department of Defense, probably the largest information processing activities are not the "far out" technological ones, but rather accounting, materiel control, personnel records, and other such mundane activities.

Local and state governments also use information processing systems, often with the financial and moral support of federal agencies. Driver information systems are being developed which can be interrogated in a matter of seconds by an on-duty highway patrol officer, with the intention that city and state systems be linked into a national one. Similarly, a national pilot program in municipal information systems, funded in part by federal agencies, is under way in several cities. Systems for delivery of services, for public safety, and for administering criminal justice are all being developed and tested. More and more, data about the world we live in are being entered into computer-accessible data bases and those data bases are being tied together into larger systems. Since public activities tend to lack means of measuring the value of a particular investment, these systems are sometimes undertaken more on the basis of faith and impassioned pleas than on the basis of an assessment of their costs and benefits.

In education, computers are used for many standard accounting applications, for student and facilities scheduling, and to some extent (though much less than publicity to date might indicate) as a teaching device interacting with students in a question and answer mode or as a simulated laboratory. Future growth in the use of computers in teaching will depend on the comparative costs of alternative modes of education, the ability to measure the effectiveness of different forms of education, and social decisions as to appropriate goals, form, extent, and levels of support for education.

In science and engineering, uses of computers are limited only by the imagination of the investigator and the availability of the computer. Any task of computation, of trying out possibilities in a regular and exhaustive manner, of modeling a real or proposed physical system is a candidate for computer application. Engineers use computers to study the details of a bridge design or a highway cut-and-fill project. Physical chemists use computers to simulate the behavior of the electrons of a molecule participating in a thermal reaction. Archeologists use the computer to scan descriptions of blocks lying scattered in Egyptian ruins and produce lists of those blocks which might have been adjacent in an ancient temple. Psychologists use computer programs as models for the thinking processes of people. Across the entire range of scientific activity, we find the computer widely used as an investigative tool. And in the arts and humanities also, computers are being employed. Experimental artists use computers to produce films; architects use computers in the design process; and modern poets use computers to help produce verse.

Finally, beyond those work activities, there are many ways in which the computer enters into the personal lives of each of us. You can purchase computer-produced diets, horoscopes, and even lists of possible spouses, jobs, or houses. The computer is the subject of humor, including many cartoons and jokes. At the same time, it is a subject of concern. Most of us are familiar with the joke whose punch line is the computer's response to the question "Is there a God?", the answer being "There is now!" How many science fiction stories and films have a computer, in malice or for our own good, taking over control of the world from people? And such uses of the computer as an impersonal force "out there" are not confined to fiction. How often have you been told that some foul-up or mistreatment was due to "computer error"? The silent computer behind the scenes has become our society's scapegoat, the commonly evoked excuse for human failure or the indifference of bureaucracy.

The computer has pervaded our current society in many ways, some obvious, some subtle. Still, it is a device of man's making to be used by man. And, on a global scale, each of us can influence how man uses it. But to exert that influence can require that each of us determine for himself when in our daily activities the exercise of human judgment, intuition, and feeling is essential, and then actively resist the attempts of technologists and bureaucrats to prematurely reduce those activities to computerized decision making.

We have introduced a simple conceptual model of the computer as a procedure-follower, with a central processing unit, memory, and input-output devices. While this simple model is sufficient for most of the purposes of this book, it is not adequate for understanding the role of computers in modern life. How could this simple device carry out the applications discussed in the previous section? It could not by itself. In fact, most computers are only one component of larger information processing and transfer systems. And while the computer may be the exciting component (partly because it is the programmable component) of these systems, characteristics of the systems as a whole determine what can be accomplished. We now examine two additional aspects of such systems: data files and communications networks.

Most large computer systems include many millions of characters of mass storage for data files. The physical media for such storage are typically magnetic tapes or magnetic disks. While the exact storage characteristics of magnetic tapes and disks vary with different manufacturers and models, a tape or disk can store approximately 25–50 million characters. Since even one tape or disk provides far more information than is directly available in the computer's memory, retrieving information from the mass storage medium depends on mechanical motion of the tape or disk and so is considerably slower than the purely electronic speed of the computer itself.

Computers may have many such mass storage devices attached to them. To get a feeling for the magnitude of data requirements in large information storage systems, consider that a book contains on the average 1–1.5 million characters. To store the books of a relatively small, say, 10,000 volume library would require 200–500 magnetic tapes for the contents alone, plus requirements for indexing information to keep track of where in the tapes each book is stored. For a technical collection, indexing requirements would be quite high. Can you visualize how browsing might be accomplished in such a library? Or look at your driver's license. How many characters on it? And how many licensed drivers in your state? Multiply those two numbers, add some percentage for minimal indexing, and you have a first (low) estimate of the size of the data bank required for a driver's license information system. (Not all that information need be "immediately" available to the computer, but it must be ultimately accessible.) The data banks of the social security or Internal Revenue Service systems are enormous. (Of course, the visual image evoked by these examples is entirely dependent on current technology, and so is subject to the rate of growth phenomenon discussed later in this chapter. It is virtually certain that the appropriate physical visualization 5 or 10 years from now will be a small slab that fits in the palm of your hand or, at most, in a desktop box.)

Similarly, many computer systems, such as that for the highway patrol, are part of a communications network. Using such a network, information can be transferred from one computer to another, input and output devices can be located in distant places, and large data files can be accessed by several remote computers. The increase in transmission circuits suitable for data has been so rapid that their capacity is now approximately twice that for voice alone. Data transmission is becoming the major business of the communications industry.

In this book, our emphasis and examples will primarily be based on the simple model of the computer as procedure-follower presented earlier. Most important concepts about computers and programming can be introduced more clearly in that context. However, remember that most uses of computers today involve the computer acting within a larger system including mass storage data banks and a communications network.

IMPORTANT CHARACTERISTICS OF COMPUTERS

What characteristics of the computer as procedure-follower have led to their current use? While the opinion of experts may differ, most would agree on the importance of the following characteristics.

Speed

Modern computers perform millions of multiplications in a second. Such speed makes possible, for example, the calculations in real time needed for control of space shots. Indeed, even many applications without such time pressures (for example, detailed analysis of income tax returns, requiring thousands of separate steps for each return) would not be feasible if computers were significantly slower.

Reliability

Computers in the 1970s are much more reliable than those of even 10 years ago. Extremely complicated pieces of electronic gear operate without error for hours, days, or even weeks. Some applications such as a moon shot with human passengers, or monitoring a patient's condition in a hospital's intensive care ward, obviously require such reliability. But even for noncritical applications, economical use of the speed mentioned above demands that computers continue without error for many millions of operations. Even a failure rate of once every 1 billion operations would mean the computer stopping every few minutes.

Automaticity

A computer can repeat the same process over and over thousands of times without human intervention. Again, the processing of income tax returns is a case where the computer's speed would be of little avail if human intervention, at speeds measured in seconds or minutes rather than millionths of seconds, were necessary with each case.

Memory

This automaticity and the capability for its effective use derive from two aspects of the computer's memory system. One, the availability of large data files accessible by the computer, was discussed earlier. The other is that the computer is a stored program device; its program is kept in memory along with data and so is immediately available for repeated interpretation and execution.

Conditional control

The power of the stored program to automatically handle many cases depends in part on conditional control of the program sequence—the ability to select different parts of the stored program as appropriate to different data cases. This is the test capability of the procedure-follower discussed in Chap. 1. Thus, the program can pay overtime, issue no bill if your charge balance is zero, or signal an alarm if the patient's oxygen consumption rate is too high.

Nonnumerical processing

Many early applications of computers were numerical, e.g., ballistics calculations, and such applications had a strong influence on the design of computers. But even so, today's general purpose digital computer can handle nonnumerical as well as numerical data. Its set of operations includes comparing characters for equality and alphabetic order as well as addition or multiplication. Many of the applications discussed earlier, from interrogating files of driver's licenses to computer dating, involve little if any numerical computing.

Preserving intellectual skills

Perhaps most important in the long run, the computer serves as a means to record and transmit intellectual skills. Programs written by experts, or data files structured by them, can be used for many years by others who do not have the knowledge or skill to carry out the original task. Programs are in many ways more varied and more variable than machinery, and so provide a richer form in which the craftsman and technician can pass on his achievements.

RATE OF GROWTH

The computer has come "from nowhere" to its present position of influence in a relatively short time. The characteristics described above suggest some reasons why such a growth has occurred. Just how great is this growth?

In 1948, total computer industry sales were on the order of $0. In 1968, total computer industry sales were on the order of $6½ billion. In 1970, there were approximately 70,000 computers in use in the United States. How do we comprehend such growth?

Richard W. Hamming suggests that we look at the "order of magnitude" growth of such phenomena. By an order of magnitude increase we mean an increase by a factor of 10. Ten times greater is one order of magnitude; one hundred times greater is two orders of magnitude; one thousand times greater is three. If we were to represent such growth on a graph with time (e.g., years) measured in equal units (years equally distant) and sales, number of computers, or whatever measured in order of magnitude units (the distance from 1 to 10 the same as from 10 to 100), then order of magnitude growth would appear as a straight line. Figure 2-1 depicts order of magnitude growth.

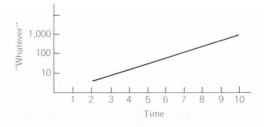

FIGURE 2-1
Order of magnitude (logarithmic) scale.

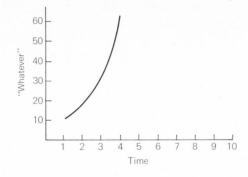

FIGURE 2-2
Equally spaced (linear) scale.

We use this order of magnitude scale on the "whatever" axis to permit us to graph data which would not fit conveniently on equally spaced scales. A portion of Fig. 2-1 is graphed on an equally spaced scale in Fig. 2-2. Note that in the same amount of space only a small portion of the data represented in Fig. 2-1 can be shown.

The surprising fact is that data on the growth of most aspects of computer technology looks roughly like the first graph — be it speed, memory size, transmission capacity, number of operations per second, or amount of memory per dollar.

What does an order of magnitude increase mean? What impact could it have on society? Perhaps we can understand that impact by looking at a more familiar analogous situation. Consider the effect of an order of magnitude increase in transportation speed. Surely the technology of the automobile has resulted in a fundamental change in our civilization, even in many ways not directly related to transportation. Compared to walking, the automobile is *one* order of magnitude increase in speed (5–50 miles per hour). The jet plane represents another order of magnitude increase. Indeed, from walking to the space vehicle, the increase in speed is approximately four orders of magnitude. The speed of multiplication by computer has increased by the same four to five orders of magnitude, *since 1948.* Indeed, compared to hand computations, present computer speeds represent an increase of *seven* orders of magnitude. If our analogy with transportation has any validity at all, much greater and wider-ranging effects of the computer are to come.

Or consider another comparison with transportation. If the *cost* of transportation decreased by four orders of magnitude, cars would cost $0.25 to $0.50. At those prices, cars would be discarded after use like paper towels, and many more people would travel by jet to foreign countries for the weekend. The cost of computation, measured in cost per multiplication, has decreased by three to four orders of magnitude over the past 20 years. At least from this perspective, computation is incredibly cheap.

Although what has occurred is most impressive, few forecasters would predict that this rate of growth will continue forever. Raw computing is only a small part of any total information system. Perhaps one reason that changes in computing have not been reflected by changes in society of the same order of magnitude is that other parts of information systems have not yet improved as sharply. (Much of the effect of automobiles could come only as the highway systems were improved.)

HISTORICAL INFLUENCES

This growth phenomenon in computing is the current manifestation of developments going back to the beginnings of recorded history. The present state of computing derives from the confluence of many diverse ideas and technologies.

Man has been calculating for many thousands of years. Measuring, holding one length up against another, is a form of analog calculation. Counting, with fingers or a pile of pebbles, is an ancestor of digital calculations. Early civilizations developed logic and notations for these concepts and in some civilizations devices for calculating appeared, such as the abacus with beads strung on wires to keep track of the counting. While the development of the first mechanical calculators is commonly credited to Leibnitz and Pascal (1650–1700), the pegged-wheel mechanism which underlay their machines had appeared several centuries earlier. However, a feasible technology for producing such mechanical devices in quantity was not available for another 200 years.

Two extensions of the mechanical calculator truly magnificent in conception were made by an Englishman, Charles Babbage (1792–1871). Babbage's difference engine calculated the squares of numbers by adding differences. (The difference between successive squares 1,4,9,16,25,36, . . . is 3,5,7,9,11, . . . ; and the difference between those terms is 2,2,2,2,2, ... Thus, the series of successive squares can be calculated by adding two the proper number of times to the proper subtotal.) Babbage abandoned the development of the difference engine to work on a more powerful calculator called the analytic engine, which was never completed. His conceptions far outstripped the metalworking technology of his day and could not be fabricated with sufficient precision to realize the devices. Two other aspects of his developments are worth noting. For controlling his machines, Babbage adopted the punched cards used by Jacquard a half-century before to control the weaving pattern of looms. This was a forerunner of the widespread use of punched cards in computing. And Babbage's support by the British government for the development of his two machines (projects that were never completed) foreshadows similar governmental support in most countries of the development of the electronic digital computer.

Mechanical punched card equipment for digital calculating was first developed by a statistician, Herman Hollerith, for use in processing the results of the 1890 United States census. Related but different punched cards developed by James Powers were used in the 1910 census. Hollerith's inventions provided the basis for the equipment marketed by International Business Machines; and Power's, the basis for Remington Rand (now Sperry Rand Univac). In the first half of the twentieth century there was widespread adoption of punched card equipment (punches, sorters, calculators, tabulators) for business and governmental accounting.

As in so many other technological areas, World War II was an incentive to apply new developments in science and technology to create useful computing devices. An automatic sequence-controlled calculator was developed under the leadership of Prof. Howard Aiken of Harvard University. The machine, called the Mark I, was completed in 1944. A group at the Moore School of Electrical Engineering of the University of Pennsylvania, working with government scientists to produce an electronic device for making ballistics calculations, completed another calculator, the ENIAC, in 1945. This group included J. Presper Eckert and John Mauchly of the Moore School, Herman Goldstine of the U.S. Army, and John von Neumann of the Institute for Advanced Study. Eckert and Mauchly later led the development of the first commercial computer, the UNIVAC.

The early computers were not stored programmed devices; their calculations were controlled by preset instructions wired into a patchboard, punched into a paper tape, or some similar device. The first stored program computers were EDSAC, built in Cambridge, and later the EDVAC, built by the Moore School group. At this point the mushrooming growth described in the previous section began.

We have described developments leading up to today's computer in terms of computing devices. Such a focus overlooks other factors which are also major contributors to present computer technology. For example, an Irish clergyman, George Boole, developed a system for describing "the laws of thought" in terms of variables having two values—true or false, zero or one, on or off. His Boolean algebra is a basic concept in the design and use of computers. Another contribution was the development of double-entry bookkeeping in the Italian city states, which led to a business community with a ready market for information processing devices. The precision machine tool technology that followed from the industrial revolution was necessary for fabricating these devices, and the electronic technology which originally focused on the development of radar was borrowed in great quantity.

In addition to Boole, other mathematicians have contributed to the conceptual framework of computer technology. An early paper by Burks, Goldstine, and von Neumann on the design of digital computers spelled out solutions still in use to many of the issues of computer design. And an English mathematician, Alan Turing, an early contributor to design and programming of computers, initiated a tradition of abstract formal analysis of computation through the use of mathematical models which has spawned much of the activity of computer science.

Such a discussion of important developments could go on for many pages and be in great danger of stressing much in the recent past that will prove tangential in the long run, while ignoring real determining issues. For so much has happened so recently that no true perspective is yet possible. And in one extremely important area, that of the computer systems programs to support the programmer in preparing his application procedures, little agreement as to "great advances" exists. Until that part of computing's first 20 years of history can be written, our retrospective view must be faulty.

THE FUTURE Predicting the future of computing in any detail requires precise prediction of a rapidly changing technology. While we forego that pleasure for the present, you may wish to extrapolate the data just presented in this chapter for your own amusement and benefit.

Among the many predictions of the future of computing, we are taken with that presented by James Martin and Adrian Norman in their book *The Computerized Society.* The following quotation gives a flavor for their view of this future. The reader who wishes to explore these notions in more depth will find much interesting material in the Martin and Norman book and in Frederic Withington's *The Real Computer.*

In the years immediately ahead, there will be a sudden, massive spread of computer usage that will affect the lives of almost everyone. Several factors will cause this. First, there will be mass production of the machines with a very sharp drop in cost. Second, there will be many areas of standardization that will have a snowball effect as programs used in an installation spread to others. Programs can be reproduced almost as cheaply as newsprint. Third, staggeringly large computer files are being developed in which every item stored can be retrieved in a fraction of a second. Fourth, and this may be the most important factor, the machines are becoming linked to the telephone network so that computers will be able to communicate with other computers. Small devices with a screen like a television set are enabling us to "converse" with computers, and these devices will become cheap enough to allow many people to have one in their home.

Indeed, when the machines do eventually become much more capable we may someday talk not about separate computers, but rather about a vast organism interconnected by telecommunication links.

One final comment: the computer industry has come to speak of generations of computers. These generations are distinguished by the underlying electronic technology. The first generation are vacuum-tube machines with their bulk and high power usage and heat dissipation; the second generation are transistorized machines; and the third use integrated circuits. Perhaps this has been a reasonable basis for distinguishing significant differences, or perhaps merely little more than an advertising gimmick. And even if it is a reasonable way of describing the past, the fourth (now appearing in advertising), fifth, and future generations may well be based not so much on electronic technology as on some other factor such as programming technology or system organization.

1 For one day, be alert to contacts with computers in your general life, whether it be bills received in the mail, comments by salespeople, newspaper stories, or whatever. Keep a log of all such contacts.

2 How many numbers associated with computer-related systems do you have? For example, social security number, driver's license number, bank account number, telephone number, etc. Make a list of all such numbers. How many do you carry with you, say, in your wallet? How much would it be worth to you to have all systems convert to a single number? How much do you estimate such a conversion would cost?

3 There have been, and undoubtedly will continue to be, proposals for a National Data Bank, combining duplicate information in the computer-based files of a number of governing agencies. Give at least two arguments *that you really accept and support* for such a data bank. Give at least two *that you also believe in* against the concept. What information would you like your congressional representative to have the next time such a proposal comes up?

4 The text speaks of the computer as a means of preserving intellectual skills. What are some specific intellectual skills that you lack and would make use of if generally available on computers?

5 List some specific ways in which your campus library might employ computers to assist you in using the library. How much would such computer services be worth to you in out-of-pocket cost at the time of use?

6 Suppose that some amount of computing service were available fairly cheaply in every home, say using the television screen for output and using telephone or cable television lines. What are some ways in which such capability would be used in your home? In most homes?

Goldstine, Herman H.: *The Computer from Pascal to Von Neumann,* Princeton University Press, Princeton, N.J., 1972, 378 p.

Hamming, Richard W.: *Computers and Society,* McGraw-Hill, New York, 1972, 284 p.

Martin, James, and Adrian R. D. Norman: *The Computerized Society: An Appraisal of the Impact of Computers on Society over the Next Fifteen Years,* Prentice-Hall, Englewood Cliffs, N.J., 1970, 560 p.

Rosen, Saul: Electronic computers: A historical survey, *Computing Surveys,* **1:**7–36 (1969).

Rothman, Stanley, and Charles Mosmann: *Computers and Society: The Technology and Its Social Implications,* Science Research Associates, Chicago, 1972, 337 p.

Withington, Frederic G.: *The Real Computer: Its Influences, Uses, and Effects,* Addison-Wesley, Reading, Mass., 1969, 350 p.

COMPUTERS AND PROBLEM SOLVING

Computers are often referred to as "thinking machines" or "giant brains." Computers are also described as nothing more than high-speed morons, with less thinking ability than any clerk. Computers are credited with vast problem-solving ability and also are characterized as machines that can only do what they are instructed to do, no more and no less. In this chapter we examine the role of the computer in problem solving, particularly the computer as a member of a problem-solving team—you and the computer.

ARE COMPUTERS PROBLEM SOLVERS?

Our answer to the question, "Are computers problem solvers?" is "No." Computers are not problem solvers. Computers carry out solution procedures; those who devised the solution procedures are the problem solvers. Thus, the computer program which produces an analysis of a proposed bridge design including specification of particular structural members is not a problem solver. Rather, the engineers who developed the procedure for analysis of bridge design and the programmers who translated that (probably loosely worded) procedure into a working program are the problem solvers.

But, what about the teachers and colleagues who trained the engineer in analysis and design? And the parents and friends with whom he developed a sense of values? In some sense they programmed the engineer to design bridges in a certain way. Are they then the problem solvers? Is the engineer merely the instrument for executing their problem-solving procedure? Does the fact that many "programmers" were involved, often working independently of each other, change the question of whose procedure it really is?

This line of questioning leads to deep philosophical arguments which we are willing to pose but prefer not to pursue here. We leave this topic for your further discussion with the following two reservations on our opening stand. First, we may occasionally refer to the computer as a problem solver, realizing at the same time that we really are referring to the computer as a procedure-follower carrying out problem-solving procedures specified by some programmer. And second, we reserve the right to revise our stand and include computers in the company of problem solvers as the full meaning of "computers only can do what they are programmed to do" becomes more clear. The discussion of artificial intelligence in the final section of this chapter is relevant to this point.

Despite science fiction stories to the contrary, the role of the computer in problem solving thus far has been as a partner to human beings.

> In some cases, a program is developed by a person to carry out a complete solution procedure, with perhaps a final checkout and revision of the solution by a person. Examples of this kind of activity are the bridge and highway calculations mentioned earlier, oil refinery scheduling using linear programming techniques, or comprehensive payroll calculations which generate paychecks, distribute costs to department and product, prepare necessary legal records, etc. Obviously, creating and testing these complete procedures is a difficult and time-consuming task, requiring consideration of many requirements, of special cases that may arise, of efficient use of the computer, and so forth.

> In other cases, the computer is used to carry out some subpart of a problem-solving task. For example, the accountant may use a computer to make a simple interest rate calculation in order to help decide which depreciation method to recommend to a client. A theoretical physicist may use a formula manipulation routine to attempt to simplify an algebraic equation he is studying. As mentioned before, an archeologist may use computer programs to produce lists of possible matches of adjoining building blocks in a ruined temple. In these cases, the problem solver must select those parts of his procedure he considers appropriate for computer processing and then program the computer to solve the subproblem (possibly using a previously prepared program).

> The task of developing solution procedures and programming the computer to carry them out is itself problem solving—the kind of problem solving that you as a programmer will be carrying out in working with the computer. Most of the remainder of this chapter will be devoted to this aspect of problem solving.

THE ROLE OF THE COMPUTER

The process of using a computer in problem solving is straightforward and obvious. This is not to deny that the process is difficult; sometimes it is very difficult. Nor is it to deny that sometimes programmers forget and deviate from this process; they do, usually to the detriment of their problem solving. But, the basic framework for problem solving using the computer is simple and direct:

1 Define the problem.
2 Develop a solution procedure.

STEPS IN PROBLEM SOLVING USING THE COMPUTER

3 Test the procedure to verify it.

4 Carry out the procedure to produce the solution.

Simple, is it not?

Obviously, you cannot solve a problem if you are not sure what the problem is. So, first, get a clear statement of the problem. Then, develop a solution procedure for solving that problem or, rather, a procedure that is intended to solve the problem. To be sure, try out that procedure for various test cases until you are sure that it does work as claimed. And then use it.

Of course, nothing, and certainly not computer programming, goes that smoothly in real life. The preceding list in neatly numbered order gives a false sense of how programming actually occurs. Typically, there will be many false starts and loops back to earlier steps before a correct procedure is produced. For example, in the process of developing a solution procedure, you may see that you have defined the problem so that no solution, or only a very difficult and expensive one, is allowed. Perhaps you must "return to go" and, with the consent of all parties involved, redefine the problem. In testing your procedure you will almost always turn up cases where it does not work quite right, so that you must go back and revise the procedure. This oscillation between the programming and testing phases is called "debugging" in computerese, since it is a process of removing "bugs" from the program. And finally, even when you use the procedure "for real," you are likely to run into situations you did not anticipate in the test phase, so that you must revise once again your "perfectly working" program.

HOW DO COMPUTERS AFFECT THIS PROCESS?

The above steps apply to the problem-solving process necessary to develop any procedure, whether it is expressed as a computer program or not. But the fact that the procedure-follower in question is to be a computer does affect the process and the resulting procedure in several ways.

The use of the computer forces us to make the solution procedure more explicit. The "hand-waving" vagueness sufficient for communicating the sense of what we want done to a colleague, secretary, or technician is not enough for the computer. Each step in a procedure to be followed by a computer must be spelled out in precise detail.

Also, the computer allows us to use different kinds of procedures, such as those involving enumeration of large numbers of possibilities. The speed and accuracy of the computer permit approaches to problems which would not be feasible with only human procedure-followers. For example, using the computer makes possible a different approach to mass health care through large-scale prescreening of the population.

Further, the computer enables us to attempt solutions to problems that could not be approached directly before. Some of the examples cited in the previous chapter are in this category, such as control of space missions or nationwide automobile registration systems. As time passes and more engineers, scientists, and other problem solvers become aware of the potential and capabilities of the computer, more solutions for such problems will be attempted.

Finally, the fact that preparing a procedure as a computer program, which may be preserved, transported, sold, and in other ways become a commodity for multiple use, changes both the economics and the social values that enter into deciding which problems shall be solved and how.

Not all procedures that can be carried out using a computer should be. For some, it just does not make sense, either in terms of the time required to prepare the program (sometimes a very long process, as you will see) or the time required by the computer to execute the program. The fact that some activity can be done does not mean that it should be done.

We shall return to examples of this throughout the book, but let us consider one illustration here. Beware of the combinatoric growth of numbers of possibilities. Suppose, for example, you were asked to make up all the English words that could be composed out of the letters in ANDY. In fact, there are 64 possible sequences of one, two, three, or four letters (not all of which are words). Perhaps you would not bother writing a computer program to find this answer, since you could do so rather quickly with a pencil and paper anyway. Even using the computer, you would have to scan the final list to pick out those letter sequences which were legal English words. But what about making up all the English words in PALINDROME? Surely here the computer would be useful. But there are in the neighborhood of 10 million possible sequences in this case, which would require a large amount of paper just to print and, at 100 possibilities per second, would require more than one day around the clock to compute. Just because there is a big, fast computer available does not mean that all problems can now be solved by brute force.

In several of his writings on the art of computer programming, Fred Gruenberger gives a list of the characteristics that you as a programmer should look for in a problem before setting forth to solve it using the computer. At the price of some repetition of what has been said above, we repeat his list here.

1 The problem must be *useful*. Useful perhaps as a learning device, perhaps as a demonstration, but not just "for the heck of it." (This requirement seems to rest on the fact that computer time is not a free good in infinite supply, although it may appear that way to those who do not pay the bill.)
2 The problem must be *defined*. If not, postpone deciding whether to solve the problem using a computer until you find out what the problem is.
3 There must be a *solution method* known for solving the problem. The program you are going to write must be based on some method for solving the problem. If you do not know of any, then it is best to find one before starting to program.
4 There should be a *match* between the requirements of the problem and the available capabilities of the machine. These capabilities are expressed typically in terms of storage space and execution time required. Our "Find the number of different words in PALIN-

PROBLEMS FOR COMPUTER SOLUTION

DROME" example is a good case of failure to match. This characteristic suggests that the programmer should make some estimates of what will be involved in a solution before he starts programming.

5 The problem should probably require *repetition* of the same process many times. Presence of this requirement for repetition makes it likely that there will be a good match with those characteristics of the computer (mentioned in Chap. 2) which make it a powerful tool in problem solving.

6 There should be a *payoff* from using the computer to solve the problem rather than some other approach. Even if solving the problem would be useful, you should also ask whether the comparative value of using the computer exceeds that of using a hand calculator, 1,000 clerks, or whatever.

HOW TO DEVELOP A SOLUTION PROCEDURE

From the standpoint of programming, the key step in the earlier framework for problem solving is that of developing a solution procedure. So, the key section of this chapter, and indeed of the entire book, must be this one. The principal theme of this book is the development of solution procedures. And yet problem solving is an activity that we as people do not understand very well. We can only talk around the subject, make vague comments about techniques, and try in examples throughout the book to demonstrate both good problem-solving practice and good solutions.

An observation we can make is that practice seems to help, particularly thoughtful practice. When you are involved in solving a problem, take time to examine what you are doing, what has worked and what has not, and learn from that. A book by George Polya, *How To Solve It,* is an extremely valuable guide to thoughtful problem solving.

One technique for problem solving is *working backwards,* starting with the final values and deriving from them what is needed. Thus, if asked to prepare a list of students in a class ordered by average performance on tests, we could work backwards to specify the input data needed and the computations, averaging and sorting, to be performed on that data.

The reverse of that technique, *working forward,* is also useful. Thus, in trying to prove a theorem in logic we start from the givens and apply legal steps of inference, checking every so often to see if we seem to be getting any closer to the desired result. Or, in chess, we usually cannot work backwards from a mate to the present situation in search of a good move, but we can work forward from this situation to a hopefully better one. Most solution procedures using complete or selective enumeration employ working forward.

A technique particularly stressed by Polya is that of working from an *analogous problem* already solved. Knowing the formula for computing the area of a triangle and how it was derived might help you in finding the area of an irregular four-sided figure. Or, if you are a football quarterback, knowing how you scored against this team last time might help in finding a long yardage play now.

Another common technique for dealing with problems is to divide the problem up into *smaller subproblems* to be dealt with separately and later combined. Most people cannot find a good chess move by considering the entire board at one and the same time; they have to consider different attacks and threats one at a time, while simultaneously looking for interconnections and interrelations.

One final technique, often used in dealing with large projects, is *planning,* i.e., ignoring all but what are thought to be the pertinent characteristics of the problem, solving the simplified problem, and then checking the solution to see that some temporarily ignored constraint was not violated.

Of course, a problem solver rarely uses these techniques in a pure form. He combines them, using one and then another on the same problem as they seem appropriate. These general descriptions leave open for each technique a great many questions as to just how to proceed, what to do next. For example, which characteristics should be ignored in simplifying, what sub-problems should be selected out in dividing up a problem, which of the possible next steps should be taken in working forwards. Most problem solvers have a collection of rules-of-thumb, or *heuristics,* for use in these situations. Chess players usually follow up mentally on the possibility of a check, as it may lead to mate. And students of trigonometry soon learn that reducing all terms to sines and cosines is a good start in proving identities. *Heuristics* are defined as "rules or devices that, on the average, lead to reduction of search in problem solving." Since they work on the average, heuristics are not a guaranteed method of solution, but rather a good idea about how to proceed. One of the things you have done as you developed problem-solving skills in various areas has been to acquire both a collection of heuristics, some general and some very specific, and also a sense for when their use is appropriate. In developing your skill at programming, continued attention to acquiring new heuristics can be beneficial.

ARTIFICIAL INTELLIGENCE

Any discussion of computers and problem solving would be incomplete if it did not at least acknowledge the active research work in the artificial intelligence area of computer science. Artificial intelligence is concerned with, in the words of one researcher in the field, getting computers to do things that, if people did them, would be considered to require intelligence. As such, it is a great intellectual challenge.

What is the likelihood of being able to program a computer to solve problems, in the sense of making it behave in a way that if a person behaved in that way we would call the behavior intelligent? The answer from science is that if we knew how to solve problems in the sense of scientific knowledge, we could construct a procedure to do just that. Lord Kelvin once wrote, "Knowledge cannot become science unless it can be recorded, reproduced, distributed, stored, and hence studied at leisure." To say that we understand problem solving in a scientific way would mean meeting these conditions and thus being able to program a computer to prepare its own problem-solving procedures.

On the other hand, some scientists view knowledge not as a substance to be passed around but rather as an experiential process. Heinz von Foerster writes, "Information is, of course, the process by which knowledge is acquired and knowledge are [sic] the processes that integrate past and present experiences to form new activities, either as nervous activity internally perceived as thought and will, or externally perceived as speech and movement." This viewpoint, while not common among workers in artificial intelligence or among scientists in general, suggests a rather different definition of what is meant by problem-solving behavior and how it might be recognized. It would lead us to seek out the components of an "experiencer" in the same way that we sought those of a "procedure-follower."

To date artificial intelligence has had some success in constructing procedures which display intelligent behavior (as defined above) in several specific areas. There are programs that play good chess or championship checkers, design electric motors, balance assembly lines, select a stock portfolio, control a moving robot, analyze mass spectrographs, and so forth. Researchers have had considerably less success in producing "general purpose" problem solvers, but work toward these continues as does debate about the limits of what may ever be achieved.

The range of approaches used in constructing these programs varies from imitation of human cognitive processes in solving the same problems to using randomness (selective trial and error), exhaustive enumeration in selected circumstances, or anything else that works. At present, the field is open and eclectic—the major constraints on research are the large amounts of computer time and memory and the human ingenuity needed for this work. Predictions of both striking success and dismal failure for artificial intelligence have been published, buttressed with justifying arguments in either case. Each reader interested in making his own judgments should read and weigh these words for himself.

EXERCISES

1 Using the problem-solving process given in this chapter, develop and test in some detail a procedure for finding the largest in a list of numbers. Pay attention to what problem-solving techniques you use in finding a solution procedure. (If you asked, "What set of operations is available to the procedure-follower," congratulations.)

2 Now, using the answer to exercise 1 as a basis, develop a procedure to find the third largest number in a list.

3 How many English words can you produce using the letters in ANDY? What problem-solving techniques did you use?

4 If Char was twice as old as Su four years ago and will be five years older than Su next year, how old are the two girls? What problem-solving techniques did you use to solve this problem?

5 Develop and test a procedure to test if a word is a palindrome (that is, reads the same forward and backward). Again, pay attention to the problem-solving process and techniques that you use.

6 In one version of the missionaries and cannibals problem, there are three missionaries and three cannibals on one bank

of a river. They all wish to cross the river, but the available boat will hold only two people at a time. If at any time the missionaries on a bank are outnumbered by cannibals, the cannibals eat the missionaries. What sequence of boatloads back and forth will transport all parties to the other side without losing any missionaries? (There must be at least one person in the boat each way. And cannibals are quite cooperative about rowing the boat alone, perhaps in hopes of a future meal.) Try solving this problem using several of the problem-solving techniques given in the chapter.

7 At what interest rate has the value of Manhattan Island appreciated since it was purchased from the Indians? Pay attention to the process and techniques that you use in solving this problem, including those for identifying and procuring necessary additional data.

REFERENCES

Feigenbaum, Edward A., and Julian Feldman (eds.): *Computers and Thought,* McGraw-Hill, New York, 1963, 535 p.

Gruenberger, Fred: *Computing: An Introduction,* Harcourt, New York, 1969, 296 p.

Gruenberger, Fred, and George Jaffray: *Problems for Computer Solution,* Wiley, New York, 1965, 401 p.

Hunt, Earl B., and R. Quinlan: *Artificial Intelligence,* Academic Press, New York, 1974.

Newell, Allen, and Herbert A. Simon: *Human Problem Solving,* Prentice-Hall, Englewood Cliffs, N.J., 1971.

Polya, George: *How to Solve It,* Doubleday-Anchor, New York, 2d ed., 1957.

Von Foerster, Heinz: Perception of the Future and the Future of Perception, *Instructional Science,* **1**(1): 31–43 (1972).

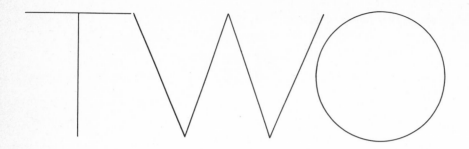

TWO

PROCEDURES AND
PROBLEM SOLVING

Our emphasis in the following chapters is on formulating problem-solving procedures and expressing them as effective computer programs. We begin in Chap. 4 with several computer-independent methods of representing procedures. These can be useful tools in the process of formulating computer programs.

Next, we present a particular procedure description language. This language, while intended primarily for describing procedures rather than for programming them for computer execution, is similar to many higher-level computer programming languages (called higher-level because they conceal the details of computer operation). Examples of translating simple procedures in this language to common higher-level programming languages are given in the appendixes. In general, we assume that the reader has access to a computer on which he can test programs written in a higher-level language. In Chaps. 5 and 6, we illustrate the use of a higher-level language and at the same time develop notions of the structure and organization of computer programs. The structure and organization of the data to be processed is equally important and is the subject of Chaps. 7 and 8.

In Chaps. 9 and 10 we focus on improving our use of the concepts presented above, first examining different computing strategies and then examining techniques for making particular programs more effective.

The final two chapters serve as a bridge to the subject of Part Three: how computer systems work. In Chap. 11 we study the detailed representation of values in computer memory, and then in Chap. 12 the approximations and errors resulting from that representation. This latter topic is an important part of any discussion of effective use of the computer.

We have illustrated many of these concepts with programs in our procedure description language, so that the study of problem-solving procedures can also be exercises in their use.

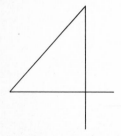

METHODS FOR
REPRESENTING PROCEDURES

Procedures can be represented at many different levels of detail. At the most detailed level, the procedure is represented directly in the language of the procedure-follower. Because procedures represented in computer language may be very long and not easily understood by people other than the programmer, such procedures are often summarized or abstracted. For example, a 20-page computer program for calculating a payroll might be represented more abstractly by a page of prose, or by two pages of flow diagram depicting only the major functions of the program (e.g., calculate income tax, calculate social security, calculate overtime).

The appropriate level of abstraction (suppression of detail) in stating a procedure depends on the sophistication of the intended procedure-follower. For example, if the procedure-follower knows how to take the square root of a number, the procedure to take the square root of 17 need consist only of the one instruction: "take the square root of 17." If the procedure-follower does not know how to take the square root of a number but only how to perform the arithmetic operations of adding, subtracting, multiplying, and dividing, the procedure to take the square root will consist of a series of instructions using those operations.

In this chapter we present several alternative representations for computer procedures. The details of a representative procedural language are given in the following chapter. But first, consider why these other methods of stating procedures are useful, even when they are followed by rewriting the procedure in more detailed form.

First, for even the most logical programmer only the simplest procedures can be written directly in the form of a computer program. Virtually all procedures are too long and too complicated to write directly as programs. And so, in the same way that we use outlines and notes in writing essays and themes, programmers use outlines, diagrams, and specifications as guides in creating procedures.

Second, the first version of even the most carefully programmed procedure probably contains errors, and these errors will only be detected and corrected by a combination of analysis of the program, tracing the program by hand (the programmer playing computer), and actually running the program on a computer. (The preceding sentence describes the experience not just of beginners but also of experienced and talented programmers, and not only for complicated problems but also for simple ones. Good programming practice involves writing procedures so as to facilitate error detection and correction, rather than putting all one's energy into "getting it right" the first time.) This process of error detection and correction is called "debugging" and is an important part of programming. Finding the errors ("bugs") in programs is greatly facilitated by the availability of less detailed descriptions of the program in prose, tables, and diagrams. Logical errors in procedures are often easier to detect in higher-level representations.

Third, the intent of the programmer in writing a particular section of procedure is not always clear from the final program, even if that program works correctly. For example, it is not immediately obvious that the following expression:

A − B * (integer-part-of A/B)

computes the remainder when dividing A by B. Many methods of representing procedures facilitate conceptualizing the procedure at a more abstract level than that required in stating it for a computer, thus recording the intent of a computation rather than its details.

Fourth, a brief description of a procedure in standard form using a standard set of symbols is usually easier to communicate to others (teachers, supervisors, coworkers, assistants, etc.). While preparing such descriptions may seem to be just extra work for simple programming exercises, it is particularly important when a number of programmers are working together on a large project.

Such methods of representation provide a methodology for documentation of programs, for yourself and for others, so that the programs can be understood, maintained, and modified later. (Nothing is more frustrating than to go back to a program you yourself wrote a month or two ago and not be able to understand it. But this happens frequently.)

The above comments will become more meaningful to you after you have written and debugged a few programs, because you will have experienced the problems described. Since for different people different methods of representation appear comfortable and effective, try out several and use those that are helpful.

The different forms in which procedures can be represented are related to different levels of abstraction and detail. Procedures are often summarized in natural language prose. Natural language is used because it is readily understood by people who will use and be affected by the procedure, even though they do not understand or need to understand the details of the procedure.

NATURAL LANGUAGE

For example, a university registrar may summarize a registration-enrollment program so that students can understand why they are asked to fill out certain forms and how certain responses on their part are treated. Natural language abstracts of computer procedures are often prepared by administrators or systems analysts (who do not write computer programs themselves) and used as outlines for programmers. These outlines of computer procedures are used in much the same way as outlines of essays or themes, as guides to writers and as summaries of the finished product.

Often it is useful to write out the procedure in prose form, with special attention to indentation and sequencing rules. The several forms of directions in Chap. 1 are examples of this method.

FLOWCHARTS

A *flowchart* is a pictorial representation of a procedure. A major purpose of representing the procedure as a flowchart is to indicate the structure (flow, order, sequence) of the procedure. Flowcharts are widely used both as problem-solving aids and for documentation of programs.

We shall use seven flowchart symbols to distinguish among types of actions.

1 Processes (computations) are enclosed in rectangular outlines, e.g.,

Drive one block

2 Tests are enclosed in diamond shapes, e.g.,

3 Input-output operations, i.e., reading data or printing data, are enclosed in trapezoidal outlines, e.g.,

4 Execution (evocation) of a procedure is represented by enclosing the action in an irregular hexagon, e.g.,

5 The *beginning* or *end* of a procedure is indicated by a suitable expression enclosed in an elongated oval outline, e.g.,

⊂ START ⊃   ⊂ DONE ⊃

6 The *order* in which the actions are performed will be indicated by connecting the symbols with directed line segments to indicate flow, e.g.,

Print paycheck

⊂ DONE ⊃

7 *Connectors* are used to enclose labels. A set of two connectors is used to represent a continued flow or order when continuous lines cannot be used (as between pages). The connector is a small circle.

②

One possible flowchart corresponding to the directions procedure is given in Fig. 4-1.

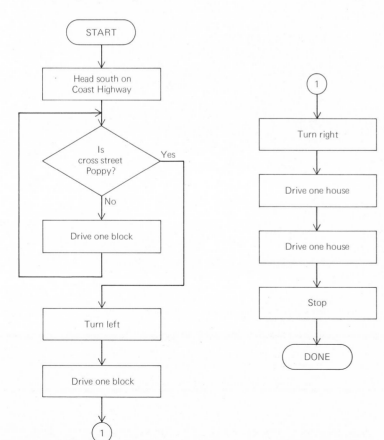

FIGURE 4-1
Flowchart of directions procedure.

compound interest *n* : interest computed on the sum of an original principal and accrued interest

compound leaf *n* : a leaf in which the blade is divided to the midrib forming two or more leaflets on a common axis

compound microscope *n* : a microscope consisting of an objective and an eyepiece mounted in a drawtube

compound number *n* : a number (as 2 ft. 5 in.) involving different denominations or more than one unit

com·pra·dor \\kam-prə-'do(ə)r\ *or* **com·pra·dore** \-'do(ə)r, -'do(ə)r\ *n* [Pg *comprador*, lit., buyer] : a Chinese agent engaged by a foreign establishment in China to have charge of its Chinese employees and to act as an intermediary in business affairs

com·pre·hend \\kam-pri-'hend\ *vt* [ME *comprehenden*, fr. L *comprehendere*, fr. *com-* + *prehendere* to grasp — more at PREHENSILE] **1** : to grasp the nature, significance, or meaning of **2** : to include as an integral part <philosophy's scope ~s the truth of everything which man may understand —H. O. Taylor> **3** : to include by construction or implication : COMPRISE *syn* see UNDERSTAND, INCLUDE — **com·pre·hend·ible** \-'hen-də-bəl\ *adj*

com·pre·hen·si·ble \-'hen(t)-sə-bəl\ *adj* : capable of being comprehended : INTELLIGIBLE — **com·pre·hen·si·bil·i·ty** \-,hen(t)-sə-'bil-ət-e\ *n* — **com·pre·hen·si·ble·ness** \-'hen(t)-sə-bəl-nəs\ *n* — **com·pre·hen·si·bly** \-ble\ *adv*

com·pre·hen·sion \\kam-pri-'hen-chən\ *n* [MF & L; MF, fr. L *comprehension-, comprehensio*, fr. *comprehensus*, pp. of *comprehendere* to understand, comprise] **1 a** : the act or process of comprising **b** : the faculty or capability of including : COMPREHENSIVENESS **2 a** : the act or action of grasping with the intellect : UNDERSTANDING **b** : knowledge gained by comprehending **c** : the capacity for understanding fully **3** : CONNOTATION 3

com·pre·hen·sive \-'hen(t)-siv\ *adj* **1** : covering completely or broadly : INCLUSIVE <~ examinations> <~ insurance> **2** : having or exhibiting wide mental grasp <~ knowledge> — **com·pre·hen·sive·ly** *adv* — **com·pre·hen·sive·ness** *n*

¹com·press \\kam-'pres\ *vb* [ME *compressen*, fr. LL *compressare* to press hard, fr. L *compressus*, pp. of *comprimere* to compress, fr. *com-* + *premere* to press] *vt* **1** : to press or squeeze together **2** : to reduce in size or volume as if by squeezing ~ *vi* : to undergo compression *syn* see CONTRACT *ant* stretch, spread

²com·press \\kam-,pres\ *n* [MF *compresse*, fr. *compresser* to compress, fr. LL *compressare*] **1** : a folded cloth or pad applied so as to press upon a body part **2** : a machine for compressing

com·pressed \\kam-'prest *also* -kam-\ *adj* **1** : pressed together : reduced in size or volume (as by pressure) **2** : flattened as though subjected to compression: **a** : flattened laterally <petioles ~> **b** : narrow from side to side and deep in a dorsoventral direction — **com·pressed·ly** \\kam-'prest-le, -'pres-əd-le\ *adv*

compressed air *n* : air under pressure greater than that of the atmosphere

com·press·ible \\kam-'pres-ə-bəl\ *adj* : capable of being compressed — **com·press·ibil·i·ty** \-,pres-ə-'bil-ət-e\ *n*

com·pres·sion \\kam-'presh-ən\ *n* **1 a** : the act, process, or result of compressing **b** : the state of being compressed **2** : the process of compressing the fuel mixture in a cylinder of an internal combustion engine (as in an automobile) **3** : a much compressed fossil plant — **com·pres·sion·al** \-'presh-nəl, -ən-ᵊl\ *adj*

compressional wave *n* : a longitudinal wave (as a sound wave) propagated by the elastic compression of the medium — called also *compression wave*

com·pres·sive \\kam-'pres-iv\ *adj* **1** : of or relating to compression **2** : tending to compress — **com·pres·sive·ly** *adv*

com·pres·sor \-'pres-ər\ *n* : one that compresses: as **a** : a muscle that compresses a part **b** : a machine that compresses gases

com·prise \\kam-'priz\ *vt* **com·prised; com·pris·ing** [ME *comprisen*, fr. MF *compris*, pp. of *comprendre*, fr. L *comprehendere*] **1** : INCLUDE, CONTAIN **2** : to be made up of **3** : to make up : CONSTITUTE

¹com·pro·mise \\kam-prə-,miz\ *n* [ME, mutual promise to abide by an arbiter's decision, fr. MF *compromis*, fr. L *compromissum*, fr. neut. of *compromissus*, pp. of *compromittere* to promise mutually, fr. *com-* + *promittere* to promise — more at PROMISE] **1 a** : settlement of differences by arbitration or by consent reached by mutual concessions **b** : something blending qualities of two different things **2** : a concession to something derogatory or prejudicial <a ~ of principles>

²compromise *vb* **-mised; -mis·ing** *vt* **1** *obs* : to bind by mutual agreement **2** : to adjust or settle by mutual concessions **3** : to expose to discredit or mischief ~ *vi* **1** : to come to agreement by mutual concession **2** : to make a shameful or disreputable concession — **com·pro·mis·er** *n*

compt \\kaunt, 'kam(p)t\ *archaic var of* COUNT

comp·trol·ler \\kan-'tro-lər, 'kam(p)-,, kam(p)-'\ *n* [ME, alter. of *conterroller* controller] **1** : a royal-household official who examines and supervises expenditures **2** : a public official who audits government accounts and sometimes certifies expenditures **3** : CONTROLLER 1c — **comp·trol·ler·ship** \-,ship\ *n*

com·pul·sion \\kam-'pəl-shən\ *n* [ME, fr. MF or LL; MF, fr. LL *compulsion-, compulsio*, fr. L *compulsus*, pp. of *compellere* to compel] **1** : an act of compelling : the state of being compelled **b** : a force or agency that compels **2** : an irresistible impulse to perform an irrational act

com·pul·sive \-'pəl-siv\ *adj* **1** : having power to compel <a strangely ~, resonant voice —L. C. Douglas> **2** : of, relating to, caused by, or suggestive of psychological compulsion or obsession <~ actions> — **com·pul·sive·ly** *adv* — **com·pul·sive·ness** *n* — **com·pul·siv·i·ty** \\kam-,pəl-'siv-ət-e, ,kam-\ *n*

com·pul·so·ry \\kam-'pəls-(ə-)re\ *adj* **1** : MANDATORY, ENFORCED <~ arbitration> **2** : COERCIVE, COMPELLING — **com·pul·so·ri·ly** \-(ə-)rə-le\ *adv*

com·punc·tion \\kam-'pən(k)-shən\ *n* [ME *compunccioun*, fr. MF *componction*, fr. LL *compunction-, compunctio*, fr. L *compunctus*, pp. of *compungere* to prick hard, sting, fr. *com-* + *pungere* to prick — more at PUNGENT] **1 a** : anxiety arising from awareness of guilt <~s of conscience> **b** : distress of mind over an anticipated action or result <he showed no ~ in planning devilish engines of destruction —Havelock Ellis> **2** : a twinge of misgiving : SCRUPLE <cheated without ~> *syn* see PENITENCE, QUALM — **com·punc·tious** \-shəs\ *adj*

com·pur·ga·tion \\kam-(,)pər-'ga-shən\ *n* [LL *compurgation-, compurgatio*, fr. L *compurgatus*, pp. of *compurgare* to clear completely, fr. *com-* + *purgare* to purge] : the clearing of an accused person by oaths of persons who swear to his veracity or innocence

com·pur·ga·tor \\kam-(,)pər-,gat-ər\ *n* : one that under oath vouches for the character or conduct of an accused person

com·put·able \\kam-'pyüt-ə-bəl\ *adj* : capable of being computed — **com·put·abil·i·ty** \-,pyüt-ə-'bil-ət-e\ *n*

com·pu·ta·tion \\kam-pyü-'ta-shən\ *n* **1 a** : the act or action of computing : CALCULATION **b** : the use or operation of a computer **2** : a system or reckoning **3** : an amount computed — **com·pu·ta·tion·al** \-shnəl, -shən-ᵊl\ *adj*

¹com·pute \\kam-'pyüt\ *n* : COMPUTATION <numbers beyond ~>

²compute *vb* **com·put·ed; com·put·ing** [L *computare* — more at COUNT] *vt* : to determine esp. by mathematical means <~ your income tax>; *also* : to determine or calculate by means of a computer ~ *vi* **1** : to make calculation : RECKON **2** : to use a computer

com·put·er \\kam-'pyüt-ər\ *n* : one that computes; *specif* : an automatic electronic machine for performing calculations — **com·put·er·like** \-,lik\ *adj*

com·put·er·ese \-,pyüt-ə-'rez, -'res\ *n* **1** : MACHINE LANGUAGE **2** : jargon used by computer technologists

com·put·er·ise *chiefly Brit var of* COMPUTERIZE

com·put·er·ite \-'pyüt-ə-,rit\ *n* : COMPUTERNIK

com·put·er·ize \\kam-'pyüt-ə-,riz\ *vt* **-ized; -iz·ing** **1** : to carry out, control, or conduct by means of a computer **2** : to equip with computers — **com·put·er·iz·able** \-,ri-zə-bəl\ *adj* — **com·put·er·iza·tion** \-,pyüt-ə-rə-'za-shən\ *n*

com·put·er·nik \\kam-'pyüt-ər-,nik\ *n* [*computer* + *-nik*] : a person who works with or has a deep interest in computers

comr *abbr* commissioner

com·rade \\kam-,rad, -rəd, *esp Brit* -,räd\ *n* [MF *camarade* group sleeping in one room, roommate, companion, fr. OSp *camarada*, fr. *cámara* room, fr. LL *camera, camara*] **1 a** : an intimate friend or associate : COMPANION **b** : a fellow soldier **2** [fr. its use as a form of address by communists] : COMMUNIST — **com·rade·ship** \-,ship\ *n*

com·rade·ly \-le\ *adj* : of or resembling a comrade or partner — **com·rade·li·ness** *n*

com·rad·ery \\kam-,rad-(ə-)re, rəd-re, -,räd-(ə-)re\ *n* : CAMARADERIE

comsat \\kam-,sat\ *n* [*communication satellite*] : an artificial satellite of the earth used for reflecting or relaying radio waves (as for intercontinental communication)

Com·stock·ery \\kam-,stak-ə-re *also* 'kam-\ *n* [Anthony *Comstock* + E *-ery*] **1** : strict censorship of materials (as books and plays) considered obscene **2** : censorious opposition to alleged immorality in art, literature, and the theater

Com·stock·ian \\kam-'stak-e-ən *also* 'kam-\ *adj* : of or relating to Comstockery

Comt·ian *or* **Comt·ean** \\kam(p)-te-ən, 'koⁿ(n)t-e-\ *adj* : of or relating to Auguste Comte or his doctrines — **Comt·ism** \'kam(p)-,tiz-əm, 'koⁿ(n)t-,iz-\ *n* — **Comt·ist** \'kam(p)-təst, 'koⁿ(n)t-əst\ *adj or n*

¹con \'kan\ *vt* **conned; con·ning** [ME *connen* to know, learn, study, alter. of *cunnen* to know, infin. of *can* — more at CAN] **1** : to study or examine closely : PERUSE **2** : to commit to memory

²con *var of* CONN

³con *adv* [ME, short for *contra*] : on the negative side : in opposition <so much has been written pro and ~>

⁴con *n* **1** : an argument or evidence in opposition **2** : the negative position or one holding it <an appraisal of the pros and ~s>

⁵con *adj* : CONFIDENCE

⁶con *vt* **conned; con·ning** [⁵con] **1** : SWINDLE **2** : PERSUADE, CAJOLE

⁷con *n* : CONVICT

⁸con *n* [short for *consumption*] *slang* : a destructive disease of the lungs; *esp* : TUBERCULOSIS

⁹con *abbr* **1** [L *conjunx*] consort **2** consolidated **3** consul **4** continued

con- — see COM-

con amo·re \\kan-ə-'mor-e, ,kon-ə-'mor-(,)ā, -'mor-e\ *adv* [It] **1** : with love, devotion, or zest **2** : in a tender manner — used as a direction in music

con ani·ma \\ka-'nan-ə-,mä, ko-'nän-i-\ *adv* [It, lit., with spirit] : in a spirited manner : with animation — used as a direction in music

co·na·tion \\ko-'na-shən\ *n* [L *conation-, conatio* act of attempting, fr. *conatus*, pp. of *conari* to attempt — more at DEACON] : an inclination (as an instinct, a drive, a wish, or a craving) to act purposefully : IMPULSE **3** — **co·na·tion·al** \-shnəl, -shən-ᵊl\ *adj* — **co·na·tive** \'ko-nət-iv, -,nät-; 'kän-ət-\ *adj*

co·na·tus \\ko-'nät-əs, -'nät-\ *n, pl* **co·na·tus** \-əs; -'na-,tüs, -'na-\ [NL, fr. L attempt, effort, fr. *conatus*, pp.] : a natural tendency, impulse, or striving

con brio \\kan-'bre-(,)o, ,kon-\ *adv* [It, lit., with vigor] : in a vigorous or brisk manner — used as a direction in music

conc *abbr* **1** concentrate; concentrated; concentration **2** concrete

con·ca·nav·a·lin \\kan-kə-'nav-ə-lən\ *n* [*con-* + *canavalin* (a noncrystalline globulin found in the jack bean), fr. NL *Canavalia*, genus name of the jack bean] : either of two crystalline globulins occurring in the jack bean; *esp* : one that is a potent hemagglutinin

¹con·cat·e·nate \\kan-'kat-ə-nət, kən-\ *adj* [ME, fr. LL *concatenatus*, pp. of *concatenare* to link together, fr. L *com-* + *catena* chain — more at CHAIN] : linked together

²concatenate *vt* **-nat·ed; -nat·ing** : to link together in a series or chain — **con·cat·e·na·tion** \(,)kan-,kat-ə-'na-shən, kən-\ *n*

FIGURE 4-2

Page from a dictionary. By permission. From *Webster's New Collegiate Dictionary,* © **1974 by G & C Merriam Co., Publisher of the Merriam-Webster Dictionaries.**

Another example is a flowchart for a procedure to look up a word in a dictionary. There are several possible procedures for searching a dictionary. A very simple one starts with the first word and examines each word until the undefined word is found or passed (i.e., you discover it is not in the dictionary). A slightly more sophisticated search technique starts on page one and examines whether a word might be on the page. The dictionary page is usually arranged to facilitate this examination (see Fig. 4-2). The first word on each page is reproduced in the upper left-hand corner of each page in large letters. The last word on the page is reproduced in the upper right-hand corner. A quick check of these two words will reveal whether the desired word is between them. If the word is between them, the searcher can examine each word on the page starting with the first to look for the desired word. Either he finds the desired word or he finds that it is not in the dictionary. Such a procedure is given in Fig. 4-3.

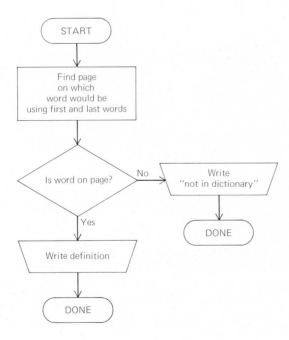

FIGURE 4-3
Flowchart of a dictionary search procedure.

Often it is desirable to draw several flowcharts for the same procedure, at several levels of complexity. Thus, a high-level or macro flowchart for searching the dictionary for a word includes a process box with the content "find the page on which the word would be. . . ." In another lower-level or micro flowchart the details for finding the remainder would be spelled out. Such a lower-level flowchart is given in Fig. 4-4. For many purposes, the macro flowchart with its clearer representation of intention is sufficient. The following is a prose summary of that lower-level procedure:

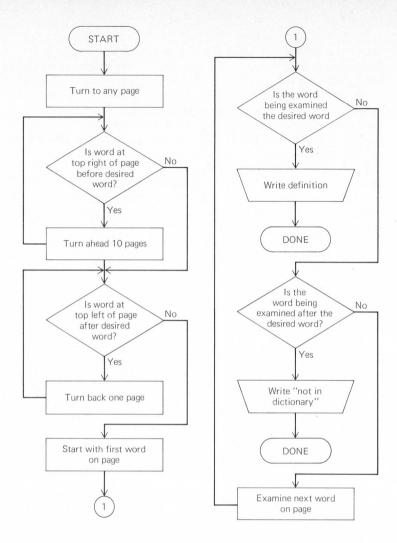

FIGURE 4-4
Lower-level flowchart of a dictionary search procedure.

Start at any page. If the desired word is after this page turn ahead 10 pages at a time until you pass the page the word might be on. If the word is before this page, turn back one page at a time until you find the page the word might be on. Starting with the first word, examine each word on this page until you find the desired word or pass where it would be. If you find the word, write out its definition and stop. If you pass the place where the word would be, write "word not in dictionary" and stop.

Other more sophisticated and more efficient techniques for searching an ordered set of items are discussed in Chap. 17.

As a final example of flowcharts, consider Euclid's algorithm for finding the greatest common divisor of two positive integers. The *greatest common divisor* (GCD) is the largest integer that divides evenly into the two integers. The procedure is as follows:

Divide the smaller integer into the larger. If the remainder is zero, the smaller is the GCD. If not, take as the two integers to be divided the smaller and the remainder and repeat the procedure with them.

For example, if the two integers are 42 and 30, then the procedure would produce results as given below, ending with six as the greatest common divisor.

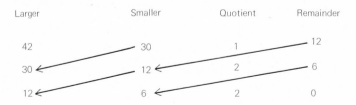

Larger	Smaller	Quotient	Remainder
42	30	1	12
30	12	2	6
12	6	2	0

One possible flowchart for Euclid's algorithm is presented in Fig. 4-5.

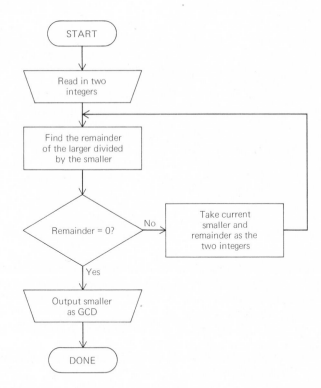

FIGURE 4-5
Macro flowchart for greatest common divisor (GCD) procedure.

DECISION TABLES

Another method of representing procedures is the decision table. A simple decision table consists of a series of lines, each line containing a condition and an action to be taken if that condition is true. The table is scanned from top to bottom and the action associated with the first condition found to be true is carried out. The process is then repeated until the action "Done." is encoun-

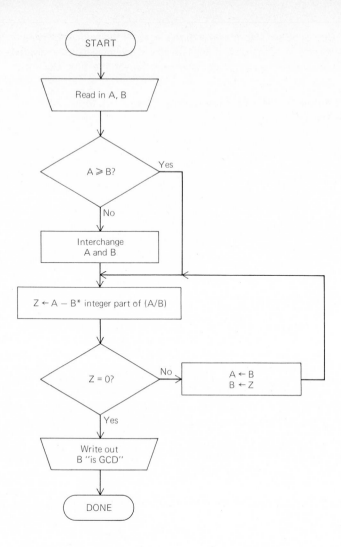

START

Read in A, B

A ≥ B? — Yes

No

Interchange
A and B

$Z \leftarrow A - B^*$ integer part of (A/B)

Z = 0? — No — $A \leftarrow B$ / $B \leftarrow Z$

Yes

Write out
B "is GCD"

DONE

FIGURE 4-6
Lower-level flowchart.

tered or no condition is true. (In more complicated versions, each line may direct the procedure-follower to a different decision table for the next scan.)

Decision tables are given for the directions, the greatest common divisor, and the dictionary lookup examples in Figs. 4-7, 4-8, and 4-9 respectively.

As you can see from these examples, the usefulness of decision tables varies among problems, depending in part on the complexity of the logical structure of the problem. For some problems, the method is quite helpful, and translators (computer programs) are available for translating decision tables constructed according to certain stylized rules directly into computer programs. Also, decision tables are often easier for someone unfamiliar with programming to understand than are flowcharts. While we do not emphasize decision tables in this text, you may want to use them in working out some exercises. You may encounter them in other programming situations.

CONDITION	ACTION
At start	Go south on Coast Highway one block
Cross street is Poppy	Turn left; drive one block; Turn right; Drive two houses; Stop
Cross street is not Poppy	Go south on Coast Highway one block

FIGURE 4-7
Decision table for directions procedure.

CONDITION	ACTION
No data	Read in two integers
Remainder of larger/smaller $\neq 0$	Take former smaller as larger; Take remainder as smaller
Remainder of larger/smaller $= 0$	Write out smaller as greatest common divisor; Stop

FIGURE 4-8
Decision table for greatest common divisor procedure.

CONDITION	ACTION
Dictionary closed	Turn to any page
Word at top right before desired word	Turn ahead 10 pages
Word at top left after desired word	Turn back one page
First word on page not yet examined	Examine first word on page
Word being examined is desired word	Write out definition; Stop
Word being examined is after unknown word	Write "not in dictionary"; Stop
Word being examined is before desired word	Examine next word on page

FIGURE 4-9
Decision table for dictionary lookup procedure.

EXERCISES

1 Prepare a flowchart for some method (your choice) of finding the square root of a number.

2 English words are translated into pig latin by the following rules:

   a For words beginning with a vowel, add the letters "nay."

   b For words beginning with a consonant, move all consonants preceding the first vowel to the end and add the letters "ay."

   Thus, "This is pig latin." would become "Isthay isnay igpay atinlay."

   Flowchart this procedure to translate a sentence from English into pig latin.

3 Prepare a decision table for either of the above problems.

4 Prepare a flowchart or a decision table for starting a car. Which technique, flowchart or decision table, seems more appropriate for expressing this procedure?

5 Flowchart the method you use to choose what nonrequired courses to take this quarter. Is your flowchart sufficiently detailed that you can turn it over to some other person to follow (and you will be satisfied with the result)? If not, now prepare a micro flowchart specifying the additional details.

6 Prepare a decision table describing the behavior of the elevator in a building you frequent (cf., Knuth, Donald E.: *The Art of Computer Programming,* vol. 1, *Fundamental Algorithms,* pp. 280–295, Addison-Wesley, Reading, Mass., 1968).

REFERENCES   Montalbano, Michael: *Decision Tables,* Science Research Associates, Chicago, 1974.

Schriber, Thomas J.: *Fundamentals of Flowcharting,* Wiley, New York, 1969.

A PROCEDURE DESCRIPTION LANGUAGE

The most common method of presenting procedures for computer execution is to write a program in a higher-level programming language such as FORTRAN, ALGOL, BASIC, PL/1, or COBOL. Programs written in these higher-level languages are first translated into the language of the machine by a translator program (called a *compiler*) and are then executed by the computer. Because one can create almost any higher-level language for which a program can be conceived to translate it into machine language, there are many different higher-level languages available. And because languages are created to allow easier expression of problem-solving procedures in particular problem areas (to close the gap between intention and details of programming), some of the operations and data types each language allows are often distinctive to that language. Yet the essential properties of these languages are quite similar.

We now introduce a higher-level language for use in the remainder of this book. This language (called *TL*) has been chosen as a vehicle for presenting and illustrating the basic notions of computer programming. We refer to TL as a procedure description language because it is intended as a language for publishing programs, rather than one for which a translator is immediately available. Many readers as they proceed through this book will be writing programs in a higher-level programming language available on their local computer. TL is designed in part to allow easy rewriting of programming examples in many common languages. The appendixes contain examples of simple TL programs rewritten in FORTRAN, BASIC, PL/1, APL, and ALGOL.

Even in working with simple exercises, however, you will discover cases in which constructs easily expressed in TL are cumbersome in your own available programming language, and also that your language contains powerful features which are not easily approximated in TL. Each higher-level programming language was designed and implemented by different individuals with different classes of problems in mind. Each designer had different ideas about how to adapt his language to make efficient use of the computer hardware. Because TL is a procedure description language, a publication language, we are able to ignore concerns of computer efficiency and of entering, editing, and debugging programs. Because this language is intended primarily for presentation and construction of simple procedures, some powerful concepts available in many programming languages are omitted (or postponed for description in later chapters). Thus, our description of TL can be somewhat less precise and more intuitive than is required for a language to be interpreted by computers as well as by people. Your understanding of TL can be more at the level of grasping the basic principles it incorporates than at the level of learning many specific details of grammar and sentence structure (details which you must master to use an implemented programming language).

ON READING THIS CHAPTER

Most of the concepts of TL are presented in this and the following chapter. The presentation here consists of four sections. The first section describes the structure of TL statements and procedures. A formal notation for describing the form of statements is also introduced here and used in later sections. The second section describes the types of data available in TL. The third section presents most of the statement types available in TL. The fourth section contains two example TL programs and commentary on those programs.

Those readers who prefer to proceed from the abstract to the specific can read this material in the order presented. Those who prefer to study from examples might start with the sample programs in the final section and then return to the earlier three sections.

STRUCTURE

A *program* in TL is made up of a series of statements separated by semicolons. A *label,* which may be any sequence of characters not including punctuation marks, may precede any statement. A label is followed by a colon. Using these conventions, we can rewrite the driving directions in Chap. 1 as follows:

> go: go south on Coast Highway through Corona del Mar; drive until the cross street is Poppy Street; turn left; drive one block; turn right; drive one house; drive one house; stop

Note that we are quite free in using indentation and in moving from one line to the next. Most programming languages *as actually entered* into the computer cannot allow as much freedom; many have rules about starting each statement on a new line, or at least indicating with a special punctuation mark when a statement runs over to the next line.

Punctuation marks we have used so far are colon, semicolon, and space. In addition, because the rules describing legitimate statements in TL programs are phrased in terms of single statements (as you will see shortly), we often wish to group several statements together into a single compound statement (called a *block*). This is done by using the punctuation marks left bracket "[" and right bracket "]" to enclose the group of statements. For example, in the above program, there is one label. The first statement is labeled "go." If we wished to treat the entire program as a single compound statement labeled "go," we might do so as follows:

> go: [go south on Coast Highway through Corona del Mar; drive until the cross street is Poppy Street; turn left; drive one block; turn right; drive one house; drive one house; stop]

The remaining bit of structure, branching out of the normal sequence of interpreting one statement after another, is provided in TL in several ways. The *repetition, conditional, block evocation,* and *to* statements all provide means for specifying some arbitrary (possibly compound) statement as the next statement to be executed. The conditional, block evocation, and to statements are presented later in this chapter. The repetition statement is more complex and is discussed in Chap. 6. We present one form of it here for illustrative purposes. This form is the word **until** followed by a logical expression (an expression that is either true or false) followed by an included statement to be repeated until the value of the logical expression is **true.** For example:

> **until** $x > 3$ **read** x;

or

> **until** $i = 17$ $[i \leftarrow i + 1;$ **write** $i]$;

or, as in the above example,

> **until** $cross_street = $"Poppy" **drive_one_block;**

More generally, we can describe the form or syntax of the **until** statement by using a notation called *BNF form* (Backus-Naur form), as follows:

> ⟨until⟩ ::= **until** ⟨logical⟩ ⟨statement⟩

to be read as, "A member of the class of untils (statements) is constructed of the string of characters **until** followed by a member of the class of logicals (expressions) followed by a member of the class of statements." While we would have to be more precise in constructing the BNF description of a language actually to be run on the computer (for example, just where may or must there be spaces), this description will suffice for now. We shall use BNF to describe the structure of all statements in TL.

Note that the BNF description says nothing of what the **until** statement *does*. BNF describes only form; additional comments must be added to describe the meaning or semantics of a construct. Just because *you,* from past associations with the word **until** and some notion of logical expressions being either true or false (which does not appear in the description of form at all), have an idea what the **until** statement must do, does not mean that you know the meaning of the statement. Only a precise statement of the action to be taken by the procedure-follower when interpreting the statement can provide that meaning. In TL, the meanings of constructs are often simple and clear (that is, close to everyday associations with the symbols used), but with more sophisticated languages the user can be quite misled by relying on associations.

So more precisely, upon interpreting the **until** statement the procedure-follower evaluates the logical expression and, if it is not true, executes the included statement, repeating that sequence of steps until the logical expression is true.

DATA TYPES

The TL programmer may work with three types of data: numbers, strings of characters, and logical values. In each of these cases, constants may be expressed in the language, variables may be assigned values of this type, and more complex expressions of constants and variables may be constructed.

As a first approximation, we mean by numbers what are commonly called integers and mixed fractions. (The question of exactly what numbers can be represented within a computer and how they can be represented is the subject of Chap. 11.) Thus, the following are numerical constants:

```
3
−7
13.214
+3.1415928
```

String constants are sequences of characters enclosed within quotation marks. Any characters, even other punctuation, may be within a string, except of course quotation marks. Thus, the following are string constants:

```
"Joe"
"429 Social Science Bldg."
"Igpay Atinlay"
"#$⟨_⟩' ()*+!"
```

Note that we are adding the quotation mark to our list of punctuation marks.

There are two logical constants, **true** and **false.** The value of any logical variable or expression is one of the two.

Variables, as introduced in Chap. 1, have both a name and a value to which that name refers. Variable names may be any sequence of characters excluding punctuation marks but may not be numerical or logical constants. (Most implemented programming languages require that the first character of a variable name be alphabetic, and we shall follow that practice here.) Thus, some allowable variable names are:

```
dan
x71365229
gross_pay
```

The type of a variable is the type of its value — numerical, string, or logical — and so may change as a procedure is carried out and different values assigned to the variable. It may also be true that a variable has not yet been assigned a value by the procedure. In that case, we say the variable's value (or, for short, the variable) is *undefined.*

For each data type, there is a set of operators and connectives which may be used to join constants and variables together into expressions. Also, parentheses may be used to form groupings within expressions.

The numerical (arithmetic) operators are as follows:

+   Addition
−   Subtraction
*   Multiplication
/   Division
↑   Exponentiation

These are used in the normal way to form expressions whose value is numerical. The following are legitimate numerical expressions in TL (assuming the variables have numerical values):

$3 * (2 + alpha)$

$x - y$

$4 - 6/2.3$

(All of the operators used above are called *binary operators* because they operate on two values, called *operands*. Operators need not be binary; for example, in ordinary arithmetic the square-root operator involves only one operand, as $\sqrt{23}$.)

The *string operators* are not as familiar as are the numerical operators, and so require considerably more explanation and examples. (That does not mean that the string operators are more difficult, just that they are unfamiliar.) For each we give an informal description of the operator. Then we shall give the operator symbol, its name, the BNF description, and an example of usage.

NAME	MEANING
Length	Operand is a string; value is the length of number of characters in the operand string.
Substring	Operands are a string and a pair of numbers enclosed in parentheses; value is the string taken from the operand string starting at the position of the first number and with length given by the second number. If the second number of the pair is omitted, the remainder of the string is taken as the value.
Concatenate	Operands are two strings; value is the string formed by adjoining the second operand to the end of the first.

SYMBOL	NAME	BNF	EXAMPLE	RESULT
#	Length	#⟨string⟩	# "abcde"	5
@	Substring	⟨string⟩@(⟨number⟩,⟨number⟩)	"abcde" @ (2,3)	"bcd"
@	Substring	⟨string⟩@(⟨number⟩)	"abcde" @ (4)	"de"
&	Concatenate	⟨string & string⟩	"abcde" & "fg"	"abcdefg"

Some examples of string expressions are:

"abcde" & "xyz" & "nuts"

"frank" & "lingle" @ (1,3)

"the" @ (2) & "well" @ (4) & "porch" @ (1,1)

(If you are wondering at this point how one can possibly arrive at the value of expressions such as the above, good question! We return to that point after discussing logical expressions.)

The *logical operators and connectives* are all familiar and their meanings are as you might expect from looking at them or reading their names. They consist of relational operators, used to compare two data items, and logical connectives used to combine two logical values.

not	Not
$=$	Equal
$\neq$	Not equal
$>$	Greater than
$\geq$	Greater than or equal
$<$	Less than
$\leq$	Less than or equal
and	And
or	Or

Some examples of logical expressions follow:

$3 > (a+b)$ **or** $x < y$

$a-b=2$

$boy=$"John" **or** $girl=$"Mary"

Finally (important), for the purposes of determining what are legal variable names, labels, etc., *all* of the operators for all three data types, including parentheses, are considered punctuation marks and, therefore, cannot be used as part of a variable name or label.

In addition to the operators given above, most higher-level programming languages include another form of operator, called a *function*. The typical functional format consists of the function name followed by a list of the operands needed, in parentheses and separated by commas. Examples might be **sin**(*alpha*) for the sine of *alpha;* **max**(3,*x*) for the larger of 3 and *x*; **abs**(−27) for the absolute value of −27. Indeed, in many languages the string operators described above are written as string functions, such as **length**("abc").

If TL were being implemented, we would need to give a complete list of the functions available to the user. However, for the purposes of this text we can be less formal and simply introduce functions as needed for our examples.

We have now introduced enough new concepts that all sorts of potentially messy little problems of meaning have been suggested and left unresolved. It is at this point that a programming language designer must make a number of small, sometimes difficult decisions which may, in the long run, do more to determine the usefulness of his language than any of the grand concepts it embodies. We have a great deal more freedom in solving these problems than the designer who is actually implementing his language on a computer and who, therefore, must be more precise and must also worry about efficiency of execution and ease of debugging.

What are some of the problems left open?

1 In what order are the operators in an expression applied to produce a value for the expression as a whole? For example, is the value of $3+2*6$ equal to 15 or to 30? And if that seems easy, since the arithmetic operators are familiar, what about "frank" **&** "lingle" **@** (2,3)? Is the value "ran" or "franking"?

2 What is the value of a comparison of values other than numerical? For example, is "3" > "2", or "abc" < "xyz", or **true ≥ false?**

3 What is the value of an expression in which the data type of an operand is inconsistent with other operands or with that required by the operator? For example, what is the value of "abc" **&** 3 or $2+$"5"?

4 What is the value of an expression in which one of the variables is undefined?

Let us consider these questions in order.

1 Although most of us would say that $3+2*6$ equals 15 (that is, do multiplication before addition), the choice of order of evaluation is essentially arbitrary. Some programming languages apply all operators left to right, some right to left, and some in a varied order depending on the operators themselves. In most languages, parentheses can be used to vary the order of evaluation, expressions within parentheses being evaluated before those outside. In TL we use a hierarchy of operations to determine order of evaluation. The hierarchy is given below, operations at the "top" of the list being applied before those further down; again, parentheses can be used to vary the order so indicated. In case of equal hierarchy, operators are evaluated from left to right. (The hierarchy given here has been chosen to appear "natural" in most conditions. Do not be afraid to use parentheses at any point; they can only clarify your intention.)

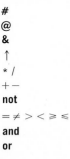

  #
  @
  &
  ↑
  * /
  + −
  not
  = ≠ > < ≥ ≤
  and
  or

2 For logical values, equality and inequality can be indicated; but greater than or less than comparisons result in undefined values. For strings, most programming languages and most computer hardware specify an ordering of characters, generally a, . . . , z, A, . . . , Z, 0, 1, . . . , 9 with other characters interspersed at various points. We shall simply use the above ordering and be careful not to use examples in which other characters would be compared. For the language in which you are actually programming, this ordering (typically called a *collating sequence*) will be given in the functional specifications manual.

3 If the data type of an operand is inconsistent with that required, the value of the expression is undefined. However, we define the following TL functions to help deal with this problem.

string (⟨operand⟩) converts the operand, numerical or logical, to a string.

number (⟨operand⟩) converts a string whose form is that of a number to a numerical.

logical (⟨operand⟩) converts a string of the form of a logical value (e.g., "true" or "false") to a logical value.

If the operand of any of the above functions is not as specified above, the value of the function is undefined.

4 If one of the variables in an expression is undefined, the value of the expression is undefined. More generally (which is to be desired, since generality often leads to fewer rules to remember), if the above rules lead to any subpart of an expression being undefined, the value of the expression is undefined.

If we were discussing a particular implementation of this language, we would now have to specify how an undefined value would be represented and how the computer would act on finding such a value. For our purposes, let us just say that interpretation of the program ceases.

Our particular choices of how to handle the above problems represent only one possible solution, one not constrained by either efficiency of implementation or providing error detection and debugging aids for the user. For example, many cases of undefined values in TL will only become known as the procedure is being carried out. In some languages, a particular variable must be declared to be a certain data type and can only take on values of that type. With that additional information, many type errors can be detected by a preliminary scan of the program, thus making debugging easier and (on most contemporary hardware) allowing more efficient code to be produced by the translator. But the programmer must add such declarations to his program and must not change the type of a variable. Thus, as with most things, type declarations have both advantages and disadvantages.

STATEMENT TYPES

TL has 11 statement types. Eight of these types are presented in this section. One of these eight, the block evocation statement, is also extended in Chap. 6. The remaining three types, the repetition statement, the local statement, and the return statement, are presented entirely in Chap. 6.

The *assignment statement* assigns the value of an expression to a variable. Its BNF is as follows:

⟨assignment⟩ ::= ⟨variable⟩ ← ⟨expression⟩

Examples of assignment statements are as follows:

$x \leftarrow 3 * alpha + 2/beta$
word ← **string** @ (*i*) **&** "nay"
truth_value ← $a > 2$ **or** $(x+y=3)$

The *conditional statement* evaluates a logical expression and then executes one of two included statements depending on whether the logical expression is true or false. Its BNF description is:

⟨conditional⟩ ::=**if** ⟨logical⟩ **then** ⟨statement⟩ **else** ⟨statement⟩

An alternative form of the conditional omits the else clause:

⟨conditional⟩ ::=**if** ⟨logical⟩ **then** ⟨statement⟩

Examples of conditional statements are:

if $x > y$ **then** *larger* $\leftarrow x$ **else** *larger* $\leftarrow y$

if $a < b$ **then** $[a \leftarrow b; z \leftarrow 0]$

Note that use of the shorter form of the conditional as an included statement in another conditional can lead to ambiguity (another form of undefined value) as in:

if $x > y$ **then if** $i = j$ **then** $z \leftarrow 3$ **else** $z \leftarrow 5$

With which **if** does the **else** belong? A particular implementation would either choose one grouping of **then**'s and **else**'s or treat the statement as undefined. We can avoid such ambiguities by using brackets.

The *read statement* causes input data to be read in by the procedure-follower and assigned as values to the variables named in the read statement. Its BNF is:

⟨read⟩ ::=**read** ⟨variable⟩,⟨variable⟩, . . .

The read and write statements are among the most complex in implemented programming languages, since they must deal with the format of data on actual input media such as punched cards, magnetic tapes, teletype tape, etc., or output media such as printed pages with line and column spacing. Since we are not concerned with a particular implementation, we can define simple read and write statements which ignore details of format. (Some implemented programming languages also include simplified input and output statements, restricting control of data format in return for programming ease.) An example of the read statement is:

read *a,b,c*

The *write statement* causes the values of the specified data to be written out or displayed by the procedure-follower. (Computer people use the word *output* as a verb, and so would say ". . . causes the data to be output . . . .") Its BNF is:

⟨write⟩ ::=**write** ⟨expression⟩,⟨expression⟩, . . .

Again, an implementation language would have to specify much more format detail. Examples of the write statement are:

write "the answers are", *alpha, bater*

write "x=", *x*

The *block evocation statement* causes the statement (block) whose label is indicated to be executed, after which execution continues with the statement after the block evocation statement. Its BNF is:

⟨block-evocation⟩ ::= ⟨statement-label⟩

Examples of the block evocation statement are:

> *Go*
> *Drive*
> *Loop*

The *to statement* causes the procedure-follower to continue the sequence of statements at that statement whose label is specified in the to statement. Its BNF is:

⟨to⟩ ::=**to** ⟨statement-label⟩

As always, if evaluation of the statement label results in an undefined value, interpretation of the program ceases. Examples of the to statement are:

> **to** *Again*
> **to** *Label*

The *done statement* causes termination of the block within which the done statement occurs. Execution continues with the statement following that block or following the statement that evoked that block, as appropriate. Its BNF is:

⟨done⟩::=**done**

The *comment statement* is treated as a null operation (in computer talk, a no-op) by the procedure-follower, and so may be used to add commentary at any point in the program at which a statement may occur. Its BNF form is:

"⟨any string excluding quotation marks⟩"

EXAMPLE PROGRAMS

Following are TL programs to reverse the letters in a word and to find the largest common divisor of the two numbers using Euclid's algorithm. Be sure you understand each step in these procedures. In these examples we shall use some conventions to make the program easier to read and make the meaning of the programs clearer.

1. Reserved words, words which have a special meaning in TL, will be printed in lowercase, boldface. Examples: **read, write, until, to, true, sin.**
2. Variable names will be printed in lowercase italics. Examples: *word, alpha, x.*
3. Labels will be printed in italics with the first letter capitalized. Examples: *Biga, Bigb.*

EXAMPLE 1
REVERSE A WORD

TL Program
"Reverse a word";
"This program reads in a word and writes out that word spelled backwards";

> **read** *word;*
> *rev* ← "";
> **until** *word*="" [*rev* ← *word* **@** (1,1) **&** *rev; word* ← *word* **@** (2)];
> **write** *rev;*

COMMENTARY ON
EXAMPLE 1

"This program reads in a word and writes out that word spelled backwards";

This comment statement describes the program's intended function for the reader. It is ignored by the computer.

read *word*

This read statement obtains a value, in this case a character string, from a source outside the program (such as a punched card reader or teletype keyboard) and assigns that value to the variable *word*. This is the word to be reversed.

rev ← " "

This assignment statement assigns the null string (nothing between the two quotation marks) as the value of the variable *rev*. This is the initial value of the reversed word.

until *word* = " " [*rev ← word* **@** (1,1) **&** *rev; word ← word* **@** (2)]

This until form of the repetition statement (mentioned in the earlier section on structure), repeats the included statement until the logical expression *word*=" " is true (that is, until the value of *word* is a null string).

The included statement is a compound statement made up of two assignment statements. The first assignment statement sets as the new value of *rev* the first character of *word* (that is, starting at position one, one character in length) followed by the previous value of *rev*. The second assignment statement sets as the new value of *word* the previous value of *word* starting with the second character; thus it discards from the value of *word* the character just added to the beginning of *rev*.

The total effect of the repetition is to move through *word* from beginning to end, adding each character to the beginning of *rev*, so that at any point the latest character encountered in *word* is the first character of *rev*.

write *rev*

This write statement transmits the value of the variable *rev* to an output medium outside the program, such as a line printer, television-type display, or teletype printer.

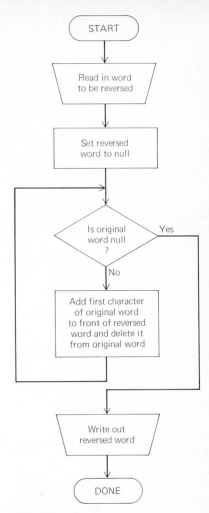

FIGURE 5-1

Flowchart for procedure to reverse a word.

TL Program

"Find greatest common divisor";

"This program reads in two numbers, *a* and *b,* and writes out their greatest common divisor found using Euclid's algorithm. The program uses the function **int,** which returns as its value the largest integer not greater than its input. The program assumes that the two numbers read in are positive integers. The program uses variable *z* as the remainder on division";

    read *a,b;*

    if *a < b* **then to** *Bigb* **else to** *Biga;*

Biga:

    z ← a − b * **int**(*a/b*);

    if *z*=0 **then write** *b* **else** [*a ← z;* **to** *Bigb*]; **done;**

Bigb:

    z ← b − a * **int**(*b/a*);

    if *z*=0 **then write** *a* **else** [*b ← z;* **to** *Biga*]; **done;**

EXAMPLE 2
FIND GREATEST
COMMON DIVISOR

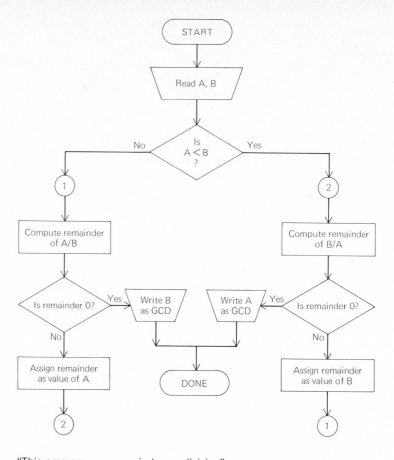

FIGURE 5-2
Flowchart for procedure to find greatest common divisor.

"This program . . . remainder on division"

This comment statement describes the program's function, the variables and the functions that it uses, and the assumed restriction that the inputs be positive.

read *a,b*

This read statement obtains values for *a* and *b* from some outside source. The first value read is assigned to *a*, the second to *b*.

if *a < b* **then to** *Bigb* **else to** *Biga*

This conditional statement tests whether the logical expression *a < b* is true. If the expression is true and *a* is less than *b* then the included statement following **then** is executed. If the expression is false, then the included statement following **else** is executed.

The two included statements are both **to** statements. The first specifies transferring the sequence of control to the statement labeled *Bigb* (in the case that *a* is less than *b*); the second specifies transfer to the statement labeled *Biga* (in the case that *b* is less than or equal to *a*).

Biga: $z \leftarrow a - b *$ **int**(a/b)

Biga is the label, or name, of this assignment statement. The statement sets the value of *z* as the value of the expression on the right of the assignment sign. That expression is evaluated by first taking the integer part of *a/b*. **int** is a function whose value is the largest integer not greater than its argument, the expression in parentheses. The value of **int**(a/b) is then multiplied by *b* and the product subtracted from *a*. Verify that if *a* and *b* are both positive integers, as assumed, the value assigned to z will be the integer remainder from dividing *a* by *b*.

if $z=0$ **then write** *b* **else** [$a \leftarrow z$; **to** *Bigb*]

This conditional statement tests to see if the remainder just computed is zero. If so, according to Euclid's algorithm the previous divisor is the greatest common divisor. In that case, the included statement is executed to write out the value of *b*, the greatest common divisor. If the remainder is not zero, then the process is to be repeated using as the two integers the previous divisor and the remainder. In that case, the included statement assigns the remainder as the value of *a* (the previous divisor is already the value of *b*) and then transfers to the statement labeled *Bigb* (since the remainder is known to be less than the divisor).

done

This **done** statement terminates the program. It is executed in the normal sequence of control if the **then** clause of the preceding conditional statement is carried out. If the preceding **else** clause is executed instead, it transfers control to *Bigb*, bypassing the **done**. If the **done** statement were omitted, the program would continue with *Bigb* after writing out *b*, rather than terminating as desired.

Bigb: $z \leftarrow b - a * \textbf{int}(b/a)$

if $z=0$ **then write** *a* **else** [$b \leftarrow z$; to *Biga*]; **done**;

These three statements parallel the preceding three except that *a* is known to be less than *b* rather than the reverse.

EXERCISES

1 Prepare a program to determine if three line segments can form a triangle. Inputs to the program are three segment lengths; assume these are entered in sorted order from shortest to longest. The output is to be a message as to whether a triangle is possible or not. Note that if the line segments are named *a, b,* and *c* from shortest to longest, it must be true that $a + b > c$ if they are to form a triangle.

2 Extend the program in exercise 1 by having it also determine, in the cases where a triangle can be formed, if that triangle is a right triangle (one angle is 90 degrees, $a \uparrow 2 + b \uparrow 2 = c \uparrow 2$), or acute (all angles less than 90 degrees, $a \uparrow 2 + b \uparrow 2 > c \uparrow 2$), or obtuse (one angle greater than 90 degrees, $a \uparrow 2 + b \uparrow 2 > c \uparrow 2$). Also, have the program check if the triangle possibly is equilateral (all sides the same length) or isosceles (two sides the same length).

3 In exercises 1 and 2 we assumed that the input data were in sorted order. Extend that program to handle input data in unsorted order; add some statements at the beginning to order the inputs.

4 Write a program that reads in a word and prints out the input in "triangular" form. For example, for the input "word", the output would be:

w
wo
wor
word

5 A worker makes $3.50 per hour, with time and a half ($5.25) for all time over 40 hours per week. Prepare a program to

read in number of hours worked in a week and print out the worker's gross and net pay. Net pay is gross pay less deductions of 4.3 percent for federal taxes, 1 percent for state disability insurance, and 3.6 percent for the retirement fund.

6 Prepare a program that prints out the first N terms of the Fibonacci sequence. That sequence has the property that each number (after the first two) is the sum of the previous two numbers; that is, 1,1,2,3,5,8,13, ... The input to the program is n, the number of terms to be printed.

7 Write a program to add a sequence of numbers. The first input is the number of terms to be added. The remaining inputs are the numbers themselves. The output is the sum of the input terms.

8 Extend the program in exercise 7 to also compute and print out the largest and smallest numbers, the average of the numbers (sum divided by number of terms), and the range of the numbers (largest less smallest plus one).

9 Write a program that reads in a word and prints out "yes" or "no" depending on whether or not the word is a palindrome. A palindrome is a word that is spelled the same backwards and forwards. ROTOR, SEES, BIB, DAD, MOM are palindromes.

10 Prepare a program to calculate the change that should be given to customers in a supermarket. Change is made up from $1.00 bills, quarters, dimes, nickels, and pennies, and is given in the largest possible denominations. The two inputs to the program are the cost of purchase and the amount tendered by the customer. Outputs are the numbers of each denomination to be given as change.

For example, if the cost of purchase was $1.53, and the customer offered $5.00 in payment, then his change would be three $1.00 bills, one quarter, two dimes, and two pennies. (*Hint:* Use the **int** function.)

11 A sequence of numbers represents the ages of persons responding to a questionnaire. Construct a program to determine how many of the respondents are 21 or younger, how many between 22 and 44 inclusive, and how many 45 and older. Input data are the sequence of ages, terminated by a value of zero. Output data are the count for each category.

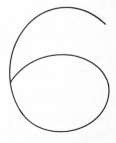

STRUCTURE OF PROCEDURES

As you develop skill in programming, the way in which you express procedures changes. Similarly, different programmers preparing procedures to effect the same action by a procedure-follower may produce quite different procedures, even though the procedures "do the same thing." The procedures, while identical in input and output, may differ in many dimensions—number of statements, time required, number of variables, etc. One of these dimensions, the structure of the procedure, is the focus of this chapter.

While it would be desirable if we could state, "Good style in programming is . . . ," or even "Style in programming is . . . ," this subject is better treated by example and illustration than by discussion. Each programmer develops his own sense of style in the process of programming and of studying other programs. For us, style involves simplifying, generalizing, combining, shortening, and abbreviating. The basic ideas introduced in this chapter—repetition statements and the use of functions and subroutines—are powerful tools for achieving this style. As you read this material, look for these and other dimensions.

GREATEST COMMON DIVISOR

As a start, let us examine the procedure from Chap. 5 for finding the greatest common divisor of two positive integers. The informal statement of the procedure was:

> Divide the smaller integer into the larger. If the remainder is zero, the smaller is the GCD. If not, take as the two integers the smaller and the remainder and repeat the procedure with them.

The program itself is repeated in Fig. 6-1 for convenience.

This program is a fairly straightforward translation of the informal statement. Such complications as exist result from the need to be more precise in describing the handling of "smaller" and "larger," (a task which people as procedure-followers seem to deal with "automatically"). The above treatment of the possibility that sometimes a is larger and sometimes b leads to a procedure

"Greatest common divisor—version 1";

Find the greatest common divisor of two positive integers, a and b, using Euclid's algorithm.

    read a,b;

Read in. Positive integers provided from an input device are assigned as the values of a and b.

    if $a < b$

Test for larger.

        then to Bigb

If $a < b$, then go to step labeled Bigb.

        else to Biga;

If $a \geq b$, then go to step labeled Biga.

Biga:

    $z \leftarrow a - b * \textbf{int}(a/b)$;

Find remainder of a/b. The remainder is calculated by multiplying the integer portion of the quotient of a/b by b and then subtracting the product from a. The remainder is assigned as the value of z.

    if $z = 0$

Is z zero?

        then write b

If $z = 0$, write out the answer, b, and terminate at the done step.

        else [$a \leftarrow z$; **to** Bigb];

If $z \neq 0$, set a to the value of z, i.e., the remainder, and go to step Bigb.

    done;

Bigb:

    $z \leftarrow b - a * \textbf{int}(b/a)$;

Find remainder of b/a.

    if $z = 0$

Is z zero?

        then write a

If $z = 0$, write out the answer, a, and terminate at the done step.

        else [$b \leftarrow z$; **to** Biga];

If $z \neq 0$, set b to the value of z, i.e., the remainder, and go to step Biga.

    done;

FIGURE 6-1

in which most statements are repeated twice, once for the case of larger a and once for larger b. How might the procedure be shortened by reducing or eliminating this duplication? (This duplication is also obvious from the flowchart describing the procedure.)

One answer would be to decide arbitrarily that the procedure would only work correctly if a is larger (more precisely, not smaller) than b, just as it now is assumed that both a and b are positive integers. While this is a perfectly legitimate answer, and in some cases a desirable one, from a more general standpoint that solution seems overly restrictive. It lacks class.

Another solution would be to write the algorithm as though a were always larger, but include at the beginning a test for the case of b larger, followed if necessary by "appropriate adjustments." Such a procedure keeps track of which variable is larger by always making a larger rather than (as above) by using different segments of program (see Fig. 6-2). This second version of the greatest common divisor program corresponds to the flowchart in Fig. 4-5 for this procedure.

Note that this version is shorter in the sense of containing fewer statements. It may not be shorter in terms of the number of statements executed for any particular pair of integers. And it also uses the variable z for exchanging. (It is not possible to

"Greatest common divisor — version 2";

  read *a,b*;   Read in. Assign values to *a* and *b*.

  if $a < b$ Insure $a \geqslant b$. If $a < b$, exchange *a* and *b*.

    then $[z \leftarrow a; a \leftarrow b; b \leftarrow z]$; Note this exchange required the use of a third variable, *z*.

Loop:

    $z \leftarrow a - b * \mathbf{int}(a/b)$; Find remainder of *a/b*. Same method as earlier version of this procedure.

    if $z = 0$ Is *z* zero?

      then write *b*   If $z = 0$, then write answer, *b*, and terminate at done.

      else $[a \leftarrow b; b \leftarrow z; \mathbf{to}\ Loop]$; If $z \neq 0$, then set *a* to *b*, *b* to *z*, and go to step *Loop*.

  done;

FIGURE 6-2

exchange the values of two variables without using a third. Try it.) In what other ways do the two procedures differ?

  These are two rather different approaches to the same problem, using only those statement types already presented. Both use loops to repeat certain sections of the program. In fact, the use of loops is so common that a special statement type to control the repetition of program segments is found in most higher-level programming languages. The *repetition* (or *iteration*) statement is typical of this construct.

REPETITION STATEMENT

In TL the repetition statement is made up of a control clause followed by an included statement to be repeated as determined by the control clause. The control clause has two basic forms: **until** followed by a logical expresssion or **for** followed by a variable and a list or range of values to be assigned to that variable.

  Before giving formal BNF descriptions of these constructs, we present a simple example of each. Each statement in Fig. 6-3 will write out the value and square of every odd integer less than 10.

$[i \leftarrow 1;\ \mathbf{until}\ i > 10\ [\mathbf{write}\ i, i \uparrow 2; i \leftarrow i+2]]$
$\mathbf{for}\ i \leftarrow 1,3,5,7,9\ [\mathbf{write}\ i, i \uparrow 2]$
$\mathbf{for}\ i \leftarrow 1\ \mathbf{thru}\ 10\ \mathbf{by}\ 2\ [\mathbf{write}\ i, i \uparrow 2]$
$\mathbf{for}\ i \leftarrow 1,3,5\ \mathbf{thru}\ 10\ \mathbf{by}\ 2\ [\mathbf{write}\ i, i \uparrow 2]$

FIGURE 6-3

  The BNF description of the repetition statement follows. Note the use of a new piece of notation, the vertical bar, to indicate alternative forms.

    ⟨repetition⟩ ::= ⟨control clause⟩ ⟨statement⟩
    ⟨control clause⟩ ::= ⟨until⟩ | ⟨for⟩
    ⟨until⟩ ::= **until** ⟨logical-expression⟩
    ⟨for⟩ ::= **for** ⟨variable⟩ ← ⟨for-list⟩
    ⟨for-list⟩ ::= ⟨for-element⟩ | ⟨for-element⟩, ⟨for-list⟩
    ⟨for-element⟩ ::= ⟨arith-expr⟩ | ⟨arith-expr⟩ **thru** ⟨arith-expr⟩ |
        ⟨arith-expr⟩ **thru** ⟨arith-expr⟩ **by**
        ⟨arith-expr⟩

  Some semantic notes on these constructs are in order. In the **for** statement, if a limiting value is given using **thru** but no increment value is specified using **by,** an increment of one (1) is

```
"Greatest common divisor—version 3";        Greatest common divisor program using repetition statement.

    read a,b ; z←a;

    if a < b                                 Insure a ≥ b by exchanging a and b if a < b.

        then [a←b; b←z];

    until z=0                                Repeat the bracketed statements, i.e., find remainder and assign new values to a and b,
                                             until the remainder, z, is 0.

      [z←a−b * int(a/b);

      a←b; b←z];

    write a;
```

FIGURE 6-4

assumed. The test for ending repetition is made each time *before* the included statement is executed, including before the first possible execution. (Thus, the bracketed statement in $i←2$; **until** $i>1$ [----], would never be executed, since i is already greater than one.) The included statement is repeated *until* the **until** clause is true or *for* each of the values in the **for** list as long as the *iteration* or *index* value does not exceed (or become less than, for a negative increment) the limit value specified by a **thru.** Some programming languages include a **while** construct analogous to this **until.**

Revised procedures utilizing repetition statements for the greatest common divisor and the reverse-a-word algorithms from Chap. 5 are given in Figs. 6-4 and 6-5.

Thus, one common way of shortening a procedure is by encapsulating loops in a repetition statement. Often this abbreviation also renders the procedure more readable. We return in Chap. 7 to other uses of the repetition statement, particularly for handling arrays of data. But first we extend the concept of the block evocation statement to provide another powerful means for abbreviating segments of program.

FUNCTIONS, SUBROUTINES, PROCEDURES

The block evocation statement as defined in Chap. 5 allows commonly used segments of code to be grouped into labeled blocks, which can then be evoked at any point in the program simply by using the label. For example, the greatest common divisor program above could be made into such a block and then used within another procedure.

```
"Reverse a word—version 2";              Reverse-a-word program using repetition
                                         statement.

    read word;

    rev←"";                              Initialize rev to a blank string.

    for i←1 thru #word                   Successively concatenate each letter of
                                         word to rev.

      [rev←word @ (i,1) & rev];

    write rev;
```

FIGURE 6-5

However, this block evocation facility has several deficiencies. First, a block can only be called (evoked) as a separate statement, not as a component (operand) within an expression. Second, before evoking a block one must first assign values to particular variables used within the block, rather than freely specifying the values to be processed at the time of evocation. And third, the variables used, within the block, whether as inputs or as working variables, must be distinct from those in the program evoking the block. This possibility of conflict in variable names reduces the generality of functional blocks. In the following we extend the block evocation facility to remedy these shortcomings. The construct which we thus create is referred to in different programming languages by various names: subroutines, functions, or procedures. Often there are distinctions among these, and almost always they mean different things in different languages. For our informal purposes, we use the terms *function* and *subroutine* more or less interchangeably and continue to use the term *procedure* in a more general sense.

The extensions we make to TL are to allow parameters, dummy and local variables, and a means of returning a result from a block. Let us consider each of these in order.

By *parameters* we mean those values to be processed by the block. Parameters are indicated by listing them in parentheses following the label of the subroutine. The variable names thus used are *dummy variables,* and are distinct from any uses of the same variable names in the evoking (calling) program. Thus, to rewrite the greatest common divisor routine as a subroutine using dummy variables a and b, we would write it as a block with the label $Gcd(a,b)$. While we then use a and b as variable names within Gcd, they are distinct uses of a and b, differing from and not interfering with values of a and b outside the block. In effect, at the time Gcd is evoked, all occurrences of a and b are temporarily replaced by the values in the call.

For example, if we rewrote Gcd using a and b as dummy variables, the following sequence of program could occur:

$a \leftarrow 8;$

$b \leftarrow 9;$

$c \leftarrow Gcd(14,6);$

write $c,a,b;$

The output produced by the **write** statement would be:

2 8 9

Even though a and b had been used within Gcd in computing its output, that usage would not alter the values assigned in the calling program.

(In implemented programming languages, there are several ways in which an argument, i.e., a value of a parameter, may be passed on to a subroutine. First note that an argument may be an arbitrary expression. Thus, in the above example the third statement could have been

$$c \leftarrow Gcd\,(a+6,\ b-3)$$

The first argument, for example, could be calculated and its value, 14, passed on to the Gcd subroutine; this is referred to as *call-by-value.* Or the argument expression could be copied and that copy passed on to the subroutine; this is *call-by-name.* Or, for arguments which are single variables, the location in computer memory associated with that variable could be passed on; this is *call-by-location.* For TL, we assume that inputs to a subroutine are handled call-by-value and outputs call-by-location.)

We can also illustrate the use of *local variables* with Gcd. As programmed earlier, Gcd uses the variable z. If it were not possible to declare this use of z to be local to Gcd, the evocation of Gcd would also change any value of z within the calling routine (since z is not a dummy variable) even though it is not obvious from the intent or calling form of Gcd that z is even mentioned within the block. Gcd could only be used by routines that did not use the variable name z. This shortcoming (lack of generality) is solved by creating a new statement type, the **local** statement, which declares that the variables listed are distinct within that block, to be treated in the same manner as dummy variables. Common programming terminology (except for FORTRAN) is to refer to those variables not specifically declared local as *global,* meaning that they have the same value throughout all blocks where not declared local. Thus, we would add to Gcd the statement **local** z to seal off this local use of z from affecting the calling routine. (You may wish to think of dummy and local variables as having their values copied and stored away just before execution of the block begins, with the old values copied back into the variables just after the block is completed.)

A more concise statement of this is that a variable is global unless declared local, and that a local variable is local to the block in which it is declared and any blocks called by that block.

Finally, for the subroutine Gcd to be generally useful, we would not want it to write out the greatest common divisor, but rather to produce that result as a value, so that Gcd could be used as an element (operand) in an arithmetic expression. (Subroutines so used are often called functions.) We allow sub-

"Greatest common divisor—version 4";   Greatest common divisor subroutine.

Gcd(a,b):

    [**local** z; $z \leftarrow a$;   z is declared a local variable and initialized to a.

    if $a < b$

      then $[a \leftarrow b;\ b \leftarrow z]$;

    until $z = 0$

      $[z \leftarrow a - b * \textbf{int}\,(a/b)$;

      $a \leftarrow b;\ b \leftarrow z]$;

    return $a]$ The answer is returned to the calling sequence.

"Reverse a word—version 3";   Reverse-a-word subroutine.

Reverse(*word*):

   [**local** *rev*; *rev* ← "";   *rev* is declared a local variable and initialized to a blank string.

   until *word* = "";

     [*rev* ← *word* **@** (1,1) **&** *rev*;   Until *word* is exhausted, repeat the following [add first letter of *word* to front of rev; strip off first letter of *word*].

    word ← *word* **@** (2)];

   return *rev*]

FIGURE 6-7

---

routines to return a value by using a **return** statement, which specifies the value to be returned. Thus, in *Gcd,* we would replace the statement **write** *a* by **return** *a.* (Again, a number of questions of precision and semantics arise, such as what value pertains if two such **return** statements are executed within a single subroutine. We ignore these for now.)

Using these constructs, we can now rewrite the greatest common divisor procedure as a subroutine (see Fig. 6-6). We can also use the subroutine construction to rewrite our earlier procedure for reversing a word (see Fig. 6-7). Note that the value produced by this function is a string rather than a number.

BNF descriptions of the new statement types introduced into TL as extensions to block evocation are given below, together with the alternative forms specified earlier.

    ⟨block-evocation⟩ ::= ⟨statement-label⟩ |

              ⟨statement-label⟩ (⟨argument-list⟩)

    ⟨local⟩ ::= **local** ⟨variable-list⟩

    ⟨return⟩ ::= **return** ⟨expression⟩

Note also that in defining a subroutine, parameters (dummy variables) are specified in parentheses immediately following the block label and before the colon.

RECURSIVE SUBROUTINES

Often it is convenient to conceive of subroutines doing their job by using (evoking) themselves on a smaller or different set of

"Greatest common divisor—version 5";   Recursive version of *Gcd* subroutine.

Gcd(*a,b*):

   [**if** *a* < *b*   Insure *a* > *b* by calling *Gcd* with arguments reversed if *a* < *b*.

   then [**return** *Gcd*(*b,a*)]

   else

     [*a* ← *a* − *b* * **int**(*a/b*);   Compute remainder.

   if *a* = 0

     then return *b*   If remainder = 0, answer is *b*.

     else return *Gcd*(*b,a*)]]   If remainder ≠ 0, call *Gcd*(*b,a*).

FIGURE 6-8

"Reverse a word — version 4";

Reverse(*word*):

    [**if** *word*=""   If *word* is null, return null string and quit.

      then return ""

      else return *Reverse*(*word* @ (2)) **&** *word* @ (1,1)]   If *word* is not blank return the output of *Reverse* (*word* less the first letter) concatenated to the first letter of *word*.

FIGURE 6-9

data. For example, the *Gcd* subroutine is written in this manner in Fig. 6-8.

Trace this procedure through by hand to verify that it does indeed compute the greatest common divisor of its inputs. (How does this version of *Gcd* compare with earlier ones in the chapter in terms of programming style?)

The reverse-a-word function is written similarly in Fig. 6-9.

Such functions, defined in terms of themselves, are called *recursive* functions. In many implemented programming languages recursive functions are not allowed, or give incorrect results, because of the manner in which the handling of dummy and local variables and returns is implemented in machine language. A correct implementation of recursive functions usually is more expensive in terms of machine time and space than nonrecursive functions. To see why, trace through for some test data the *Gcd* or *Reverse* functions using the notion of copying the old values of variables and later restoring them, and see what complications arise.

SUBROUTINES AND PROGRAMMING

Grouping statements into blocks and subroutines is a natural part of several different approaches to programming. In the "top down" approach, we begin with the top level of activity in a procedure, assuming that there are or will be subroutines for the various major parts of the procedure, and then treat each of those parts in a similar manner in turn. For example, we might begin to write a chess-playing program with the procedure in Fig. 6-10.

Note that in writing this high-level chess procedure we have assumed the existence of subroutines to determine if a position

Chess:

    [*Setup*;   Call subroutine *Setup* for initialization.

    if *position*="checkmate"   If the last move produces a board position which is checkmate, then the game is over.

      then done

      else

        if *move*="black"   If no checkmate, then next move is made.

          then *Blackmove*

          else *Whitemove*]

"Greatest common divisor—version 6";

Gcd(*a*,*b*):

    [**local** *z*;

    z ←**mod** (**max**(*a*,*b*), **min**(*a*,*b*));   *z* is set to the remainder of **max**(*a*/*b*, *b*/*a*).

    if *z*=0

        then return min(*a*,*b*)   If remainder = 0, done.

        else return *Gcd*(**min**(*a*,*b*),*z*)]   If remainder ≠ 0, return the result of *Gcd*(. . .).

FIGURE 6-11

is a checkmate, to determine whose move it is, to make a move for black, and to make a move for white. We can now continue by taking these subroutines in turn and programming them.

As another example, we could approach the job of creating a greatest common divisor program in a straightforward way by assuming functions for the maximum, minimum, and modulo (remainder after dividing), of two numbers (see Fig. 6-11). Then we would proceed by defining the functions **max, min,** and **mod.**

In the "bottom up" approach, we begin by identifying and defining useful "lower-level" routines, combining these into larger packages until finally we have the desired total procedure. Thus, in chess, we might create routines to check if a given move is legal, to make a given move, to check if a specified square is under attack, and so forth. Or, if using the computer in numerical work, we could start out defining **max, min, mod,** and other functions that might prove useful. Of course, most programmers use a mixture of these approaches; the important point is that the use of blocks and subroutines to structure a programming task fits naturally with either problem-solving tactic.

Much is being written about an approach to programming, called *structured programming,* which extends the notions expressed above on top down programming and the use of subroutines. There is no agreed-upon definition of structured programming. For our purposes, structured programming is a state of mind in which the programming task is approached.

This state of mind emphasizes "formalization" of a "top-level" statement of the procedure and of the statements (analogous to mathematical theorems) which must be true about the data at each step of execution to guarantee that the procedure will always produce the desired outputs. Under structured programming, procedures are written in several stages or levels, with the performance of each level "proven" before its sublevels are written. If this approach were carried to the extreme of formal mathematical proof (in those cases where possible), there would be no need to debug the resulting program; any bugs would have had to be corrected to enable a proof. (See exercise 12, Chap. 10, for a small example of this approach.)

STRUCTURED PROGRAMMING

STRUCTURE OF PROCEDURES

To follow the structural programming approach in detail may seem tedious and wasteful on small problems (at least for skilled programmers), and formally impossible for procedures of any complexity. Yet by using the approach as far as possible, there is evidently much to be gained in ease of debugging and of fitting together separately produced segments of larger systems.

Thus, structured programming involves working from the top down, making heavy use at each level of modules whose inputs and outputs are carefully defined, and with a great deal of attention to verifying for each level of program or module that (assuming the correctness of the submodules) the program works.

Not only must the inputs and outputs of each module be defined, but it is also desirable to structure the flow of control so that each module has a single entry and exit. Multiple entries and exits greatly complicate the statement of inputs and outputs, and thus the verification process. This structuring can be done by emphasizing the use of normal sequencing and of conditional and repetition statements and by minimizing the use of simple branching (go to) statements. The extreme of this approach, so-called gotoless programming, can be a natural if not necessary aspect of structured programming.

EXERCISES

1 Write a program to read in a sequence of numbers and print out the difference between successive items in the sequence. The first input is the number of items in the sequence; the remaining inputs are the items themselves. For example, if the input sequence were:

    5 4 −7 23 0 18

it would be followed by the output sequence:

    11 −30 23 −18

2 Now extend your program for exercise 1 (if necessary) so that it behaves properly for "extreme" data cases, such as zero or only one data item.

3 Many programming languages include a string-processing function called *index*. Index takes as its inputs two strings and searches the first input string for the first occurrence within that string of the second input. The output is the character position within the first string at which the second string starts, if it does occur within the first string, and zero if it does not occur. For example:

    index ("abcdbc","bc")=2

    index ("forever","eve")=4

    index ("hello_there","elf")=0

Program an **index** function.

4 The recursive version of the greatest common divisor program given in this chapter repeatedly tests which of its two inputs is larger. (*Gcd* makes this test each time it is evoked.) However, once we have identified which of the initial values is larger, we do not need to test for relative size again; the remainder is always smaller than the divisor. Rewrite *Gcd,* still using recursion, so as to omit unnecessary tests. (*Hint:* Your answer may use more than one block.)

5 A scientist has a series of readings of the concentration in solution of a certain substance. The readings were made at regular intervals and were subject to fluctuations due to uncontrollable factors. The scientist wishes to examine the data for trends by averaging out the fluctuations. Write a program to read in the sequence of data and write out a corresponding sequence in which each item is replaced by the average of itself and the preceding and following items. (The first and last items of the original sequence will not appear in the output.) The inputs are the sequence of data, terminated by a reading of zero. The outputs are the sequence of averages. Thus, for the input sequence

    4 4.2 3.8 4.3 5.1 4.4 4.6 0

The output sequence would be

    4 4.1 4.4 4.6 4.7

6 Prepare a program that determines the number of letters which two words have in common. The letters need not be in the same character position in the words. Assume that no letters appear more than once in a word. For example, "slept" and "wrong" have no letters in common, "wakes" and "aches" have three. The input is two words; the output is the number of common letters.

7 Extend your program for exercise 6 to include the possibility that letters may be repeated within a word. For example, "need" and "indeed" have four letters in common, "appear" and "potatoes" have three.

8 Write a program that reads in a word and counts the number of vowels. The input is a word; the output is the count.

Kernighan, Brian W., and P. J. Plauger: *The Elements of Programming Style,* McGraw-Hill, New York, 1974.

Wirth, Niklaus: *Systematic Programming: An Introduction,* Prentice-Hall, Englewood Cliffs, N.J., 1973.

REFERENCES

ARRAYS AND LOOPS

Loops are one of the most common structural constructs in programming. Even with a variety of repetition statements available, it is sometimes necessary to "program out" a loop using conditional and to statements. Whether spelled out or compacted into a repetition statement, a loop consists of four parts: initialization of variables, test for completion, computation, and modification of variables. Can you identify each of these components in the flowchart in Fig. 7-1 for computing the sum of the first *n* integers?

A TL procedure realizing this flowchart is given in Fig. 7-2(*a*) and a version using the **for** statement is in Fig. 7-2(*b*). Identify the four loop components—initialization, test for termination, computation, and modification—in these two programs.

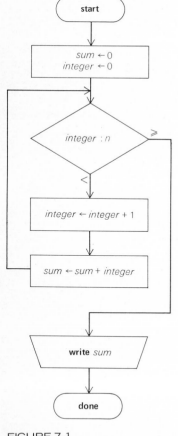

FIGURE 7-1
Add the first *n* integers.

"Add the first *n* integers—version 1";

    $sum \leftarrow 0$; $integer \leftarrow 0$;   Initialize values of *sum* and *integer*.

Loop:

    if $integer \geqslant n$ Test for termination.

        then write *sum*   If index exceeds limit, write answer.

        else   If not, increment index, add in next value, and return to test for termination.

        $[integer \leftarrow integer + 1;$

        $sum \leftarrow sum + integer;$

        to *Loop*];

(*a*)

"Add the first *n* integers—version 2";

    $sum \leftarrow 0$;   Initialization.

    for $integer \leftarrow 1$ **thru** *n*   Test and modify.

        $sum \leftarrow sum + integer;$ Computation.

    write *sum*;

FIGURE 7-2   (*b*)

Often the data to be processed are or can be considered a sequence. Most higher-level languages allow a data structure called an *array,* consisting of a sequence of items with one name but with each item having a distinct index or subscript. For example, we could consider the sequence of elements 3,5,7,22,9 as the values of an array named *a,* with $a_1 = 3$, $a_2 = 5$, and so forth. This array can be pictured as a row of cells containing the numbers (see Fig. 7-3).

Such subscripted arrays are particularly useful because arithmetic and ordering operations can be done on the subscripts. In particular, **for** type repetition statements, often called *iteration* statements, can be used to move through the array using the subscript as the index variable. To see the power of this approach, consider how you would have to program even the simple task of writing out a sequence of 50 values if they were the values of 50 distinct, unrelated variables.

In TL, we specify array elements by enclosing the subscript of an array entry in parentheses following the array name, as in $a(1)$ for a_1. Many implemented programming languages use this format, at least in part because it has been difficult on keypunches, teletypes, line printers and other typical input-output devices to indicate subscripts by dropping down a half line. As you will see in the next section, the array notion can be extended to several dimensions, with corresponding subscripts.

(In some implemented languages, the programmer is required to declare, in a special type of statement at the beginning of a procedure, the maximum and minimum subscripts of each array. This *dimension* statement is used to produce more efficient use of space and time in the final machine language program. For TL we ignore such considerations.)

Now let us look at an example of the use of arrays. A flowchart for a procedure to search a sequence of *n* values stored in array *a* looking for cases where the numbers are not in increasing order is provided in Fig. 7-4. Such a procedure might be used to check if a list of numbers that is supposed to be sorted really is. The procedure prints out each value that is less than its predecessor and its position in the list.

A segment of TL program for carrying out this checking follows:

for $j \leftarrow 1$ **thru** $n - 1$ **if** $a(j) > a(j+1)$ **then write** $j+1, a(j+1)$;
Try writing a program to do the same checking if the *n* values in sequence were not stored as values in an array, but as distinct variables, $a, b, \ldots, n$. And how would you modify that program if the number of values were changed? In the above, only a new value for *n* need be assigned.

As another example of the use of arrays, consider the problem of finding the earliest and latest (alphabetically) words in a sequence of words, and then writing out the message "⟨earliest⟩ through ⟨latest⟩". The flowchart in Fig. 7-5 shows a procedure for solving that problem, assuming that the words are stored (not necessarily in order) as values of the array *w.* A straightforward translation of this flowchart into TL is given in Fig. 7-6.

a_1 a_2 a_3 a_4 a_5

| 3 | 5 | 7 | 22 | 9 |

FIGURE 7-3

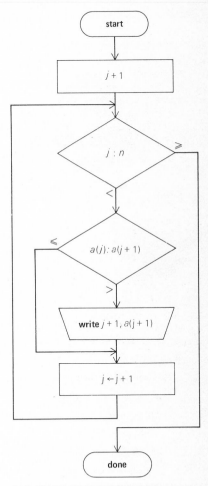

FIGURE 7-4
Check if a sequence is in order.

ARRAYS AND LOOPS

67

FIGURE 7-5
Find the earliest and latest words.

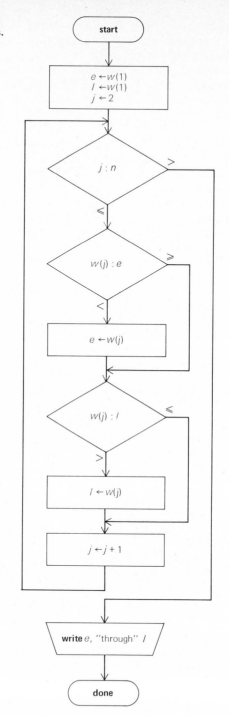

w = array of words
j = index
n = number of words
l = latest value
e = earliest value

"Find the earliest and latest words";
   $e \leftarrow w(1)$; $l \leftarrow w(1)$; $j \leftarrow 2$;
Loop:
   if $j > n$
      then write e, "through", l
      else
         [**if** $w(j) < e$
            then $e \leftarrow w(j)$;
         if $w(j) > l$
            then $l \leftarrow w(j)$;
         $j \leftarrow j + 1$;
         to *Loop*];

FIGURE 7-6

68

Try rewriting the above program to correct some of its obvious deficiencies. For example, in some cases the program makes tests whose outcome is known from previous tests.

Now we extend the structural concept of the TL array to multiple dimensions. As an example, consider the following situation. Professor Q wishes to get some feedback as to how he and his lectures in Introductory Aesthetics are affecting the 31 students in that class. So each week he hands out a 20-item questionnaire to the students. Each item is a simple yes-no, agree-disagree question. (For example, one item is "This week Professor Q's answers to student questions were generally responsive to what the student was asking. Agree _____. Disagree _____.") At the end of the quarter, Q has 10 stacks of questionnaires, one for each week, with 31 questionnaires in each stack. Of course, he has been looking at them each week to see how he is doing, but now Professor Q would like to analyze some of the items over time. How would you represent this data for processing by programs written in TL?

The raw data consists of separate *marks* for each *item* on a *questionnaire sheet* for a particular *week*. In order to have all of this data available within the computer, we must distinguish each datum along three dimensions: questionnaire, item, week. But assume for now that we are not interested in the distinction among individual questionnaires and will work only with total responses (total number of "yesses," say) for each item on a particular week. Then we might represent the data in a two-dimensional array as in Fig. 7-7.

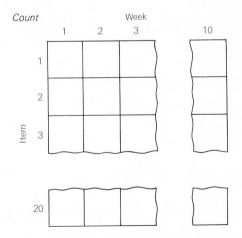

FIGURE 7-7

For 20 items and 10 weeks, if the data were presented one questionnaire at a time, all 31 questionnaires for a week together, in increasing order of items within a questionnaire and in increasing order of weeks, the flowchart in Fig. 7-8 describes a procedure to read in and total the data.

ARRAYS AND LOOPS

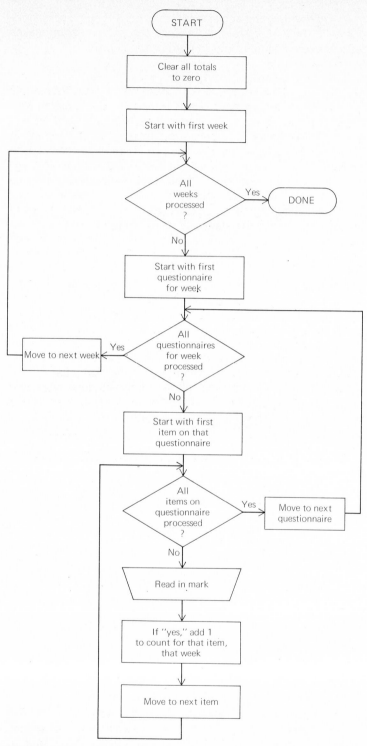

FIGURE 7-8
Data totaling procedure.

The TL program in Fig. 7-9 realizes the flowchart of Fig. 7-8. It assumes that marks in the "yes," "agree," space are entered as one and "no," "disagree" marks as zero.

"Read in and total questionnaire data";	Initialize totals.
for $i \leftarrow 1$ **thru** 20	For each row (item),
for $j \leftarrow 1$ **thru** 10	for each column (week),
$count\ (i,j) \leftarrow 0$;	set total variable to zero.
	Now read in and total questionnaires.
for $j \leftarrow 1$ **thru** 10	For each week,
for $k \leftarrow 1$ **thru** 31	for each questionnaire for that week,
for $i \leftarrow 1$ **thru** 20	for each item on that questionnaire,
[**read** *mark*;	read value and add it
$count\ (i,j) \leftarrow count\ (i,j) + mark$];	to appropriate total.

FIGURE 7-9

(Be sure that you can follow this procedure. For example, in what order are the items in *count* set to zero initially, all of one row at a time or all of one column at a time? Play computer to check your answer.)

Note that i and j are used as indices on the rows of *count* (items) and columns of *count* (weeks) respectively. While k is also an iteration variable, it is used to count the number of questionnaire sheets each week, not to index *count*.

SOME IMPORTANT POINTS

This program illustrates several important concepts about data structuring. First, the program does not "know" that each row of data represents an item or each column a week. That may be indicated in comments, flowcharts, drawings, etc., but this information is only meaningful to you or other people. To the computer, an array is an array is an array. Any further meaning is in the intent of the programmer and in his interpretation of the results of executing the program. *You* may know that this array is a grouping of totals, but even the array name has no meaning to the program; *count* is just another two-dimensional array. And in more complicated cases these meanings that are so clear in the programmer's head may not even be apparent to other human readers unless the programmer writes them down. Do not expect the computer to behave in a certain way because of what the data means *to you*. The computer will behave as the program instructs—no more, no less.

Second, the order in which data are to be read in, and so the order of statements in the program, depends on the order in which that data is presented in the input media. If the physical order is changed (for example, all 10 questionnaires from one student are read in before the next student's), then the program must be changed to reflect that order. The programmer must make sure that whoever is entering data for the program knows the order that the program is expecting, or that the program reminds him of that order, or that the data is self-identifying. (For example, if each questionnaire sheet had as its first data item the number of the week in which it was administered, the value of j could be read from the questionnaire. If that were done, the questionnaires need not be in order.)

Third, the usefulness of data often depends on careful planning in gathering it. In our example, the average positive count by week across all items may or may not be meaningful. If Professor Q had worded all items positively, so that a "yes" or "agree" is always a positive comment on his teaching, then such an analysis would be easy and possibly meaningful. If the items are mixed positive and negative, however, further adjusting must be done before that analysis could be carried out. The job of data analysis begins not with programming but with *planning the gathering of the data*.

The program fragment in Fig. 7-10 will compute and write out the average count (number of positive responses) for each item across the quarter. If we wished to make these programs more general (usually a good idea), we could replace the specific numbers of weeks, items, and questionnaires, by variables with the appropriate value. Then, if we should decide to skip one week, or disqualify an item as ambiguous, we need only change one variable rather than many constants throughout the program.

"Compute average count";

for $i \leftarrow 1$ **thru** 20

   [$ave \leftarrow 0$;

    for $j \leftarrow 1$ **thru** 10

      $ave \leftarrow ave + count\ (i,j)$;

    write "for item", i, "ave=", $ave/10$];

FIGURE 7-10

EXERCISES

1 The crossproduct of two arrays is the sum of the products of their individual terms in order. For example, the crossproduct of 3 4 5 and 12 −2 7 is 63. Write a program to read in first the length of the array, then the first array, and then the second, and to print out their crossproduct.

2 For exercise 10 in Chap. 5, making change, store the information as to which denominations may be used for making change in an array, and rewrite your program so that it works from that array. Add $5.00 bills and 50 cent pieces to the denominations available.

3 One method for sorting an array in decreasing order is as follows. Start with the first value of the array. Go through the remaining values, exchanging any one larger than the first with the first. At the end of this pass through all values, the largest will be first. Now, start with the second value of the array and repeat going through the remainder and exchanging. At the end of this pass, the second largest value will be second. Repeat this procedure for all positions from first to last. For example, the state of the following five-value array after each pass is as shown.

Initially:	4 −3 6 8 0
After first pass:	8 −3 4 6 0
(exchanged 4 and 6, then 6 and 8)	
After second pass:	8 6 −3 4 0
(exchanged −3 and 4, then 6 and 4)	

After third pass:	8 6 4 −3 0
(exchanged 4 and −3)	
After fourth pass:	8 6 4 0 −3
(exchanged −3 and 0)	

Write a program to read in an array of numbers, sort it using this method, and print out the resulting ordered sequence.

4 A botanist is investigating the relationship between the amount of light exposure and the total growth of 20 species of African violet. The total growth ranges from 1 to 5 inches and the exposure from 8 to 22 hours. Prepare a program to read in and tabulate this information. Group the growth into intervals of 1 inch and the exposure hours into 3-hour intervals. Be sure to specify the format of input data.

5 Extend your program for exercise 4, if necessary, to check the validity of input data and print out an appropriate message for each invalid set of data.

6 A supermarket manager wishes to determine how men and women differ in their shopping hours. He has collected information in the form (sex, time) for each customer entering the store over the last week. The market was open from 0900–2100 hours each day. The information is encoded 1 if the customer was male and 2 if female. Write a program to accumulate this information in a table of the following form. Print the table.

| | HOURS | | |
SEX	9–11	11–1	1–3
Male			
Female			

7 The manager of the market in exercise 6 also wants a tabulation of his data by sex and by time period. The desired output is the number of men and women customers, and of men and women together for each time period. Extend your program to produce those totals also.

8 Revise the questionnaire analysis program given in this chapter to record in memory each individual raw data item, rather than summarizing on input. (*Hint:* Use a three-dimensional array.)

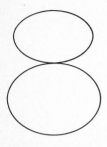

REPRESENTING THE STRUCTURE OF DATA

Most problems involve more complex structures of data than the simple single numbers or words in our previous examples. Except for the array, the data facilities available directly in many higher-level languages to which TL is similar are at the level of single values—a number, a string of characters, **true** or **false.** The programmer must construct a representation of the problem data out of these elements. This choice of data representation is as important a part of the programming task as specification of the procedure. Indeed, as you will see in many examples, specification of data structure and specification of procedure are closely related.

In this chapter we examine some common methods of structuring complex problem data. Because we are using TL as our procedure description language, we must ultimately state each structure in TL constructs—numbers, strings, or logical values, as single items or grouped as elements of an array. This restriction on possible solutions is typical of many current higher-level programming languages.

LISTS   One of the most powerful features of arrays is that they provide a means of associating and ordering data items. Because the *names* of the variables are *not* symbols available to be operated on by the program, there is no *easy* way (there is almost always *some* way) of ordering five data items with separate names, even if those names are alphabetically consecutive, such as *a,b,c,d,e,* or *a*1, *a*2, *a*3, *a*4, *a*5. But if the five items are the values of *a*(1) through *a*(5), we can find the next or previous one by adding or subtracting one to the index variable.

However, using an array in a straightforward way to keep a number of items in order sometimes results in excessive moving of values. Using the notion of a *linked list* may lead to a "better" program.

Suppose, for example, that rather than writing out the average for each item as earlier (see Fig. 7-10), we had stored those averages in a new array *ave* (see Fig. 8-1). Now we wish to

"Complete averages and store them in an array";

for $i \leftarrow 1$ **thru** 20

$\quad [ave(i) \leftarrow 0;$

$\quad$ **for** $j \leftarrow 1$ **thru** 10

$\quad\quad ave(i) \leftarrow ave(i) + count\ (i,j);$

$\quad ave(i) \leftarrow ave(i)/10];$

FIGURE 8-1

arrange and print out the item averages in order, largest first. To get the averages in this new order, by magnitude rather than by item, we must compare them. Also, if we use *ave* as a one-dimensional array, we must move the averages around, placing the largest in *ave*(1), etc. (The whole question of sorting will be discussed in some detail in Chap. 17.) But, using a linked list, we can represent the order without physically rearranging the data elements themselves.

One possible linked-list representation for our example is shown in Fig. 8-2. We have added a second piece of data to each row of the array *ave*. The first column in a row still holds the average value itself. The second column holds a *pointer* (also called a *link*) to the next data element *in order.* Thus, order is no longer represented implicitly by consecutive row numbers but rather is represented explicitly by the link. In TL, a convenient way to represent the link is by the index of the row it points to. Thus, as shown in Fig. 8-3, the second column of each row contains the row number of the next item in order.

How might we construct this ordering in *ave* assuming that the average values are already available? Or even more simply, what would be a program to write out the elements of *ave* once it is in order? Immediately we have a problem. We know that the next element after the element in row *i* is in row *ave*(*i*,2) (that is the purpose of the link), but how do we know in which row to find the *first* element, and how do we know when we have reached the end of the list? If an array is being used to represent a linked list, row one need not hold the first element on the list, and the highest numbered row need not hold the last. There must be some other means of indicating these positions.

The "standard" way of handling these problems is to define for each list a *head* and an *end* or *termination symbol.* The head, which points to (holds a link to) the first row in order, may be a separate variable or it may be a specially designated row of the

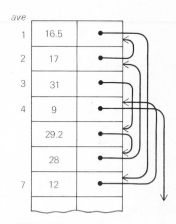

FIGURE 8-2

ave		
1	16.5	7
2	17	1
3	31	5
4	9	11
5	29.2	6
6	28	2
7	12	4

FIGURE 8-3
A list in an array.

"Print arrays in order";

$i \leftarrow avehead;$ — Set *i* to the pointer to the first row.

until $i = 0$ — Test for end of list.

$\quad [$**write** "item", *i*, "average", *ave*(*i*,1); — If $i \neq 0$, then print information and advance down list.

$\quad i \leftarrow ave(i,2)];$

REPRESENTING THE STRUCTURE OF DATA

FIGURE 8-4

array (often row 0). In this example we use a variable *avehead* to hold the head. Since we agree that row 0 will never hold a data item (either because we use it as the head or we leave it empty), we can use the link value 0 as an end symbol. Now it is straightforward to construct a procedure for writing out the averages in order (see Fig. 8-4).

Basic list operations

The three basic operations in processing a list are *advance* or *locate next, insert* an item, and *delete* an item. The statement $i \leftarrow ave(i,2)$ in Fig. 8-4 is an example of advancing (following the link). The effects of insertion and deletion are depicted in Fig. 8-5.

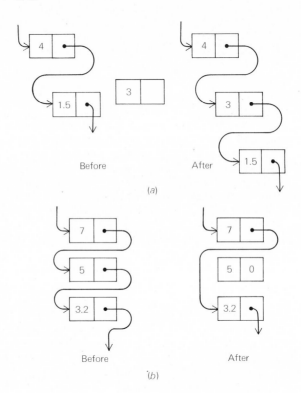

FIGURE 8-5
Basic operations on lists. (*a*) Insertion, (*b*) deletion.

Constructing a list in order

The flowchart in Fig. 8-6 gives a procedure for constructing in array *ave* a list of the items in decreasing order by average, assuming that the array is represented as shown in Fig. 8-2.

The program fragment in Fig. 8-7 carries out this procedure. It assumes that the value of *last_ave* is the number of data rows in *ave* and that there is at least one data item. Note that the procedure uses a repetition statement on index variable *i* to go through the unordered rows, but detects the last list row by a test for zero on link variable *j*. Note also that it must use two distinct insert functions, one if the element is to go first on the list and another if the element is to go after some other element.

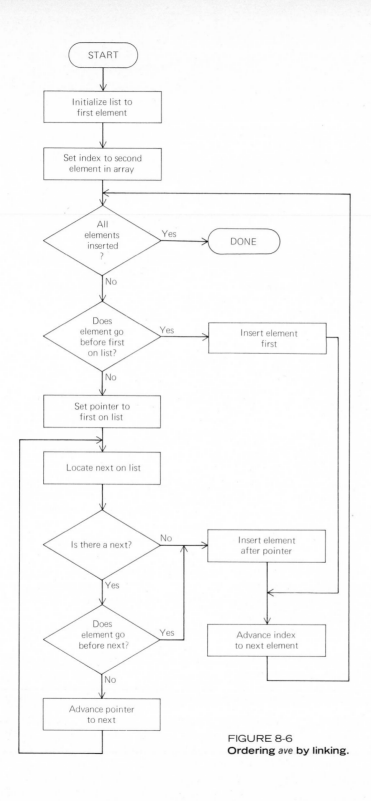

FIGURE 8-6
Ordering *ave* **by linking.**

```
avehead ← 1; ave(1,2) ← 0;                    Initialize, set link of head list to one and link of first row to zero.

for i ← 2 thru last_ave                       For each element in turn, search through list for place to insert.

  if ave(i,1) ≥ ave(avehead,1)                If current candidate for insertion (ave(i,1)) is greater than the first item in the list,
                                              then insert candidate in front of list and get next candidate.


    then Headinsert(i)
    else

      [ j ← avehead;                          Else advance down list.
Loop:

        next ← ave(j,2);

        if next=0 or ave(i,1) ≥ ave(next,1)   If encounter end of list or candidate greater than current item, insert,

          then Insert(i,j)                    else advance down list and go to Loop.

          else [ j ← next; to Loop]]; done;

Insert(x,y):

  [ave(x,2) ← ave(y,2);                       Insert row x into list at position previously held by row y by replacing link of x with
                                              link of y and link of y with x.

  ave(y,2) ← x];

Headinsert(x):

  [ave(x,2) ← avehead;

  avehead ← x];
```

FIGURE 8-7

Follow through this program with pencil and paper to be sure that you understand it. Perhaps you can find some improvements.

Often the order among a set of data elements that we wish to record is not a numerical function of the elements at all, but rather reflects some other consideration. For example, we could use a list (or an array) to store the words in a sentence in order of occurrence, or the names of students waiting to get into a course in order of eligibility. The same comparisons of the relative advantages of lists and arrays still hold, and the same basic list operations are still relevant.

We shall say more about lists and pointers in this and later chapters, as they are a very powerful programming technique. Also, our simple example gives a limited impression both of their uses and of some of the problems that arise. For example, insertion in a list may occur at several points in a procedure, or may be spread out over several procedures, as may deletion. If new items are being created and added to a list by several different procedures, how does one keep track of empty (available) slots for holding them? And if items are being deleted from the list, what happens to the slots that formerly held those items? Or, as another example, if we wish to go from an item to that *preceding* it on a list, should we use two links per item—one forward and one backward? And so forth.

If our problem data exists in space and so can be visualized as a grid of points, as say a checkerboard, then an array seems a natural data structure. Most board games, such as tic-tac-toe in two or more dimensions and other such pastimes, fit this situation. An array might also be a natural way for representing a map or a maze for running rats. However, there are alternatives. For example, another way of representing a map besides overlaying it with a grid is suggested in Fig. 8-8. Particularly if use of a grid results in a number of empty spaces or zero values, pointers may require considerably less data space and running time. Part of the challenge in programming is to find a better representation of the data.

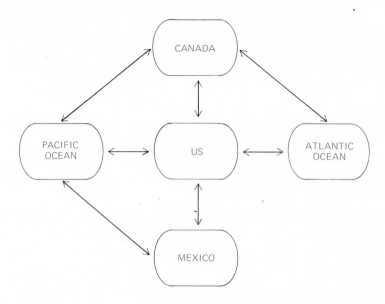

FIGURE 8-8
Another representation of a map.

Often the basic relationship among data elements is logical rather than physical. Common types of such logical relationships are hierarchies and branching processes. These relationships have a common underlying structure as shown in Fig. 8-9. This structure is called a *tree.*

Examples of trees, all shown in Fig. 8-10, include an organization chart, a partial genealogy, the outline of a term paper, a parsing of a sentence, and a strategy for playing blackjack. These all are trees because (1) each data element, or *node,* has one and

TREES

FIGURE 8-9
A tree.

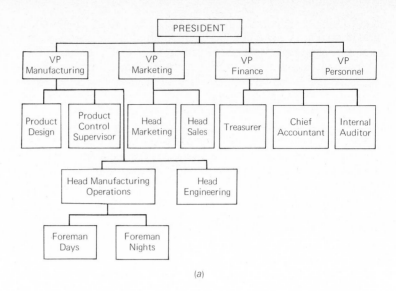

(a)

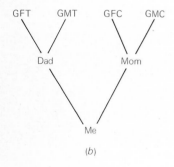

(b)

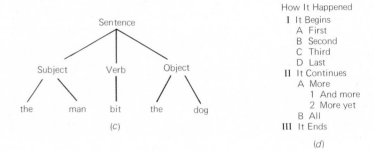

(c)

How It Happened
  I It Begins
     A First
     B Second
     C Third
     D Last
 II It Continues
     A More
        1 And more
        2 More yet
     B All
III It Ends

(d)

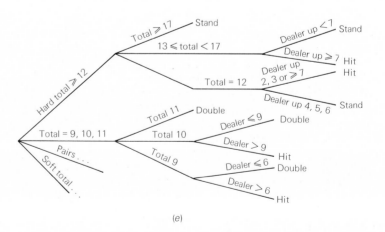

(e)

FIGURE 8-10
Examples of trees. (a) Organization chart; (b) genealogy; (c) parse of a sentence; (d) term paper outline; (e) blackjack strategy.

only one *ancestor* or *root,* excepting (2) one distinguished node, which has no ancestor and is the root of the entire tree. Each node is a root for a subtree of its descendants and their descendants. Those nodes with no descendants are called *leaves* or *terminal nodes.* All nodes with the same immediate ancestor are called *siblings.*

Because so many different problem situations can be represented as trees, computer scientists have devoted a great deal of attention to studying the formal properties of trees. However, we shall not discuss that work here, but rather concentrate on ways in which trees can be represented in an array.

In the general case, a particular node may have an arbitrary number of descendants. We can put all descendants of a node on a list, and use a pointer to connect the node to the list. In Fig. 8-11 we represent our parsed sentence [Fig. 8-10(c)] in an array. Each row represents an element of the parse tree, with data in the first column, pointer to descendants in the second, and link to siblings (other descendants of the same ancestor) in the third.

	DATA	POINTER TO DESCENDANTS	LINK TO SIBLINGS
0		9	0
1	the	0	2
2	man	0	0
3	bit	0	0
4	the	0	5
5	dog	0	0
6	object	4	0
7	subject	1	8
8	verb	3	6
9	sentence	7	0

FIGURE 8-11
Representing a tree in an array.

In a tree where each node has at most two descendants, we can use the same array structure, but using the second column for one descendant and the third column for the other (see Fig. 8-12).

Often we can use trees to reduce computing by encoding in the structure of the tree hierarchical information that it would be difficult to compute directly. For example, consider the following logical expression in TL:

$$(a+b \uparrow 2 * c > 3 \textbf{ or } (x-y/2 < z-1) \textbf{ and } b \geqslant 17$$

Obviously, a correct evaluation of the entire expression requires that its various parts be evaluated in the proper order. In Chap. 5 we gave rules for determining the precedence of the various operators in TL. We could represent this expression as a

0		4	0
1	Mom	3	2
2	Grandma C.	0	0
3	Grandad C.	0	0
4	Me	5	1
5	Dad	7	6
6	Grandma T.	0	0
7	Grandad T.	0	0

FIGURE 8-12
Representing a two-descendant tree in an array.

string of characters, and prepare a TL procedure to scan and rescan it picking out subexpressions in the proper order for evaluation. Or we could represent the expression as a tree of characters as in Fig. 8-13, from which the proper order of evaluation would be obvious. (In Chap. 14, we demonstrate how to construct such a tree from the expression in *one* scan. For now, we take the tree as given.)

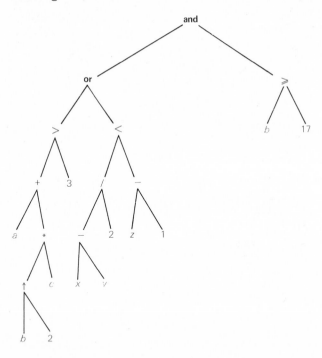

FIGURE 8-13
Logical expression as a tree.

Because TL operators never have more than two operands, we can use the scheme illustrated in Fig. 8-12 for representing TL expressions as data. Our example would then be as shown in Fig. 8-14, pointing to the left subtree and then to the right. Since each node in a tree has at most one ancestor, it is possible to record that information also, and we have done so in a fourth column labeled UP.

logex		LEFT	RIGHT	UP
0		1	1	0
1	**and**	2	3	0
2	**or**	4	5	1
3	$\geq$	6	7	1
4	$>$	8	9	2
5	$<$	10	11	2
6	b	0	0	3
7	17	0	0	3
8	+	12	13	4
9	3	0	0	4
10	/	14	15	5
11	−	16	17	5
12	a	0	0	8
13	*	18	19	8
14	−	20	21	10
15	2	0	0	10
16	z	0	0	11
17	1	0	0	11
18	↑	22	23	13
19	c	0	0	13
20	x	0	0	14
21	y	0	0	14
22	b	0	0	18
23	2	0	0	18

FIGURE 8-14
Logical expression tree encoded in an array.

The flowchart in Fig. 8-15 represents a procedure for counting the number of nodes in a two-descendant tree. In particular, this procedure could be used to count the number of symbols in the example logical expression.

A TL program fragment realizing this flowchart for the case of counting the number of symbols in the logical expression encoded in *logex* (Fig. 8-14) is given in Fig. 8-16. Note how the UP column is used to keep track of position in the tree. However, this flowchart and program are not the easiest way to program counting nodes. Because of the hierarchical structure of trees, it is natural to think of processing them by hierarchically pro-

SOME TREE-PROCESSING PROGRAMS

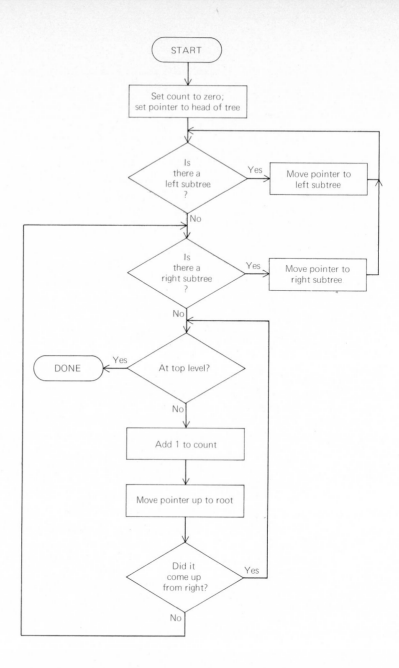

FIGURE 8-15
Counting the nodes in a tree.

cessing their subtrees, that is, to process them recursively. A recursive procedure for the counting is given in Fig. 8-17. The value of *nodes* (*logex*(0,2)) will be the count of nodes for the tree.

We can also treat the name of the (array holding the) tree as a parameter, giving the procedure(s) in Fig. 8-18, which will count the nodes in any tree, not just *logex*.

Of course, the procedures in Figs. 8-17 and 8-18 are somewhat inefficient in that they call themselves recursively even for links of zero. This can be avoided at the expense of making the

```
nodes ←0; i ←0                    Initialization.

Left:
    if logex(i,2) ≠ 0
    then [j ← logex(i,2); to Left];
Right:                            Go down to left.
    if logex(i,3) ≠ 0
        then [i ← logex(i,3); to Left];   Go down to right.
Up:
    if logex(i,4) ≠ 0
        then                      Count node and back up.
        [nodes ← nodes + 1; j ← i; i ← logex(i,4);
        if logex(i,2) = j
            then to Right          Come from left.
            else to Up];           Come from right.          FIGURE 8-16
```

procedure somewhat more complex; we leave that extension as an exercise.

As a final example, the program in Fig. 8-19 produces as its value a string of the symbols (data values) in the tree in their original linear order. Note that the procedure in Fig. 8-19 does *not* reintroduce those necessary parentheses that appeared in the original linear version of the expression. If we assume a function *Hier* of two arguments whose value is **true** if the first argument is a symbol of higher precedence order than the second, and **false** otherwise, we can rewrite our procedure for stringing out a tree to produce necessary parentheses also (see Fig. 8-20). (Functions which produce a logical value are called *predicates*.)

One last digression on the problem of representing a TL expression as a tree within an array. Suppose that the language in which you are working does not allow, as TL does, mixed data

```
Nodes(i):
    if i = 0
        then return 0
        else
            return Nodes(logex(i,2))
                +Nodes(logex(i,3))+1;
```
FIGURE 8-17

```
Nodes(tree):
    return Nd(tree,tree(0,2));
Nd(t,i):
    if i = 0
        then return 0
        else
            return Nd(t,t(i,2))
                +Nd(t,t(i,3))+1;
```
FIGURE 8-18

```
String_tree(tree):
    if tree(0,2) = 0
        then return ""
        else
            return St(tree,tree(0,2));
St(t,i):
    if i = 0
        then return ""
        else
            return St(t,t(i,2))      Return everything to the left of the ith sym-
                                      bol, the ith symbol, and
                & t(i,1)
                & St(t,t(i,3));       everything to the right of the ith symbol.   FIGURE 8-19
```

String_tree(tree):

   if tree(0,2)=0

     then return ""

     else

       return St(tree,tree(0,2));

St(t,i):

  if i=0

    then return ""

    else

  if Hier(t(t(i,4),1), t(i,1))

    then return "(" & Stt(t,i) & ")"

    else return Stt(t,i);

Stt(t,i):

  return St(t,t(i,2))

    &t(i,1)

    &Stt(t,t(i,3));

FIGURE 8-20

tree

0	
1	and
2	or
3	

links

0	1	1	
1	2	3	0
2	4	5	1
3	6	7	1

FIGURE 8-21
Trees as parallel arrays.

types within the same array. One solution, shown in Fig. 8-21, is to use "parallel" arrays, one (with one column) for the symbols which are strings and another (with three columns) for the links which are numerical. (Another possibility is to use a separate array for each column.)

As was pointed out in Chap. 6, many higher-level programming languages do not allow recursive procedures. In expressing procedures such as those in Figs. 8-17 to 8-20 in those languages, the programmer must use an approach like that of the first version of the node counting procedure (see Fig. 8-16). This is sometimes unfortunate because the recursive approach is a powerful one and often greatly simplifies the programming task.

GRAPHS (NETWORKS)

Trees are a special case of graphs. In graphs any node can be connected (linked) to any other node. Graphs can be used to model electrical networks, or airline routes among cities, or the linked representation of a map suggested earlier. In the general case of a graph, no node stands in the privileged relationship of root or ancestor. Recursive procedures are not as generally applicable to graphs since there is the possibility of loops, which by definition cannot occur in a tree. The basic representational approach for graphs is to associate with each node a list of those nodes to which it is connected.

CENTRALIZATION OF KNOWLEDGE ABOUT THE STRUCTURE

As we indicated earlier, it is often desirable to arrange a program so that the programmer's decisions about how to represent the data are reflected in as few places as possible. For example, in the preceding logical expression example, knowledge of which data is stored in which column is reflected in every program fragment given. That knowledge could have been centralized into a few functions as in Fig. 8-22. Now the various routines could be rewritten as shown in Fig. 8-23.

What advantages does such centralization into functions offer? First, since the form may be more meaningful to the programmer, it can lead to fewer coding errors; e.g., you are more likely to write down the wrong column number than to write *Right* when you mean *Up*. Further, within the general approach of en-

Symb(tree,i):

    return tree(i,1);

Left(tree,i):

    return tree(i,2);

Right(tree,i):

    return tree(i,3);

Up(tree,i):

    return tree(i,4);

FIGURE 8-22

Nodes(tree):

    return Nd(tree,Left(tree,0));

Nd(t,i):

    if $i=0$

    then return 0

    else

        return Nd(t,Left(t,i))

          $+Nd(t,Right(t,i))+1$;

FIGURE 8-23

coding the tree in the rows of an array, this use of functions allows changes in the data structuring scheme as new requirements arise or errors are found, without having to make many changes throughout the program. Because there are fewer changes, errors are less likely here also. Further, this format makes it clearer to the reader of the program, including the programmer himself at a later date, just what is going on.

What disadvantages does this centralization have? It requires defining these additional functions, which require space. And the additional evocations of functions may take more computing time. If the program is completed, debugged, and not subject to change, such disadvantages may outweigh the advantages. More discussion on this general subject follows in the next two sections, after another example.

Sometimes centralization can also offer space savings. (The following example indicates the spirit of such possibilities, although the size of the example itself is not great enough to really cause much concern about space.) Suppose we are constructing a program to play bridge and we want a minimum space representation of each card. Generally we are interested in the suit and value of a card, but the minimum representation might be just the integers 1,2, . . . ,52. Using that approach, 1 for the TWO OF CLUBS through 52 for the ACE OF SPADES, we can create the functions to produce the card values (2 through 14 for the deuce through the ace) and its suit (1 for clubs, 2 for diamonds, 3 for hearts, and 4 for spades). (See Fig. 8-24. **frac** produces the fractional part of its argument; **int,** the integer part.) Such functions could well take less space than explicitly representing the suit and value for each card as separate numbers.

In bridge, when two cards are played, that with the greater face value is higher if they are of the same suit; otherwise, if one is of the suit currently named trumps, it is higher; otherwise the first one played is higher. Using the above functions and assuming the existence of a global variable *trump* which has as its value the trump suit, we can construct a predicate *High* indicating whether its first argument is higher than its second (see Fig. 8-25). Note that the value to be returned is found by evaluating a logical expression which will be either true or false.

Value(card):

    return frac((card-1)/13) * 13+2;

Suit(card):

    return int((card-1)/13)+1;

FIGURE 8-24

High(card1,card2):

  if suit(card1) = suit(card2)   If suit of card1 is same as suit of card2, then return **true** if value of card1 > value of card2.

  then return (Value(card1) > Value(card2))

  else return (suit(card2) ≠ trump);   If suit of card2 is different from that of card1, then return **true** if suit of card2 is not trump.

FIGURE 8-25

TIME VERSUS SPACE

In choosing a data representation and constructing a procedure, the programmer is constantly trading off execution time and storage space. If there are no constraints on either, he can be less careful in his choices; but that is a rare situation for realistic problems. Indeed, it has been said that time and space are the essence of programming.

We have seen a number of examples of this tradeoff in this chapter: In representing bridge cards, whether to use more space to represent the card suits and values or whether to encode them and use more time in function evocation to decode them. In going back up a list to previous items, whether to take the space to keep a backward link with each item also, or to take the time to start from the beginning of the list again, or to otherwise complicate the procedure. In sorting data items in order, whether to use up space for links or to spend more time physically rearranging the items. Or, if only the largest data item is required, and that not too often, to search the data again each time the largest is requested.

In each case, the tradeoff can only be made by analysis of the requirements—how much space, how much more time, how often? And because there is no single metric for measuring both time and space, the choice is ultimately a matter of judgment.

EFFICIENCY

Even if there were some numerical method of establishing a tradeoff between execution time and storage space, the question of the most efficient representation would not be settled. The question remains: Efficient for whom? The program that is ultimately efficient in execution may not be worth the extra time taken to program it. Or, if a program is not to be run too often, choices which improve debugging may be more efficient in machine time alone (let alone programmer time) than more sophisticated coding that does not quite work the first few times. Each pass through the translator may take more time than actually doing the final computations. (This is often true for student exercises, for example.)

So program efficiency involves, at the least, efficient use of storage space, execution time, translation time, and programmer time. Its complicated nature is not an excuse for ignoring the problem, but rather is even more reason for planning and analysis in choosing a data representation and procedure.

Some programming languages have additional facilities for structuring data that simplify many of the examples above. We have not included these capabilities in TL primarily because examples using them would not be easily translatable into many of the common higher-level programming languages. However, we do mention them here because they are very useful facilities that should be and no doubt will be more generally available.

In some languages, such as PL/1 and the specialized list-processing languages, a data type for pointers (essentially, addresses of data items) is available. Single variables can have as their values pointers to other variables, and so forth. This capability can greatly increase the programmer's facility in using list structures.

In some languages, such as PL/1 and COBOL, data may be structured into records with addressable subgroupings of fields. For example, consider a record called *pay_master,* including a field called *start_date,* which in turn has subfields named *day, month,* and *year.* The *day* field could be treated as a variable in PL/1, addressed as *pay_master.start_date.day.* In COBOL the field would be addressed as *day* of *start_date* of *pay_master.* For file processing in particular, such structuring ability is quite valuable.

Further, in some experimental languages, the programmer is allowed to define new data types as arbitrary groupings of given ones and to define new operators for such types or to indicate the action of previously defined operators on them. As an example, a type "complex number" might be defined as made up of two numeric parts, with the arithmetic operators redefined appropriately. While such a facility requires additional time and space, it also greatly eases the programming task for certain problems.

1 Write programs to *insert* a new item into and *delete* an item from a linked list such as that in Fig. 8-2.
2 Write a program to read in a sequence of data items and construct from them a doubly linked list. In a doubly linked list each element in the list has two pointers. One pointer is to the element following, the other preceding each element. The items are to be linked initially in the order in which they are read in. Encode the list in an array, as was done for singly linked lists in Fig. 8-2.

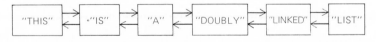

3 Write *insert* and *delete* functions for a doubly linked list. How do they differ from those of a singly linked list? Test your

functions on an actual data list and check that they reorder the elements on the list appropriately without actually changing their location.

4 Write a program to count the number of times a given symbol appears in the tree of an expression. Use the data structure given for *logex* in Fig. 8-14.

5 Write a program to determine the greatest depth of a tree. Use the data structure given in Fig. 8-14.

6 The *Nodes* procedure given in Fig. 8-17 is inefficient in that it evokes itself recursively even for links of zero. Revise the procedure so that it does not evoke itself for zero subtrees.

7 Write a program to compare two binary trees and output whether or not they are the same. Use any tree representation you wish, but be sure to describe the structure and provide a sample diagram.

8 Program the *Hier* function described on page 85.

9 Design a data structure for representing a bridge hand so that it is "easy" (requires little processing) to locate a card that will take (be of higher rank than, as defined by the predicate *High*) another specified card.

10 The TL program in Fig. 8-7 which follows from the flowchart in Fig. 8-6 requires two insert functions, one for use at the head of the list and another for use within the list. However, if the head of the list were kept in some row of the array (such as row zero), the program would be simplified and only one insert function would be required. Revise the program in Fig. 8-7 using some row of the array as the list head.

11 Prepare a procedure to construct a binary tree, where the data items to be input are an unordered list of numbers. To determine where to place a number in the tree, apply the following rules.

Let r be the root node
   ls be the left subtree
   rs be the right subtree
   0 represent empty subtree
   n be node being examined
   i be value of number to insert

  I $n \leftarrow r$
  II **if** $i > n$ **then to** V
  III $n \leftarrow ls(n)$
  IV **if** $n = 0$
       then *Insert at this leaf*
       else to II
  V $n \leftarrow rs(n)$, **to** IV

(These rules state that smaller numbers go into the left subtree and larger numbers into the right.)

12 The procedure described in exercise 11 builds a *sorted binary tree*. The tree can now be scanned and the data items of each node printed out such that an ordered list of numbers is produced. The required scan is called a *postorder traversal* and is defined (recursively) as:

traverse the left subtree (if any) in postorder; visit (print out the data item of) the root; traverse the right subtree (if any) in postorder;

Write a program to traverse a binary tree in postorder. It need not be a recursive. For example, the tree shown below would lead to the indicated output.

13 Design a data structure for representing general graphs (i.e., a node can be connected to any number of other nodes) as TL data.

Berztiss, A. T.: *Data Structures: Theory and Practice,* Academic, New York, 1971.
Knuth, Donald E.: *The Art of Computer Programming,* vol. 1, *Fundamental Algorithms,* Addison-Wesley, Reading, Mass., 1968. See especially chap. 2, "Information Structures," pp. 228–463.

REFERENCES

COMPUTING STRATEGIES
In Chap 3 we discussed some approaches to problem solving, particularly solving programming problems. If successful, this problem solving leads to a program to do the necessary computations. In this chapter, we will discuss several ways in which these computer programs can be organized — strategies for computing the solution to a problem. These computing strategies are closely connected with the problem-solving methods discussed earlier, and often seem to follow naturally from a particular way of viewing the problem. The four strategies that follow are not entirely distinct, but merge with one another in various combinations. Since this classification of strategies is intended to help you use the computer effectively, not just as a list to memorize, you may find this blending useful in suggesting alternative approaches to a particular problem.

The four computing strategies we will discuss (adapted from a similar list in *Introduction to Computer Science* by Rice and Rice) are *direct solution, enumeration, trial and error,* and *simulation.* The direct-solution method computes the answer to a problem by evaluating some expression that produces the answer. Direct solution is the strategy most generally used, when possible; other computing strategies are used when no direct-solution method is available.

Enumeration and trial and error both generate and evaluate many possible alternative answers searching for the best solution. In enumeration, the generation of alternatives is systematic and, in some cases, exhaustive. In trial and error, the generation of alternatives is more selective than in enumeration, often relying on information from previously computed alternatives to suggest what alternative to try next.

If no direct-solution method is available and if the number of possible answers is too large for enumeration or trial and error to be appropriate, then simulation techniques may be useful. In simulation a model is constructed of the problem situation being studied and then the model is exercised. The model's behavior may produce a solution directly, or further study of that behavior by those interested in the problem may result.

This distinction among solution methods can also be stated in terms of a set or space of possible solutions to a problem.

Direct computation and simulation are similar in that they generate only one possible solution to the problem. Direct computation produces the best answer; simulation produces some one answer. Enumeration and trial and error are similar in that they generate many possible solutions. Enumeration produces all possible answers (possibly rigorously excluding some as being less desirable); trial and error produces a sequence of trial answers.

Typically, direct-solution and simulation procedures are quite specific to the particular problem being solved, while enumeration and trial-and-error procedures often incorporate problem-independent search techniques. One's confidence in the answer produced by a direct computation or by simulation is derived from confidence in the problem-solving procedure. One's confidence in answers produced by procedures relying on search among many alternatives (enumeration and trial and error) is based on the ability to recognize the "right" answer when it is generated. The choice among computing strategies often resolves into a choice between investing effort in searching for a good solution procedure (direct computation or simulation) or in searching among alternative solutions (enumeration and trial and error).

DIRECT SOLUTION

If the problem situation can be formalized into a specific set of solvable equations or a straightforward guaranteed procedure, the program can then use direct solution to compute an answer. The process of formalizing the problem, of constructing a framework, may involve any of the problem-solving strategies discussed earlier—working forward, working backward, analogy, and so forth. Most of the example problems used in this text have been solved by the direct-solution method. For example, both Euclid's algorithm for finding greatest common divisors and the procedure for reversing a word produce a result directly, without generating and evaluating possible alternative answers. In most cases, the task in direct solution is to develop the equations or procedure for which a direct solution can be computed; writing the program itself is relatively less difficult.

Card-ordering example

Suppose that you are responsible for ordering boxes of punched cards for the bookstore. Over the year the total number of cards sold will be many boxes, and let us suppose that sales are about the same each week. Should you order a total year's supply at once? Probably not, since there is a limited amount of space available for storing various supplies. In fact, if you know the cost per box of holding it in inventory (storage space and interest on money tied up in stock) and the cost to the bookstore of writing and processing an order for more cards, you can compute the total cost of handling boxes of punched cards for the year as follows:

$$\text{total cost} = (\text{ordering cost}) * (\text{number of orders})$$
$$+ (\text{inventory cost}) * (\text{average stock})$$

Since sales are roughly even throughout the year, average stock would be one-half the size of an order, or

$$\text{average stock} = \frac{1}{2} * \frac{(\text{yearly sales})}{(\text{number of orders})}$$

from this, the expression for total cost becomes:

$$\text{total cost} = (\text{ordering cost}) * (\text{number of orders})$$
$$+ \frac{(\text{inventory cost}) * (\text{yearly sales})}{2 * (\text{number of orders})}$$

Thus, if you order a smaller amount more frequently, ordering costs go up and inventory holding costs go down. This situation is depicted in Fig. 9-1. The problem is to find the number of orders that minimizes their sum.

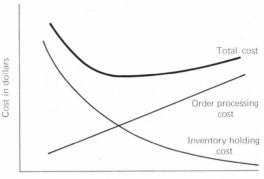

FIGURE 9-1
Total inventory cost.

Using calculus, or just reasoning about the effects on total cost of a small change in number of orders, leads to the following expression for the optimum number of orders (the number that minimizes total cost).

$$\text{number of orders} = \sqrt{\frac{(\text{inventory cost}) * (\text{yearly sales})}{2 * (\text{ordering cost})}}$$

Now the problem can be solved using direct solution, for example with the following TL program segment.

> *number* ← **sqrt** (*inv_cost* * *sales*/ (2 * *order_cost*))

Pig latin example

As another example, consider a program to respond to an input word with its equivalent in pig latin. A straightforward procedure for doing this would be to check if the first letter of the word is a vowel, if so to append "nay" to the word, and otherwise find the first vowel in the word and append all letters preceding that vowel to the end of the word followed by "ay." Again, once a direct-solution procedure can be stated, the program follows easily (if you are familiar with the elements of the programming language being used). The TL program in Fig. 9-2 goes through the word letter by letter searching for the first vowel and takes appropriate action depending on where in the word that first vowel occurred. The predicate *Vowel* returns as its result the value of a logical expression testing the specified letter against the vowels. (Note that the value of *Pig_Latin* is undefined if the word has no vowels.)

Pig_Latin(*word*):

    for $k \leftarrow 1$ **thru** # *word*   Scan each letter of *word* until a vowel is found.

       if *Vowel*(*word* **@** (*k*,1))

      then   If the vowel is the first letter, then answer is *word* and "nay."

      [**if** *k*=1]

        then return *word* & "nay"

        else   If the vowel is not the first letter, then answer is the first vowel and the remaining characters followed by the letters preceding the first vowel and the "ay."

           return *word* **@** (*k*)

              & *word* **@** (1,*k*-1)

              & "ay"];

Vowel(*x*):   Answer is **true** if letter is a vowel.

    return x="a" **or** x="e"

    or x="i" **or** x="o" **or** x="u";

FIGURE 9-2

ENUMERATION

The computing strategy of enumeration is used when the program does not have a direct-solution method for the problem at hand. Enumeration consists of *systematic* generation and evaluation of alternative answers, i.e., a series of different cases. Each case may be evaluated using direct solution or some other method, but the essence of the method is the enumeration of a number of cases.

Card-ordering example

Consider the punched card–ordering problem just discussed. If an expression for the optimum number of orders did not exist (as is often true with more complicated problems), the program could systematically compute the total cost for different numbers of orders, starting with once a year, until we found that for which the cost is lowest.

    The equation for total cost is such that its value will decrease as the number of orders increases, up to a point (the optimum), and then it will increase (see Fig. 9-1). Thus, the enumeration need continue only until total costs start rising. Note that this approach produces an integer number of orders per year, while the value of the equation used in direct solution need not be an integer. The TL segment in Fig. 9-3 uses enumeration to find the least total cost number of orders, and also prints out the total cost for each number of orders considered.

    You may want to try out this approach for some specific data. If yearly sales are 10,000 boxes, the cost per order is $10.00, and the holding cost per box is $0.10 per year, direct solution gives us 7.07 orders (to the nearest hundredth) as the optimum. The TL segment above for enumeration will produce total costs for one through eight orders per year before it stops; the values for six, seven, and eight are as follows:

    6   143.33
    7   141.43
    8   142.50

"Card ordering by enumeration";

$prev \leftarrow 10 \uparrow 6$; $cost \leftarrow 10 \uparrow 6$;	Initialize costs to large numbers for comparison.
$number \leftarrow 1$;	Number set to one.
until $cost > prev$	Repeat the following steps until costs start increasing.
$[prev \leftarrow cost$;	
$cost \leftarrow order\_cost * number$	Set $prev \leftarrow cost$;
$+ inv\_cost * sales/(2 * number)$;	Compute $cost$ for new $number$.
write $number, cost$;	Write $number$ and $cost$.
$number \leftarrow number + 1]$;	Increase $number$ by one.

FIGURE 9-3

Assignment example

Many of the problems that arise in managing an operation, whether a business, hospital, school, or commune, can be dealt with using enumeration. Basically, many of the quantitative techniques of management science are enumeration techniques. The following situation is a classic management science paradigm, the assignment problem.

Arnie, Bonnie, Clyde, Dee, and Fran have five tasks to be done on Saturday as shown in Fig. 9-4. Because each one is interested in and skilled at different things, the five require different amounts of time to do any job. And they get bored doing the same thing each week. For this Saturday at least, they have agreed to assign jobs so that the total amount of work for all is the least. Who should do what?

One systematic way to compute an answer to this problem using enumeration would be to assign each job in turn to Arnie; for each such assignment assign each remaining job in turn to Bonnie; for each such pair of assignments assign each job of the remaining three to Clyde, and so forth. Whichever assignment required the least total time would be best.

It turns out that actually programming this enumeration procedure is not as simple as the above statement might lead one to expect. A great deal of thought was given to how to represent the data before arriving at the solution given below.

Let us imagine a one-dimensional array, say *a*, each of whose rows corresponds to a job and whose value in a row is the

FIGURE 9-4
Assignment problem data.

time	Arnie	Bonnie	Clyde	Dee	Fran
clean house	2	3	1	2	2
shopping	2	3	3	3	2
cook dinner	4	3	2	3	4
chop wood	1	2	5	2	3
feed animal	4	4	4	2	4

identification of the person assigned to the corresponding job. For example, the values in *a* depicted in Fig. 9-5 correspond to Arnie cleaning house, Bonnie shopping, . . . , and Fran feeding the animals. Then the task of generating all assignments is identical to the task of generating all orderings (also called *permutations*) of the elements of array *a*. For the remainder of this discussion, we focus on this more general problem of generating orderings. For the assignment problem each of these orderings could be evaluated using the data in Fig. 9-4 and the best one selected.

The flowchart of the ordering procedure is given in Fig. 9-6 and the TL version of the procedure is in Fig. 9-7. It uses two one-

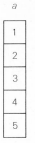

FIGURE 9-5
One possible assignment.

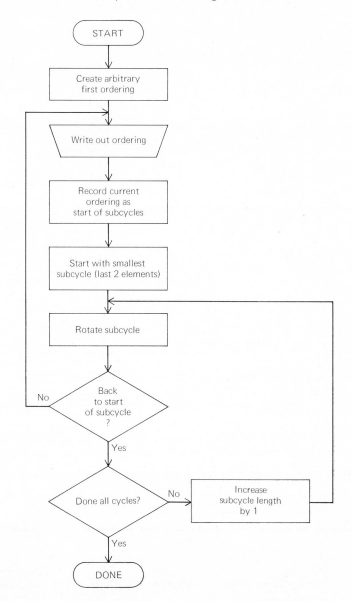

FIGURE 9-6
Procedure to generate orderings.

"Enumerate alternative solutions
to assignment problem";

for $i \leftarrow 1$ **thru** n Make arbitrary first ordering.

$a(i) \leftarrow i$;

$i \leftarrow 0$;

New:

Output;   Write out new ordering.

Record; $i \leftarrow n-1$;   Record start of subcycles beginning
                                                         with smallest subcycle.

Change:

Rotate;   Rotate subcycle.

if $a(i) \neq f(i)$ If not back to beginning of sub-
                                                         cycle, then to *New*.

then to *New*;

if $i \neq 1$ If all cycles not completed, to
                                                         Change.

then $[i \leftarrow i-1$; **to** *Change*];   If all cycles completed, move to
                                                         larger subcycle.

done;

Record:

$[$**for** $k \leftarrow i+1$ **thru** $n-1$ $f(k) \leftarrow a(k)]$;

Rotate:

$[x \leftarrow a(i)$;

for $k \leftarrow i$ **thru** $n-1$

$a(k) \leftarrow a(k+1)$;

$a(n) \leftarrow x]$;

Output:

FIGURE 9-7 $[$**for** $k \leftarrow 1$ **thru** n **write** $a(k)]$;

dimensional arrays. *a* holds the current assignment; position $a(i)$
holds the column number (from Fig. 9-4) of the person assigned
to the job in row *i*. *f* controls the systematic cycling of persons
among jobs. Each position in *a* is treated as the beginning of a
cycle consisting of the rest of *a*, that cycle being advanced one
step each time all included cycles are completely recycled. For
example, the cycle of positions 3,4,5 is rotated one position each
time the cycle of positions 4,5 is completely recycled. *f* records
the beginning assignment of each cycle and is used to test
completion of cycles.

The first 10 orderings, permutations of $a(i)$, produced by the
procedure are as shown in Fig. 9-8. Note that the third, sixth,
ninth, and tenth are not written out but rather are a signal to
include one more element in the next cycle. Simulate the program by hand to be sure that you understand how these results
are produced.

clean	1	1		1	1		1	1		
shop	2	2	2	2	2	2	2	2	2	2
cook	3	3	3	4	4	4	5	5	5	5
chop	4	5	4	5	3	5	3	4	3	4
feed	5	4	5	3	5	3	4	3	4	5

FIGURE 9-8
First 10 orderings generated.

These two examples, optimum number of orders and assignment, illustrate basic issues that arise when using the enumeration approach to computing a solution.

A major concern is the number of cases to be enumerated. Complete enumeration is not always possible, even if the procedure is relatively simple and direct, because of the time or space involved. The assignment example above requires generating and evaluating 5! = 120 complete orderings. If the commune involved eight people, the number of possible assignments would be 8! or approximately 40,000 orderings. Twice that number of people would increase the number of possible distinct orderings to approximately 21 trillion. Such factorial growth makes exhaustive enumeration impossible for many realistic problems.

Fortunately, it is often possible to control the number of enumerations to be performed, by means of (1) some rule for choosing the next possibility to be considered, and/or (2) some rule for skipping enumeration of some cases because they clearly do not contain the answer.

Rules for choosing the next possible enumeration may be *heuristic,* not guaranteeing to be the best but hopefully better on the average, or *optimal,* guaranteeing that the next enumeration will be better than the previous one. A heuristic for the assignment problem would be to try out possible assignments in increasing order of time required. (Obviously such a rule must be combined with one for specifying when the enumeraton process is to stop; if you are going to examine *all* possibilities anyway, the order does not matter.)

A rule which guarantees an improvement on the next enumeration itself provides a stopping rule. In the card-ordering problem such a rule is obvious—stop when total costs begin to rise. [Indeed such a rule exists for the assignment problem (we shall not give it here) making it possible to compute assignments of many more than 16 people and tasks with very little computer time.]

Rules for skipping some cases often depend on using the results of earlier enumerations as a bound against which to measure future possibilities. Again, the stopping rule in the card-ordering problem allows skipping most possible numbers of orders. Or, for the assignment problem, an approach which eliminated partial assignments with a larger time than the best found so far would incorporate such a rule.

The method of trial and error involves generating a number of alternative answers just as does enumeration. However, rather than proceeding in a systematically exhaustive manner, successive at-

TRIAL AND ERROR

tempts at the solution (often, approximations to the solution) are related in a different way. While there is sometimes occasion to use "blind" trial and error (for example, randomly-generating assignments in the preceding problem), more often a selective process is used to relate successive trials. The method could better be called selective or controlled trial and error. Information about the solution learned or inferred from the change in output value between trials can be used to change the input parameters of the next trial. Most computer-based search processes are of that sort. We devote much of Chaps. 17 and 18 to this kind of search.

Card-ordering example

The following procedure uses trial-and-error search in our previous problem of finding the number of times to order punched cards. The procedure differs from exhaustive enumeration in that it uses a variable difference (step size) between successive order frequencies computed.

The procedure works as follows. Some arbitrary step size is chosen. Then the total cost of handling punched cards is computed for several numbers of orders, starting from one order per year and increasing by that step size until the total cost increases from one trial to the next. When cost increases, the step size is cut in half (to the next lower integer) and the direction of search reversed, again computing cases until there is an increase in total cost. The step size is again divided in two, the direction changed, and the procedure repeated, until a step size of one is reached. Thus, for the example data given earlier, and arbitrarily starting with a step size of five, the sequence of trials shown in Fig. 9-9 would be computed before arriving at seven as the optimum number of orders.

NUMBER OF ORDERS	TOTAL COST
1	510.00
6	143.33
11	155.45
8	142.50
5	150.00
6	143.33
7	141.43
8	142.50

FIGURE 9-9
Search computation – card ordering.

Much more sophisticated search schemes can be constructed, ones which keep more history and limit the search more severely (at the cost of a more complex procedure). In some cases (where the computing effort in evaluating each trial is high relative to the computing effort of setting up the next trial), it may be worthwhile to store the results of each case and avoid duplicate computations. However, we have kept this illustrative procedure simple. The TL segment in Fig. 9-10 implements this procedure. (Note that the sequence of step sizes is 5, −3, 1. The value −3 occurs instead of the −2 that you might expect. For TL, as for most programming languages, the integer

"Search procedure for card ordering examples";

    step ← 5; *prev* ← 1; *prev_cost* ← *Tc*(1)   Initialize.

Loop:

    number ← *prev* + *step;*   Compute next value of number and cost of that number of orders.

    cost ← *Tc*(*number*);

    if *cost* > *prev_cost*   Test for cost increase.

      then

        [**if abs**(*step*) = 1   If *cost* is increasing, then if the absolute value of step size is one, then write answer and quit.

          then

            [**write** *prev, prev_cost;*   If the absolute value of step size is not one, then compute next step size and change sign.

            to *End*]

          else

            step ← **int**(*step*/−2)];

      prev ← *number; prev_cost* ← *cost;*

    to *Loop;*

End:

    done;

Tc(*n*):

    return *order_cost* * *n* + *inv_cost* * *sales*/(2 * *n*);   Total cost subroutine. Assumes initialization.

FIGURE 9-10

part of a number is defined as the next smaller integer, and the next smaller integer of −2.5 is −3. Also, note that we must compare the *absolute value* of *step* against 1, since the step size may be −1.)

As an example of a trial-and-error computing strategy involving cooperation between the computer and a human being during the actual problem solving, consider the problem of decoding an encoded message. Suppose that the message is formed by a simple substitution of one letter for another, without changing the spacing or punctuation marks. (The "Literary Crypt" problems in the magazine *Saturday Review* were of this form.) An example of such a cryptogram is the following encoding of the sentence you are now reading:

SA NOSTHEN RX MPLF S LIDHCRUIST GM CFN XREERYGAU
NALRWGAU RX CFN MNACNALN DRP SIN ARY INSWGAU.

    How might a cryptographic analyst use the computer to help discover the encoding? There is available for English a listing of the average frequency of occurrence of each letter, of each letter following a given letter, of each letter following the more common pairs of letters, and so forth. This data, with lists of the most common one-, two-, and three-letter words, could be

Cryptogram example

used to generate a number of possible solutions based on frequency counts and word sizes within the encoded message. The human being could examine these possible decodings and suggest other substitutions based on his analysis and possible recognition of more complex words.

SIMULATION

In simulation we construct a symbolic model of the situation being studied and then "operate" the model through time to discover the answer to whatever questions have been asked. The model itself may involve direct solution to find its behavior each period, or there may be random elements requiring repeated runs of the model in a trial-and-error process, or the model may even incorporate enumeration of some key factor. But the basic notion of the simulation computing strategy is that of running a model through time (and/or space). The two examples of simulation that follow are deterministic, with no random elements; simulation of random events is discussed in Chap. 19.

Billiards example

Imagine a 3 by 6 foot billiard table with a single ball on it. Suppose that the ball were at rest at a specified point and were hit in a specified direction imparting to it a specified amount of energy. Suppose further that rolling 1 foot uses up 2 units of the ball's energy, and that rebounding from a cushion on the edge of the table uses up 3 units of energy. (We have simplified the physics of the situation since our emphasis here is on the simulation computing strategy.) Question: If the ball were sitting in the exact center of the table and were hit "due northeast" with an impact of 52 units of energy, where would it come to rest?

   Rather than answering that specific question directly, we proceed (as we often do in using computers) to analyze the situation in general and construct a general model to use in answering that question and similar ones. Our thought processes might go as follows. We can see that at any time the situation is summarized by the ball's position, direction, and energy. We need more precise ways of describing each of these. Energy can be measured directly in units as above. Direction can be described in degrees, and we shall take "due East" as 0 degrees. Position can be described using a coordinate system as in Fig. 9-11.

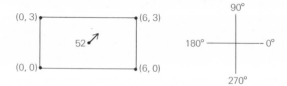

FIGURE 9-11
Coordinate systems – billiard ball simulation.

The key questions to be asked concern the collision of the ball with an edge. Given the ball's position and direction, which edge will it hit and where (if it has enough energy to travel that far), and in which direction will it rebound? If we consider the ball as moving in any of four general directions (northeast, northwest, southwest, or southeast), for each direction it might hit one of two edges depending on exact position and direction. Trigonometric

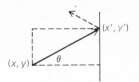

$$\text{Dist} = (6 - x)/\cos(\theta)$$
$$x' = 6$$
$$y' = y + (6 - x) \tan \theta$$
New direction = $180° - \theta$

$$\text{Dist} = (3 - y)/\sin \theta$$
$$x' = x + (3 - y) \cot \theta$$
$$y' = 3$$
New direction = $360° - \theta$

FIGURE 9-12
Analysis of direction and distance.

"New position of billiard ball";

   if *angle* < 90   Series of tests to determine which direction is expected.

      then to *Ne*

      else

         if *angle* < 180

            then to *Nw*

            else

               if *angle* < 270

                  then to *Sw*

                  else to *Se;*

Ne:

   dist1 ← (6−x)/**cos**(*angle*);   Compute distance to eastern edge.

   dist2 ← (3−y)/**sin**(*angle*);   Compute distance to northern edge.

   min_dist ← *energy*/2;   Compute distance of roll given that it takes 2 units of energy to roll 1 foot.

   if *min_dist* < **min**(*dist1,dist2*)

      then

            [*x*← *x* + **cos**(*angle*) * *min_dist;*   If distance of roll will not get the ball to an edge, then the coordinates of the new position are computed.

            y ← *y* + **sin**(*angle*) * *min_dist;*

            energy ← 0]

      else   If distance of roll will get the ball to an edge and if distance to eastern edge is shorter, compute position on eastern edge, new angle, and new energy level.

         if *dist1* < *dist2*

            then

                [*x* ← 6; *y* ← *y* + (6−x) * **tan**(*angle*);

                angle ← 180−*angle;*

                energy ← **max**(*energy* − 2 * *dist*/1 − 3, 0)]

            else   If distance to northern edge is shorter, then compute position on northern edge, new angle, and new energy level.

                [*x* ← *x* + (3−y) * **cot**(*angle*);

                y ← 3; *angle* ← 360−*angle;*

                energy ← **max**(*energy* − 2 * *dist2* − 3, 0)];   FIGURE 9-13 analysis for each case gives formulas for the distance to each edge, the position at which the edge is hit, and the angle of rebound from the edge. Such an analysis for a ball heading northeast is given in Fig. 9-12.

Thus we can imagine a procedure which, for a given position, direction, and energy, determines which of the two appropriate edges is closer, whether the ball has sufficient energy to reach that edge, and the ball's new position, direction, and energy after either stopping or reaching an edge. Such a TL program segment is given in Fig. 9-13, including only the case where the ball is heading northeast. It assumes sine, cosine, tangent, and cotangent functions which take input in degrees, and it assumes that the appropriate variable values have been defined previously.

This segment could then be imbedded in a larger procedure which would repeat the new position computation until the energy of the ball became zero. (The answer to our original question is that the ball would stop in the middle of the table, where it started, after bounding off each of the narrow ends exactly once and each long end exactly twice.)

This is a relatively simple simulation (even though the direct computation required for each step is complicated) because the movement of the model through time is quite straightforward. In the next example, the handling of time is somewhat more complex.

Game of life example

The mathematician John Conway has developed a simulation model of the life and death of a population. One can imagine the model as a game played on an extremely large checkerboard, with each individual being in the population represented by a piece on one square. Each being can have up to eight neighbors in the eight adjoining squares. Three rules describe the behavior of a population from one time period (generation) to the next.

Birth. A new being appears for the next time period in any empty square with exactly three neighbors.

Death. A being dies because of isolation (disappears before the next time period) if he has zero or one neighbors. A being dies because of overpopulation before the next time period if he has four or more neighbors.

Survival. A being continues living in the next time period if he has two or three neighbors.

These simple rules lead to quite varied behavior for different initial populations. An initial population of two beings must die immediately from isolation, since no one has more than one neighbor. Some three-being populations move into a nonchanging state, some others into a periodic state. Initial populations have been discovered which shift their positions across the board endlessly, or grow in number without limit. Three examples of three-being populations are given in Fig. 9-14.

Those interested in learning more about this game will find further examples, discussion, and analysis in several articles in Martin Gardner's column in *Scientific American* (see references).

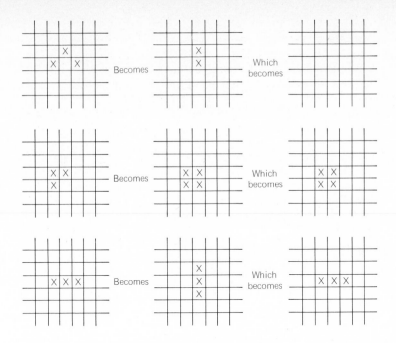

FIGURE 9-14
Examples of three-being popula-tion.

For now, however, just consider writing a program to carry out the above rules.

The first step in writing such a program is to choose a representation for the problem data. A two-dimensional array seems a natural way of representing the board, using values of zero to

New(i,j):

    [**local** *k, l, n;*

      n ← # − board(i,j);   Initialize *n* by subtracting the value of *board*
                                          (i,j) which will be added in later. (This is done to
                                          simplify the tally of neighbors.)

      for *k ← i−1* **thru** *i+1*

          for *l ← j−1* **thru** *j+1*   Tally neighbors, count the beings in the squares
                                          touching *board(i,j)* and add in *board(i,j)*.

        n ← n + board(k,l);

    if *board(i,j) = 0*

      then

          if *n = 3*

             then return 1   Birth: a new being is born if an empty square
                                         has exactly three neighbors.

             else return 0

      else   Death: a being dies from isolation (fewer than
                                         two neighbors) or overpopulation (more than
                                         three neighbors).

          if *n < 2* **or** *n > 3*

             then return 0   Survival: a being survives if it has two or three
                                         neighbors.

             else return 1];

indicate an empty square and one to represent an occupied square. The TL procedure in Fig. 9-15 will compute a new (next time period) value for square $board(i,j)$. The program in Fig. 9-15 ignores for now the complication that any representation of the board within the computer must be of finite size, and so would have squares along the edge for which this procedure must be modified.

However, when applied in a straightforward manner, this program does not compute correctly. For example, locate a row of three beings in the middle of a small board and call the program as in Fig. 9-16. The computed result is incorrect. (Take a few moments to follow through the procedure by hand for this case and verify that the result is as shown.)

Before

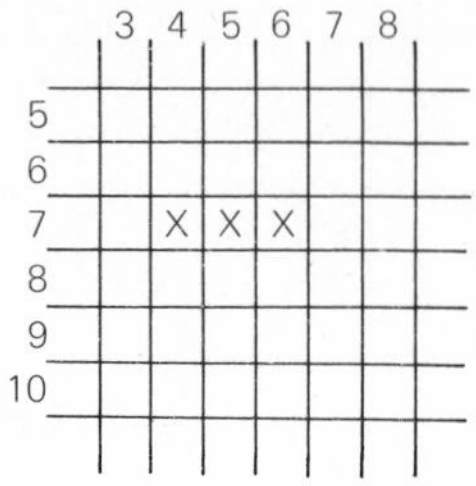

for $j \leftarrow 3$ **thru** 7 **for** $i \leftarrow 5$ **thru** 9 $board\,(i, j) \leftarrow New\,(i, j)$;

After

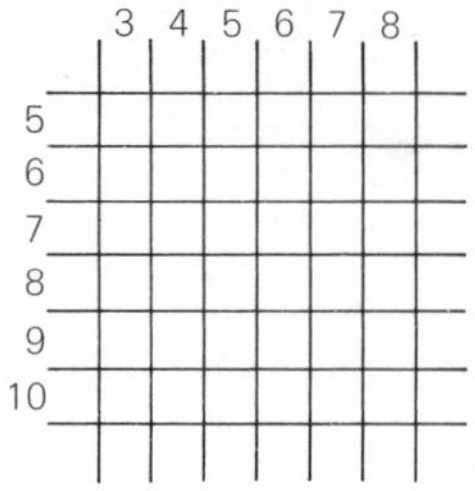

FIGURE 9-16
An erroneous computation.

The earlier examples in Fig. 9-14 show that, according to the rules, a horizontal row of three beings should become in the next time period a vertical row of three beings, with the same "middle" being in each. Why did that result not occur?

The problem is that the rules for birth, death, and survival define the state of a square at a particular time period as depending on the state of all of its neighbors at the previous time period. The value of $board(i,j)$ at time $t + 1$ depends on the value of $board(i+1,j)$ at time t; and likewise the value of $board(i+1,j)$ at time $t + 1$ depends on the value of $board(i,j)$ at time t. Our program produces the wrong result because it uses the values of some squares at time period $t + 1$ to compute the values of other squares at $t + 1$. If the program computes the value for $board(i,j)$ at time period $t + 1$ and immediately changes $board(i,j)$, it will use that (possibly wrong) value in computing $board(i+1,j)$ at time $t + 1$. Computing $board(i+1,j)$ first will not correct the situation, for then $board(i,j)$ at $t + 1$ might be computed incorrectly. The rules assume that all squares will change simultaneously.

This problem of having to carry out a number of interrelated computations simultaneously arises in many simulations of reality, because reality contains a multitude of procedure-followers acting in parallel. However, most computers must simulate these parallel activities sequentially, one after another, and so the programmer must develop some sequential way of achieving the correct result.

The basic approach to achieving this simultaneity is to substitute parallelism in some other dimension (say, storage space) for parallelism in time. Thus, one general solution for our problem would be to create a separate two-dimensional array for each time period. *Board* could have three dimensions — row, column, and time period. But since in this problem the values for the next time period depend *only* on current values, the program really needs only two arrays, one for the current period (say, *board*) and one for the next period (say, *bb*). The program could first compute the new values (values at time $t + 1$) and store them in *bb,* and then copy *bb* into *board* only after *all* new values are computed. The following TL segment does just that.

for $i \leftarrow 3$ **thru** 7 **for** $j \leftarrow 5$ **thru** 9 $bb(i,j) \leftarrow New(i,j)$;
for $i \leftarrow 3$ **thru** 7 **for** $j \leftarrow 5$ **thru** 9 $board(i,j) \leftarrow bb(i,j)$;

There are many further issues which arise in the correct and efficient handling of simulations, some of them suggested by even this simple problem. As an example, in a very large board most of the squares would be empty, and so most of the computing time would be spent adding up zeros. How could one represent the data so that these computations would be avoided? Chapter 10, on using the computer effectively, deals with such problems.

1 The Fibonacci series, (see exercise 6, Chap. 5) was originally proposed to answer the question, "How many pairs of rabbits are produced from a single pair after k months." This particular answer assumes that rabbits bear a new pair of offspring each month, that each pair becomes fertile at age 1 month, and that rabbits live forever. Suppose that each rabbit needs 3 square feet of living space. In how many months will the rabbits fill a 250 by 180 foot rabbit yard?

2 It has been noted that the terms in the Fibonacci sequence tend to increase by a constant ratio. Use this information to help improve your computing strategy in solving exercise 1. (For example, if you were using enumeration, can this ratio be the basis for a selective trial-and-error approach?) Program and test your revised procedure.

3 The Newton-Raphson method for finding an approximate solution to a function can be specialized to the problem of finding the square root x of a number a by computing a sequence of approximations to a as follows:

$$x_{k+1} = \frac{(x_k + a/x_k)}{2}$$

where x_{k+1} is the $k + 1$st approximation to the square root of a. Program and test this procedure. With what value does your sequence of approximations begin? How does your procedure determine when the approximation is close enough? How does this approximation compare with the answer produced by the square-root function that is part of your programming system?

4 The TL procedure given in Fig. 9-7 for solving the assignment problem by enumeration can be used to produce all orderings (permutations) of a set of elements. For example, it could be used to generate all orderings of the letters in the word FEAST. Program the procedure in the programming language available to you, and use it to generate all orderings of FEAST.

5 Another general combinatorial problem is that of producing all combinations of n elements taken m at a time. For example, what are the three letter groupings that can be made out of FEAST (five letters taken three at a time)? Since ordering does not matter in combinations ("eas" and "sea" are considered to be the same combination), one straightforward answer would be: fea, fes, fet, fas, fat, fst, eas, eat, est, ast. Program a general procedure to produce all combinations of n elements taken m at a time.

6 The combination and permutation programs developed in exercises 5 and 4 can be combined into a procedure to solve the following problem. Prepare a program to list all possible letter sequences that can be generated from a given input. (For example, if the input were FEAST, the answer should include a, seat, sea, esa, among others.)

7 Program and test on your local computer the Game of Life simulation given in the last section of this chapter. What interesting patterns can you discover?

8 Modify the ordering program given in Fig. 9-7 so that it will find the best assignment of jobs to persons for the data in Fig. 9-4. (*Hint:* Replace the output subroutine with one that keeps track of the best assignment found so far.)

9 The dice game of craps has the following rules. The player rolls two dice.

   a If the shooter rolls 7 or 11, he wins.

   b If the shooter rolls 2, 3, or 12 on the first roll, he loses.

   c If the shooter rolls any other combination on the first roll, the number becomes his "point." He continues rolling until either he again rolls his point, in which case he wins, or he first rolls 7, in which case he loses.

To play craps, the computer must generate random numbers simulating the roll of dice. Most programming languages have a function for generating pseudo-random numbers; typically this function generates a fraction in the range $0 < n < 1$. Such a function (call it **rnd**) could be used to simulate the throw of a die with the expression

$$\text{int}(\text{rnd} * 6) + 1$$

Program and test a simulation of playing craps using whatever random-number-generating capability is available on your computer.

An interesting addition to the program is to input at the beginning the amount of money you have to bet (your stake), and to input at the beginning of each play the amount you wish to bet on that roll. The computer can then keep track of your winnings (or of when you go broke).

10 Suppose you are given the distance between a group of cities. For example, the data for five cities might be as shown below. Note that it is not possible to get directly from all cities to all others. Develop a procedure for finding the shortest distance between two given cities. Program and test that procedure. Your program should first read in the distance data, and then the two cities between which the distance is to be found.

	A	B	C	D	E
A	0	15	—	19	13
B		0	40	38	29
C			0	—	27
D				0	—
E					0

REFERENCES

Gardner, M.: "Mathematical Games" in *Scientific American,* Oct. 1970, Feb. 1971.

Rice, John K., and John R. Rice: *Introduction to Computer Science,* chap. 7, pp. 249–308, Holt, New York, 1969.

EFFECTIVE USE OF THE COMPUTER

EFFECTIVENESS AND EFFICIENCY IN PROGRAMMING

In programming, as in all uses of resources to accomplish goals, there are two general considerations: effectiveness and efficiency. *Effectiveness* is concerned with doing *what ought to be done*—accomplishing the goals. *Efficiency* is concerned with doing *whatever is done* at least cost.

It would seem obvious that effectiveness, doing what ought to be done, should be the primary consideration. But because problem statements and goals are often vague and because discrepancies from them are less easily measured and controlled than are costs, it is often easier to attend to efficiency than it is to effectiveness. Of course, there are returns from efficiency, but these returns diminish as the costs of obtaining additional efficiency mount. Furthermore, overemphasis on efficiency—doing whatever is being done at lower cost—can obscure issues of effectiveness—doing what ought to be done. The computer carries out its program, efficient or not, effective or not; the programmer must take care not to lose sight of effective use in a search for further efficiency.

The cost of developing a computer program includes costs of both human and computing resources. The human resources include the time required by the programmer or programmers to specify the problem, to develop the solution procedure, to write the program, to debug the program, and to maintain the program. The computing resources include central processor time, main memory, file storage, and input-output operations.

In getting the job done, the programmer has to estimate how much of each of these resources, both human and computing, will be required, to determine the cost of each resource, and to calculate the total cost of different strategies. Because there are always different mixes of resources that will be effective, that is, different ways of getting the same job done, costs must be estimated for several strategies. These cost estimates are complicated by the uncertainties involved—how long will it take to write the program? to debug it? how much will computing resources cost?

Most programmers do not make careful, detailed cost estimates for small programs which will only be run once or twice; the cost of such analyses would exceed any possible benefits. For major programming tasks the need for cost estimates is great; but the difficulty of making them is also great.

In this chapter we provide some rules, hints, examples, and words of wisdom about programming effectiveness and efficiency. But we cannot provide wisdom itself. You will have to find your own answers fitting your own problems. And your answers will be affected by how quickly the computation is required and by how important the solution is.

The epitome of ineffectiveness is the program that does not produce correct answers. Dealing with the errors in programs, both before they occur and after, is the subject of two sections of this chapter. A major source of inefficiency in computing is poor (inappropriate) data organization. Good data organization can also be helpful in reducing the human resources required and in debugging. Another section of the chapter is concerned with data organization, and a final section is concerned with efficiency in the use of computer time itself.

1 Think first. Of course.

What can you do to ease the job of finding errors in your running program by detecting them before the run, by programming in such a way that errors are less likely to occur, or by devising test cases to "catch them in the act"?

2 *Hand simulate, desk check the program.* Hand simulation can be a lot of work—boring, repetitive and demanding of attention to details. And, like other aids, it can be overused. But a fresh, careful look at a program, a look from the standpoint of the computer, almost always turns up both gross and subtle errors.

3 *Choose test data so as to exercise decisions, distinctions, boundary conditions, etc.* Rather than just running the program to see what happens, give some thought to its internal workings and construct test cases to exercise those workings.

Consider, for example, the billiard ball simulation in Chap. 9. The test data should check movement in each quadrant to see that the right subprogram is activated, and in each subquadrant, collision with both of the possible edges should be checked. But what about hitting an edge perpendicularly (moving "due east," for example)? Does the ball rebound in the opposite direction? And what if the ball strikes exactly in a corner? Does it behave as it should? In the case of moving in at "45 degrees"? At 60 degrees? In fact, how many different cases of hitting in the corner can be distinguished and so must be checked?

Then there is the computation of the ball's energy. Does the program compute correctly when the ball does not have enough energy to reach a wall? When it has enough to reach an edge but not to rebound? When it has exactly enough to reach and/or to rebound? And what about the change in energy when the ball strikes exactly in a corner? And so forth.

Also include some random cases, in hopes of testing conditions otherwise overlooked.

4 *Compute the results of test data beforehand — know what answers to expect.* Obvious? Perhaps, but failure to do this is the common reason for not noticing errors that test runs do turn up. Taking the billard ball example again, what results would you expect in each of the cases mentioned above? What about striking in the corner, for example? What should be the change in energy from hitting there — the same as hitting an edge, or as hitting two edges? If you do not know which it should be, how can you tell if the program is performing correctly? Or will you just accept whatever the program does as correct, letting ease of programming (laziness?) determine the model?

5 *Incorporate in the program checks that the input data is reasonable.* As the saying states, "Garbage In, Garbage Out." Often the computer is an expensive and frustrating means for rearranging garbage (particularly frustrating if you are sitting by the output device waiting for fruitcake). One way to minimize garbage processing is to check that the input makes sense. The need for this in, say, a payroll program or a space mission control program is clear. But input checking can help in simpler problems also. In the billiard ball case, is the ball starting out off the table? With negative energy? Does your program check the plausibility of the input data? If the data look suspicious, the best thing may be to have the program stop and request proper input.

CORRECTIVE DEBUGGING

Even the most careful programmer, using the most careful methods, will occasionally find that his program *almost* runs, and he does not know why it does not run. Often it helps to make another desk check of the program, after a good night's sleep. As with most problem solving, letting your subconscious work on the problem for a while can help. Also, you might try the following.

6 *Use output statements throughout the program to show just what is happening.* Many good programmers put such output statements in from the beginning, even before any problems turn up. A version of the billiard ball program, with output statements inserted (and circled) to facilitate debugging, is given in Fig. 10-1.

Writing out the intermediate values allows both the detection of a possible erroneous statement in the program and a double check on the computation of your test answers. (Many programmer and computer hours have been spent trying to find bugs that did not exist; only the precomputed test results were in error.)

7 *Explain what the program is supposed to do and how it is supposed to do it to someone else.* This technique is particularly effective if the other person understands programming but knows very little about the particular problem. Often a programmer will "miss the obvious" in desk checking his program because of hidden assumptions he has made and is not even aware of. (For example, he may expect certain inputs to be positive when they need not be.) The

"Billiard ball computation with output statements";

write *angle;*

> Print value of *angle* before calculation begins.

if *angle* < 90 **then to** *Ne*
  else if *angle* < 180 **then to** *Nw*
    else if *angle* < 270 **then to** *Se*
      else to *Sw;*

write 'nowhere'; **done;**

> Somehow an error has occurred if control reaches this point in the program.

Ne:

write 'Ne';

> Control is now in *Ne* block.

dist 1 ← (6 − *x*)/**cos**(*angle*);
dist2 ← (3 − *y*)/**sin**(*angle*);
min_dist ← *energy*/2;

write *dist1, dist2, min_dist;*

> Calculated values of these three variables are printed.

if *min_dist* ≤ **min**(*dist1,dist2*)
  then [. . .]
  else [. . .]
energy ← **max**(*energy* − 2, * *dist2* − 3, 0);

write *x, y, angle, energy;*

> New values of these variables are printed.

FIGURE 10-1

discipline of explaining what is supposed to occur and why often brings these details to light. In fact, it seems that in many cases "the light" suddenly appears without the other party saying a word.

DATA ORGANIZATION

While some changes in data organization can greatly reduce computing time (see the next section for example), others are beneficial primarily in the reduction of time spent in programming and tracking down errors. Indeed, they may increase running time.

8 *Use parameters and generalized common segments where possible.* We have already discussed a number of examples of parameterizing programs and using common subroutines as a way of localizing possible changes and making programs more general. A further example, from the billiard table simulation, would be to use variables for the size of the table and the energy losses from rolling 1 foot and from hitting a cushion. Then, by changing the values of these variables one could simulate a number of different physical situations. Even more general would be to use procedures that, given two points as inputs, would output the energy required to move from the first to the second. Under this approach the entire method of computing energy use could be changed (for example,

making it a nonlinear function of distance) merely by changing a few procedures.

9 *Organize the program into modules that conceal the details of data structures where possible.* In particular, try to conceal from the main flow of the program the exact storage representation of data. This point is closely related to the preceding one, since the use of common procedures is a major tool in sealing off storage structure. There were several examples of this concept in earlier chapters. As another example, consider the assignment problem described in Chap. 9. Suppose that we wish to experiment with procedures that try the shortest job for each person first, rather than an arbitrary initial assignment.

We can consider possible data representations for the assignment problem by ignoring the details of storage representation and focussing on what must be known about the data—what functions must be performed. For each person-job combination (each element in a particular ordering), the program must require the time for that person to perform that job. Also, to consider jobs in increasing order of time, the program requires for each person and job rank (first, second, etc.) the corresponding job. This suggests specifying two functions whose inputs and outputs are as given in Fig. 10-2. At this point we need not be concerned with how these functions represent the data or form their outputs. Their existence is enough to allow us to program the main procedure.

FUNCTION	INPUTS	OUTPUT
time	Person, job rank	Job
job	Person, job	Time

FIGURE 10-2

USE OF COMPUTER TIME

Sometimes changes in the representation of a problem or in the computing strategy can greatly reduce the amount of computer time used without making the programming task that much more difficult.

10 *Rearrange the data representation to make the "active" data more accessible, to avoid considering "meaningless" cases.* For example, consider the population simulation at the end of Chap. 9. While it is not possible to represent an infinite board within the computer, one may want a fairly large board to study the growth of different initial colonies. Suppose the program starts off with a 50×50 board. For a beginning population of, say, six beings fairly close together in space, most of the board will be empty (at least for a while). If the computer program checks each square on the board each time period, most computing time will be spent adding zeros. In this case, the "active" data are the squares near the colony, and the other squares are "meaningless" cases.

One simple way to reduce the number of squares considered would be to use variable limits on the area to be scanned each period. These could be set one row "above" the row of the "highest" being, one column to the "left" of the "leftmost" being, and so forth. With each birth, the limits could be checked to see if they must be increased. This simple strategy would never reduce the area checked, but even so, in some cases, it could reduce greatly the amount of computing. For example, in the case of a horizontal row of three adjacent beings, the limits would start off including 15 squares, expand to 25, and stay there. Checking an entire 50×50 board would include *one hundred times* that many squares each period, and probably close to one hundred times as much computer time.

11 *Precompute, before the high repetition loops in the program, any different encoding or rearrangement of the data that will eliminate recomputing or re-searching the same results.* As an example, consider the earlier discussion of an assignment problem approach which involved selecting possible assignments in increasing order of time required. If the basic data describing the problem were kept in the form of the array of persons and jobs given with the problem statement, that array would have to be searched and re-searched many times in finding the next best job for each person. But if the data were ordered at the beginning of the program, that searching could be eliminated. One representation that encodes this ordering information is shown in Fig. 10-3.

This representation uses a three-dimensional array, one dimension referring to jobs in increasing order of time required, another dimension to people, and the third having two entries—job number and time required. (For example, the least time job for *A* is job 4; it requires 1 hour. The worst is job 3; it requires 4 hours.) Thus, the data is arranged in sorted order for each person (though not for each job).

As another example, consider a program to simulate experiments with rats moving through a maze. We are concerned for now only with the problem of representing the maze itself. The problem statement reads as follows.

The maze is laid out on a 10×10 grid, with one starting point and one goal. For each experiment, the program is to read in a specification of the maze as a list of squares, each specified by a pair of coordinates. (For example, the start square in the maze in Fig. 10-4 is specified as 5,1.) At any square there will be at most two possible directions for the rat to go (not counting that from which he came). Call these "left" and "right."

Further details of the statement describe the rules of movement, the rat's propensity to go right or left, rules governing learning by the rat, the number of trials to be run for each experiment, and so forth.

How should the maze be represented in the computer? One way would be as an array, just as it was specified. However, using that representation, before each move the program must search the squares surrounding the occupied square to determine the "left" and "right" paths. Much of the computer time on each trial would be spent in this search to rediscover data that had not changed since input.

As an alternative, the program could "preprocess" the maze data into a form which would eliminate all searches. Since this

FIGURE 10-3

C	JOB	TIME	
	1	1	Least

B	JOB	TIME	
	4	2	Least
	1	3	Second

A	JOB	TIME	
	4	1	Least
	1	2	Second
	2	2	Third
	5	3	Fourth
	3	4	Most

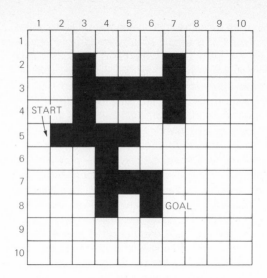

FIGURE 10-4

preprocessing would only require as much time as one or two complete searches, it could amount to considerable savings in a 30-trial experiment. One approach would be to associate with each square, for each direction from which it could be entered, its "left" and "right" neighbors. The data could be viewed as a three-dimensional array—one dimension being the square identification, another the direction from which entered, and the third having two pieces of information—the "left" and "right" neighbors. (For this purpose it is simpler just to number the squares from 1 to 100, going left to right, top to bottom, than to use a coordinate system.) The array would be as pictured in Fig. 10-5, and the state of the rat in the maze could be recorded by two pieces of information—square number and direction. Thus, if the rat were in square 43 coming from the left, a "left" turn would take it to square 33.

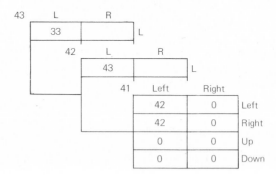

FIGURE 10-5

An even greater simplification could be achieved by numbering only the squares that actually make up the maze, using different numbers for the same square when approached from different directions. Using this approach, the example maze would be numbered as in Fig. 10-6, and the data recorded in the corresponding array shown in Fig. 10-7. In this case, only a single square

	1	2	3	4	5	6	7	8	9	10
1										
2			13↑				23↑			
3			10↑ 11↓ 12←	14→ 15←	16→ 17←	18→ 19←	20↑ 21↓ 22→			
4			8↑ 9↓				24↓			
5	1←	3→ 4←	5→ 6← 7↓	25→ 26← 27↑	28→					
6				29↑ 30↓						
7				31↑ 32↓ 33←	35→ 36←	37→ 38↑				
8				34↓		39↓	→2			
9										
10										

FIGURE 10-6

number is needed to record the state of the trial. (For example, being in square 5 here corresponds to being in square 43 coming from the left in the preceding representation.)

12 *Look for heuristics that eliminate considering some cases on the average.* The consideration of jobs in increasing order of time in the assignment problem is one such heuristic. Another heuristic introduced in Chap. 9 is the variable step size used in searching for the optimum order size for punched cards. In many problems, a little thought can turn up simple heuristics that speed up search or enumeration.

13 *Consider using other computing strategies besides the "obvious" one.* Again, the use of search instead of enumeration in finding the optimum order size is an example. As another example, consider the following situation. For each of 200 students in an introductory programming class, two pieces of information are available: the average grade on the first three quizzes and the amount of computer time used. The instructor would like to form a 2×2 table for the data, showing how many students are high on both grade average and time used, how many low on both, and so forth, as in Fig. 10-8. One can construct this table by finding the median grade and median time used, and then tally each student's data into the appropriate one of the four cells in the table.

The obvious procedure for finding the median of a set of data is to sort it and take the middle value. In this case, two sorts of 200 items would be required. This sorting would require a large number of comparisons and could take a noticeable amount of

Square	"Left"	"Right"	Square	"Left"	"Right"
1	3	3	21	24	19
2	0	0	22	23	24
3	5	1	23	21	21
4	1	5	24	20	20
5	8	25	25	28	30
6	4	8	26	30	6
7	25	4	27	6	28
8	10	7	28	26	26
9	7	10	29	27	32
10	13	14	30	32	27
11	14	9	31	29	35
12	9	13	32	35	34
13	11	11	33	34	29
14	16	12	34	31	31
15	12	16	35	37	33
16	18	15	36	33	37
17	15	18	37	39	36
18	22	17	38	36	39
19	17	22	39	2	38
20	19	23			

FIGURE 10-7

GRADE

	High	Low
TIME High		
Low		

FIGURE 10-8

computer time and, on an interactive system, possibly a large amount of elapsed time also. The best possible sorting procedures require $n * \log(n)$ comparisons to sort n items, or about 3000 comparisons in this case for both sorts.

As an alternative, consider searching for the two medians, perhaps using the average grade and average time used as a first guess. Each pass through the data would compare the items with the current guess and count the number higher and lower. With a good searching strategy, such an approach could be noticeably faster, and would certainly use less storage space.

14 *Use human interaction to handle exceptions, special cases, or judgments that are difficult to program.* One example of this is the literary cryptogram program mentioned in Chap. 9. Another is the 2 × 2 table just considered. Having a human being guess the median value to try next might be even more efficient than a search program, particularly if the task were being done interactively anyway.

The moral of this chapter is of course where we began.

1 *Think first.*

1 Keep a journal of a programming task. Keep track of how much of your time and how much computing time you spend (*a*) analyzing the problem and developing an algorithm, (*b*) writing the program, (*c*) debugging the program, and (*d*) obtaining results. Place a reasonable value on your own time and calculate the cost of each of the four steps. What tradeoffs could you have made between your time and machine resources?

2 For some years now there has been a debate among computer users about the costs and benefits of interactive computing services versus batch computing services. In interactive mode the programmer develops, enters, and debugs his program from a typewriterlike terminal. In batch mode, the programmer enters his program on punched cards and has the deck read into the computer. The results of the batch job are printed on a line printer and returned to the programmer some time later. What do you think are the relative advantages and disadvantages of those two modes of program preparation? Terminal service is usually more expensive than batch service. How much more would you be willing to pay for terminal service?

3 Prepare a form (table) to record the intermediate results obtained from a hand simulation of the greatest common divisor program (use any of the versions discussed in Chaps. 5 and 6). What variable values have to be recorded? Use your table as a teaching aid in explaining how the program works to somebody else. What modifications would you make in your table to improve its value as a teaching aid? As a debugging tool?

4 Modify the greatest common divisor program to produce the same intermediate results as you developed in the table prepared in exercise 3, including column headings.

5 Using the information under point 3 in this chapter as a guide, develop a set of test data for the billiard ball simulation program of Chap. 9. Indicate which aspect of the program is tested by each set of test data. What interesting test cases were not mentioned in the text?

6 Write a TL program to check a list of numbers to see if they are all positive, less than 1 million, and greater than 10.

7 Write a program to play tic-tac-toe against a human being or against another program. Represent the board as a two-dimensional array and the player's moves as *X*'s and *O*'s.

8 Rewrite the tic-tac-toe program of exercise 7 using an alternative representation of moves, e.g., numbers and possibly an alternative representation of the board, in an effort to reduce the amount of computation required by the program.

9 Rewrite the tic-tac-toe program so it is independent of the representation of the board and the player's moves.

10 In Figs. 10-6 and 10-7 a method is suggested for representing the maze in simulated rat experiments. This method reduces substantially the computing on each trial. Develop and program a procedure that converts from an input description of

the maze using a coordinate system (see Fig. 10-4) to the internal representation of Figs. 10-6 and 10-7.

11 Develop and program a procedure to conduct experiments with simulated rats in a maze (see exercise 10). The maze would be at most 10 × 10, with at least one route to the goal, at least three dead ends, and no more than two choices of forward motion at any one point. Design the maze so that when the choice is available, right turns will result in reaching the goal (see Fig. 10-9). A stat-rat (statistical rat) being trained in the maze moves forward one unit per time interval. If he has a choice, his choice of direction is governed by some random process, with probability p that he will move to the right. p is initially set at .5 and is changed as follows any time a choice is made to go right: new $p \leftarrow .08 * (1 - p) + .02 * p$.

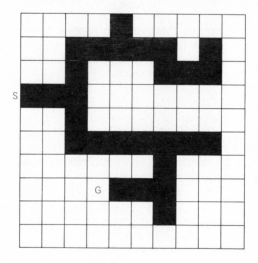

FIGURE 10-9
Sample maze.

Run 10 stat-rats, 25 trials each. For each rat, output a graph indicating the number of moves needed for each trial and two mazes showing where the rat is on the tenth unit move of the first and thirteenth trials. (See Fig. 10-10.)

FIGURE 10-10
Sample output of stat-rat simulation.

12 Another suggested approach to ensuring the correctness of programs (and thus minimizing debugging) is to verify the program (or flowchart) logically, independent of the computer. This might be done by attaching one or more assertions to each branch in the flowchart, those at the beginning and end corresponding to the input and output specifications of the program. The next task is to show that the validity of the assertions attached to the branch leading into a program step or flowchart box, together with the operations carried out in that step, implies the validity of the assertions on the branch leading out. If that implication can be demonstrated for each step in the procedure, the validity of the entire procedure is established (given proper inputs). The difficult and creative part of this approach often is to find the appropriate assertions. Consider for example the loop from the first example of Chap. 5, reversing a word.

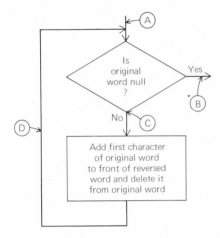

The assertions at point *D* might be as follows.

1 All characters read into the original word are either in the original word or in the reversed word. (No characters lost.)
2 Only characters from the original word are in the reversed word. (No characters added.)
3 Any character in the reversed word precedes all characters that preceded it in the original word. (Order reversed.)

What assertions would be appropriate at *A, B, C?* Can you "prove" (by informal argument) the output assertions for each step? Can you extend this proof to the entire procedure in the first example? Can you prove that the procedure must terminate?

Weinberg, Gerald M.: *The Psychology of Computer Programming,* Van Nostrand Reinhold, New York, 1971.

REFERENCE

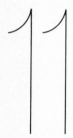

REPRESENTATION OF VALUES

Most of Part Two is concerned with learning to use the computer in problem solving A simple model of the computer is assumed with most of the detail postponed to a later section. Thus far the data being processed have been discussed in terms of aggregate structures of data items, assuming the reader to be familiar with the properties of basic constructs such as numbers and characters.

These final two chapters of Part Two, on the representation of basic data items in the computer and on the approximations and errors that arise from their representation, logically could be located either in Part Two or in Part Three. In the latter, because they are concerned with some details of how computers function; here, because the programmer must know the characteristics of computer arithmetic if complex numerical procedures are to behave as desired. In particular, all of us have learned many general principles about arithmetic operations that just *are not true* for computers. For example, most people "know" that the sum of a sequence of 10 numbers is independent of the order in which the numbers are added. Or that $3 * (1/3)$ is equal to one. These need not hold true in computer arithmetic. In a very real sense, Chap. 10 on effective use of the computer is incomplete without the discussion in Chap. 12 of arithmetic accuracy and errors.

Thus, Chaps. 11 and 12 form a bridge between our introduction to procedures and problem solving and a more detailed examination of how computers work.

BASIC VALUES AND TOKENS

The basic (lowest level) values to which the programmer can refer in TL are numbers, strings of characters, and the two logical values. But one cannot actually write down, keypunch, type, etc., any of these values; what one can do is set down a *token* referring to a value. For example, "nine," 9, IX, are different tokens referring to the value nine. [Note that while one can think of a variable named *a* being assigned the value 9 (e.g., $a \leftarrow 9$), what is actually written down in a TL program—and also manipulated within the computer—are tokens for the variable name and for its value.]

In normal affairs, such as writing this book or preparing procedures in TL, these tokens are constructed from an alphabet (set of markings) made up of letters, digits, and some special characters. If the construction is a program, then that program when entered into the computer is represented with a different set of tokens, constructed from an alphabet internal to the computer. The processes evoked by that program are carried out on these other tokens, and the results translated back into "our" alphabet for output. This chapter and the next are concerned with the characteristics of this internal representation of basic values and with the errors and approximations that may arise because of its use.

Of course, human beings can and do construct larger groupings of values and groupings of tokens to represent them. Strings of characters interpreted as English words can be grouped into sentences, or grocery lists, or novels. Numbers can be grouped into tables, as for example, "acres of wheat planted by state in 1948," or "mean temperature readings at major airports." And combinations of letters and numbers become driver's licenses, or paychecks, or personnel files. Some of the possible structures for representing these groupings have been discussed in earlier chapters. At the lowest level, however, these groupings too must be constructed from the basic values and represented by tokens from the basic alphabet.

COMPUTER MEMORY

One constraint on the formation of tokens within the computer, at the machine hardware level, is that the computer's memory is made up of individual storage slots (usually called *words*), each having a name (usually called an *address*). Typically, each token is stored in one slot, and each slot holds one token. (While there are exceptions to this one-slot one-token correspondence, it is true for many cases and provides a useful first view of computer memory.)

The details of computer memory are discussed more thoroughly in a later section of this text. For now, however, keep in mind the concept of fixed-sized slots (words) of memory, each holding a token representing a value (and thus, each corresponding to some variable in the program).

POSITIONAL NOTATION

Most of the following discussion of the representation of values will be about the representation of numbers. We begin by reviewing positional notation. As most school children today learn several times, positional notation is one of the great intellectual creations of mankind, allowing (compared to Roman numerals, for example) much more complicated arithmetic operations to be carried out with comparative ease.

Consider the number (more precisely, of course, token for a number) 203. This is made up of the three numbers (tokens) 2, 0, 3. Their combination is commonly understood to refer to the value two hundred and three because they signify two hundreds plus zero tens plus three ones, or:

REPRESENTATION OF VALUES

$$2 * 100 + 0 * 10 + 3 * 1$$

This can also be written as:

$$2 * 10 * 10 + 0 * 10 + 3 * 1$$

or

$$2 * 10^2 + 0 * 10^1 + 3 * 10^0$$

This use of a base (in this case 10) and the use of the position or column of each digit to show the power to which the base is raised is very powerful. It requires comparatively few symbols and also aligns the digits in a way that allows relatively simple procedures for arithmetic operations. Note the contribution of zero as a placeholder, keeping straight the position of each digit. This notation also applies to fractions, as in

203.48

or

$$2 * 10^2 + 0 * 10^1 + 3 * 10^0 + 4 * 10^{-1} + 8 * 10^{-2}$$

NOTATIONS FOR DECIMAL NUMBERS IN PROGRAMMING LANGUAGES

There are, of course, many different tokens for the same number, even restricting oneself to the decimal (base 10) system. Consider for example the number twenty three and one-half.

23.5 The so-called mixed numbers are commonly used in programming languages, although the existence of a fixed word size within the computer limits the number of meaningful digits.

$23\frac{1}{2}$ On most computer input-output devices, special symbols such as $\frac{1}{2}$ and $\frac{1}{4}$ are not available, nor are half-space positions, and so this notation is excluded from most higher-level languages. Of course, one could use the notation 1/2 for one-half, but that already has been defined as indicating the (result of the) operation of dividing one by two. Most programming languages, including TL, take that token as a command to divide, thus producing the indicated value.

2.35 * 10 ↑ 1 Called *scientific notation,* this notation has advantages in representing very large or very small numbers without explicitly showing all zeros. Thus, 12,346,000,000,000.00 becomes 1.2346 * 10 ↑ 13, and 0.000000078 becomes 7.8 * 10 ↑ −8.

.235 * 10 ↑ 2 In computing, the custom is to use a notation like scientific notation, except that the number is scaled to lie in value between .1 and 1, rather than between 1 and 10. This is called *floating-point notation.* Of course, the representation given at the beginning of this paragraph would be interpreted by TL as an arithmetic expression to be evaluated, rather than as a single token for a number. Many programming languages add an additional symbol (such as "E" or "$_{10}$") to allow direct expression of floating-point numbers. (In such languages, .235 * 10 ↑ 2 could be written as .235E2 or .235$_{10}$2.)

Floating-point notation is of particular interest because many computers, including almost all larger ones, have special hardware for performing arithmetic operations on numbers in floating-point form. And many computers that lack such hardware use special programming procedures to process floating-point numbers.

What do we mean by "numbers in floating-point form"? We mean that the token in a storage slot, the internal representation, is organized in a special way to represent a floating-point number. Suppose, for example, that each word in computer memory can hold 10 decimal digits. The number 203.48 could be represented as shown in Fig. 11-1 (usually called *fixed-point format*), with the programmer knowing that the decimal point lies between the eighth and ninth digits from the left.

0	0	0	0	0	2	0	3	4	8

FIGURE 11-1
Fixed-point representation.

Or the representation might be as in Fig. 11-2, where the first two digits are used to show the exponent and the remaining eight the magnitude of the number, with the magnitude always understood to be a fraction.

Exponent   Magnitude

0	3	2	0	3	4	8	0	0	0

FIGURE 11-2
Floating-point representation.

Using this representation, the hardware can keep track of the decimal point and of aligning numbers for arithmetic operations. (This is an application of the principle of making explicit in the data as much of its structure as possible.)

Given the same size word, the number of digits in the magnitude of a token in floating-point form will be smaller than in fixed-point form, but the range of magnitudes possible is much greater. Also, as illustrated in Fig. 11-3, for one-third in decimal, there are some numbers that cannot be represented exactly in a fixed-word-size memory in either fixed- or floating-point form, no matter *how big* the word size.

One-third in fixed-point (decimal point understood at left)

One-third in floating-point

FIGURE 11-3
Internal representations of one-third.

The effects on computer arithmetic of these two representations, and of the fixed maximum (and minimum) size for tokens, are discussed in Chap. 12.

We are accustomed to using tokens in the base 10 or decimal system, but in fact any number can be used as the base for a counting system. Because computers are constructed from two-state (On-Off) devices, tokens in a base 2 or *binary number system* are used within most computers. (Thus, for example, word size is measured in binary digits.)

In the decimal number system, the distinct digits are 0,1,2, . . . ,9, the largest being one less than the base. Similarly, in the binary system each digit (usually called *bit* for *bi*nary digi*t*) is either 0 or 1.

How could one write two hundred and three in binary? Just as each position in decimal denotes a power of 10 (1, 10, 100, 1000, . . .), each position in binary denotes a power of two (1,2,4,8,16,32,64, . . .). So one way to write decimal 203 in binary would be as follows:

$$1 * 128 + 1 * 64 + 0 * 32 + 0 * 16 + 1 * 8 + 0 * 4 + 1 * 2 + 1 * 1$$

or

$$1 * 2^7 + 1 * 2^6 + 0 * 2^5 + 0 * 2^4 + 1 * 2^3 + 0 * 2^2 + 1 * 2^1 + 1 * 2^0$$

or

11001011

Can you prove that this is the *only* way to write two hundred and three in binary? (It had best be!)

Similarly, the fractional positions in binary are one-half, one-fourth, one-eighth, one-sixteenth, and so forth. Decimal 203.48 would be represented in binary as:

11001011.01111010111000010100 . . . (Repeats)

Note that not only are there fractions that cannot be represented exactly in either decimal or binary (for example, one-third), there are also fractions that can be represented exactly in one but not in the other (for example, decimal .48 or .1). Are there fractions that can be represented exactly in binary but not in decimal?

We have generated a possible source of confusion by talking about decimal and binary numbers at the same time. Is 10 the token for ten or two; is .1 the token for one-tenth or one-half? In general, if confusion is possible, we shall indicate the base in parentheses, following the number, for bases other than decimal. Thus, 203 = 11001011 (base 2).

CONVERTING A DECIMAL NUMBER TO BINARY

Of course, as the statement 203 = 11001011 (base 2) indicates, the "decimal number" and the corresponding "binary number" are equal; at the level of value no conversion is needed. What we can convert is the decimal token representing a number into the binary token representing the same number. One scheme for this conversion, for integers, is as follows:

1 Divide the decimal number (token) by 2 (the base of the number system *into* which you are converting).
2 The remainder after division is the next (larger) digit of the number (token) in base 2 (the new number system).
3 If the quotient is zero then stop, otherwise take the quotient as the new decimal number and go to step 1.

The intermediate steps in finding the binary equivalent of decimal 203 are shown in Fig. 11-4.

Note that the first remainder produced becomes the low-order digit of the result. Note also that the division is carried out in the number system of the original base. That is, to convert a number from decimal, use decimal division.

A TL program to carry out this conversion procedure is given in Fig. 11-5. The program assumes the existence of integer part **(int)** and fractional part **(frac)** functions. The only difficult part of the program is setting up the binary token properly. Because numerical output from TL is in decimal, the program must position each binary digit as if it were a decimal digit; that is, each digit must be in the appropriate base-10 column. (As you may have already discovered in earlier exercises, input and output are often as difficult as the problem-solving procedure itself.) A more compact and elegant version of this procedure is given in Fig. 11-6.

203/2 = 101 and remainder of 1
101/2 = 50 and remainder of 1
50/2 = 25 and remainder of 0
25/2 = 12 and remainder of 1
12/2 =   6 and remainder of 0
6/2 =   3 and remainder of 0
3/2 =   1 and remainder of 1
1/2 =   0 and remainder of 1

or

11001011(base 2)

FIGURE 11-4

Bin_int(n):   Produces a binary token equivalent to n.

  [**local** p, r, answer, q;

  p←0; answer←0; q←n;   p is position of next digit in answer.

  until q=0

    [r←**frac**(q/2) * 2;   Compute remainder.

    q←**int**(q/2);   Compute quotient.

    answer←(r * 10 ↑ p)+answer;   Remainder is tacked on to front of answer.

    p←p+1];   Increment p.

  return answer];

FIGURE 11-5

Bin_int(n):   Produces a binary token equivalent to n.

  [**local** a, p;

  a←0; p←2;   Initialize a and p.

  until n=0

    [a←a+**frac**(n/2) * p;   Remainder is calculated for p = 2. In successive repetitions, remainder is multiplied also by appropriate power of 10 for correct positioning thereby combining two steps of previous program.

    n←**int**(n/2);

    p←p * 10];

  return a];   Power of 10 is included in p.

FIGURE 11-6

A similar conversion procedure exists for decimal to binary fractions, with the arithmetic again carried out in decimal.

  1 Multiply the decimal fraction by 2 (the base of the *new* number system).
  2 The integer part of the product is the next smaller digit of the fraction in base 2 (the new number system).
  3 If the fractional part is zero or enough digits have been developed, then stop, otherwise take the fractional part of the product as the new decimal fraction and go to step 1.

REPRESENTATION
OF VALUES

The first steps of the never terminating conversion of decimal .48 to binary are shown in Fig. 11-7.

$$.48 * 2 \rightarrow \underline{0}.96 * 2 \rightarrow \underline{1}.92 * 2 \rightarrow \underline{1}.84 * 2 \rightarrow \underline{1}.68 * 2 \rightarrow \underline{1}.36 * 2 \rightarrow \underline{0}.72 \ldots$$

FIGURE 11-7

$$.011110 \ldots$$

The TL procedure for the decimal-to-binary fraction conversion is given in Fig. 11-8. Because fractions of arbitrary length may occur, such procedures typically stop after producing a given number of digits in the result. This TL procedure produces a binary token of eight digits (an arbitrary choice for illustrative purposes).

Bin_frac(n):	Produces binary token equivalent to n.
[**local** a, p;	
a ← 0; p ← .1;	
until p < 10 ↑ −8	Sets limit of repetition.
[a ← a + **int**(n * 2) * p;	Take integer part of n * 2 and then multiply by p for positioning.
n ← **frac**(n * 2);	
p ← p/10];	
return a];	

FIGURE 11-8

OTHER BASES

A number can be represented in any base system. We are interested in binary because many computers use base 2 for internal representation and for arithmetic operations. Even though computers may include circuitry to carry out the above conversion procedures, and so type out numerical results directly in decimal, the programmer needs to be familiar with binary in order to understand word length in memory, accuracy of arithmetic results, and such considerations.

Two other bases commonly used in computing are base 8 (called *octal*) and base 16 (called *hexadecimal*). Because 8 and 16 are powers of 2, these correspond to taking binary digits in groups of 3 and 4 bits, respectively, per character. Circuitry to accomplish such grouping is relatively trivial, allowing input and output in octal or hexadecimal to be converted easily to internal binary representation. The advantage of these bases over binary is that fewer characters are needed to construct the token representing a number. (Some machines, such as the IBM 360-370 series, actually use hexadecimal representation internally for some operations. See the discussion of floating-point normalization in Chap. 12.) Figure 11-9 gives the tokens in these systems for 0 through 19. Note that in each system the base is also the number of distinct numerals (including zero) employed. For any base greater than 10, such as hexadecimal, additional numerals beyond the 10 used in decimal must be defined; common prac-

DECIMAL	BINARY	OCTAL	HEXADECIMAL
0	0	0	0
1	1	1	1
2	10	2	2
3	11	3	3
4	100	4	4
5	101	5	5
6	110	6	6
7	111	7	7
8	1000	10	8
9	1001	11	9
10	1010	12	A
11	1011	13	B
12	1100	14	C
13	1101	15	D
14	1110	16	E
15	1111	17	F
16	10000	20	10
17	10001	21	11
18	10010	22	12
19	10011	23	13

FIGURE 11-9
Number tokens in several bases.

tice for hexadecimal (as in the IBM 360-370 series) is to use the letters A through F for 10 through 15.

The decimal-to-binary conversion procedures given above can be modified so as to convert to other number bases, by making the new base a parameter. A TL program for generalized integer conversion procedure is given in Fig. 11-10. Given this general routine, procedures for specific bases are easily defined:

Bin_int(n):Gen_int(n,2)

Oct_int(n):Gen_int(n,8)

Of course, this general routine will not work as it stands for new bases greater than 10, such as hexadecimal, since the process of reconstructing the new token by shifting to a new decimal position and adding does not accommodate numerals greater than 9. In fact, to represent hexadecimal numbers in output from TL, we must use character strings rather than decimal number tokens.

Gen_int(n,b):

[local a, p;

a ← 0; p ← b;

until n=0

[a ← a + **frac**(n/b) * p;

n ← **int**(n/b);

p ← p * 10];

return a];

Produces a token in base b equivalent to n (base 10).

FIGURE 11-10

Procedure is same as in Fig. 11-6 except that 2 is replaced by b.

REPRESENTATION
OF VALUES

129

None of the examples above have mentioned negative numbers. How should these conversion procedures be modified so as to work for negative numbers?

Although numbers are usually read into the computer and written out as sign and magnitude of value, there are three major schemes used for representing signed numbers within computer memory—sign and magnitude, base complement, and base-less-one complement. Each has certain advantages, and the choice of which to use is made by hardware designers as part of an overall system design. Normally the programmer working in a higher-level language is not aware of this choice. The programmer working in machine language will need to know which representation is being used, but it will have little effect on his programming activities. We illustrate each of these concepts by assuming a binary memory with a word length of 4 bits, and initially we consider fixed-point numbers only.

In *sign and magnitude,* 1 bit (usually the high-order one) is used to indicate the sign, typically 0 for positive and 1 for negative. The remaining bits of the word are used for the magnitude of the number. Thus, in our 4-bit machine, numbers can range from positive seven to negative seven, since seven is the largest magnitude that can be represented in three bits.

In *base complement,* a negative number is represented by the difference between the modulus number (the largest that can be represented in a word plus one) and the magnitude of the negative number. For example, in our 4-bit binary machine the modulus is 16, that is, 10000 (base 2); thus negative three would be represented as $10000 - 0011$ or 1101. This representation is used because it simplifies the circuitry needed to perform subtraction. To see why, notice that $p+(-q)$ is the same as $p+(m-q)-m$, or $(p-m)+(m-q)$, where the term $(m-q)$ is our base complement. Subtracting the modulus m is the same as discarding a bit one higher than the word length, and so subtraction can be implemented without the comparisons of magnitude needed for sign-and-magnitude arithmetic. Some examples of base-complement arithmetic are given in Fig. 11-11.

```
0111  7     1011 −5    0110  6
1011 −5     1110 −2    0001  1
────────    ────────   ────────
0010  2     1001 −7    0111  7
```

FIGURE 11-11
Examples of base-complement arithmetic.

```
−5  1011     −5  1011     5  0101
 5 |0101     −5 |1011     5 |0101
   10000        10110       01010

   |0           |6          |−6
```

FIGURE 11-12
More examples of base-complement arithmetic.

However, some cases of addition using base-complement arithmetic need further processing beyond that illustrated above. For example, consider the cases shown in Fig. 11-12. The carry into the fifth bit position generated in adding negative five and five is the modulus, and so is subtracted (by discarding it). However, the carry generated in adding negative five and negative five is not just the modulus, but rather is an indication that the result is in error. And in the case of adding positive five and positive five, the result is too large for 3 bits plus sign, and so is incorrect, even though no such carry is generated. Can you determine the rule for deciding when the result of a base-complement addition is valid, and when the result is too large in magnitude? (*Hint:* It depends on carry both into and out of the high-order-digit position.)

In *base-less-one complement,* a negative number is represented by the difference between the largest possible number that can be represented in a word and the magnitude of the number. For example, in our 4-bit machines the largest possible number is 15, that is, 1111 (base 2); thus, negative three would be represented as $1111 - 0011$ or 1100. This complement is even easier to create than the base complement; on a binary machine it is found by inverting each bit — 1's become 0's and 0's become 1's. However, addition itself is slightly more complicated. On binary machines, the base-less-one complement is usually referred to as the *one's complement,* and the base complement as the *two's complement.*

The representations of several positive and negative numbers are given in Fig. 11-13. Note that in each system one 4-bit combination is not used. In sign and magnitude and one's complement, this is negative (as distinct from positive) zero; in two's complement both positive and negative zero (whatever the distinction may mean) have the same representation, and the unused combination has a different meaning.

DECIMAL	SIGN AND MAGNITUDE	TWO'S COMPLEMENT	ONE'S COMPLEMENT
7	0111	0111	0111
4	0100	0100	0100
1	0001	0001	0001
0	0000	0000	0000
−1	1001	1111	1110
−4	1100	1100	1011
−7	1111	1001	1000
Unused	1000	1000	1111

FIGURE 11-13
Internal representations of negative integers.

NEGATIVE FLOATING-POINT NUMBERS

As was discussed earlier, floating-point numbers are usually represented by two number tokens packed into one word, one representing the exponent of the number and the other the magnitude. Provision must be made for either or both of these to be negative. Typically, the magnitude of the number and its sign are represented by one of the schemes given above, but the exponent is handled differently. A new number called the *characteristic* is formed by adding to the exponent a constant chosen so as to make the resulting characteristic always nonnegative. For example, if 4 bits were assigned to the characteristic, then exponents from negative eight to positive seven could be handled by adding eight to the exponent to form a characteristic between 0 and 15. The programmer using a higher-level language such as TL is not concerned with these details of internal representation.

OTHER ENCODINGS OF NUMBERS

Many other encodings besides base 2 tokens are possible on a binary machine. One common approach is to use groupings of 4 bits to represent the decimal digits of a number. In this system, called *binary-coded decimal or BCD,* the bit configurations 0000 through 1001 represent the numerals 0 through 9, and the configurations 1010 through 1111 are "illegal." Circuitry can be built to do arithmetic directly on this encoding, but it is more complex than that for straight binary because it must translate any illegal groupings generated into legal ones.

Another possibility is an encoding that includes all characters, whether numbers, letters, punctuation, or whatever. If this is to allow both upper- and lowercase letters, then $2 * 26 + 10 = 62$ separate groupings are required for numbers and letters alone. Six-bit groupings permit 64 distinct characters (since $2^6 = 64$); but since there are many more than two additional characters we wish to use, at least 7 bits per character are necessary. Current practice is to use 8-bit groupings since eight, being a power of two, is a much "nicer" group size than seven; two 4-bit BCD or hexadecimal groupings can be packed into one 8-bit grouping, and so forth. The two common encoding schemes for 8-bit groups, commonly called *bytes,* are ASCII-8, developed by a national standards activity, and EBCDIC, used by IBM and so a de facto standard.

The choice of which encoding scheme or schemes to use is an economic one, made by system designers to satisfy cost and usability constraints. For example, while bytes permit letters and other characters in the same encoding as digits, and so may simplify both programs and input-output circuitry, they require 8 bits in memory for the equivalent of each decimal digit. In binary, each decimal digit requires a theoretical lower limit of ~ 3.3 bits (since $2^{3.3} \simeq 10$), and even BCD requires only four. The use of byte encoding leads to greater memory requirements to store the same numerical information. But not all information is numerical.

Some computers use several encodings and provide appropriate machine-level operations to process each. For example, the IBM 360-370 uses bytes, BCD, binary, and hexadecimal floating point, and the machine instruction set includes operations for converting from one encoding to another. Again, most of these details may be concealed from the programmer working in a higher-level language such as TL.

REPRESENTATION
OF LOGICAL
VALUES

Each logical variable can have one of two values only, and so a single bit is sufficient to represent that value. The choice of whether to devote an entire word to each value or to pack several into one word depends on the tradeoff between memory space and processing time. Again, these details are typically hidden from the user of a higher-level language, who only knows that logical variables have two possible values—in TL, **true** and **false.**

REPRESENTATION
OF CHARACTER
STRINGS

Each character is encoded in some bit grouping, the two 8-bit alternatives discussed above being the most common ones. Again, the decision as to whether to use one entire word for each character or to pack several characters into a word is a design decision trading off the perceived relative worth of time and space.

Both the hardware designer and the system programmer who constructs translators in machine language for higher-level languages make these decisions. Typically, the user of a higher-level language such as TL knows only that character strings exist and is not concerned with how they are encoded.

Most computers do not have circuitry to generate functions such as square root or sine of a number. Rather, procedures (usually written in machine language) are used. For example, the sine of an angle (measured in radians) is given by the following infinite Taylor's series:

$$\sin z = \frac{z}{1!} - \frac{z}{3!} + \frac{z}{5!} - \frac{z}{7!} + \ldots$$

An approximation to the sine can be obtained by computing the first few terms of this series. Numerical analysts have studied the choice of series and of number of terms to use so as to minimize the error for a given amount of computing. Again, the user of a higher-level language is only concerned with using the function and, typically, does not know how the value is computed. However, if high accuracy is important, the programmer must look into the approximation used and its error characteristics.

REPRESENTATION OF FUNCTIONS

The individual elements of an array are represented in storage by one of the methods described above, but the structure of the array as a whole must also be represented. For each individual variable in a higher-level language such as TL, the language translator assigns a corresponding storage slot. For an array, the translator must assign a group of slots. One method is to make this group a sequence of slots with consecutive addresses. For example, in the array pictured in Fig. 11-14, the element *array*(3) would be found in the fourth slot.

REPRESENTATION OF ARRAYS

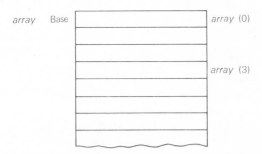

FIGURE 11-14
An array.

  If the address of the first or *base* element of the array, *array*(0), is known, then the address of any element *array*(i) can be computed as:

   address of element with subscript $i = base + i$

This equation computing the location of an array element given the array base and element subscript is called a *mapping function*.

REPRESENTATION OF VALUES

133

For multidimensional arrays, the mapping function is somewhat more complicated. As an example, we look at the two-dimensional case; the notions generalize easily to more dimensions.

Assume the common practice of mapping the array elements into consecutive storage slots in some orderly manner. This orderly manner could be to put all elements with the same first (sometimes called *major*) index together, or it could be to put all elements with the same second (*minor*) index together. Both possibilities for a 2×3 array *a* are shown in Fig. 11-15.

a	0	1	2
0	*a*(0,0)	*a*(0, 1)	*a*(0, 2)
1	*a*(1, 0)	*a*(1, 1)	*a*(1, 2)

	By major index
Base	*a*(0, 0)
	a(0, 1)
	a(0, 2)
	a(1, 0)
	a(1, 1)
	a(1, 2)

	By minor index
Base	*a*(0, 0)
	a(1, 0)
	a(0, 1)
	a(1, 1)
	a(0, 2)
	a(1, 2)

FIGURE 11-15
Storage mapping of two-dimensional array.

The mapping function now depends not only on the minimum index value for each dimension (here assumed to be zero), but also on the maximum value. Let us call these maximum values *majormax* and *minormax*. Then the mapping function for the major-index-first case is

$$\text{location of } a(i,j) = base + i * (minormax + 1) + j$$

Of course, the user of a higher-level language is not concerned with this mapping any more than he is with the storage slots assigned to individual variables. The language translator does the mapping computation as it translates if the information is available (that is, if the subscripts are constants), or it generates program statements to do the mapping computation during execution of the problem program if the subscripts are variables.

EXERCISES

1 Combine the TL procedures for *Bin_int* and *Bin_frac* into a single procedure that converts a decimal mixed number into a single binary token (of total length, say, eight digits).

2 Make the TL procedure that you produced in exercise 1 work for negative as well as positive numbers. Use sign-and-magnitude representation for negative numbers.

3 Program the procedure from exercise 2 in your local programming language and test it. (In some programming languages, it is much easier to produce a representation of a binary number by using a character string than by using a decimal number.)

4 Expand the procedure and program of exercises 1, 2, and 3 to convert a mixed number from decimal into an arbitrary base (less than 10). What are the problems with using your procedure to convert to a base greater than 10?

5 Prove that there is only one representation for a number in binary. For example, 203 decimal is 11001011 in binary and no other binary number = 203(base 10).

6 Write a program that inputs a decimal integer and produces as its result a character-string token representing the number in hexadecimal.

7 Program a procedure for converting decimal integers into base-complement notation. Assume a word length of eight decimal digits. Program a procedure for adding two numbers in that notation; for subtracting two numbers.

8 Answer the following questions with regard to your local computer and language.

a What is the word size?

b What is the largest possible integer value? The smallest?

c What are the largest and smallest floating-point numbers?

d What representation is used for negative numbers: sign and magnitude, base complement, base-less-one complement?

e How does (a) relate to (b) and (c)?

f What would be the answers to (b) and (c) if the other two representations from (d) were used?

9 Change the two-dimensional mapping function given in this chapter to handle arbitrary values for the minimum index values *majormin* and *minormin*.

10 a Find out the internal character representation used on your computer. What are the encodings for the characters A, . . . Z, blank, etc.?

b If your local programming language includes a function producing the numerical value of a character (say, as a binary number), use that function and your knowledge from part (a) to write a program that tabulates the number of times each character appears in some character input data. Tabulate these totals in an array, using the values of the characters to index the array. (*Hint:* If the value of the characters were A=21, B=22, C=23, . . . , what mapping function would map the character A into the first element of an array, B to the second, etc.?)

Bartee, T. C.: *Digital Computer Fundamentals,* McGraw-Hill, New York, 1972.

REFERENCE

APPROXIMATIONS AND ERRORS

As was demonstrated in Chap. 11, data values as conceived outside the computer cannot always be represented exactly in storage. This need for an approximate representation can lead to errors—to final values from a computational process different from those obtained by carrying out the same process on the same data by hand.

In this chapter, we consider three sources of error in the results of a computation which are present *even if the program and data being processed are entirely correct*. These sources of error are: change in representation of data, fixed-length representation determined by memory structure, and system error. Our intention is to create in the reader an awareness of how and why such errors occur, of the need for careful evaluation and analysis of possible errors, and of the possibilities in structuring procedures so as to limit such errors. The actual techniques of evaluation and analysis are a technical area of study (for numerical data, called *numerical analysis*) beyond the scope of this book. We concentrate here on presenting examples of what can happen.

ERRORS IN NONNUMERICAL VALUES

There has been very little study of errors in value arising from the processing of nonnumerical data. The traditional approach in computing has been to represent such data exactly, with a distinct internal character representation for each external character (using encodings as shown in Chap. 11, for example). Further, the representation usually has reproduced the entire data value, no matter what its length, using as many memory slots as were necessary. Such abbreviations as are used are introduced before the data are input and are not modified by any computational process. There have been a few studies relevant to errors in nonnumerical values, such as those concerning confusion of abbreviated names in airline reservations systems, but not enough analysis to permit any systematic treatment of the area. It seems likely that this situation will change in the next few years. For example, the English language contains some redundancy, as measured by the differing probabilities of particular letters occurring in certain positions or with certain frequencies. The increasing size of data files may make economical the use of probabilistic encodings taking advantage of these redundancies, and so introduce the possibility of errors in decoding. But for now our examples are numerical.

As noted earlier, there is no exact binary equivalent of many exact decimal fractions, such as 0.48 or 0.1. Therefore, even the process of converting a fraction from decimal to binary and immediately back to decimal (for example, input to a binary memory followed by output) may produce an output token different from that input. Thus, 0.1(base 10) becomes 0.0001100110011 . . . (base 2) which converts back to 0.0999999999999. . . . Of course, the binary fraction will not repeat infinitely, but will have some particular length in memory, as will its exact decimal equivalent. Generally, that exact decimal equivalent will not be 0.1. For example, with 10 bits available for the binary representation, 0.1(base 10) converts into 0.0001100110(base 2), which converts into (is exactly equivalent to) 0.099609375(base 10).

This error due to change of representation is further illustrated in Fig. 12-1. Note that the *existence* of conversion errors does *not* depend on the details of the conversion process nor on the length of number tokens in the two systems, although the *particular* errors and confusions in any instance will depend on those factors. One decimal digit can encode 10 distinct values and three binary digits can distinguish eight values; in going from one decimal digit to three binary digits, two distinctions *must* be lost. One decimal digit can encode 10 distinct values and four binary digits can distinguish 16 values; in this case although all of the decimal distinctions can be preserved in binary, six possible distinctions that can arise in arithmetic processing must be lost in converting back to decimal.

CHANGE IN REPRESENTATION

DECIMAL	BINARY	BINARY—3 BITS	BINARY—4 BITS
.0	.0	.000	.0000
.1	.00011001100 . . .	.000	.0001
.2	.00110011 . . .	.001	.0011
.3	.0100110011 . . .	.010	.0100
.4	.011001100 . . .	.011	.0110
.5	.1	.100	.1000
.6	.100110011 . . .	.100	.1001
.7	.1011001100 . . .	.101	.1011
.8	.11001100 . . .	.110	.1100
.9	.11100110011 . . .	.111	.1110

FIGURE 12-1

You may be asking, "So what?" The only distinctions that matter are those in decimal, and besides most computers use far more than 4 bits to represent numbers. Furthermore, change of representation occurs only at the beginning and end of processing, so it cannot introduce much error relative to that from the processing itself. There is some truth in this viewpoint, but the accumulation of a very small error introduced on input conversion may have a significant effect in determining the flow of control of a program.

For example, consider the effect of the following TL segment.

$a \leftarrow 0$;
for $n \leftarrow 0$ **thru** 1 **by** .1
  $a \leftarrow a + 1$;
write a;

If this were carried out on a three-digit binary machine as above, the computation would never finish since .1(base 10) is represented by .000(base 2). And for the 4-bit machine, the value of a written out would be 16. Of course, with longer number tokens in binary, the effect may not be as startling; but it can (and will) still occur.

Another caution should be observed here. Just because two values appear to be identical on output (the same number tokens are printed out) does not mean they are identical within the computer. (Remember the 4-bit case above.) It is quite conceivable that, after executing the equivalent of the TL segment given above on a particular computer, the following additional statements

write n;
write $(n = 1)$;

would produce the additional and seemingly contradictory outputs

1
FALSE

This can arise from the output conversion process printing out a rounded (see next section) and possibly shortened version of the actual value.

One other related point. The above construction **for** $n \leftarrow 0$ **thru** 1 **by** .1 would stop iteration as soon as n equalled or exceeded 1; that is the definition of **thru**. Therefore, n need not even exactly equal one, and indeed would not on most machines (even though the output routine might print out decimal one as the value). However, a loop programmed out using the conditional statement **until** $n = 1$ looks for exact equality, and so might never stop. Be very careful about using exact equality in testing for the end of processes.

ROUNDING AND TRUNCATION

As just illustrated, it is often necessary to discard some part of a number token arising from a conversion process. This discarding can also occur as the result of arithmetic processes. For example, multiplication of two 4-bit numbers can result in a product of up to 8 bits. But if the word size in memory is 4 bits, then the four least bits of every product must be thrown away. Or if 1 is divided by 10 in binary, an infinite continuing fraction results, but the fraction must be shortened to fit the available word size in memory.

This cutting off and discarding can be done in two ways—truncation (chopping off) and rounding. In *truncation,* those digits below the smallest are simply discarded. The 3-bit and 4-bit tokens for .1 through .9 in Fig. 12-1 were generated in that way. In *rounding,* one-half (.1 in binary) is added at the digit position just smaller than the smallest kept in the result. This may generate a carry, thus increasing the value of the resulting shortened token. For example, if this procedure were used to generate the 3-bit equivalents of .1 through .9 given in Fig. 12-1, the tokens for decimal .1, .2, .6, and .7 would be 1 bit larger in value. The 3-bit token for .1(base 10) would be found as follows:

.0001100110 . . .

.0001

.001

The particular errors and confusions among values that arise from rounding are different from those arising from truncation; the number of distinct tokens is the same.

As another example, recall that the 10-bit representation of one-tenth is .0001100110(base 2). (Since the next smaller bit would be 0, this token would be the result of either truncation or rounding.) Suppose that output were to be three decimal digits. The exact decimal equivalent of the above binary fraction is 0.099609375. Using truncation, this becomes .099. Rounding to three digits is accomplished by adding .0005, which generates .100109375, and then chopping to three digits, resulting in .100.

While no general statement is true for all cases, most often the discarding done by hardware is truncation, while that done by software systems (for example, input-output conversion procedures) is rounding.

FINITE LENGTH OF TOKENS

As just demonstrated, errors can be introduced by the finite length of words in computer memory. Such errors can arise without the presence of nonterminating fractions. These errors can be introduced while carrying out normal arithmetic processes on *correctly represented initial values.* Further, the particular error present at the completion of a series of arithmetic operations may depend on the order in which the operations are performed. The *commutative, associative, and distributive laws for addition and multiplication need not hold for computer arithmetic.*

As an example, consider the following four-digit decimal numbers: 100.0, −99.00, .0001, −.0002. Their true sum is a four-digit decimal number, .9999. Now suppose that they are added one sum at a time on a machine with four-digit numbers, rounding after each partial sum to find the nearest four-digit result. The rounding takes place in the fifth place over from the first nonzero digit or decimal point, using negative one-half if the partial sum is negative, and four digits of the result starting with

100.0	−	.0002
− 99.00		.0001
1.0000	−	.0001
5	−	5
1.000	−	.0001
+ .0001	−	99.00
1.0001	−	99.0001
5	−	5
1.000	−	99.00
− .0002		100.0
.9998		1.000
5		5
.9998		1.000

FIGURE 12-2

the largest nonnegative digit are kept for the next addition. For four terms, there are 24 orderings in which they could be added. The detailed process for two cases, the order given above and its reverse, are given in Fig. 12-2. Neither of the two orderings in Fig. 12-2 produces the true result. In fact, only two of the 24 possible orderings give the true result of .9999, six of them giving .9998 and 16 giving 1.000.

As an even more startling example of the problems of finite token length, consider evaluating the following expression using a more realistic word length—eight decimal digits:

$$a^2 - b^2 - c$$

where $a = 1.0002$
$b = 1.0001$
$c = .00020001$

This expression is evaluated using eight-digit arithmetic in Fig. 12-3. However, the true value, calculated using as many digits as needed, is shown in Fig. 12-4. The approximate number, −.00000001, and the true value, .00000002, differ by a factor of 2 and are of opposite sign!

(1) a^2

$$
\begin{array}{r}
1.0002 \\
* 1.0002 \\
\hline
20004 \\
10002000 \\
\hline
1.00040004
\end{array}
$$

(2) b^2

$$
\begin{array}{r}
1.0001 \\
* 1.0001 \\
\hline
10001 \\
10001000 \\
\hline
1.00020001
\end{array}
$$

(3) $a^2 - b^2$

$$
\begin{array}{r}
1.0004000 \\
-1.0002000 \\
\hline
.0002000
\end{array}
$$

(4) $a^2 - b^2 - c$

$$
\begin{array}{r}
.0002000 \\
-.00020001 \\
\hline
-.00000001
\end{array}
$$

FIGURE 12-3

(3) $a^2 - b^2$

$$
\begin{array}{r}
1.00040004 \\
-1.00020001 \\
\hline
.00020003
\end{array}
$$

(4) $a^2 - b^2 - c$

$$
\begin{array}{r}
.00020003 \\
-.00020001 \\
\hline
.00000002
\end{array}
$$

FIGURE 12-4

(1) $a+b$

$$
\begin{array}{r}
1.0002 \\
1.0001 \\
\hline
2.0003
\end{array}
$$

(2) $a-b$

$$
\begin{array}{r}
1.0002 \\
1.0001 \\
\hline
.0001
\end{array}
$$

(3) $(a+b)*(a-b)$

$$
\begin{array}{r}
2.0003 \\
\times .0001 \\
\hline
.00020003
\end{array}
$$

(4) $(a+b)*(a-b)-c$

$$
\begin{array}{r}
.00020003 \\
-.00020001 \\
\hline
.00000002
\end{array}
$$

FIGURE 12-5

In this case the error can be eliminated by rewriting the expression as follows:

$$a^2-b^2-c=(a+b)*(a-b)-c$$

Evaluating this form of the expression will produce the correct result even with eight-digit arithmetic (see Fig. 12-5).

We have been discussing numerical errors informally, relying on examples to illustrate what can occur in processing. Now we introduce some formal concepts of errors and approximations, not to exploit them here in further analysis, but rather because they point out more generally some dangers to be avoided. In particular, we look at the concepts of *significant digits,* of *absolute* and *relative error,* and at the accumulation of these two types of error under the common arithmetic processes.

Significant digits

A number (token) has *n* significant digits if the value which it represents (the true number) rounded to *n* digits produces that token. For example, rounding 12345.67 to five digits generates 12346. In this case, 12346 is an approximate number with five significant digits. In discussing errors, the converse case is of more interest. Given an *n*-digit approximate number, the true value that it represents lies in the range of the approximate number ±5 in the *n*-plus-first digit position. For example, the true value represented by the five-digit approximate number 12346 lies between 12345.5 and 12346.4999 . . . inclusive. (These definitions are changed in the obvious way for bases other than decimal.)

If the programmer knows the number of significant digits in input data and if he knows the effect on significance of arithmetic operations, he may be able to predict the number of significant digits in the results of his computations. Of course, such statements about significance give only limits on the number of significant digits, but they can indicate when the computer is in danger of producing meaningless numbers.

Scientists often use the convention of recording only significant digits, except for trailing zeros before the decimal point. Such zeros can be eliminated by using scientific notation, thus removing any ambiguity as to whether zeros are significant or not. For example, if a number is known to the nearest hundred as 2300, it has in fact only two significant digits and could be written in scientific notation as 2.3 * 10 ↑ 3. This makes it clear that the true value lies in the range 2250 to 2349.999 . . . , not 2299.5 to 2300.499 . . . . By following this convention through a series of hand calculations, recording only significant digits, one can easily determine the significance of a result.

However, in using the computer, the programmer must calculate and verify significance outside of the machine. The computer reads in and writes out number tokens not according to their significance but rather according to the conventions of its input and output procedures. If the output procedure calls for writing out up to eight digits and there are at least that many non-zero digits, those eight digits will be printed whether significant or not, and trailing zeros may be suppressed even when significant. Indeed, the results of a computation may be completely without significance, as the second example of the previous section shows. *Just because numbers are printed as computer output does not make them meaningful.*

Measurement of errors

The *absolute error* of a computation or series of computations is defined as the difference between the approximate number resulting from the computation and the true value that the number represents. Using $\underline{a}$ for absolute error, (A) for approximate number, and A for true value, this definition is:

$$\underline{a} = (A) - A$$

Thus, if .14285714 is the approximate representation (as it would be in eight-decimal-digit arithmetic) of one-seventh, (which is truly .142857142857142857 . . .), then the error in the computation 1/7 (also, reasonably speaking, the error in the approximate number .14285714) is $-2.85714 . . . * 10 \uparrow -9$. If the true value that this approximate number represents is not known, but assuming that all eight digits are significant (a strong assumption indeed), then the absolute error lies within the limits $\pm .5 * 10 \uparrow -8$.

The relative error $\underline{r}$ is the ratio of the absolute error to the true value. Thus,

$$\underline{r} = \underline{a}/A$$

For the above case of .14285714 approximating 1/7,

$$\underline{r} = (2.85714 . . . * 10 \uparrow -9) / (1/7) = 1.9999 . . . * 10 \uparrow -8$$

Since in general neither the absolute error nor the true value is known, limits for the value of the relative error can be found by using our estimate of the absolute error and the approximate value.

$$\underline{r} = \underline{a}/A = (.5 * 10 \uparrow -8) / .1485714 = 3.5 . . . * 10 \uparrow -8$$

Accumulation of errors

The above definitions can be used to develop expressions for the errors resulting from arithmetic operations. In the following, let us represent approximate numbers as the sum of their true value plus some (absolute) error, as in:

$$(A) = A + \underline{a} \quad \text{and} \quad (B) = B + \underline{b}$$

For addition and subtraction, (which is simply addition with a change of signs):

$$(A) + (B) = [A + \underline{a}] + [B + \underline{b}] = [A + B] + [\underline{a} + \underline{b}]$$

Thus, the absolute error of the sum or difference can be as large as $[\underline{a} + \underline{b}]$, the sum of the absolute errors of the terms.

For addition and subtraction, the relative error is given as:

$$\underline{r} = \frac{[\underline{a} + \underline{b}]}{[A + B]}$$

If $[A + B]$ is very small, as it would be in the case of the sum of numbers of approximately the same magnitude but opposite sign, the relative error may be very large, possibly many times the magnitude of the sum. *The loss of significance in the subtraction of two nearly equal numbers is the greatest source of inaccuracy in most calculations.* Automatic scaling, as in floating-point arithmetic, provides almost no protection against this loss. If such subtractions are possible, even (or particularly) in a sequence of calculations, the programmer should take special precautions to avoid the difficulty or at least to make the user of the output aware that a potentially large loss of significance has occurred. These special precautions could include reordering the data and/or printing out warning messages at appropriate points.

As an example, consider the two approximate numbers, with one digit of significance each, 1 and .9. The former could range from .5 to 1.5, and the latter from .85 to .95. While their computed difference is .1 their true difference could range from .65 to −.35, with the relative error at the extremes approximately one. That is, the error in the result could be as large as the true value itself. For this particular data, in fact, the error relative to the computed value could be as much as approximately five.

The danger is that many numerical processes, such as matrix inversion, correlation or regression computations, and so forth, include many thousands of arithmetic operations. Even though initial data items may not be very close in value, such numbers may arise (and be subtracted) in the course of the computation. There is no way to know if this has happened except by checking if the results are close to the true value. (Final results may often be checked for consistency by entering them back into the original equations being solved, but such checks do not indicate how to adjust erroneous results.)

In multiplication:

$$[A+\underline{a}] * [B+\underline{b}] = [A*B] + [\underline{a}*B] + [A*\underline{b}] + [\underline{a}*\underline{b}]$$

The $[\underline{a}*\underline{b}]$ term is generally very small relative to the others and so is ignored. (If this is not true, then the original data will be of little significance, as in the example with 1 and .9.) Then, the absolute error is given by the terms $[\underline{a}*B] + [A*\underline{b}]$, and the relative error is that sum divided by $[A*B]$, or $[\underline{a}/A+\underline{b}/B]$. Thus, as an upper limit, the relative error for multiplication is the sum of the absolute values of the relative errors of the numbers involved. The same limit on relative error holds for division.

For any fixed limit to the number of digits in a token, there is the possibility that an arithmetic process will generate a value larger than can be represented within that fixed length. For example, in eight-decimal-digit arithmetic the sum of 90,000,000 and 10,000,000, both legal numbers, is 100,000,000, requiring nine digits. This generation of a value too large to be represented is called *overflow*. Note that this possibility is present with tokens in floating point also. No matter how the digits are allocated between magnitude and characteristic, there will be some largest value that can be represented, and adding any positive value to that largest one will generate overflow.

Of course, the computer user should be made aware when overflow occurs, as there is no direct way of representing the resulting value. Some hardware-software systems terminate processing by halting the machine or, more likely, by transferring

FLOATING-POINT PROCESSES

control to another process specified by the programmer or by those operating the computer system.

In working with floating-point numbers there is another possibility for developing a nonrepresentable value. Arithmetic processes may lead to a value smaller than the smallest nonzero magnitude representable. For example, using eight decimal digits for magnitude and two for characteristic, the smallest positive value that theoretically can be represented is .00000001 * 10 ↑ −50. Generation of positive values smaller than that limit (or negative values larger) is called *underflow*. Underflow may be signalled by the means discussed above for overflow or, in some systems, the value zero is taken automatically.

Another aspect of floating-point computations is *normalization*. By normalization is meant shifting the magnitude (and appropriately adjusting the characteristic) so that the most significant (leftmost) digit of the magnitude is nonzero. On many computers this is done automatically; on others, the programmer in machine language has the choice of normalized or unnormalized results. On binary machines, for example, normalization results in the most significant digit of the magnitude being a one. Of course, one must know just what normalization takes place in order to calculate the significance of computed results.

SYSTEM ERRORS

By system errors are meant those errors due to failures of the hardware and/or software system. While such failures are not nearly as common as programmers would like to believe, they do sometimes occur, particularly as large software systems become more complex and difficult to debug.

System errors are, of course, not due to the representation used, but sometimes that representation can be adjusted to aid in detecting and/or correcting errors. The most common representational device, employed in checking for errors in transmission, is the use of additional bits for parity. Parity bits are added to a unit of information (say, a character) so as to make the total number of bits odd (called *odd parity*) or even (called *even parity*). Transmission errors that result in changing a bit can be detected since parity will no longer be odd (or even). Examples of odd parity for three different 8-bit character codes are given in Fig. 12-6. In some hardware systems such parity bits are kept in memory with each character or word (although hidden from the programmer), and in almost every system parity bits are generated and included as part of each character recorded on file storage or transmitted over communication lines.

The parity scheme just described detects single-bit errors, but not cases of simultaneous errors in 2 bits. More complicated schemes, involving more parity bits, can detect more subtle errors and/or determine in which bit position the error occurred.

If the file-handling hardware-software system does not automatically generate parity checking, the programmer may wish to add it to his program. For example, the following TL segment

CODE	PARITY BIT
11010010	1
01000011	0
00000000	1

FIGURE 12-6

computes a parity value for the array a, with elements from $a(1)$ to $a(n)$. The parity value is stored as value $a(n + 1)$, and is such that all elements of the extended array sum to zero. If this extended array is recorded on disk or transmitted over communication lines, error-free transfer can be checked by adding up the $n + 1$ elements and seeing if they total zero.

$a(n+1) \leftarrow 0;$

for $i \leftarrow 1$ **thru** n

$\quad a(n+1) \leftarrow a(n+1) - a(i);$

1 What rules are used in converting numbers for output in your local programming language? Are values rounded or truncated, and at which digit position? How many digits are printed out in different cases, and what are the different cases? What is the largest possible difference between two values that will appear equal on output?

2 In your local programming language, test (using conditional statements or some similar means) to see if n, **sqrt** $(n * n)$, and $(n \uparrow 2) \uparrow .5$ all have the same value. Test this for integer values of n from 1 to 10. If your language has some means for changing the precision of output so as to show more digits before truncation or rounding, use that means to print the values computed with more precision.

3 On page 138 a TL segment is given in which the number of repetitions of a loop is not as expected. Experiment with an analogous program in your local programming language to produce the same effect.

4 Try the eight-digit arithmetic examples of Figs. 12-3 and 12-4 on your local computer system. Explain why you got the result you did in terms of your answer to exercise 8, Chap. 11 and exercise 1, Chap. 12.

5 For some trigonometric functions such as sine or cosine, compute on your local system 8 or 10 different values for angles between 0 and 90 degrees. Compare these answers with a standard table of trigonometric functions. What is the accuracy of the computer's function calculation?

6 Compute the value of 1/7, 2/7, 3/7, . . . , 7/7 on your local system. What are the absolute and relative errors of these computations compared to the true value? Are these errors the same for all of the above, or do the errors fluctuate?

Hamming, Richard W.: *Introduction to Applied Numerical Analysis,* McGraw-Hill, New York, 1971.

Pennington, Ralph, H.: *Introductory Computer Methods and Numerical Analysis,* 2d ed., Macmillan, New York, 1970.

HOW COMPUTER SYSTEMS WORK

From the first moment that one person began describing to another what computers are and what they can do, a debate has continued about the correct order of presenting that information. Some teachers believe that learning is best motivated by first showing just how computers work, at the "basic" level, and so they begin with the details of computer organization and machine language programming. Others believe that problem solving and the logic of programming, independent of the details of computer operation, should come first, and so they begin with programming in a higher-level language. The authors of this book are of the latter persuasion. (You may well ask, what do belief and persuasion have to do with learning?)

But just as the historical development and current uses of computers form a context within which computer programming and problem solving can be better understood, so too the details of the systems making up computers and of the systems of which computers are a component also form a context within which effective problem solving must operate. Part Three presents a part of that context.

Chapter 13 specifies further the details of computer organization first mentioned in Chap. 1. It also describes the nature of programming a computer at that level of detail, in the machine's own language as it were. Chapter 14 describes the programs, called *language translators,* which have been developed to ease the problem of programming in machine language, in the extreme by translating from a higher-level language such as TL into machine language. Together these two chapters relate the reality of the computer as viewed by the second approach mentioned above (and in Part Two of this text) to the reality of the first approach. Chapter 15 is concerned with moving up a level of organization to the hardware and software making up today's larger and more complex computer systems. And Chap. 16 moves down a level from Chap. 13, to a consideration of the logical basis of circuits making up the computer. Together these two chapters define some of the technological context surrounding our simplified image of the computer.

And what of the reader who does not care for these matters, who wants only to write programs? Consider the Middle Eastern tale of the man who went to a rich acquaintance. "Give me some money," he said. "Why?" asked the acquaintance. "I want to buy . . . an elephant." "If you have no money, you cannot afford to keep an elephant." "I came here," said the man, "to get money, not advice."

COMPUTER ORGANIZATION AND
MACHINE LANGUAGE

Up to this point a very simple and sketchy model of the inner workings of the computer has been sufficient because we have been concerned mainly with the functions that a computer can perform and with the way in which those functions can be specified in a higher-level language. Now we turn our attention to a more detailed examination of "what really goes on" inside the computer. Of course, explaining is like unpeeling an onion. We can explain how higher-level language programs work in terms of computer organization and machine language programs, as we shall do in this chapter; but these concepts can then be explained in terms of more basic hardware configurations—circuits for computing logical combinations of signals, adders and shifters, etc., and these logical elements can further be explained in terms of physical phenomena of electricity and magnetism. Each level of explanation requires implicit acceptance of those lower levels. But for now, we concentrate on the next layer of the onion, the basic computer organization as programmed in machine language—raw hardware unaccompanied by the typical software assistance.

Our approach is to review and describe in more detail the four major components of a computer, showing the information flows among them. We then combine those components into a simple computer and spell out its cycle of execution—the steps required to execute a single machine instruction. Next, we construct a program in TL to simulate this simple computer. To do so requires specifying even more details including a set of machine language operations. Given this simulation of the simple computer, we can prepare and test machine language programs. Finally, we modify our simulated computer to incorporate several additional hardware features available on most real machines.

In practice, the range of computers available is limited only by the laws of physics, the state of technology, and the designer's ingenuity. Our simulated computer is not exactly like any one real machine, but it is typical of early computers and of some of the smaller machines available today.

Consider the computer as having four components—memory, arithmetic and logical unit, control unit, and input-output—as shown in Fig. 13-1. The solid lines indicate the flow of data and instructions; the dotted lines, the flow of control signals. Let us examine each of these components in more detail.

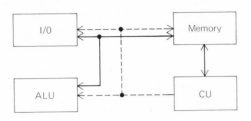

FIGURE 13-1

The memory consists of a set of *cells* or *locations,* each of which holds a single piece of program or data. (Often these pieces of program or data, and/or the locations that hold them, are called *words*.) Each location has an *address* by which it and its contents can be referenced. Typically these addresses are consecutive integers starting with zero, like a group of post office boxes. Associated with the memory are two special registers, the *memory address register* and the *memory data register.* Data to be read from or written into the memory pass through the memory data register. The address at which reading or writing takes place is given in the memory address register. This part of the computer is shown in more detail in Fig. 13-2.

Memory

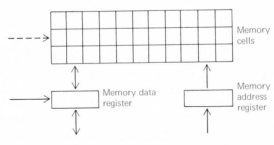

FIGURE 13-2
Memory detail.

Note that both data and instructions (*program steps*) are stored in memory and so can be intermixed. This feature is true of most current computers, although a few have separate program stores. Also, the size of the addressable memory unit varies widely, from a single character to a word of, say, 64 bits (eight characters), with most possible combinations in between those extremes to be found in some machines. Indeed, many computer designs allow several different-sized groupings of bits or characters to be addressed.

The arithmetic and logical unit (ALU) contains the hardware necessary to carry out machine-level operations—such hardware as adders, shifters, logical comparators, counters for multiplication by repeated addition, and so forth. In many computer designs,

Arithmetic and logical unit

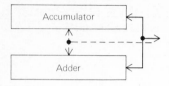

FIGURE 13-3
Arithmetic and logical unit detail.

including this simple computer, the ALU also contains a register, called the *accumulator,* which holds one of the words of data (*operands*) entering into most instructions. The arithmetic and logical unit is diagrammed in Fig. 13-3, though simplified by showing just the adder to stand for the full set of operations hardware. A typical machine operation set is given later in this chapter. Add, Store in Memory, Branch, and Write, are examples of such operations.

Control unit

The control unit decodes instructions, initiates the flow of data to and from memory, and controls the order in which instructions are executed. Among its components are a register holding the operation being executed (the *operation register*), a register holding the address or operand part of the current instruction (the *data address register*), a register holding the address in memory of the next instruction to be executed (the *control counter* or *next instruction address register*), and hardware for decoding the operation. These components are shown in Fig. 13-4. Often the control unit and arithmetic and logical unit taken together are referred to as the *central processing unit* (*CPU*).

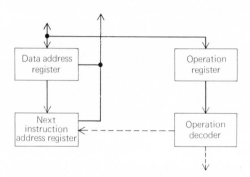

FIGURE 13-4
Control unit detail.

Input-output

The input-output units are such devices as teletypes, punched card readers, printers, magnetic tape and disk drives, optical scanners, etc. For this chapter their nature need not be specified in any more detail.

Total system

The information flow diagrams of these individual components can be combined into a single total system information flow diagram as shown in Fig. 13-5.

FETCH-EXECUTE CYCLE

The operation of our computer is comprised of a sequence of individual information transfer steps among these components. These steps are grouped into two phases—Fetch and Execute. Together the two phases are called the *Fetch-Execute cycle.* During the Fetch phase of the cycle, the next instruction is fetched from memory and decoded; during the Execute phase, that instruction is carried out. The Fetch-Execute cycle is spelled

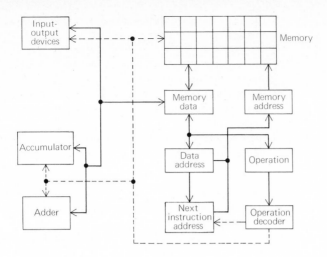

FIGURE 13-5
Detailed information flow.

out in more detail in the following steps.

Fetch phase

1 The contents of the next instruction address register are transferred to the memory address register.
2 The contents of the memory location whose address is given in the memory address register are transferred to the memory data register.
3 The operation part of the contents of the memory data register is transferred to the operation register; the operand part is transferred to the data address register.
4 The contents of the next instruction address register are increased by one.
5 The contents of the operation register are sent to the operation decoder, initiating the Execute phase of the cycle.

The exact details of the Execute phase depend on the particular operation being executed. Some examples are given below.

**Execute phase
(Add to Accumulator)**

6 The contents of the data address register are transferred to the memory address register.
7 The contents of the memory location whose address is given in the memory address register are transferred to the memory data register.
8 The contents of the memory data register and the contents of the accumulator are transferred together through the adder, and the sum produced by the adder is transferred back to the accumulator.

**Execute phase
(Store Contents of
Accumulator in Memory)**

6 The contents of the data address register are transferred to the memory address register.
7 The contents of the accumulator are transferred to the memory data register.
8 The contents of the memory data register are written into the memory location whose address is given in the memory address register.

151

Execute phase (Branch)	6 The contents of the data address register are transferred to the next instruction address register.
Execute phase (Write)	6 The contents of the data address register are transferred to the memory address register.
	7 The contents of the memory location whose address is given in the memory address register are transferred to the memory data register.
	8 The contents of the memory data register are transferred to the output device.

MEMORY FORMAT AND INSTRUCTIONS

The above step-by-step listing of the Fetch-Execute cycle specifies most of the details required to program a simulation in TL of this simple machine. The most important additional specifications are of the format in memory of data and instruction words and of the set of operations available. We consider memory format next and postpone specifying the operation set until after programming the Fetch phase.

Assume that each word in memory contains six characters. For numerical data, these can be five digits preceded by a sign. For instructions, these five characters can specify a single instruction. We shall use a single operand (single address) instruction format, with the contents of the accumulator implied as a second operand in most instructions. More precisely, four characters of each instruction word are used to specify an operand, such as the memory address of data. (Thus, using decimal numbers, there can be up to 10,000 locations in memory, addressed from 0 to 9999.) One character is used to specify the operation to be performed. For now, the remaining character is left blank; some uses are introduced for it later. The format of an instruction word is pictured in Fig. 13-6.

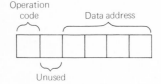

FIGURE 13-6
Instruction word format.

Several features of this instruction format should be noted. First, it is an example of a *single-address* machine organization (that is, one operand per instruction); this is only one of several possibilities. Some computers have two addresses per instruction, others three or four. And some (such as the IBM 360-370 series) allow several of these possibilities, depending on the particular operation. However, most small, simple machines have a single-address instruction format.

Also, this instruction format, arbitrarily chosen for easier understanding of the machine, is extremely wasteful of information capacity. For example, since there are 8 bits per character, this format uses 4 times 8 or 32 bits to address 10,000 memory locations. By using binary rather than decimal number tokens for addresses, 10,000 locations (indeed, more than 16,000 locations) can be addressed with 14 bits. This format uses over twice as many bits as are needed for addresses. As will be seen later, the format also wastes bits in the operation code. The computer designer, conscious of the cost of hardware and the need to provide the most computer per dollar in order to compete in the marketplace, will pack binary addresses and operation codes together so as to maximize the amount of information contained in a given word size. Such a format may be harder for the machine language programmer to use, but few programmers use machine language anyway (see discussion of assemblers in Chap. 14). For our purposes, to make clearer just what is going on in the machine's operation and to make easier the task of simulating the machine, we use a less economical design.

Next the programmer must decide how much detail is needed to represent the computer in this simulation. Must all of the registers and data flows given above be represented or can some be omitted? Since the simulation is intended to make clear the inner operation of the computer and since some as yet unspecified additional details will be introduced later in the chapter, we choose to include all of the machine's registers as distinct variables. However, the operational hardware, such as the adder and operation decoder, can be represented by the appropriate steps in the TL simulation program, as can the input-output devices.

DATA STRUCTURES OF THE SIMULATION

The TL variables chosen to represent each of these computer components are given in Fig. 13-7. A TL segment simulating the Fetch phase follows directly.

Fetch:
    mar ← nia;
    mdr ← mem(mar);
    opr ← mdr @ (1,1);
    dar ← mdr @ (3);
    nia ← nia + 1;

nia and *mar* must be numerical variables in TL, even though in the computer being simulated all data are in character form. The other TL variables are character strings.

COMPUTER COMPONENT	TL VARIABLE
Memory	*mem* (an array)
Memory data register	*mdr*
Memory address register	*mar*
Data address register	*dar*
Operation register	*opr*
Next instruction address register	*nia*
Accumulator	*acc*

FIGURE 13-7
Computer simulation data structures.

The next phase to be simulated is the Execute phase. Since that phase depends on the particular operations being executed, an operation set for our simple computer must be specified next.

OPERATION SET

We begin with a set of 11 operations, and later add six more to illustrate additional features of current machines. The initial 11 operations are presented in Fig. 13-8, giving for each a simple name, a brief explanation of the operation, a hardware operation

OPERATION	OP CODE	BRIEF DESCRIPTION	TL PROGRAM SEGMENT
Load	0	$\mathbf{C}mem \Rightarrow acc$	$mar \leftarrow \mathbf{num}(dar);$ $mdr \leftarrow mem(mar);$ $acc \leftarrow mdr;$
Store	1	$\mathbf{C}acc \Rightarrow mem$	$mar \leftarrow \mathbf{num}(dar);$ $mdr \leftarrow acc;$ $mem(mar) \leftarrow mdr;$
Add	2	$\mathbf{C}acc + \mathbf{C}mem \Rightarrow acc$	$mar \leftarrow \mathbf{num}(dar);$ $mdr \leftarrow mem(mar);$ $acc \leftarrow \mathbf{str}[\mathbf{num}(acc) + \mathbf{num}(mdr)];$
Subtract	3	$\mathbf{C}acc - \mathbf{C}mem \Rightarrow acc$	$mar \leftarrow \mathbf{num}(dar);$ $mdr \leftarrow mem(mar);$ $acc \leftarrow \mathbf{str}[\mathbf{num}(acc) - \mathbf{num}(mdr)];$
Multiply	4	$\mathbf{C}acc * \mathbf{C}mem \Rightarrow acc$	$mar \leftarrow \mathbf{num}(dar);$ $mdr \leftarrow mem(mar);$ $acc \leftarrow \mathbf{str}[\mathbf{num}(acc) * \mathbf{num}(mdr)];$
Branch zero	5	Branch if $acc=0$	$\mathbf{if}\ \mathbf{num}(acc)=0\ \mathbf{then}\ nia \leftarrow \mathbf{num}(dar);$
Branch negative	6	Branch if $acc<0$	$\mathbf{if}\ \mathbf{num}(acc)<0\ \mathbf{then}\ nia \leftarrow \mathbf{num}(dar);$
Branch	7	Branch unconditionally	$nia \leftarrow \mathbf{num}(dar);$
Halt and continue	8	Halt; if restarted continue with data address	$nia \leftarrow \mathbf{num}(dar);\ \mathbf{done};$
Read	A	Input data into mem	$mar \leftarrow \mathbf{num}(dar);$ $\mathbf{read}\ mdr;$ $mem(mar) \leftarrow mdr;$
Write	B	Output $\mathbf{C}mem$	$mar \leftarrow \mathbf{num}(dar);$ $mdr \leftarrow mem(mar);$ $\mathbf{write}\ mdr;$

FIGURE 13-8

code, and a corresponding TL program segment. Because TL requires numerical data for subscripts and for numerical operations, the functions **num** (which converts a string to the corresponding number) and **str** (which converts a number to the corresponding string) are used widely.

(The following abbreviations are used throughout this chapter: *mem* for the specified memory location, *acc* for the accumulator, **C**mem for the contents of the specified memory location, **C**acc for the contents of the accumulator, and ⇒ for "is transferred into." More generally, **C**xxx denotes the contents of *xxx*.)

These program segments indicate several opportunities for introducing useful subroutines. For example, all references to memory include a sequence for getting the memory address into *mar,* and all operations which fetch data from memory include the above memory address setup followed by a transfer into *mdr.* Further, each operation itself should probably be constructed as a named subroutine. These changes are introduced in Fig. 13-10.

The one remaining segment of TL program required to complete the simulation is that representing the operation decoder, selecting the appropriate segment of operation code. The language TL does not include a convenient and compact way of selecting among multiple branches; TL requires multiple conditional statements. (Some higher-level languages include a construct which selects one of a set of next statements or subroutines according to the value of a variable. It would be easy enough to add such a construct to TL, but since many languages with which TL should be consistent lack such a construct, it has been omitted.) An operation-decoding procedure which assumes subroutines for each operation and uses the facilities available in TL is presented in Fig. 13-9.

The total simulation program consists of the Fetch phase given earlier, followed by the decoding statement just developed, followed by the subroutines representing the various operations. Additional operations can be inserted by extending *Decode* and adding the appropriate subroutines. The entire simulation, re-coded to use subroutines, is given in Fig. 13-10.

Decode:
      if *opr*="0" **then** *Ld* **else**
      if *opr*="1" **then** *St* **else**
      if *opr*="2" **then** *Ad* **else**
      if *opr*="3" **then** *Su* **else**
      if *opr*="4" **then** *Mu* **else**
      if *opr*="5" **then** *Bz* **else**
      if *opr*="6" **then** *Bn* **else**
      if *opr*="7" **then** *Bu* **else**
      if *opr*="8" **then** *Ht* **else**
      if *opr*="A" **then** *Rd* **else**
      if *opr*="B" **then** *Wr;*
      to *Fetch;*

FIGURE 13-9

Fetch:
    mar ← *nia;*
    mdr ← *mem(mar);*
    opr ← *mdr* **@** (1,1);
    dar ← *mdr* **@** (3);
    nia ← *nia* +1;

Decode:
      if *opr*="0" **then** *Ld* **else**
      if *opr*="1" **then** *St* **else**
      if *opr*="2" **then** *Ad* **else**
      if *opr*="3" **then** *Su* **else**
      if *opr*="4" **then** *Mu* **else**
      if *opr*="5" **then** *Bz* **else**
      if *opr*="6" **then** *Bn* **else**
      if *opr*="7" **then** *Bu* **else**
      if *opr*="8" **then** *Ht* **else**
      if *opr*="A" **then** *Rd* **else**
      if *opr*="B" **then** *Wr;*
      to *Fetch;*

Addr:
    [*mar* ← **num**(*dar*)];

Datr:
    [*Addr; mdr* ← *mem(mar)*];

Ld:
    [*Datr; acc* ← *mdr*];

St:
    [*Addr; mdr* ← *acc; mem(mar)* ← *mdr*];

Ad:
    [*Datr; acc* ← **str**[**num**(*acc*)+**num**(*mdr*)]];

Su:
    [*Datr; acc* ← **str**[**num**(*acc*)−**num**(*mdr*)]];

Mu:
    [*Datr; acc* ← **str**[**num**(*acc*) * **num**(*mdr*)]];

Bz:
    [**if num**(*acc*)=0 **then** *Bu*];

Bn:
    [**if num**(*acc*) < 0 **then** *Bu*];

Bu:
    [*nia* ← **num**(*dar*)];

Ht:
    [*Bu;* **done**];

Rd:
    [*Addr;* **read** *mdr; mem(mar)* ← *mdr*];

Wr:
    [*Datr;* **write** *mdr*];

FIGURE 13-10

155

Now, given a program written in machine language, with that program stored in *mem* and with *nia* set to the location of the first step of the program one could follow the above procedure to simulate executing that machine language program. Let us now write some simple machine language (ML) programs to indicate the detail of thinking required when programming at that level.

PROGRAMMING IN MACHINE LANGUAGE

First, consider a program to read in two values and write out the larger. A TL segment to do that task would be:

read *a;*

read *b;*

if *a > b*

   then write *a*

   else write *b;*

However, in using ML, the programmer must choose which specific memory locations are to hold the program and the data. Arbitrarily, assume that the program is stored beginning in location 0100 and that the two items of data are to be stored in locations 0200 and 0201. One possible ML program to write out the larger value is given in Fig. 13-11. Notice the form in which instructions are written. Typically, coding sheets with such columns marked off are used when programming in machine language for transcription to punched cards.

LOCATION	OP	ADDRESS/DATA	COMMENTS
0100	A	0200	Read A
0101	A	0201	Read B
0102	0	0200	Load A
0103	3	0201	Subtract B
0104	6	0107	Branch negative if B larger
0105	B	0200	Write A
0106	8	0100	Halt and repeat
0107	B	0201	Write B
0108	8	0100	Halt and repeat
0200			Location of A
0201			Location of B

FIGURE 13-11
Example ML program—find larger value.

If *nia* were set to 0100 (in real computers, usually done by keys from the operator's console) and the appropriate data were available to be read, this program should write out the larger datum. Note that the branch address in location 0104 could not be specified until later parts of the program were completed. The programmer must remember to go back to 0104 and complete it later. This is a trivial example of the bookkeeping problems that arise in machine language programming.

Next consider an ML program to evaluate the function $3x^2 + 4x - 7$, first reading a value of *x*. The TL program segment to carry out this task is as follows:

read *x;* **write** $3 * x \uparrow 2 + 4 * x - 7;$

LOCATION	OP	ADDRESS/DATA	COMMENTS
0100	A	0200	Read in x
0101	0	0200	Load x
0102	4	0200	Times x
0103	4	0201	Times 3
0104	1	0202	Store $3 * x \uparrow 2$
0105	0	0200	Load x
0106	4	0203	Times 4
0107	2	0202	Plus $3 * x \uparrow 2$
0108	3	0204	Minus 7
0109	1	0202	Store $3 * x \uparrow 2 + 4 * x - 7$
0110	B	0202	Write out value
0111	8	0100	Halt and repeat
0200			Location of x
0201		3	Constant 3
0202			Working storage
0203		4	Constant 4
0204		7	Constant 7

FIGURE 13-12
Example ML program—evaluate function.

A possible ML program, again starting in location 0100, is given in Fig. 13-12. (A shorter version of this program can be constructed based on rewriting the function to be evaluated as $(3 * x + 4) * x - 7$. Can you write that program?)

As a third example of machine language programming, consider the problem of summing 100 values already stored in memory, say in locations 0200 through 0299, and storing the sum in location 0300. One would prefer not to write out 100 Add instructions, but rather use a loop of some sort, just as in TL one would use an iteration statement. Such a loop can be constructed

LOCATION	OP	ADDRESS/DATA	COMMENTS
0100	0	0301	Load zero
0101	1	0300	Set sum to zero
0102	0	0302	Load initial add instruction
0103	1	0105	Store in place
0104	0	0300	Load sum
0105			Add number
0106	1	0300	Store sum plus number
0107	0	0105	Load add instruction
0108	3	0303	Subtract final instruction
0109	5	0112	Branch if done
0110	2	0304	Add instruction plus one
0111	7	0103	Loop back to add next number
0112	8	0100	Halt, done
0200			Data in 0200−0299
. . .			
0299			
0300			Sum
0301		0000	Constant zero
0302	2	0200	Initial add instruction
0303	2	0299	Final add instruction
0304	2	0300	Add instruction plus one

FIGURE 13-13
Example ML program—summing 100 values.

in ML based on the fact that instructions are stored in memory and can be processed just like data. The same Add instruction can be used for all 100 of the data items, by doing arithmetic on the instruction to modify its address portion. This technique of programmed address modification is illustrated in the program in Fig. 13-13.

Note that both the sum and the Add instruction are initialized by the first steps of the program, rather than by writing initial values on the coding sheet. In this way, the program can be repeated just by starting execution at location 0100, rather than having to reload those locations. Note also that, although the program is much shorter than a version with 100 distinct Add instructions, it will take much longer to execute, since adding each number requires seven instructions. This is another example of the tradeoff between time and space.

INDEX REGISTERS

Programming experience with early computers made it clear that loops are an important programming technique; so computer designers invented hardware features to implement loops more directly than with programmed address modification as illustrated above. Probably the most common of these features is the index register. An *index register* is a register within the control unit whose contents are added to the address portion of an instruction (when so indicated) to give the *effective data address*. For example, if the index register held the value 0023 and the instruction in question had as its address portion 0210, the effective address would be $0210 + 0023 = 0233$.

In order to implement an index register in our simulated machine, it is necessary to specify both how the instruction format is to be modified to indicate that indexing is to take place and how the Execute phase is to be modified to accomplish indexing. Also, additional instructions must be created to transfer data into and out of the index register.

Let us simulate the index register with a TL numerical variable named *ixr*. The unused character in the instruction word can be used as a control character to indicate indexing: if it is zero, no indexing; if it is one, indexing is to take place. A review of the Execute phase of our simulation indicates that indexing can be introduced by modifying the subroutines *Addr* and *Bu*. In order to localize the implementation of indexing (although possibly making the simulation of branching slightly less realistic), *Addr* can be changed to accomplish indexing and *Bu* changed to make use of *Addr*. Also, a new register, *ccr* (for control character register), is added to the control unit to hold the previously unused character in instructions, and *Fetch* modified to transfer that character to *ccr*.

Thus, the changes to accomplish indexing are as follows:

1 Add to *Fetch,* after the statements that assign values to *opr* and *dar,* the statement

$ccr \leftarrow mdr$ **@** (2,1);

2 Redefine *Addr* as

Addr:

    [*mar* ← **num**(*dar*);

      if *ccr*="1"

        then *mar* ← *mar* + *ixr*];

3 And redefine *Bu* as

    Bu:

    [*Addr; nia* ← *mar*];

The net effect of these changes is to use as the data address the sum of the address given in the instruction and the contents of the index register, in those cases where the control character in the instruction is "1."

Finally, some additional instructions are needed to transfer data into and out of the index register. A typical set is the three given in Fig. 13-14. Note that because of the nature of the decrement and test operation, which is typical of single-address machines, loops tend to work through data "backwards"—from high address to low, rather than from low to high. The segment of the simulation labeled *Decode* in Fig. 13-10 must also be extended to accommodate these new operation subroutines.

OPERATION	OP CODE	BRIEF DESCRIPTION	TL SUBROUTINE

Load index	C	**C**mem ⟹ ixr	*Li:*
			  [*Datr;*
			   ixr ← **num**(*mdr*)];

Store index	D	**C**ixr ⟹ mem	*Si:*
			  [*Addr;*
			   mdr ← **str**(*ixr*);
			   mem(*mar*) ← *mdr*];

Decrement index and test	E	The contents of the index register are decreased by one; if the resulting value is zero or greater, control branches to the address given in the instruction	*Di:*
			  [*ixr* ← *ixr* − 1;
			  if *ixr* ⩾ 0 **then** *Bu*];

FIGURE 13-14

Using this new indexing facility, a program to add 100 numbers in a straightforward manner is shown in Fig. 13-15. Be sure that you understand why the initial index register value is 99 rather than 100. Another advantage of indexing is that the program as stored in memory is not modified, which often simplifies debugging.

LOCA-TION	OP	CC	ADDRESS/DATA	COMMENTS
0100	0	0	0301	Load zero sum
0101	C	0	0302	Initialize index register
0102	2	1	0200	Add indexed
0103	E	0	0102	Decrement, branch if not done
0104	8	0	0100	Halt, done
0200				Data in 0200–0299
0300				Sum
0301			0	Constant zero
0302			99	Initial index register value

FIGURE 13-15
Example ML program using indexing.

You may have noticed that no examples so far involved character string data; indeed, it would be clumsy to process characters using the operations described. A minimum capability to manipulate such strings can be obtained with operations to shift a character string left or right, and so we introduce such operations in Fig. 13-16. Again, modifications are necessary for *Decode* to incorporate these subroutines.

OPERATION	OP CODE	BRIEF DESCRIPTION	TL SUBROUTINE
Shift left	F	**C**acc is shifted left the number of character positions specified in the data part of the instruction; zeros fill in from the right	Sl: [Addr; acc ← (acc & "000000") @ (mar + 1,6)];
Shift right	G	**C**acc is shifted right the number of character positions specified in the data part of the instruction; zeros fill in from the left	Sr: [Addr; acc ← ("000000" & acc) @ (7 − mar,6)];

FIGURE 13-16

As an example of the nature of character processing using shifts, consider the problem of reversing the six characters in a machine language word. This reversal can be carried out by unpacking the initial string into six locations, one character each, and then packing them back into a word in reverse order. Suppose that the initial word is in location 0200, the reversed word is to be put in location 0201, and that locations 0202 through 0207 may be used as temporary storage for characters. Then the program might begin as shown in Fig. 13-17.

FIGURE 13-17
Example ML program using shifting.

LOCATION	OP	CC	ADDRESS/ DATA	COMMENTS
0100	C	0	0208	Initialize index with 5
0101	0	0	0200	Load word
0102	F	1	0	Shift left amount of index
0103	G	0	5	Shift right 5
0104	1	1	0202	Store indexed
0105	E	0	0101	Decrement and loop

The portion of code in Fig. 13-17 unpacks the six characters in a word into six consecutive locations, one character per word. To be sure that you understand the program before proceeding to the rest of code, play computer and keep track of the status of the accumulator and index register after each instruction is carried out, as well as the effective address or data of that instruction. Such a tracing is given in Fig. 13-18 using the data "abcdef;" be sure that you understand where the results come from.

Thus, location 0207 now holds 00000f, and 0206 holds 00000e. The next steps are not shown and Fig. 13-19 continues at the point where **C***ixr* becomes zero. The remainder of the program, the portion that packs the characters into a word in reverse order, is given in Fig. 13-20. Verification of this portion of the pro-

LOCATION OF INSTRUCTION BEING EXECUTED	INSTRUCTION	EFFECTIVE ADDRESS/DATA	Cacc AFTER INSTRUCTION	Cixr AFTER INSTRUCTION
0100	C00208	0208	. . . . .	5
0101	000200	0200	abcdef	5
0102	F10000	0005	f00000	5
0103	G00005	0005	00000f	5
0104	110202	0207	00000f	5
0105	E00101	0101	00000f	4
0101	000200	0200	abcdef	4
0102	F10000	0004	ef0000	4
0103	G00005	0005	00000e	4
0104	110202	0206	00000e	4
0105	E00101	0101	00000e	3
0101	. . . . . .			

FIGURE 13-18

LOCATION OF INSTRUCTION BEING EXECUTED	INSTRUCTION	EFFECTIVE ADDRESS/DATA	Cacc AFTER INSTRUCTION	Cixr AFTER INSTRUCTION
0104	110202	0203	00000b	1
0105	E00101	0101	00000b	0
0101	000200	0200	abcdef	0
0102	F10000	0000	abcdef	0
0103	G00005	0005	00000a	0
0104	110202	0202	00000a	0
0105	E00101	0101	00000a	−1
0106	. . . .			

FIGURE 13-19

LOCA-TION	OP	CC	ADDRESS/DATA	COMMENTS
0106	0	0	0209	Load zero
0107	1	0	0201	Set reversed word to zero
0108	C	0	0208	Initialize index to 5
0109	0	1	0202	Load character, indexed
0110	F	1	0000	Shift left, indexed, into position
0111	2	0	0201	Add in word so far
0112	1	0	0201	Store partial reversed word
0113	E	0	0109	Decrement and loop
0114	8	0	0100	Halt, done
0200				Initial word
0201				Reversed word
0202				Working storage, 0202–0207
. . . .				
0207				
0208			5	Constant 5
0209			0	Constant 0

FIGURE 13-20
Another ML program segment using shifting.

gram by tracing is left to the reader. (The program does assume that in this simple machine the sum of zero and any character is that character. This is not true in many current computers, where the character representation of zero is not all zero bits.)

In most machines, operations in addition to these simple shifts are available to ease character processing. Since data are considered in binary form in most machines, shifts may be of as little as 1 bit at a time, adding flexibility in packing and unpacking characters.

SUBROUTINES

Often computer hardware features are a response to the need to increase the efficiency of commonly used programming constructs. For example, index registers increase the efficiency of programs which do counting and looping. Another common programming practice is the use of subroutines, and several hardware features have been developed to reflect this practice. The feature to be added to the simulated machine is a new operation—Branch and mark. This operation branches to the location named in the instruction, and also saves in the index register the contents of the next instruction address register, and thus the location of the instruction to which a subroutine beginning in the named location is to return. Branch and mark is defined in Fig. 13-21. Do you understand why this instruction cannot be simply [*ixr ← mar; Bu*]?

OPERATION	OP CODE	BRIEF DESCRIPTION	TL SUBROUTINE
Branch and mark	9	Unconditional branch, but with **C***nia* saved in *ixr*.	*Bm:* [*mar ← nia;* *Bu;* *ixr ← mar*];

FIGURE 13-21
Subroutine operations.

As an example of the use of the Branch and mark to implement subroutines, consider making the preceding program for reversing the characters in a word into a subroutine. Let the subroutine expect the word to be reversed in the accumulator when it is called, the return address in the index register, and the reversed word to be left in the accumulator on return. An ML program to read a word, reverse it, and write out the result could be as shown in Fig. 13-22 (assuming the reverse-a-word subroutine started in location 0098).

LOCA-TION	OP	CC	ADDRESS/DATA	COMMENTS
. . . .				
1537	A	0	2500	Read word into location 2500
1538	0	0	2500	Load into *acc*
1539	9	0	0098	Branch and mark to reverse
1540	1	0	2500	Store reversed word in 2500
1541	B	0	2500	Write out reverse word
. . . .				

FIGURE 13-22
Example of calling a subroutine in ML.

The changes that must be made in the earlier reverse-a-word program to make it into a subroutine are as shown in Fig.

LOCA-TION	OP	CC	ADDRESS/DATA	COMMENTS
0098	1	0	0200	Store word in 0200
0099	D	0	0210	Store return address
. . . .				
. . . .				
		(Instructions 0100–0113 as before)		
0114	C	0	0210	Load return address into *ixr*
0115	7	1	0000	Branch to return, indexed
. . . .				
. . . .				
		(Data 0200–0209 as before)		
0210				Working storage for return address

FIGURE 13-23
Example of a subroutine in ML.

13-23. Since the index register is used in most subroutines, good programming practice suggests that the return address be saved upon entering the subroutine and restored to the index register just before exiting the subroutine. Note also that the accumulator need not be loaded from 0201 at the end of the subroutine, since its value as last stored by instruction 0112 is still there.

Many subroutines have more than one input or output, in which case some other means than the accumulator must be used to pass arguments to and from the subroutine. Another approach, that of placing the data immediately after the subroutine call in what is known as a *calling sequence,* is illustrated next.

Consider a subroutine to compute *a* modulo *b,* that is, the remainder of *a/b.* For now, assume that *a* and *b* are both positive, that the values of *a* and *b* are in the locations immediately following the transfer to the subroutine, and that the result is to be left in the accumulator. A call of the subroutine is illustrated in Fig. 13-24, starting in location 0300. The subroutine itself begins in 0900.

LOCA-TION	OP	CC	ADDRESS/DATA	COMMENTS
0300	9	0	0900	Transfer to modulo subroutine
0301			537	Datum A
0302			193	Datum B
0303			....	Continuation of program
0900	0	1	0001	Load A indexed into *acc*
0901	3	1	0002	Subtract B
0902	5	1	0003	Return if remainder zero
0903	6	0	0905	Skip loop if remainder minus
0904	7	0	0901	Loop back to subtract again
0905	2	1	0002	Add B back for positive remainder
0906	7	1	0003	Return

FIGURE 13-24
Example ML program—modulo subroutine.

The discussion in this chapter just begins to suggest the hardware features available in current computers; a complete listing could continue for literally hundreds of pages. We mention a few

OTHER FEATURES

more of the commonly available features below to give the reader a better feeling for what a more complete repertoire of hardware features contains. But our main purpose has been to demonstrate the nature of programming at the machine language level, indicating the amount of detail that must be spelled out, the bookkeeping necessary by the programmer to keep track of machine locations of instructions and data, and the necessity to remember meaningless characters standing for meaningful operations. In Chap. 14 we examine some of the software commonly used to ease the machine language programmer's task.

Many computers have an accumulator two words in length, thus allowing full-length products from multiplication, larger dividends in division, and a greater variety of shift instructions. And some computer designs include multiple accumulators and multiple index registers, and in some cases registers that can serve as either of these. Often the hardware can process several different types of data — integers, floating-point numbers, character strings — with different sets of operations for each. Some machines have hundreds of operations, including logical operations such as And and Or (as discussed in Chap. 16).

Also, there may be a set of operations for dealing with input-output, including the capability of having separate input-output programs which run in parallel with the central processor program. Some of the operations may be restricted in use, available only when the computer is in a special state known as *executive mode.*

Indeed, the larger modern computers may seem to bear little relation to the simple machine simulated in this chapter. The search by designers to find ever more economical balances of memory, disk files, logical circuitry, teletypes, high-speed printers, etc., has led to machines with multiple memories, multiple arithmetic units, multiple central processors, microprogramming capabilities that allow the definition of new instructions in terms of the basic information flows described at the beginning of this chapter, and so forth. Some of these features are considered in Chap. 15. Each of them adds to the bookkeeping burden of the machine language programmer, and so increases the importance of the software assistance that is the subject of Chap. 14.

EXERCISES

1 Program in ML the greatest common divisor procedure presented in Chaps. 5 and 6. If you wish, use the ML modulo subroutine given in Fig. 13-24.

2 Prepare a program in ML to determine if three line segments can form a triangle. Requirements for the program are stated in exercises 1–3, Chap. 5.

3 Prepare a program in ML that reads in a word and prints out the input in "triangular" form. For example, for the input WORD, the output would be:

```
W
WO
WOR
WORD
```

4 Prepare a program in ML to calculate the change that should be given to customers in a supermarket. Requirements for the program are given in exercise 10, Chap. 5 and exercise 2, Chap. 7.

5 In some computers, execution of an indexed operation (in ML, those operations which have CC = 1) automatically decrements (or increments) the index register. Under what conditions would such a feature be useful? Under what conditions would such a feature not be advantageous?

6 Implement in your local programming language the simulation of ML given in Fig. 13-10 and extended later in the chapter for additional machine features. Use this simulation to test your ML programming exercises (such as exercises 1–4).

7 Modify the ML simulation program given in this chapter to provide a trace feature. The trace capability should print (a) the values of the accumulator and the index register both before and after execution of each instruction, (b) the location of the instruction being executed and the instruction, (c) any other information you consider important to debugging (see for example the trace of the unpacking program in this chapter). Some trace features permit the execution of a snapshot routine just before entering and/or leaving each subroutine. How would you implement such a feature? How will the simulation program know which part of the ML program to trace, i.e., when to turn the trace on and when to turn it off?

8 In the subroutine calling sequence described in this chapter, the actual data values were stored in the locations following the transfer instruction. An alternative calling sequence would store the addresses of the data (rather than the actual data) in the calling sequence. What are the advantages of using the addresses rather than the actual data in the calling sequence?

9 When a computer program fails to produce the correct result or stops unexpectedly, a knowledge of the contents of certain memory locations is usually helpful in finding the problem. Programs which list the contents of memory locations are called *dump programs*. Write a dump program in ML. Since you do not know whether the contents of a memory location will be program or data, you should print the location both ways. Some issues to consider: Where should the dump program be stored? How will the dump program get its arguments? Can the dump program be used as part of a snapshot feature of the trace?

10 Modify the ML simulation program to count the number of interpretation cycles required to execute a program. Such counts can be helpful in comparing programs and in locating

subroutines whose improvement could substantially reduce the cost of running a program.

11 Consider the problem of the computer designer who has to select the instruction set for a new machine. What factors enter into (or should enter into) the choice of an instruction set? If you knew what programs were going to be run on the machine, how would you use that knowledge to help determine the instruction set?

12 The passing of parameters in subroutine calls and the storage of return addresses for recursive subroutines can be facilitated by the use of stacks. The ML machine can be converted to a stack machine by treating the accumulator as a stack rather than as a single word. Consider some of the problems involved in such a conversion: How large should the stack be? How will the program know if the stack limit is reached? What are the advantages and disadvantages of one stack or several stacks? What instructions will have to be added to utilize the stack capability?

13 Many small computers use a 16-bit word and are able to address 32K of memory. Since 32K of memory requires a 15-bit address, there is only 1 bit left over. But designers manage to have more than two instructions. How would you reconcile these conflicting constraints, i.e., a 16-bit word, a 15-bit address, and more than two instructions? Examine manuals and descriptions of one or more 16-bit machines and propose your own solution.

REFERENCES

Bell, C. Gordon, and Allen Newell, *Computer Structures: Readings and Examples,* McGraw-Hill, New York, 1971.

Falkoff, A. O., K. E. Iverson, and E. H. Sussenguth: A Formal Description of System/360, *IBM Systems J.,* **3:**198–263 (1964).

Gear, C. William: *Computer Organization and Programming,* 2d ed., McGraw-Hill, New York, 1974.

Hellerman, Herbert: *Digital Computer System Principles,* McGraw-Hill, New York, 1967.

PROGRAMMING LANGUAGE TRANSLATORS— ASSEMBLERS AND COMPILERS

As was illustrated in Chap. 13, programming in machine language allows the programmer much greater control of the details of how his program is executed than does a higher-level language and thereby provides the possibility of greater efficiency. But programming in machine language also requires much attention to details of both syntax and content, often resulting in many errors in stating a procedure and increasing the time and effort required to find the errors. To avoid programming in machine language, computer users have developed a range of programs, commonly called *language processors* or *translators,* which translate a procedure statement from a language more natural to the human programmer into one more natural to the machine. In this chapter, we examine two classes of language processors—assemblers and compilers. The languages that these two classes of translators accept, assembly language and higher-level language, span the spectrum of current-day programming languages.

Translators take as their input data a program in one language, called the *source language,* and produce as their output a program in another language, called the *object language.* This relationship is illustrated in Fig. 14-1.

FIGURE 14-1
Translation process.

Assembly language is in some sense "close" to machine language, as we see in the following sections. That is, there is almost a one-to-one correspondence between assembly language instructions and machine language instructions. The assembly language translator or *assembler,* takes a program in assembly language and produces a corresponding program (one that does the same computation) in machine language (see Fig. 14-2).

Higher-level languages are considerably "farther" from machine language; that is, a single instruction or statement in a

Figure 14-2
Assembly process.

Program in assembly language → Assembler → Program in machine language

higher-level language usually generates several machine language instructions. Translators for such languages, often called *compilers,* take a program in the higher-level language and produce a corresponding program in assembly language. That program can then be translated in a second pass by the assembler, producing a machine language object program (see Fig. 14-3). In either case, the object program can then be executed with problem data to produce results, as in Fig. 14-4.

FIGURE 14-3
Compilation process.

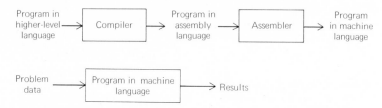

Program in higher-level language → Compiler → Program in assembly language → Assembler → Program in machine language

FIGURE 14-4
Execution process.

Problem data → Program in machine language → Results

Sometimes the above steps are chained together by the translator without human intervention, so that it appears to the user that his source language program, followed by problem data, is read in and executed. Such a translator is referred to as *load-and-go.*

ASSEMBLERS Simple assemblers relieve some of the bookkeeping burden that machine language places on the programmer, but still allow him to specify instructions at the level of machine operations. Typical functions of assemblers include keeping track of the memory location in which instructions and data are to be stored, replacement of symbolic variable names created by the programmer with the appropriate machine locations, and replacement of symbolic codes for machine operations with the appropriate internal machine codes. Thus, assembly language allows the programmer to use symbolic, mnemonic names for operations, instructions, and data; the assembler replaces those symbols with the appropriate machine encoding.

Assembly language This concept can be illustrated with a simple assembly language AL corresponding to the machine language ML introduced in Chap. 13.

Each line in an AL program corresponds to a single instruction in ML. Additional lines in AL specify necessary bookkeeping information. Machine storage locations may be represented by alphanumeric symbols of up to six characters. Operation codes are represented by the two-character mnemonic codes given in Fig. 14-6. (The length of symbolic names here and for most assembly languages is arbitrary, and often is dictated by considerations of ease in programming the assembler.) The occurrence of indexing is signaled by an asterisk following the operation code.

Within the assembler, a variable called the *location counter* keeps track of the storage address into which the next translated AL line is to be stored.

Given these rules, the first example ML program in Fig. 13-11, which reads in two values and prints out the larger, could be programmed in AL as shown in Fig. 14-5. This AL program should assemble into *exactly* the ML program given in Fig. 13-11.

LOCATION	OP CC	ADDRESS/DATA	COMMENTS
LARGER	AT	0100	Set location counter for address 0100
	RD	A	Read A
	RD	B	Read B
	LD	A	Load A
	SU	B	Subtract B
	BN	BIGB	Branch negative if B larger
	WR	A	Write A
	HT	LARGER	Halt and repeat
BIGB	WR	B	Write B
	HT	LARGER	Halt and repeat
	AT	0200	Set location counter to address 0200
A	DA		Location of A
B	DA		Location of B
	EN		End of program

FIGURE 14-5
Assembly language program—find larger.

A complete list of AL operations is given in Fig. 14-6. The above example uses three AL *pseudo-operations.* Pseudo-operations are assembler operations that do not correspond to machine language operations, but rather give information to the assembler, such as where to set the location counter (AT), or to set aside a location for data (DA), or to signal the end of the assembly language program (EN).

ML OP	AL OP	OPERATION
0	AL	Load *acc*
1	ST	Store *acc*
2	AD	Add
3	SU	Subtract
4	MU	Multiply
5	BZ	Branch zero
6	BN	Branch negative
7	BU	Branch unconditional
8	HT	Halt and continue
9	BM	Branch and mark
A	RD	Read
B	WR	Write
C	LI	Load index
D	SI	Store index
E	DT	Decrement and test
F	SL	Shift left
G	SR	Shift right
	AT	Set assembler location counter
	DA	Data
	EN	End of program

FIGURE 14-6
Definition of AL operations.

As another example of an assembly language program, study the AL version in Fig. 14-7 of the subroutine given in Chap. 13 to reverse the characters in an ML word.

LOCATION	OP CC	ADDRESS/ DATA	COMMENTS
REVERS	AT	0098	Location of program
	ST	WORD	Store initial word
	SI	RETURN	Store return address
	LI	FIVE	Initialize index to 5
LOOP	LD	WORD	Load word
	SL *	0	Shift left amount of index
	SR	5	Shift right 5
	ST *	WORK	Store indexed
	DT	LOOP	Decrement and loop
	LD	ZERO	Load 0
	ST	NEW	Set new word to zero
	LI	FIVE	Initialize index to 5
LOOP1	LD *	WORK	Load character, indexed
	SL *	0	Shift left indexed into position
	AD	NEW	Add in word so far
	ST	NEW	Store partial reversed word
	DT	LOOP1	Decrement and loop
	LI	RETURN	Load return address into *ixr*
	BU *	0	Branch to return, indexed
	AT	0200	Location of data
WORD	DA		Initial word
NEW	DA		Reversed word
WORK	DA		Working storage, 0202–0207
	AT	0208	
FIVE	DA	5	Constant 5
ZERO	DA	0	Constant 0
RETURN	DA		Return address
	EN		

FIGURE 14-7
AL program—reverse-a-word.

The assembly language specified here is in fact simpler than any you are likely to meet in practice. To give you some feeling for the additional features included in modern assemblers, some of them are described in passing, even though they are not included in later discussions of how an assembler might be implemented.

In most assemblers the programmers can refer to locations in storage by using expressions consisting of symbols plus or minus an integer. Thus an instruction could refer to the line after that whose location is LOOP by the expression LOOP +1. Also, the programmer often can refer to the current value of the location counter, typically by using for the location counter a specified symbol such as *. Thus, an instruction could refer to the address of the immediately following instruction as * +1.

Additional pseudo-operations beyond those already defined are often available. One typical pseudo-operation reserves a block of consecutive locations. For example, in the reverse-a-word subroutine, six words were set aside for working storage by defining the first using DA and then resetting the location counter ahead six locations using AT.

If a block start (BS) pseudo-operation were available, this action could be accomplished with one line: WORK BS 6. And more important, the AL program would more nearly reflect the programmer's intent in writing that line of code, thus clarifying the meaning (to people) of that part of the program. Finally, many assemblers allow the programmer to specify a data constant directly in a line of AL code, the assembler itself setting aside space for the constant. In such a system, an instruction to initialize the index register to five could be written as LI +5.

In addition to the features given above which ease the task of expressing machine instructions, most advanced assemblers include other powerful features. Many maintain libraries of subroutines, which the programmer can access to include in his program. Many include facilities for merging disparate pieces of code created by different programmers, automatically resolving any conflicts in duplicate uses of symbols and/or in overlapping instructions and data caused by inconsistent location counter settings. (Incorporating library subroutines in a program is a simple version of this latter problem.)

Macro facilities

One powerful feature of extended assemblers is that of macro definitions. Macros are sufficiently interesting to warrant a simple illustration of them here. (Again, this illustration is deliberately simplified and only hints at the capabilities available in a complete macro system.)

A *macro* is a segment of code which can be defined by the user (in this case, in assembly language) and which can be inserted on call at appropriate points in a program. Thus, the two aspects of a macro are its *definition* and its *call*. A *macro definition* consists of a *head* specifying the name of the macro and its parameters, a *body* specifying the segment of code to be substituted for a call of the macro, and a *tail* completing the definition. A *macro call* gives the name of the macro and the actual values to be substituted for the parameters. These notions are illustrated in the following example.

Suppose a procedure to be programmed often called for selecting the larger of two variable values. One could define a macro to do that task, taking as its parameters the two values and leaving the larger value in the accumulator. The definition would start with a DM (define macro) pseudo-operation, whose name is to be used in the macro call and whose data field lists the parameters of the macro. (The parameters are dummy variable names which are replaced during an actual call of the macro by the variable names or values used in the call. This is the same technique used in handling arguments for TL functions and subroutines.)

Following the macro head (the DM) would be the actual AL code needed to select the larger value. And following that macro body would be the macro tail, an EM (end macro) pseudo-operation. This macro definition might look like the one shown in Fig. 14-8. An illustration of the use of this macro is shown in Fig. 14-9, another version of our earlier program to read-in two values and print out the larger.

PROGRAMMING LANGUAGE
TRANSLATORS – ASSEMBLERS
AND COMPILERS

LOCATION	OP CC	ADDRESS/DATA	COMMENTS
MX	DM	X,Y	Macro head with parameters X,Y
	LD	X	
	SU	Y	
	BN	MX1	
	LD	X	
	BU	MX2	
MX1	LD	Y	
MX2	EM		Macro tail

FIGURE 14-8
An example macro definition.

LOCATION	OP CC	ADDRESS/DATA	COMMENTS
LARGER	AT	0100	
	RD	A	
	RD	B	
	MX	A,B	Call maximum macro
	ST	C	
	WR	C	
	HT	LARGER	
A	DA		
B	DA		
C	DA		
	EN		

FIGURE 14-9
An example macro call.

In many macro assemblers, the program segment in Fig. 14-9 would be processed by first scanning the AL program and replacing all macro calls with the body of the macro, with variables properly substituted, and then assembling the expanded program into machine language. That first step commonly is called *macro expansion;* its result in this case would appear as in Fig. 14-10.

LOCATION	OP CC	ADDRESS/DATA	COMMENTS
LARGER	AT	0100	
	RD	A	
	RD	B	
	LD	A	
	SU	B	
	BN	MX1	
	LD	X	
	BU	MX2	
MX1	LD	Y	
MX2	ST	C	
	WR	C	
	HT	LARGER	
A	DA		
B	DA		
C	DA		
	EN		

FIGURE 14-10
An example macro expansion.

Some final comments. Clearly if there were only one call of MX in a program, it would hardly be worth going to the trouble of using a macro. But if there were several calls, then several lines would have location MX1, which is not meaningful. In fact, that problem can be handled by allowing addresses relative to the location counter, as mentioned in the previous section. Then, for example, the macro body for MX would be written as in Fig. 14-11.

Macros often reduce the number of lines of program to be written, thereby reducing the tedium of assembly language programming, probably reducing the number of errors introduced, and improving the readability of the programs. Like functions and subroutines, macros are important programming tools which facilitate the development of modular procedures. Also, they allow the definition in assembly language of useful operations not actually available in machine language. For example, a stripped down model of a computer might not have certain basic operations available on most computers. (For example, the machine language introduced in Chap. 13 does not include a division operation.) By the use of macros, these operations can be provided in the assembly language even though not directly available in machine language. (In the case of division, a macro could be written to find the quotient of two numbers by repeated subtractions.) Macros are also valuable in the implementation on one computer of programs developed for another computer. With judicious use of macros, the assembly language of one machine can be made to bear a very close resemblance to the assembly language of another.

Returning to the simplest form of an assembler given earlier in this chapter, the assembly process can be described (very loosely) in the following steps (see also Fig. 14-12).

> Initialize the assembler.
> Read in the next line of AL code.
> If operation is AT, reset location counter value.
> If operation is EN, terminate assembly.
> If location is not blank, add the symbol in that field and the current location counter value to a symbol table.
> Set the location counter value as the address of this line.
> If operation is DA, store data in output line and go to write output.
> Look up the AL operation code in an OP code table and store in output (ML) line.
> Store control character for indexing or not in output line.
> Look up address-field symbol in symbol table and store in output line.
> Write out output line.
> Increase location counter value by one.
> Loop back to read-in next line.

This procedure implies three data structures within the assembler—a location counter, a table of symbols and their storage address equivalents, and a table of AL OP codes and their ML OP code equivalents. The processing itself, beyond simple testing and arithmetic, involves unpacking and reforming lines of code, and maintaining the above tables. The unpacking and reforming processes are just like those used in the earlier reverse-a-word subroutine and are not considered any further here. In fact, the

LD	X
SU	Y
BN	*+3
LD	X
BU	*+2
LD	Y

FIGURE 14-11
Macro body with relative addresses.

The assembly process

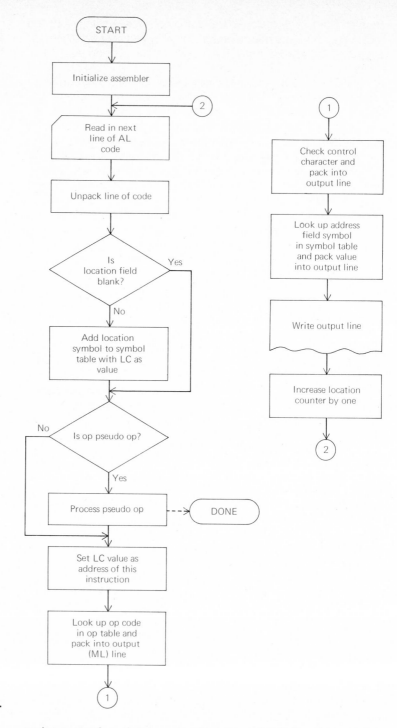

FIGURE 14-12
Assembly process.

major part of a simple assembler is maintaining the symbol table, so let us examine that problem in more detail.

Before leaving the total assembly process, however, one further comment is in order. The above outline does not indicate what to do in case a symbol is not defined (does not appear in a location field) until after it is used (appears in an address/data field). The use of BIGB in the program in Fig. 14-5 illustrates this question. BIGB is used before it is defined, whereas LARGER is defined before it is used. Some assemblers scan the entire program once to build the symbol table, then scan the program again to construct output lines. These are called *two-pass assemblers.* Others, called *one-pass assemblers,* go through the program only once, but maintain lists for each symbol of instructions referring to that symbol. When the symbol is eventually defined, the assembler traces down the list of incomplete instructions and completes them. Obviously such an assembler must have storage room for the entire program during assembly, rather than dealing with it one line at a time. On the other hand, it needs to read and write each instruction only once.

The exact form of an assembler symbol table depends on the choice of strategies for building the symbol table. For this example, assume a two-pass assembler, thus guaranteeing that any symbol will already be defined and entered into the symbol table before it is used. Consider the two processes of adding a new symbol to the table and of looking up a symbol already in the table.

In its simplest version, the symbol table can be represented in a two-column array, one row per item, the first column holding the symbol and the second column its value. Such a table could be filled in arbitrary order during the first (definition) pass, then sorted before the second pass of actually assembling instructions. The table might appear as in Fig. 14-13.

Another organization of the symbol table could be as a branching tree, with a symbol and its value at each node, symbols which occur earlier in the alphabet to the left and those which occur later to the right. Such a tree built in order from the symbols

NOW IS THE TIME FOR ALL GOOD MEN . . .

is shown in Fig. 14-14.

The symbol table

1	A	0200
2	B	0201
3	BIGB	0107
4	LARGER	0100

FIGURE 14-13
Symbol table as array.

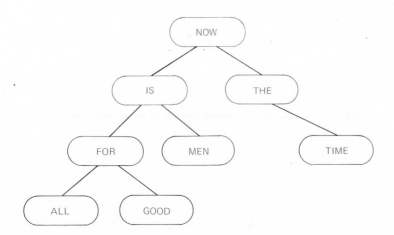

FIGURE 14-14
Symbol table as tree.

A branching tree of this form could be represented in a four-column array structure using a row for each node, with the first column holding the symbol, the second its value, the third an index to the left subtree, and the fourth an index to the right subtree. The above tree would be encoded in an array such as the one shown in Fig. 14-15. Such a symbol table is kept in sorted order as it is constructed.

1	NOW	–	2	3
2	IS	–	5	8
3	THE	–	0	4
4	TIME	–	0	0
5	FOR	–	6	7
6	ALL	–	0	0

FIGURE 14-15
Symbol table tree represented in an array.

Which of these alternatives should be used? The second requires more space, but may lead to faster processing depending on the relative speeds of sorting and searching in the two tables. Techniques for making such comparisons are considered in Chap. 17. Also the expense of writing out a sorted symbol table at the completion of assembly is relevant to the choice of alternatives. Such a sorted table is immediately available in the first case; in the second case it can be created with a systematic but more complicated procedure.

Assume the branching tree organization for our symbol table. And assume that this branching tree is encoded in an array as indicated in Fig. 14-15. TL procedures for entering a symbol into the table and for looking up a symbol are given in Figs. 14-16 and 14-17 (the actual implementation of those procedures requires an assembler and a TL compiler). In addition to the tree-array table itself (called *symtab*), these procedures use a global variable *empty,* whose value is the index of the next empty row in *symtab*. Initially, before any symbols are entered into the table, the value of *empty* is one (for row one).

This routine is quite straightforward, but leaves some opportunities for further refinement. There is no specification in the routine (nor was there in the problem statement) of what action to take if the same symbol were defined twice; whatever is to be done must be added with label *Error*. Also, the routine does not check for overflow of the table (too many symbols entered); in most implemented programming languages that could be a problem. Finally, there are obvious opportunities for simplifying and shortening the procedure using local subroutines (for example, *Left* and *Right* are almost identical).

A procedure for looking up a symbol in this table is given in Fig. 14-17. This procedure also needs a specification of an error condition, that of not finding the specified symbol in the table. Again, there are opportunities for subroutines within *Lookup*.

Enter (symbol, value):

  [**local** *line;*

    if *empty*=1   If the first line of the symbol table is empty, then place the symbol and value in the first line. If the first line is not empty start searching for the proper place to enter.

     then to *Put*

     else *line* ← 1;

Look:

    if *symtab(line, 1)=symbol*   If the symbol is in the table, there must be a mistake.

     then to *Error*

     else if *symtab(line, 1) > symbol*   If the symbol in the line being examined is greater than the symbol to be inserted, then search to left. If not, search to right.

       then to *Left*

       else to *Right;*

Left:

    if *symtab(line, 3)* ≠ 0   If there is something to the left, check it out. If nothing to the left, set "left" pointer to empty line, and go to *Put.*

     then

        [*line* ← *symtab(line, 3);* **to** *Look*]

     else

        [*symtab(line, 3)* ← *empty;* **to** *Put*];

Right:

    if *symtab(line, 4)* ≠ 0   If there is something to the right, check it out. If nothing to the right, set "right" pointer to empty line, and go to *Put.*

     then

        [*line* ← *symtab(line, 4);* **to** *Look*];

     else

        [*symtab(line, 4)* ← *empty;* **to** *Put*]:

Put:

    symtab(empty, 1) ← *symbol;*   Enter *symbol* and *value.* Set pointers to zero. Increase value of *empty* by one. Stop.

    symtab(empty, 2) ← *value;*

    symtab(empty, 3) ← 0;

    symtab(empty, 4) ← 0;

    empty ← *empty* + 1;

    done]

FIGURE 14-16

Also, there are possible subroutines common to both *Enter* and *Lookup,* ones which would even further centralize and restrict knowledge of exactly how the symbol table is represented in storage. Design of such subroutines is left as an exercise.

    Tables associating a value with some symbol are quite common across a number of computer applications [both non-

Lookup (*symbol*):
  [**local** *line*; *line* ← 1;

  Look:

    if *symtab*(*line*, 1) = *symbol*

      then

        [**return** *symtab*(*line*, 2); **done**]

      else

        if *symtab*(*line*, 1) > *symbol*

          then to *Left*

          else to *Right*;

  Left:

    if *symtab*(*line*, 3) = 0

      then to *Error*

      else

        [*line* ← *symtab*(*line*, 3);

         to *Look*];

  Right:

    if *symtab*(*line*, 4) = 0

      then to *Error*

      else

        [*line* ← *symtab*(*line*, 4);

FIGURE 14-17   **to** *Look*]]

numerical procedures such as translators and numerical procedures where they can serve (for example) as tables of the value of functions]. In the following sections on compilers, uses for such tables also occur.

COMPILERS   Even though the assembly language programmer is relieved of much of the detailed bookkeeping necessary in machine language programming, he still must operate at a level of familiarity with the details of the computer much beyond that needed to express the essence of his problem-solving procedure. Higher-level languages, such as TL, have been designed to automate much of that concern with detail. Programs for translating from a higher-level language into machine language are called *compilers*. (In fact, most compilers produce not machine language code but assembly language, and that case is assumed here.)

The compiling process   In even the simplest compilers, there are the following stages:

  Lexical analysis consists of breaking up the input program into its basic units of variable identifiers, operator symbols, punctuation marks, and so forth. The phase of the compiler carrying out lexical analysis is typically called a *recognizer,* and its output is a string of internal (to the computer) tokens standing for the lexical units in the program.

Syntactic analysis consists of analyzing the input string of tokens to determine the structure of the source language statements it represents. This phase of the compiler is called a *parser.* Many parsers work from some formal description of the source language, perhaps encoded in tables (hence the term *table-driven compiler*), and produce as output a representation of the input in which its structure as a legitimate program statement is also represented. This intermediate form of the program may take several shapes, such as a parse tree, a table of triples (which may be viewed as an encoding of the parse tree), or a string of tokens in so-called Polish postfix order, with operators following their operands. These forms for a particular input expression are illustrated in Fig. 14-18. And an illustrative procedure for parsing into Polish postfix form is given in a later section of this chapter.

Semantic analysis consists of generating the object code corresponding to the intermediate form produced by parsing. If that object code is in assembly language, it can then be processed by the assembler. An example of code generation is given in a later section.

In addition, many compilers contain a separate phase concerned with *storage allocation,* particularly if the object code is to be executed on a large, multiprogrammed computer system such as is discussed in Chap. 15. Also, following semantic analysis, there is often a phase concerned with *optimization* of the generated code. In addition to machine-specific optimizations, a number of techniques applicable to most higher-level languages are now understood by compiler builders. These include identifying common subexpressions so they need be computed only once, computing expressions made up only of constants during compiling rather than during each execution, ordering the computation of Boolean expressions so that if the first subexpression of an OR or an AND is true or false, respectively, the remainder are not computed, and so forth. Such techniques can reduce the execution time (and sometimes the size) of the compiled program. And, finally, if the generated code is in assembly language, the *assembly* phase produces machine language code.

Parsing algebraic expressions

One purpose of parsing expressions is to facilitate later evaluation (or generation of code for evaluation) of expressions, replacing a possibly complicated analysis with a relatively straightforward scan. The Polish postfix (also called *parenthesis-free*) notation mentioned above permits such a scan, since each operator is preceded by its operands. This can be seen in the example expression of Fig. 14-18 by marking off each operator and its operands, as below.

$(3 \ (xy+) \ z \uparrow \ ) *)$

One procedure for carrying out this reordering uses a target stack to hold the reordered expression, a temporary stack to hold

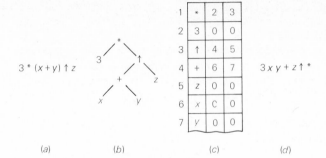

FIGURE 14-18
Examples of syntactic analysis. (*a*) Input expression; (*b*) parse tree; (*c*) triple table; (*d*) Polish postfix expression.

(*a*) (*b*) (*c*) (*d*)

certain postponed operators, and a table specifying the ordering rule to be applied for certain operator pairs.

The rules controlling reordering (omitting details of initialization and ending) are as follows:

1 If the leftmost token of the expression is an operand, move that token to the right end of the target stack.

2 If the leftmost token of the expression is an operator, select and carry out the appropriate rule from the following as governed by the rule table. (That is, select and carry out rule 2*a*, 2*b*, or 2*c* depending on the particular leftmost token of the expression and rightmost token in the temporary stack.)

   a Move the leftmost token in the expression to the right end of the temporary stack.

   b Move the rightmost token in the temporary stack to the right end of the target stack.

   c Discard the matching parentheses from the temporary stack and the expression.

3 If no tokens remain in the expression and there are tokens in the temporary stack, move the rightmost token in the temporary stack to the right end of the target stack, repeating rule 3 until the temporary stack is empty.

The table referred to in rule 2 is given in Fig. 14-19. The table in Fig. 14-20 traces the progress of applying these rules to the example expression.

Rightmost token in temporary stack

Leftmost token of expression	↑	*/	±	(	empty
(	A	A	A	A	A
↑	B	A	A	A	A
*/	B	B	A	A	A
+−	B	B	B	A	A
)	B	B	B	C	

FIGURE 14-19
Rule table for postfix ordering.

		AFTER APPLYING RULE	
EXPRESSION BEFORE APPLYING RULE	RULE APPLIED	TEMPORARY STACK	TARGET STACK
3 * (x+y) ↑ z	1		3
* (x+y) ↑ z	2*a*	*	3
(x+y) ↑ z	2*a*	* (	3
x+y) ↑ z	1	* (	3 x
+y) ↑ z	2*a*	* (+	3 x
y) ↑ z	1	* (+	3 x y
) ↑ z	2*b*	* (	3 x y+
) ↑ z	2*c*	*	3 x y+
↑ z	2*a*	* ↑	3 x y+
z	1	* ↑	3 x y+z
	3	*	3 x y+z ↑
	3		3 x y+z ↑ *

FIGURE 14-20
Trace of reordering an expression.

"Parsing program";

    [**local** *r;*

       $ep \leftarrow 1; tp \leftarrow 0; mp \leftarrow 0;$ Initialize pointers into expression, target, and temporary stacks.

      until $ep > n$ Repeat the following statements until the expression stack is exhausted.

        [**if not** *Operator*(*expr*(*ep*))

          then   If the leftmost token of the expression is an operand, then move that token to the right end of the target stack.

              $[tp \leftarrow tp + 1;$

               target(*tp*) $\leftarrow$ *expr*(*ep*);

               $ep \leftarrow ep + 1]$

          else   If the leftmost token of the expression is an operator, select the appropriate rule.

            $[r \leftarrow Rule(expr(ep), temp(mp));$

             if $r =$ "A"   If rule is "A", then move the leftmost token in the expression to the right end of the temporary stack.

              then

                  $[mp \leftarrow mp + 1;$

                   temp(*mp*) $\leftarrow$ *expr*(*ep*);

                   $ep \leftarrow ep + 1]$

              else

                if $r =$ "B"   If the rule is "B", then move the rightmost token in the temporary stack to the right end of the target stack.

                 then

                     $[tp \leftarrow tp + 1;$

                      target(*tp*) $\leftarrow$ *temp*(*mp*);

                     $mp \leftarrow mp - 1]$

                 else   If the rule is "C", discard the matching parentheses from the temporary stack and the expression.

                   $[ep \leftarrow ep + 1;$

                     $mp \leftarrow mp - 1]]];$

    until $mp = 0$ If no tokens remain in the expression and there are tokens in the temporary stack, repeat this operation until the temporary stack is exhausted: Move the rightmost token in the temporary stack to the right end of the target stack.

      $[tp \leftarrow tp + 1;$

       target(*tp*) $\leftarrow$ *temp*(*mp*);

       $mp \leftarrow mp - 1]]$

FIGURE 14-21

The TL program in Fig. 14-21 carries out the above parsing scheme. It assumes that the input expression of *n* tokens is stored one token per value in array *expr*, and that *target* and *temp* are also arrays. The variables *ep*, *tp*, and *mp* are indices into those arrays.

The above routine does not include either checks for possible error conditions or handling of the first operator. Note that knowledge of the internal encoding of input symbols into tokens is not needed by this routine, but is localized in the two functions that it uses, *Operator* to test if a token represents an operator and *Rule* to produce the rule corresponding to two operators.

Code generation

The code-generation process used in a compiler depends on the intermediate form produced by syntactic analysis. Sometimes code generation can be done at the same time as parsing. The simple scheme sketched below for generating code for evaluating an arithmetic expression from a Polish postfix intermediate form could be combined with parsing.

The code-generation process can be described in a table (see Fig. 14-22) similar to the decision table format introduced in Chap. 4. This first description ignores the details of keeping track of pointers and counters. The process distinguishes between operands, operators which are directly implemented as machine operations (such as +), and operators which must be implemented as subroutine calls (such as ↑). The process also uses a flag indicating whether the accumulator is in use or empty, a pointer (called SAVE) to an unused but already scanned operand, and a block of storage (called TEMP) for temporary results. It also assumes, for subroutines, that the subroutine expects to find its two operands in known locations (i.e., locations with known names specific to that subroutine).

TOKEN IS	acc STATUS	SAVE POINTER	ACTION
Operand	Free	Clear	Generate "LD token"
			Mark *acc* in use
Operand	Free	In use	ERROR condition
Operand	In use	Clear	Set SAVE to point to token
Operand	In use	In use	Generate "ST next temporary"
			"LD token pointed to by SAVE"
			Set SAVE to point to token
Operator	Free	....	ERROR condition
Operator	In use	Clear	Generate "ST next temporary"
			"LD previous temporary"
			"operator next temporary"
Operator	In use	In use	Generate "operator token pointed to by SAVE"
			Clear SAVE
Subroutine	Free	....	ERROR condition
Subroutine	In use	Clear	Generate "ST known location 2"
			"LD previous temporary"
			"ST known location 1"
			"BM subroutine"
Subroutine	In use	In use	Generate "ST known location 1"
			"LD token pointed to by SAVE"
			"ST known location 2"
			"BM subroutine"
			Clear SAVE

FIGURE 14-22
Rules for code generation.

For the postfix expression 3xy+z ↑ *, the assembly language code generated by the rules in Fig. 14-22 is shown in Fig. 14-23.

```
LD    +3
ST    TEMP+1
LD    X
AD    Y
ST    EXPON1                LD    X
LD    Z                     AD    Y
ST    EXPON2                ST    EXPON1
BM    EXPON                 LD    Z
ST    TEMP+2                ST    EXPON2
LD    TEMP+1                BM    EXPON
MU    TEMP+2                MU    +3
```

FIGURE 14-23   FIGURE 14-24
Example of generated object code.   **Optimized object code.**

A "smarter" set of rules, or a relatively simple optimization procedure, could eliminate the unnecessary move of the constant +3 to TEMP+1. And a set of rules which checked whether the operator in question was commutative or not could eliminate the two operations reordering the operands for multiplication. The shortened code generated by such a cleverer set of rules, that is, rules developed by a cleverer programmer, would be as in Fig. 14-24.

Of course, until one has an assembler and a compiler, programs must be written in machine language. A sophisticated assembler or compiler can be an extremely difficult program to write and debug in machine language. Often a procedure called *bootstrapping* is used to minimize machine language programming. First a simple, possibly inefficient, assembler is programmed in machine language. Next a simple, and probably highly inefficient, compiler is programmed in the assembly language and compiled and assembled using the first assembler. Then a more complete and efficient assembler can be programmed in the higher-level language and compiled and assembled. (Alternatively, the advanced assembler can be coded in assembly language before any work on a compiler.) And then an advanced version of the compiler is programmed in its own language and compiled on the first version. And so on through additional refinements as desired.

An alternative bootstrapping procedure involves using one computer to generate a translator to be run on another computer. Suppose that the compiler is written in the higher-level language and has been compiled on machine 1. The code-generation phase of the compiler is modified to produce object code for machine 2. Then the modified translator can be executed on machine 1 to produce programs to be run on machine 2. If the compiler itself is compiled using the modified compiler on machine 1, that process will produce a compiler which runs on machine 2. If machine 2 is a small computer with limited input-output equipment, it may be more convenient always to use machine 1 to translate programs into object code for machine 2.

BOOTSTRAPPING

INTERPRETERS

Compilers generate code that can be executed many times without retranslation. In some cases there are advantages to executing the source code directly upon translation, actually carrying out the code that would have been generated by a compiler. Translators that accept and execute the source language program directly, without generating code, are called *interpreters*. In fact, many translators which appear to be compilers are a mixture of both approaches; for example, FORMAT statements in FORTRAN are often passed over during compilation and interpreted at program execution time by a system program called the *FORMAT interpreter.* The flow of program and data through an interpreter appears as in Fig. 14-25.

FIGURE 14-25
Interpretation process.

Interpreters are sometimes useful as a control program between the object program and the computer itself. Such a control program can be used to make computer 1 look like computer 2, for example, as an interpreter implemented on computer 1 with a source language identical to the machine language of computer 2. In fact, the TL program given in Chap. 13 to simulate an ML machine is such an interpreter. Also, interpreters can be used to trace the execution of a program by interpreting the program statements and providing information on register status and control flags before and after instruction execution. The ability to trace programs is most helpful in debugging. Some translator systems use an interpreter for debugging and then a compiler for producing machine language programs for debugged programs. A third use of interpreters is to protect the program from itself and other programs. Even with modern hardware features and operating system safeguards, it is sometimes possible for a program to "go wild" and write over itself and/or other programs. If every instruction is interpreted, the interpreter provides another level of protection.

EXERCISES

1 Program in AL the pig latin translation procedure given in Chap. 9.

2 Program in AL the procedure given in Chap. 9 for the simulated Game of Life.

3 Program in AL the procedure given in TL in Chap. 9 for generating all orderings (permutations) of a given number of elements.

4 Implement the simple version of the assembler described in this chapter (as in Fig. 14-12).

5 In early versions of FORTRAN, the length of variable names was restricted to six characters. Why do you think this restriction was imposed? In other languages, variable names and subroutines were often of the form *Adddd* where *A* was an alphabetic character and *d* was a decimal digit. What advantages might accrue from this restriction?

6 Use the rules in the section on parsing algebraic expressions (p. 179) to reorder the expression $3 * x \uparrow 2 + 4 * x - 7$ into postfix order. Use a work table like the one in Fig. 14-20 to develop a trace of the steps in the reordering.

7 Add the features mentioned in the text (error checks and handling the first operator) to the TL parsing program given in Fig. 14-21. Implement this program and check your hand-computed answer to exercise 6 using this program.

8 Using the rules provided in Fig. 14-22, generate the AL code for the postfix form of $3 * x \uparrow 2 + 4 * x - 7$.

9 Compilers do a one time, once and for all translation of source language statements into machine language or into an object language which can be easily translated into machine language. Interpreters retain the program in source language translating and retranslating each statement whenever the program calls for execution of the statement. If you had to choose between these two types of translators, which would you choose? Under what conditions or for what purposes do you think compilers (interpreters) would be more efficient? easier to write? better for the programmer?

10 "The proliferation of machine languages with only small differences between them is a waste of resources because programs cannot be transferred easily between machines. Machine language should be standardized, and all computer manufacturers should use the same machine language." Comment.

Gries, David: *Compiler Construction for Digital Computers,* Wiley, New York, 1971.

Higman, Bryan: *A Comparative Study of Programming Languages,* American Elsevier, New York, 1967.

Lee, John A.: *The Anatomy of a Compiler,* Van Nostrand Reinhold, New York, 1967.

Rosen, Saul (ed.): *Programming Systems and Languages,* McGraw-Hill, New York, 1967.

Sammet, Jean E.: *Programming Languages: History and Fundamentals,* Prentice-Hall, Englewood Cliffs, N.J., 1969.

REFERENCES

PROGRAMMING LANGUAGE
TRANSLATORS—ASSEMBLERS
AND COMPILERS

LARGE COMPUTER SYSTEMS

INTRODUCTION

Up to this point a simple model of computers and of their uses has been sufficient. Our model of a computer has been of a central processing unit and memory configuration with simple input-output devices executing a program for one user at a time. While this model is almost true of most minicomputers in use today, it does not convey the real complexity of the manner in which medium- and large-scale computers operate. Most current computers are a much more complex organization of components, typically serving several users (executing several programs) "at the same time." In this chapter, we examine both these more complex hardware systems and the control programs, often called *executive or operating systems,* that supervise their behavior.

EFFICIENT USE OF RESOURCES

Why have computer systems become larger and more complex? A major reason has been the desire to make more efficient use of computers.

The resources needed to carry out any particular computation are rarely exactly those available from the computer or computing center at hand. For example, using a computer which rents for $20,000 a month or more to execute student programs one at a time in a beginning programming class almost certainly means that much of the computer's memory is unused (idle) during the execution of most programs. On the other hand, all of the memory may be needed during compilation of the programs. And in any case, memory comes in fixed-sized modules from computer manufacturers and so cannot be matched exactly to the demands of any particular program. (The problem is like that which arises because most of us use the same automobile for town and for freeway driving. If the automobile has the capacity to perform well on the freeway, much of that capacity is idle when driving in town or while sitting in a parking lot.)

The problem of resources not matching demands is not a new one. Early computers read in punched cards a row of punches at a time. Since cards moved at relatively slow mechanical speeds, the central processor sat idle for several computer cycles between card rows. Programmers (in machine language) spent a great deal of energy structuring their computations so as to use those otherwise wasted machine cycles. A few years later, users were concerned that the central processor had to sit idle while the machine operator changed tape reels between jobs. In some cases, the economics of the situation suggested purchasing additional tape units so that the operator could be readying the tapes for the next job while the current one was computing. Each new development in computer technology has led to new imbalances and relative inefficiencies in the use of resources, and so to further innovations to redress those imbalances.

Most computing centers are called upon to process both large and small programs; so they must have available a computer system large enough and fast enough to handle the maximum demand for service. Further, experience has shown that for many hardware components, cost increases less rapidly than capacity. For example, four times as fast a central processing unit may cost only twice as much. This too has led to justification of larger computer systems for many general purpose computer centers, followed by efforts to then use such systems effectively for small jobs. Often small jobs share a system—that is, are computed at the same time. Many argue that whatever hardware economies of scale may accrue from large machines are more than offset by the inefficiencies of the additional software complexity needed to utilize such systems. While the data necessary to resolve this dispute has not been gathered in a systematic manner, it is clear that efficient use of large computer systems requires both hardware and software innovations. Many of the recent developments in computer architecture have been motivated by this search for efficiency. In the remainder of this chapter we examine some of these developments.

But first a word about minicomputers. The computer industry has responded to users' demand for a greater and more economical range of services by developing both larger systems in which the computational resources can be shared and also smaller, stand-alone systems. These small minicomputers (that term must be taken in historical perspective; their performance is often greater than that of the largest computer available 20 years ago) are much like the simple model of a computer that we have been using. Both minicomputers and large systems are playing an important part in computing. Often the user sitting at a teletype or other remote terminal is indifferent as to which type of machine is performing his computation.

The theme underlying the many variations existent in large computer systems is that of multiplicity, of repetition of the same resource or function. Large systems can be put together in many ways to suit many different purposes, but each different design is

LARGE COMPUTER CONFIGURATIONS

a variation on the theme of parallelism of multiple units. There are computer systems with several "main" memories, or with several disk and/or tape units as auxiliary memory. There may be several input-output devices such as teletypes. There may be in the central processing unit multiple accumulators (as in the IBM 360-370 general registers). And in some systems there may even be multiple central processing units, sharing memory and input-output devices.

A particularly widespread variation on this theme is the use of a separate specialized processor to control input-output. It was apparent early in the use of computers that very often the central processing unit was idle waiting for input-output to be completed. At other times during the same programs, the main memory was idle (not being read from or written into) because the central processing unit was executing some operation (such as add or compare) for which the operands had already been fetched. During this free time, data could be read into or written out from memory to auxiliary memory such as disk or tape or to input-output devices if only there were another processing unit available to control that transfer. And so, smaller specialized processors for controlling input-output were added to computer systems for the express purpose of making more efficient use of the total system by overlapping data transfer to and from memory with computation by the central processing unit. Such specialized processors are often called *channels or peripheral processing units* (*PPU's*). The use of these specialized processors requires a system of hardware interlocks to prevent both CPU and channel from attempting to read from or write to memory at the same time.

Not only does the hardware of such large computer systems contain duplication, but also program execution can be carried out "in parallel." This is obvious for systems with multiple central processing units and also for the parallelism (interleaving might be a better term) of main computation and input-output in many modern computers. But even in systems without the several processors needed for multiprocessing, a form of parallel execution commonly called *multiprogramming* can take place. Under multiprogramming, several programs (say, one for each active remote terminal) can be within the system and partially executed at the same time. The CPU is actually executing only one of these programs at a time. When that program is waiting for data from the disk, or for a response from a remote terminal, or has exhausted its allocation of time for the moment, the CPU (or, more accurately, the control program) sets it aside in an inactive or wait status and activates another program from those now ready for further computing. Such an arrangement can result in a more efficient utilization of the total computer system even after subtracting out the time and space costs of control. Multiprogramming may also be advantageous to the user, particularly users who require fast responses and/or have only modest computing requirements. These small jobs can be interleaved between or within larger computations when "spare time" that might otherwise be wasted is available.

These comments, while not detailed, show that the behavior of a large computer system is not so much a simple repetition of the Fetch-Execute cycle as a flurry of asynchronous but interrelated activities. The implementation and coordination of these activities is achieved through a number of hardware and software features to be discussed next.

HARDWARE FEATURES

Several hardware innovations in recent years have been concerned with coordinating asynchronously interacting hardware units and with programs operating independently within a single computer.

Interrupts

A major coordinating feature is the *interrupt,* a signal generated by an independent unit (such as a remote terminal or disk control unit) and directed to the central processing unit to indicate that the independent unit in question now needs service. Generally, on reception of an interrupt, the central processor temporarily sets aside whatever task it is performing, saves the necessary status information so that it can proceed with that task at a later time, and proceeds to execute a program associated with the interrupt (for example, to activate the program associated with the terminal which just signaled completion of input). Of course, the hardware must allow interrupts to be postponed or stacked up for later processing if appropriate; for example, it often is not logically possible to interrupt the routine servicing of a prior interrupt. Thus, it must be possible to disable and enable interrupts.

Often the occurrence of an interrupt is a signal to the processor to switch from one job program to another. This switching requires that the "context" of the job just interrupted be saved (until the job is resumed) and replaced with the context of the job now to be executed. This context consists of such information as the contents of the next instruction address register, the status of interrupt-enable flags and of condition flags, the contents of the accumulator and index registers, and any other such information in central processing unit registers. Recent hardware technology contains features which facilitate saving such information. For example, in the IBM 360-370 series, much of this information is carried in a single item, called the *program status word,* which is stored automatically in main memory when an interrupt occurs. Also, some machines contain multiple general registers which can serve as both accumulators and index registers. A single instruction, Store Multiple Registers, copies their contents into memory.

Memory protection

Another problem arising under multiprogramming (or multiprocessing) is the protection of memory areas assigned to one program from accidental or deliberate change by other programs. If a program were allowed to write into or read from any location in memory, a program bug might lead to destroying part of the program or data of another job. To avoid this, various *protection* schemes have been implemented in hardware. These range from bound registers holding limits within which legal addresses must lie, against which all memory references are checked, to protection keys associated with blocks of memory and with each program, the keys being matched by the hardware on each memory reference. The variable data associated with these schemes is also status information that must be saved with each change of job. And an attempt to access protected memory generates a protection interrupt.

Supervisory mode

In a multiprogramming or multiprocessing system it would be intolerable to allow each program to arbitrarily start and terminate input or output or transfers to or from auxiliary storage overriding whatever such action was already in process. Such activities must rather be passed by the individual job programs to a portion of the control program, which can ensure that they are done in an orderly manner (for example, so that lines from two different jobs do not appear consecutively on the printer). One approach to this problem is to have two system states for the central processor, called perhaps *task mode* and *supervisory mode*. All routines for input and output, for changing protection keys, for handling interrupts, etc., are executed in supervisory mode. Indeed, some machine operations, such as those for input-output or for changing the program status word, can only be executed in supervisory mode; otherwise, they cause an illegal operation interrupt. Job programs are executed in task mode; when they need the services of a supervisory routine, they execute a special instruction, a *supervisor call.*

Memory allocation

Another problem arising in multiprogramming systems concerns the memory location of each program. If there is to be flexible intermixing of programs or of modules within programs, it should be possible to execute a program from (have it stored in) any area in memory, rather than one particular area whose machine addresses are included in the instructions. Several hardware features work toward this end.

In some systems, instruction addresses are modified by the contents of a relocation (or base) register prior to execution. Thus, all programs can be coded as if to start from location zero, but can be moved by the control program to any other block of memory by adjusting the relocation register.

However, this approach requires a single contiguous (or at least preplanned) block of memory for the program. In actuality, there might be within main memory enough storage to hold the program, but scattered in several smaller blocks. Another approach involves dividing main memory into fixed-sized blocks called *pages*. While a job is being executed, a table called the *page table* holds the correspondence between program addresses and memory pages, with that information substituted into each program reference. Now, as far as the program (and the original programmer) is concerned, the program is in consecutive storage, but as far as the hardware is concerned it can be scattered in noncontiguous blocks throughout storage.

A related idea is that of *segments* and *virtual memory.* Using this approach, the programmer conceives of his task as requiring a number of logically different blocks of consecutive memory, each block being called a *segment.* He can conceive of a virtual memory of as many of these segments as he needs; that is, he programs without memory limitation. During execution, a *segment table* (like the page table described above) is used to lead to the appropriate page table for the active segment, and that page table is then used to construct a memory address. Of course, since the programmer has proceeded as if he had virtually unlimited main memory, the final memory address may be a reference to information not actually in main memory but rather on auxiliary storage. There are several strategies for handling this problem. The programmer may be asked to specify which pages or segments are to be in main memory together. Or, under an approach called *demand paging,* when a page not in main memory is referenced, an interrupt is generated and the supervisory system transfers that page into main memory, replacing an already resident page. In this latter case, the programmer need have no concern for where pages are physically located; when a page interrupt occurs, some other job will be executed until the appropriate transfer is made. Of course, the demand paging approach can lead to a great deal of system overhead in transferring pages to and from auxiliary storage, particularly if poor choices are made of which pages to replace. A great deal of thought has been given to this problem and to how to capture the programmer's knowledge of the program's structure without requiring him to be familiar with paging details.

None of the features described above "solve" the problems toward which they are directed. Rather they are features that can be used by appropriate programs to switch between jobs, to protect against interference among programs, and so forth. They assume the existence of a set of programs which will take care of handling interrupts, allocating memory, etc. That collection of programs is the *operating system.*

We now describe four major functions of a typical operating system: input-output handling, storage management, process management, and file management. Typically, each function is handled by a separate section of system program, or module.

In many systems it is quite possible to treat information transfer requests and devices in the same manner whether they are input or output to the external world or transfers to or from auxiliary storage devices within the system itself. In either case, several programs may wish to use the same device simultaneously, and so it is necessary that the programs deal with a portion of the operating system rather than with the devices directly. The

SOFTWARE FEATURES OPERATING SYSTEM

Input-output handling

operating system module concerned with input-output handling must maintain a queue of jobs requesting use of a particular device, select a next job to service when one is finished, and initiate the appropriate information transfer routine (for example, a channel program). Also, the module must check for error conditions such as "record not located," "improper termination of transfer," "parity check error," etc., and take appropriate action. Further, the module must keep track of buffer areas used for information transfer, assigning them and freeing them as needed. And finally, the module must contain routines specific to each device to generate the appropriate timing and control signals as needed. Such a set of routines can allow the programmer to request information transfers with a minimum of detailed information about the system beyond the source and destination of the transfer.

Storage management

Another major module of modern operating systems is concerned with the management of storage. Typically, main memory and auxiliary storage are treated separately, and this discussion will also treat them separately. As new processes are started up in the system and old processes terminate, blocks of storage are requested and released. The memory management module must keep track of available blocks of storage and/or requests for storage, matching them as well as possible, and maintaining queues of waiting requests and of free blocks. Further, in a system with paging, this module must initiate the information transfers necessary to move pages between main and auxiliary memory, and must update the page and segment tables appropriately.

Process management

Another module must perform similar queuing and initiation functions with respect to the several programs in process in a multiprogramming situation. A particular program may be executing, or waiting for some system resource such as the printer, or waiting ready to proceed when the central processing unit becomes available. The process management module (program segments being computed are often referred to as *processes*) must maintain the appropriate queues and, as the required system resource becomes free, select the next process on some specified priority basis. In those systems with multiple processors, the selection process is extended to matching process and processor. (This last statement, which is consistent with current operating system practice, reflects the belief that the central processing unit is the critical limiting resource of the system, and so is accorded special treatment in resource allocation.) One feature of this scheduling decision of particular interest and study in computer science is the possibility that two processes, each using a resource the other is requesting, can create a deadlock in which neither can proceed. That this happens can be easily shown; a simple, straightforward, general solution is being sought.

The final operating system module discussed here is concerned with file management. This part of the operating system is often the largest and most complicated, particularly in multiprogramming systems. Within such a system there are a set of programs and data files belonging to the system itself, a public set available to all users, and private sets for each user. Further, the rights of access to files are generally not simple; some users may be allowed to read certain public files but not write them; some to do both; others to do neither, and most other conceivable combinations. The file management module must maintain directories associating program file names with physical locations, specifying protection and access rights, and so forth. Also, it must keep track of available file space and process requests for additional space and releases of space. Further, because auxiliary storage is typically kept on devices such as disk units which can involve time delays due to physical movement of the storage medium, different arrangements of data on the medium can lead to noticeably different processing times. Many file management systems contain routines for reorganizing file location assignments periodically so as to improve processing efficiency. And finally, this module provides generalized data access routines, so that the programmer need not know the details of how his data is physically stored, but need only ask for the next item by name or using some key as appropriate.

While large computing systems have evolved mainly as a solution to efficiency problems, there also have been other factors behind their development.

One has been the demand to solve larger problems—the increased appetite of problem solvers. In some cases (for example, weather prediction), the problems have been so large that parallel computation is suggested. In other cases more conventional computer architectures are adequate, but the complexity of a system made up of several medium-sized computers has led to a single larger one.

A second factor leading to the development of large computing systems has been technological development and the desire to use the latest technology to *build something*. In the 1950s computer designers did not have the organizational knowledge nor the components necessary to construct the large systems that they have been able to fabricate in the 1970s. Cost reduction in components and increases in their speed have made large systems economically feasible.

A third factor in the development of large systems has been the marketing strategies of major computer manufacturers. Until recently, the primary solution to possible decreased sales (due to saturation of demand) in the computing field has been to replace entire computing systems with a "new and bigger" (with "bigger" implying "better") model, rather than improve or enlarge components, or improve operating systems or programs. However, as

File management

OTHER REASONS FOR LARGE COMPUTING SYSTEMS

the computing field has become more sophisticated, alternatives to hardware replacement are becoming more popular as solutions to computing problems.

A fourth factor in the development of larger computer systems is reliability. Components and units are *replicated* not only to improve efficiency but also to improve reliability. *Redundant* and error-checking circuits are one part of the search for reliability; multiple processors and multiple peripheral units are another. There are so many components in the modern computers that the wonder is that they run as well as they do. Large systems have self-diagnosis capabilities to detect failed or marginal components and have sufficient replication that often most jobs can be run without all the components and units available in good condition. In particularly critical situations, such as moon shots or power networks, whole computer systems are duplexed so that if one fails, a second system can take over very quickly. In many applications less reliability than that provided by full duplexing is required, but some duplexing is available in most computing systems.

CONCLUSION

These comments have only surveyed the hardware and software features of large systems. Whole books are devoted to spelling out some of these issues in more detail. To the programmer using such systems, it is convenient to view the computer for which he is programming as specified by the hardware and operating system taken together; he is often indifferent to whether certain functions are performed by hardware or software. Together hardware and operating systems provide an environment, often much closer to our simple model of a computer than the base machine itself, within which he can specify his procedures.

EXERCISES

1 Schools, business firms, and governmental units frequently reassess the ways in which they have been providing computing services. Many options are available. An organization can buy or lease a computer to provide services, it can obtain computing services from some other unit in the organization, or it can obtain services from a firm which sells computing services. Within each one of these options there are suboptions, e.g., which computer, which service firm? On the basis of your knowledge and experience with computing, what criteria do you think should be used in the selection of the method of providing computing services?

2 Assume that your organization or school has decided to buy a computing system. $1 million is available for the purchase of hardware. Would you buy one system for $1 million, four for $250,000 each, or ten for $100,000 each? What considerations led you to your choice, e.g., ability to run large programs, reliability, specialization?

3 Many commercial firms which provide computing services to other organizations use several (sometimes 20 or more)

medium-sized computers rather than one or two large computers. Why do you think service firms follow this strategy? Do you think it is a good one?

4 The scheduling or process management of a multiprogramming system requires a set of decisions about who gets what services when. Should the system give priority to the small, short job? Should priorities be arranged to make best use of the processor or processors? What goals do you think are important? Who would you give priority to?

5 One partial solution to the priority problem is to set up a pricing system which permits users to pay for different priorities. If you pay more, you get better service. If you pay less, you get slower service. What do you think of such a pricing system? If a pricing system causes the CPU to be idle more than another scheduling system, do you think such a pricing system is wasting resources?

6 The manager of a multiprogramming computing system has to decide how large a program users will be permitted to run. If any one program is larger than half of the memory, it is possible that only that one program will be in memory and the CPU will be idle while the big program is swapped in or out. Many installations set a limit on program size of half of memory. If the limit is smaller, more programs can be in memory; and the chances of idle CPU time are reduced. But breaking up a large program into small parts is sometimes inefficient. How would you respond to this dilemma? How can virtual memory and demand paging help?

7 How could the linked-list data structure discussed in Chap. 8 be used to organize a file storage system? How large (how many words) should each unit (page, block) of the file system be? If a link gets destroyed, how can the file be reconstructed?

Rosin, Robert F.: Supervisory and Monitor Systems, *Computing Surveys,* **1**(3):37–54 (1969).

Watson, Richard W.: *Timesharing System Design Concepts,* McGraw-Hill, New York, 1970.

LOGICAL BASIS OF COMPUTERS

How do computers *really* work? In this chapter the focus shifts from examining the behavior of computer systems in general to examining the basic logical circuits and components underlying our simple model computer. Again, this search for understanding can go on at many levels—at the level of the circuits making up the adders and accumulators, at the level of the electronic components making up those circuits, at the level of the physical elements making up those components, etc. Here the emphasis is on circuits and components in terms of their functional characteristics without concern for the physics of the situation.

CIRCUITS

As was seen earlier, the information flow within computer circuits consists both of data and of control information. In either case, the information is encoded into sequences of two-state information units, that is, binary numbers. Thus, a control signal can be ON or OFF, an alphabetic character can be encoded as a group of 8 bits, and so forth. The student (and the computer designer) can deal strictly with information circuits transmitting 0s and 1s.

It is useful to distinguish between those circuits whose behavior (output) depends only on immediate inputs and those circuits whose behavior depends in some way on previous inputs, on what happened in the circuit at an earlier time. Circuits independent of time are usually called *combinatorial or switching circuits;* those dependent on time (and so embodying the notion of memory) are usually called *sequential circuits.*

BASIC COMBINATORIAL-CIRCUIT ELEMENTS

Combinatorial circuits for carrying out such tasks as addition of two numbers, decoding of an operation, comparison of two characters, generation of a parity bit for a character, etc., can be constructed out of three basic types of circuit elements or components.

The *AND element* produces a 1 output if and only if all of its inputs are 1s; otherwise it produces a 0. The *OR element* produces a 1 output if any of its inputs are 1; otherwise (if no inputs are 1) it produces a 0. The *NOT element* (also called an *inverter*) produces a 1 output if its input is a 0; otherwise (if the input is a 1) it produces a 0. There are several different systems for depicting these elements graphically; one such is given in Fig. 16-1. (Note that for illustrative purposes AND and OR elements are shown with two inputs; in fact, they can be constructed with more inputs if desired.)

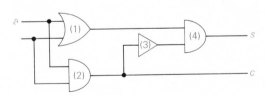

AND   OR   NOT

FIGURE 16-1
Circuit elements.

These elements are described in terms of their function, with nothing said of their physical realization. They may be constructed of transistors, vacuum tubes, mechanical relays, or a number of other physical elements; in this chapter we are not concerned with that distinction.

A common and useful way of representing the function of circuit elements and/or circuits is the truth table. A *truth table* lists all possible combinations of inputs for a circuit and for each combination the associated output. Truth tables for AND, OR, and NOT are given in Fig. 16-2.

ab	d	ab	d	a	d
00	0	00	0	0	1
01	0	01	1	1	0
10	0	10	1		
11	1	11	1		
AND		OR		NOT	

FIGURE 16-2
Truth tables for circuit elements.

Using these three components it is possible to construct a circuit to add two binary digits. Such a circuit should produce a sum of 0 for two 0 inputs, a sum of 1 for inputs of 0 and 1, and a sum of 2 for inputs of 1 and 1. Of course, the value 2 cannot be represented in a single binary digit, so in fact the adder must produce a sum and carry to the next digit position. A truth table for such an adder, calling the input digits a and b, the sum s, and the carry c, is given in Fig. 16-3.

An adder

ab	c	s
00	0	0
01	0	1
10	0	1
11	1	0

FIGURE 16-3
Truth table for adder.

FIGURE 16-4
Adder circuit.

A circuit constructed out of ANDs, ORs, and NOTs that carries out this addition is given in Fig. 16-4. How does one know that this circuit does in fact do addition, does in fact produce the correct result? One method of checking is to build such a circuit, apply all possible combinations of inputs, and observe the outputs. Another method is to construct a truth table for the circuit and compare it with the truth table for an adder given in Fig. 16-3. If the two truth tables are identical, the circuits that they describe carry out the same function. A truth table for the adder of Fig. 16-4, constructed using the truth tables for its basic elements, is given in Fig. 16-5. As can be seen, its outputs are indeed the same as those in Fig. 16-3.

INPUTS		(1)	(2)	(3)	(4)	OUTPUTS	
a	b	a OR b	a AND b	NOT (2)	(1) AND (3)	c[=(2)]	s[=(4)]
0	0	0	0	1	0	0	0
0	1	1	0	1	1	0	1
1	0	1	0	1	1	0	1
1	1	1	1	0	0	1	0

FIGURE 16-5
Truth table for adder circuit.

a	b	k	c	s
0	0	0	0	0
0	0	1	0	1
0	1	0	0	1
0	1	1	1	0
1	0	0	0	1
1	0	1	1	0
1	1	0	1	0
1	1	1	1	1

FIGURE 16-6
Truth table for full adder.

Actually, the adder circuit shown above does only part of the job of adding two binary digits; it is commonly referred to as a *half-adder*. In general, in adding numbers of more than one digit, any digit position will have as input a carry from the previous digit position. And so, a full adder should take three inputs—two digits and a previous carry (call it k)—and add them to produce a new sum and carry. The truth table for this function is shown in Fig. 16-6. A full-adder circuit is shown in Fig. 16-7. Construction of its truth table from the circuit is left to the reader.

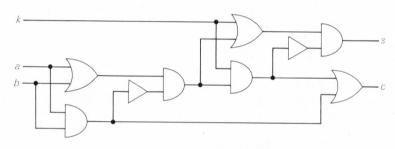

FIGURE 16-7
Full-adder circuit.

If the circuit designer is allowed the same use of abbreviation and of standard functions that is used so extensively in programming (for example, subroutines), then he can construct the same full adder out of two half-adders. Such a circuit is shown in Fig. 16-8, using rectangles labeled HA to represent half-adder circuits. Note that the truth table for the circuit component HA is given in Fig. 16-5.

FIGURE 16-8
Full-adder circuit from half-adders.

EVALUATION AND SIMPLIFICATION

A number of questions come to mind about the circuits considered above. Given a desired function, how does one know to construct a particular circuit? Or even any arbitrary circuit that works (carries out the desired function)? Given an arbitrary circuit, how does one determine what it does (what function it represents)? And how does one determine if there is a simpler (composed of fewer components) circuit that carries out that same function? All of these questions could be answered more easily if there were some formal system for describing these circuit functions, some system which could be manipulated symbolically, about which theorems could be proven, and so forth. In other words, it would be useful to have a calculus of these logical functions. Such a calculus does exist; it is called *Boolean algebra*. It can be used to describe, evaluate, and simplify functional descriptions of desired circuits.

Variables in Boolean algebra may have the values true or false, 1 or 0, or any such binary distinction. In the following, the symbols 1 and 0 are used. Two basic Boolean operations are *logical sum,* or OR, and *logical product,* or AND, symbolized by $\vee$ for logical sum and $\wedge$ for logical product. (Sometimes logical sum is symbolized as $+$ and logical product as $\cdot$; however, these can be confused in some contexts with arithmetic addition and multiplication.) These two operations are commutative, associative, and distributive, and 0 and 1 serve as the identity elements for sum and product, respectively. A third basic operation is *negation,* or NOT, symbolized by $\sim$. (Often negation is symbolized by a bar over the variable or expression negated, as in $\bar{x}$.)

Truth tables for the basic Boolean operations of logical product, logical sum, and negation are given in Fig. 16-9. These tables are, of course, identical to those for AND, OR, and NOT, respectively.

a	b	$a \wedge b$	a	b	$a \vee b$	a	$\sim a$
0	0	0	0	0	0	0	1
0	1	0	0	1	1	1	0
1	0	0	1	0	1		
1	1	1	1	1	1		
Logical product			Logical sum			Negation	

FIGURE 16-9
Truth tables for Boolean operations.

Because variables and operations in Boolean algebra correspond directly to signals and circuit elements in switching circuits, Boolean expressions can be used to represent and evaluate such circuits. For example, the half-adder circuit of Fig. 16-4 is represented by the following two expressions:

$$s = (a \vee b) \wedge \sim (a \wedge b)$$
$$c = (a \wedge b)$$

Similarly, the full-adder circuit of Fig. 16-7 can be represented as:

$$s = \{[(a \vee b) \wedge \sim (a \wedge b)] \vee k\} \wedge \sim \{[(a \vee b) \wedge \sim (a \wedge b)] \wedge k\}$$
$$c = (a \wedge b) \vee \{[(a \vee b) \wedge \sim (a \wedge b)] \wedge k\}$$

By evaluating these expressions for all combinations of the input or "independent" variables $a, b,$ and $k,$ one can construct the truth tables for the output or "dependent" variables s and c.

In those programming languages which include Boolean expressions, the truth tables for expressions such as those for s and c can be computed directly. But even in other languages such calculation is fairly simple. For example, logical product, logical

FIGURE 16-10
More truth tables.

a	b	min(a,b)	a	b	max(a,b)	a	(1−a)
0	0	0	0	0	0	0	1
0	1	0	0	1	1	1	0
1	0	0	1	0	1	1	0
1	1	1	1	1	1		

sum, and negation can also be represented by the functions **min, max,** and 1−, as the truth tables in Fig. 16-10 demonstrate.

Thus, the following TL segment calculates and writes out the truth tables for s and c (for a full adder) using the expressions given above.

> **for** *a*=0,1
>> [**for** *b*=0,1
>>> [**for** *k*=0,1
>>>> [*s*=**min(max(***k*,**min(max(***a,b***),1−min(***a,b***)))**,
>>>> 1−**min(***k*,**min(max(***a,b***),1−min(***a,b***))))**;
>>>> *c*=**max(min(***a,b***),min(***k*,**min(max(***a,b***),1−min(***a,b***))))**;
>>>> **write** *a,b,k,c,s*]]];

This approach to evaluating Boolean expressions requires that each expression be hand-coded into a program step involving **max, min,** and 1−. More generally, it would be desirable to have a form in which these expressions themselves were data for some evaluation program.

As was noted previously, a Boolean expression can be represented as a tree. The expressions for s and c would appear as the trees in Fig. 16–11.

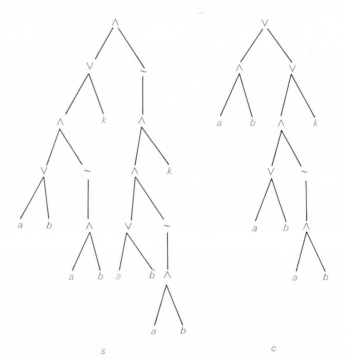

FIGURE 16-11
**Boolean expression trees for sum
and carry.**

Bex	SYMBOL	LEFT LINK	RIGHT LINK
1	∧	2	3
2	∨	4	5
3	~	13	0
4	∧	6	7
5	k	0	0
6	∨	8	9
7	~	10	0
		...	

FIGURE 16-12
Tabular representation of tree for s.

Such trees can be encoded into arrays and processed by programs like those discussed in Chap. 9. For example, if the above expressions were encoded into an array *bex* (an example of which is shown in Fig. 16-12), the following (recursive) TL procedure would compute the value of the expression (tree) starting in row i of the array.

Bool(i):

[**if** $bex(i,2)=0$ **and** $bex(i,3)=0$

then return $Varval(bex(i,1))$

else

if $bex(i,1)=$ "~"

then return $(1-Bool(bex(i,2)))$

else

if $bex(i,1)=$ "∨"

then return $\max(Bool(bex(i,2)),Bool(bex(i,3)))$

else

if $bex(i,1)=$ "∧"

then

return $\min(Bool(bex(i,2)),Bool(bex(i,3)))$];

Note that no value of the function is defined if the operation is other than ∧, ∨, or ~. Also, a function *Varval* is used which returns the value of the Boolean variable whose name is its character-string operand. (The characters "∧", "∨", and "~" have been added to TL's character set for illustrative purposes. In most real systems, other characters would have been used.)

Simplification

If one were actually going to construct the circuits associated with Boolean expressions, one would prefer the most economical circuit possible to achieve a particular function. At the simplest level (more realistic considerations are introduced later), this means the circuit that realizes a given truth table with the least number of components. And since circuit components correspond to operators in the associated Boolean expression, the search for the most economical circuit is also the search for the expression with the least number of operators.

For example, consider the expression for the carry output of a full adder:

$$c=(a \wedge b) \vee (a \wedge k) \vee (b \wedge k) \vee (a \wedge (b \wedge k))$$

This expression involves eight operators. The following expression, involving only four operators, has the same truth table and so is functionally equivalent.

$$c=(a \wedge b) \vee ((a \vee b) \wedge k)$$

How does one find the second expression given the first?

The process of finding a simpler circuit or expression is a design process, and its success depends both on the design tools available (such as theorems or graphical methods) and also on the skill of the designer in recognizing which tools are useful in any particular situation.

Some of the more commonly used theorems in simplifying Boolean expressions are the following:

1	$\sim x \vee \sim y = \sim (x \wedge y)$	7	$x \vee 0 = x$
2	$\sim x \wedge \sim y = \sim (x \vee y)$	8	$x \wedge 0 = 0$
3	$x \vee \sim x = 1$	9	$x \vee x = x$
4	$x \wedge \sim x = 0$	10	$x \wedge x = x$
5	$x \vee 1 = 1$	11	$(x \vee y) \wedge \sim y = x \wedge \sim y$
6	$x \wedge 1 = x$	12	$(x \wedge y) \vee \sim y = x \vee \sim y$

The reader can verify any of these theorems using truth tables. Theorems 1 and 2 are called De Morgan's laws; they also demonstrate the interdependence of the three "basic" Boolean operators introduced earlier.

Using these theorems and the distributive, associative, and commutative properties mentioned earlier, let us trace one possible simplification process leading to the result given above.

$(a \wedge b) \vee (a \wedge k) \vee (b \wedge k) \vee (a \wedge (b \wedge k))$	Given
$(a \wedge b) \vee (a \wedge k) \vee (1 \wedge (b \wedge k)) \vee (a \wedge (b \wedge k))$	(6)
$(a \wedge b) \vee (a \wedge k) \vee ((1 \vee a) \wedge (b \wedge k))$	Distributive
$(a \wedge b) \vee (a \wedge k) \vee (1 \wedge (b \wedge k))$	(5)
$(a \wedge b) \vee (a \wedge k) \vee (b \wedge k)$	(6)
$(a \wedge b) \vee ((a \vee b) \wedge k)$	Distributive

Computer programs have been written to carry out this kind of manipulation. Typically these are trial-and-error procedures using various search techniques for determining which laws and theorems to apply. The complexity of these procedures arises from the encoding of heuristics governing which theorem to try next, from the bookkeeping involved in keeping track of simplifications already tried (possibly a treelike structure of partial simplifications), and from the processing involved in the substitution of subexpressions for single variables in the theorems. As an example of this last point, note that Theorem 6 states simply that $x \wedge 1 = x$. However, its use in the first step of simplification involved not only recognizing that it could be used here but also substituting the expression $(b \wedge k)$ for x.

This discussion of simplification has been based on the use of AND, OR, and NOT as basic operators and circuit elements. While the principles of the simplification process may remain the same, the *definition* of simplicity depends on which circuit components are considered basic. If half-adders were available as a basic circuit element, the circuit shown in Fig. 16-8 would be a simplification of the circuit of Fig. 16-7 upon which it would indeed be difficult to improve. The next section mentions some ways in which the preceding discussions have themselves been simplifications of reality.

In actual practice the design of logical circuits has changed markedly since the introduction of integrated circuits in the 1960s. Integrated circuits can contain relatively large numbers of simple circuits (ANDs, ORs, NOTs) on a single plastic chip about the size of a thumbnail. Standard chips which contain half-adders or full adders have been available for some time. In the early 1970s, chips were introduced which contain all of the circuitry for the central processing unit of a computer comparable to the one described in Chap. 13. Modern circuit design for computers begins with the larger building blocks available in integrated circuits.

Even basic design is typically expressed in terms of NAND (NOT-AND) and NOR(NOT-OR) elements (in part because the underlying physics of transistors makes these elements simpler to manufacture). A NAND element can be diagrammed as shown in Fig. 16-13. From De Morgan's laws, we see that x NAND y is equivalent to $\sim x \vee \sim y$. NOR is analogously defined.

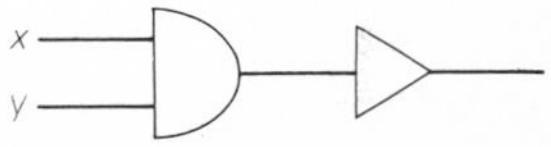

FIGURE 16-13
NAND element.

Further, the above discussion of simplification does not reflect some other constraints of using larger, more complex circuit elements on a single chip. Although the cost of such chips reflects their complexity, and so does not negate the need to minimize what is in some sense the equivalent number of basic elements, the circuit designer must also be concerned with such factors as the number of interconnections between chips, the desirability of placing all chips related to a single function close together, and the problems of finding faulty components. A more complex circuit with fewer interconnections may in fact be more economical. Placing all circuits related to a particular function in one area (e.g., on one circuit board) can simplify troubleshooting and/or changes in that function. Because the manufacturing process for circuit chips occasionally produces a marginal component or one that fails after some usage, a good design can greatly simplify finding faulty components.

Finally, this discussion ignores any considerations of the physical processes underlying these devices. It requires time and energy for circuit elements to respond to input signals, and the signals themselves must also be coordinated in time. Even for supposedly time-independent switching circuits, these considerations enter into translating logical representations into actual pieces of hardware. They are even more important in the realization of the time-dependent sequential circuits discussed next.

SEQUENTIAL CIRCUITS

In sequential circuits the output of the circuit is determined both by input signals and by previous states of the circuit. If the output at any point in time depends only on the input at that time, then the circuit can be constructed as a combinatorial circuit of the sort discussed above, together with some clock pulse for keeping track of time. (For example, the cycle of a computer is marked by the output of an internal clock, which emits a "one" pulse every fixed interval.) However, if the output of a circuit depends on its inputs at an earlier time, then some form of memory must be incorporated into the circuit. Two common logical elements for carrying over information from one time period to the next are the *delay* and the *flip-flop*.

The simple delay produces an output identical to its input, but one time period later. Longer delays can be achieved by compounding such elements.

FIGURE 16-14
Diagram of R-S flip-flop.

The flip-flop is an element with two stable states, for example an output of 0 or an output of 1. The flip-flop continues in some one state through time until switched to the other. A simple R-S flip-flop is diagrammed in Fig. 16-14. (Other more complex flip-flop designs are also used.)

The R-S flip-flop has two input lines, labeled r and s, and two output lines, say q and $\bar{q}$. $\bar{q}$ is the complement or inverse of q; if q is 1, $\bar{q}$ is 0; if q is 0, $\bar{q}$ is 1. So the R-S flip-flop in fact has only one independent output, q; the complemented output $\bar{q}$ is also provided for convenience.

The rules determining the output of the R-S flip-flop are as follows:

r	s	q_{t-1}	q_t
0	0	0	0
0	0	1	1
0	1	0	1
0	1	1	1
1	0	0	0
1	0	1	0
1	1	0	*
1	1	1	*

* Not allowed. Both r and s cannot be 1 at the same time.

FIGURE 16-15
Truth table for R-S flip-flop.

If s is 1, then the flip-flop is set, that is, q is 1.

If r is 1, then the flip-flop is reset, that is, q is 0.

Both r and s cannot be 1 at the same time.

If both r and s are 0, that is, neither set nor reset, the flip-flop does not change states.

These rules are summarized in Fig. 16-15. q is the output of the flip-flop at time t, and so indicates the state of the flip-flop at that time.

In addition to the inputs shown above, the flip-flop often has a clock input. At each clock pulse, the r and s inputs are scanned and the new state of the flip-flop is determined. The following discussion assumes a clock input without showing it explicitly.

State-transition diagrams and tables

A useful way of depicting the behavior of a simple sequential circuit is the state-transition diagram. Such a diagram is constructed from circles for each state of the circuit (each set of events that must be remembered) and arrows for each transition from one state to another. Often the transitions are labeled with the input and output symbols, separated by a slash, that are associated with that change of state.

An example device

For example, consider a simple device to count 1s in its sequence of inputs, producing an output of 0 until it has counted three 1s in the input and then producing an output of 1. The behavior of such a device is shown in Fig. 16-16, and a corresponding state-transition diagram in Fig. 16-17.

Input sequence   0 0 1 0 0 1 1 0 1 0 0 1 0 1 0 . . .
Output sequence   0 0 0 0 0 0 1 0 0 0 0 0 0 1 0 . . .

FIGURE 16-16
Input and output behavior.

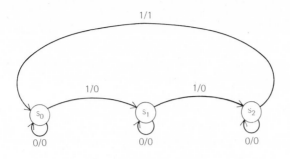

1/1

1/0   1/0

s_0 s_1 s_2

0/0   0/0   0/0

FIGURE 16-17
State-transition diagram.

In Fig. 16-17, s_0 corresponds to the state of having received no 1s since last producing a 1, s_1 to having received one 1, and s_2 to having received two 1s. The label "1/0" on the arrow from state s_0 to state s_1 indicates the following behavior: when in state s_0, if the input is a 1, then output a 0 and move to state s_1. The information represented in a state-transition diagram may also be presented in a state-transition table, similar to a truth table. A state-transition table for this example device is given in Fig. 16-18.

STATE	INPUT	OUTPUT	NEXT STATE
s_0	0	0	s_0
s_0	1	0	s_1
s_1	0	0	s_1
s_1	1	0	s_2
s_2	0	0	s_2
s_2	1	1	s_0

FIGURE 16-18
State-transition table.

Now let us consider the development of a circuit to produce the behavior described above. As a first step, what are the logical equations specifying this behavior? The following equations specify the output and the internal state of the device at any point in time as a function of its input and its state at the previous point in time.

An example circuit

$$o_t = i_t \wedge s_{2,t-1}$$
$$s_{0,t} = (i_t \wedge s_{2,t-1}) \vee (\sim i_t \wedge s_{0,t-1})$$
$$s_{1,t} = (i_t \wedge s_{0,t-1}) \vee (\sim i_t \wedge s_{1,t-1})$$
$$s_{2,t} = (i_t \wedge s_{1,t-1}) \vee (\sim i_t \wedge s_{2,t-1})$$

Note that the discussion so far has been in terms of general device or circuit characteristics, without regard to the circuit components (ANDs, ORs, R-S flip-flops, etc.) that might be used to achieve those characteristics.

A straightforward way of representing this behavior would be to use a distinct flip-flop to represent each distinct state of the circuit. (For example, FF1 being set would represent the circuit being in state s_1.) The above logical equations could then be rewritten as circuit equations, representing the circuit being in a specified state by the output of the corresponding flip-flop being set. ($q1$ denotes the output of flip-flop 1, $q2$ the output of flip-flop 2, etc.)

$$0 = i \wedge q2 \qquad s2 = i \wedge q1$$
$$s0 = i \wedge q2 \qquad r2 = i \wedge q2$$
$$r0 = i \wedge q0$$
$$s1 = i \wedge q0$$
$$r1 = i \wedge q1$$

Note that the condition of a flip-flop remaining set if the circuit input is 0 need not be represented directly, since R-S flip-flops remain set until reset. Instead, the action of resetting must be specified. A circuit realizing these equations is diagrammed in Fig. 16-19.

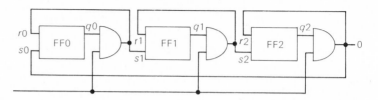

FIGURE 16-19
Example counting circuit.

This desired behavior can also be generated by a circuit using only two R-S flip-flops, by encoding the states of the device not as the states of separate flip-flops but rather as though the two flip-flops together represented a two-digit binary number. For example, s_0 would be represented as ($\sim q0 \wedge \sim q1$), s_1 by ($q0 \wedge \sim q1$), and s_2 by ($\sim q0 \wedge q1$). The details of such a circuit follow directly.

SERIAL ADDER

These concepts of combinatorial and sequential circuits are combined in our final example, an adder which adds two numbers of several digits each, one digit at a time. (Such a device is called a *serial adder* because it deals with the digits making up the numbers in serial. An adder which treats all digits at the same time must have separate circuits for each digit position and is called a *parallel adder*.) The digits (a and b) are delivered to the adder low-order position first, and the carry from each position is held for the next position in a one-time interval delay element (labeled d_1). Such an adder is shown in Fig. 16-20. (In practice, additional timing signals would be used to ensure zero carry into the first digit position and to check for overflow beyond

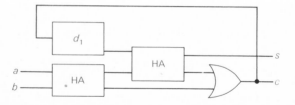

the last digit position.) Construction of the state-transition diagram and table and the logical equation corresponding to this circuit is an exercise for the reader.

1 Construct a truth table for the full-adder circuit shown in Fig. 16-7 by building it up from the truth tables for circuit components (as was done in Fig. 16-5). Compare the output columns of this truth table with those given in Fig. 16-6.

2 Construct a truth table for the full-adder circuit shown in Fig. 16-8 by building it up from the truth tables for circuit components. (A truth table for half-adders is given in Fig. 16-3.) Compare the result with your answer for exercise 1 above.

3 Diagram a circuit which will produce the outputs specified for the input combinations given below.

ab	c
00	1
01	0
10	1
11	0

Hint: For a procedure to translate a truth table to a circuit see one of the following references: McCluskey (1965, chap. 3); Hellerman (1967, chap. 4, especially pp. 173–174); and Bartee (1972, pp. 97–103, especially p. 100).

4 Construct a truth table for a circuit with three inputs and a single output defined as follows. When the number of ON inputs (1 inputs) is odd, the output is 1; when the number of 1 inputs is even, the output is 0. Design a circuit to realize that truth table.

5 Construct truth tables for the two expressions for c given in the section on simplification (p. 201) in this chapter. Are the expressions equivalent as the text asserts?

6 Verify by constructing truth tables the 12 theorems given in the section on simplification (p. 201).

7 Design a half-adder circuit using NAND elements only. Design a full-adder circuit using NAND elements only.

8 Prepare state-transition diagrams and tables for a circuit with the following behavior. The circuit has one input and one output. If the input at time t differs from the input at time $t-1$, the output at time t is 1; otherwise, the output is 0. An example of the circuit's behavior appears below.

   Input   0 0 0 1 1 1 1 0 0 . . .
   Output   . 0 0 1 0 0 0 1 0 . . .

9 Implement the circuit of exercise 8 using a one-time interval delay element. Implement the circuit using an R-S flip-flop.

10 Redesign the counting circuit given in Fig. 16-19 as suggested in the text, so that it requires only two R-S flip-flops.

11 Construct a state-transition diagram and table for the circuit shown in Fig. 16-20.

12 Games have been developed to illustrate several of the con-

cepts described in this chapter. Pick one of the games described by Englebart (1961) and present the concept to your class with the aid of your colleagues.

13 Although textbooks stress the advantages of modularity in building programs, software modularity is in its infancy compared to hardware modularity. Not only are basic circuits combined into integrated-circuit packages, but integrated circuits are combined into circuit boards and circuit boards are combined into subassemblies.

Discuss the advantages and disadvantages of the high degree of electronic modularity for the computer designer, the customer engineer (maintenance and repair), the owner of the computer, the user of the computer. Why do small- and medium-sized manufacturers of CPUs prefer to use their own electronic subassemblies in memories and peripherals even when they do not make the mechanical components?

14 Changes in the cost and effectiveness of computers have resulted from two kinds of technological development. One kind of development has changed the architecture or organization of the system, e.g., the index register, the input-output channel, the removable disk pack. The second kind of development has been the reduction in cost as a result of competition and of technological changes in circuit implementation. Survey the electronics trade journals in your library and talk to practicing electronics engineers to gather information on the current state of the art in circuit development. Is a breakthrough coming in chip design or fabrication which will drastically lower the price of computer components or drastically improve performance? Is it possible to extrapolate on past circuit developments to predict the future cost and capabilities of computers?

REFERENCES

Bartee, T. C.: *Digital Computer Fundamentals,* McGraw-Hill, New York, 1972.

Englebart, D. C.: Games that Teach the Fundamentals of Computer Operation, *IRE Trans. Electronic Computers,* **10:**31–41 (1961).

Hellerman, H.: *Digital Computer System Principles,* McGraw-Hill, New York, 1967.

McCluskey, E. J.: *Introduction to the Theory of Switching Circuits,* McGraw-Hill, New York, 1965.

Shackleford, Barry: Microelectronic Flipflops and Nand Gates Add up to a High Speed Counter, letter printed in "The Amateur Scientist" department (conducted by C. L. Strong), *Scientific American,* **228**(5):108–113 (1973).

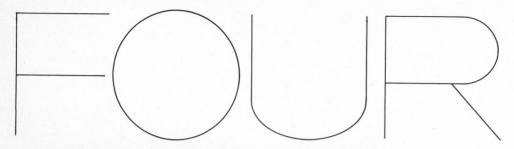

COMMONLY USED ALGORITHMS AND TECHNIQUES

The compleat procedure-writer has both knowledge of procedural languages and skill in constructing procedures to fit a given situation. His toolkit also includes a collection of algorithms developed (often by others) to solve frequently occurring problems. Effective use of these algorithms requires knowledge of their details, care in selecting from the available alternatives that algorithm most appropriate to the situation at hand, and attention to ensuring that the algorithm has been programmed correctly. The measure of appropriateness in selecting an algorithm includes its effectiveness and efficiency and also the existence of an implementation on an available computer.

In Part Four we present some common

problems arising in many contexts, together with algorithms for solving or partially solving these problems. Chapter 17 presents algorithms for searching and sorting and also elementary methods for comparing and choosing among the algorithms. Chapter 18 describes some commonly used numerical methods. Chapter 19 considers techniques involved in the implementation of simulation as a problem-solving strategy, particularly the simulation of random events. Although the problem situation in which simulation is appropriate is more general and so less well defined and structured than that of sorting or solution of equations, a number of specific techniques for simulating random processes are available.

SEARCHING AND SORTING†

Searching for an item with certain characteristics is a fundamental and frequent information processing task. Looking up a word in a dictionary to check its spelling or definition, finding the call number of a book in a library card catalog, and searching a pile of papers for last year's income tax return are everyday examples of this kind of search activity.

From a combination of instruction and experience, each of us develops techniques for search in everyday situations. Which technique is used depends on whether the items being searched (e.g., names, words, bibliographic entries) are ordered in a way which facilitates the search. The words in a dictionary are ordered to facilitate search provided one has a good idea of what letters occur in the word and in what order. In particular, if one knows the first couple of letters of the word, one can usually find the word in a conventional dictionary. But if one knows the definition (meaning) of a word and wants to find out how to spell it, the lexicographical ordering of a standard dictionary will not be very helpful.

Unordered information records can only be searched in a sequential manner. For example, in looking in a shuffled deck of cards for the "king of hearts," one must simply start at the beginning or the end of the deck and scan every card until the "king of hearts" is found. With unordered information there are only two choices, search sequentially or order the information records and then search.

Sequential search is simply the worst case of the enumeration problem-solving strategy discussed in Chap. 9. The ordering of information records, often called *sorting,* is an important preliminary to search. Sorting is usually done to convert a problem which would have to be solved by enumeration into one which can be solved by direct computation or scientific trial and error.

A procedure for searching ordered information records has already been introduced with the dictionary example of Chap. 4.

† Shortly before the final version of this chapter was written, Donald E. Knuth's treatise on this subject appeared (*The Art of Computer Programming,* vol. 3, *Sorting and Searching,* Addison-Wesley, Reading, Mass., 1973). This chapter follows Knuth's presentation closely on naming methods and on the form of procedures because we believe that Knuth's treatise will be the significant reference work in the field for some time to come. We hope that the adoption of Knuth's work as a guide improves this chapter and also makes it easier for readers of this chapter to refer to Knuth.

In this chapter, that dictionary lookup procedure is refined and generalized for computer applications. Procedures for locating information records directly, without either exhaustive or guided search, are also introduced.

The discussion of searching and sorting techniques in this chapter is limited to problems in which all of the information is available in primary memory, i.e., memory in which the access time to each word is the same. For large files of information which are wholly or partially stored on tape or disk, additional considerations apply.

The way in which data is structured has a major impact on searching and sorting. Appropriate data structures can facilitate the ordering of data by making it possible to insert and change records with only minimal changes to other information in the file. Appropriate data structures can also facilitate the search process itself. References to the material in Chap. 8 on the structure of data will be made where appropriate.

A general search procedure is represented in Fig. 17-1. This procedure assumes that the *file* or *table* to be searched consists

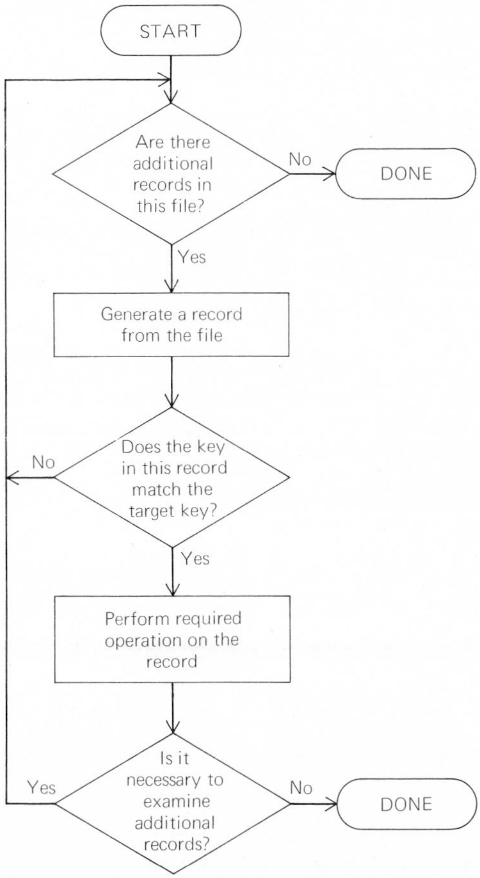

SEQUENTIAL SEARCH
A general search procedure

FIGURE 17-1
Flowchart of generalized search procedure.

of a collection of items which we call *records*. A record might be a set of numbers or a string of characters. Parts of the record are called *fields*. The search procedure is designed to search a particular field of each record, the *key*, for a match to the *argument* or *target*. If the key matches, then the procedure carries out the appropriate action, e.g., reads the definition or writes down the telephone number. If additional items with this feature are required (e.g., the goal is to find all records with a certain key), then continue searching. If no key matches, then stop without a match. The critical part of this general search procedure is that which "generates a record from the file."

Sequential search procedure

The sequential search procedure simply generates successive records from the file. The virtue of this procedure is that it is easy to program.

Programming a sequential search procedure in TL (see Fig. 17-2) using repetition statements is a simple task already done many times in previous exercises. The major problem with sequential search is its cost. For large files, sequential search can be very expensive since potentially every item must be examined.

"Sequential search";

    read *key*, *k*(1), *k*(2), *k*(3),...,*k*(*n*);

    for *i* ← 1 **thru** *n*

      [**if** *key* = *k*(*i*)

        then

          [**done**; "*key* found"]];

FIGURE 17-2   **done**; "*key* not found in file";

Estimating the cost of search

The cost of search is a function of (1) the length of the file to be searched, (2) the distribution of the desired records, (3) the number of times the file will be searched, and (4) the cost of examining a record.

In a file which is searched sequentially with a uniform distribution of targets (e.g., each record is an equally likely search target) the costs can be easily calculated. If the first record is the target, the search will require one cycle of the search program. If the second record is the target, the search will require two cycles, and so forth. If each record is the target once, the total number of search cycles required for an *n* record file will be

$$1+2+3+\cdots+n=(n*(n+1))/2$$

The average number of cycles per iteration is $(n*(n+1))/2$ divided by *n*, or $(n+1)/2$. If no information is available on how often each record will be sought, equal frequency (uniform distribution) is usually assumed, and the case just considered becomes a base line against which improvements can be measured.

If some records are sought more frequently, e.g., popular telephone numbers, these records can be moved up in the file to decrease the search effort. In fact, the record which is sought most frequently should be the first record, etc.

The cost of obtaining information should include not only the cost of the retrieval process itself but also the cost of delays in retrieval. Where appropriate and possible, costs of delay should be considered in developing the data structures and in devising search techniques. The cost of delay is the reason that emergency telephone numbers are listed in the front of telephone books even though these numbers will not be called frequently. Presumably the cost of delay in reaching the fire or police department in time of emergency is much greater than the cost of delay in reaching John Doe.

When the expected frequency of search and the cost of delay are difficult to estimate, it is often useful to consider the recency phenomenon. In many situations, the next target sought is information used recently. For example, one may telephone somebody and because he is out, call the same number again later. It saves search time to keep the telephone number handy. The recency phenomenon can be utilized to decrease file search activity by moving the most recently sought item to the beginning of the file, on the assumption that it will be searched for again soon.

Another factor to consider in estimating the cost of search is the case in which the key being sought is not in the file. For each target not in the file, all n records must be examined, increasing the average cost of search.

The cost of determining that a key is not in the file is greatly reduced if the file is ordered. In a file ordered from smallest key to largest key, the search procedure can test to see if the target is less than or equal to a given key. If the test is satisfied, then the procedure can test for equality. If the target is found, fine. If the test for equality fails, the target key is not in the file (see Fig. 17-3).

"Sequential search on ordered table";

    for $i \leftarrow 1$ **thru** n

      [**if** $key \leq k(i)$

        then

          [**if** $key = k(i)$

            then [**done**; "key found"]

            else [**done**; "key not in table"]]]   FIGURE 17-3

SORTING

The major technique available to reduce the costs of repeated searches of the same file is sorting the file. Sorting can be done either as the file is being collected or after the file is complete. A few of the basic sorting procedures are presented in this section.

Insertion   One straightforward method of sorting the file involves taking each key which has not yet been sorted, comparing it to those keys which have already been sorted, and inserting the record containing that key into its proper place in the file. Without any loss of generality, we shall assume that all files are to be ordered from smallest key to largest key, i.e., in the sorted file

$$k(1) \leq k(2) \leq k(3) \cdots \leq k(n)$$

The TL procedure for straight insertion is given in Fig. 17-4. Each key is compared to the keys preceding it (starting with the key just ahead). As long as the current key is smaller than its predecessors, the predecessors are moved down to make room for the current record. When the right slot is found, the current record is inserted.

"Straight insertion sort";

   for $j \leftarrow 2$ **thru** n

      $[i \leftarrow j-1; kk \leftarrow k(j); rr \leftarrow r(j)]$;   Initialize. i is the index. Because j is constant for each iteration, $k(j)$ and $r(j)$ can be replaced by kk and rr.

   Loop: Find a place for kk.

     if $kk \geq k(i)$

      then

         $r(i+1) \leftarrow n$ If $kk \geq k(i)$, then insert record j into position $i+1$.

      else   Else move up the list searching for the right place.

        $[r(i+1) \leftarrow r(i)$;

        $i \leftarrow i-1$;

        if $i > 0$ Test for top of table.

          then [**to** *Loop*]

FIGURE 17-4   **else** $[r(i+1) \leftarrow rr]]$;

An example of straight-insertion sorting is provided in Fig. 17-5. The 16-record file used in this example (column 0) was generated with the pseudo-random number generator provided with the BASIC translator on a Xerox SIGMA 7 computer. Each record consists of only one number which is also the key. The table in Fig. 17-5 shows snapshots of the file after the jth record is inserted into its proper place.

The alert reader will have realized that the straight-insertion procedure requires excessive moving of records. In Chap. 8 the linked-list data structure was justified for just such a situation—when it is necessary to insert a record in the middle of a table. A sorting procedure using list insertion is presented in Fig. 17-6. A link field l is added to each record; the head of the list is $r(1)$ and the actual records are $r(2)$ through $r(n)$. An example of list-insertion sorting is presented in Fig. 17-7. Again the records are numbered from 1 to 17 to permit compatibility with programming systems which do not permit use of zero subscripts. The

POSITION	ORIGINAL	2	3	4	5	6	7	8	9	10	11	12	13	14	15	16	FINAL
1	445	353	112				106	66		55							55
2	353	445	353			285	112	106		66							66
3	112		445			353	285	112		106							106
4	494			494		445	353	285		112							112
5	956				956	494	445	353		285							285
6	285					956	494	445	441	353							353
7	106						956	494	445	441	353						353
8	66							956	494	445	441						441
9	441								956	494	445						445
10	55									956	494						494
11	353										956	625	569				569
12	625											956	625		615	579	579
13	569												956	790	625	615	615
14	790													956	790	625	625
15	615														956	790	790
16	579															956	956

FIGURE 17-5
An example of straight-insertion sorting.

"List insertion sort";

$l(1) \leftarrow n; l(n) \leftarrow 0;$ — Set up linked list by initializing link (1) and link (n).

for $j \leftarrow n-1$ **thru** 2 **by** -1 — Obtain insertion candidates from bottom of table.

$[p \leftarrow l(1); q \leftarrow key; key \leftarrow k(j)];$ — p points to next record, q points to last record. key 1 is key of record to be inserted.

Test:

if $key \leq k(p)$ — If key of record to be inserted is less than or equal to key of record pointed at, then to *Insert*.

    then [**to** *Insert*]

    else

      $[q \leftarrow p; p \leftarrow l(q);$

      if $p > 0$ — If get to bottom of list and insertion has not taken place, insert at bottom.

        then [**to** *Test*]];

Insert:

  $[l(q) \leftarrow j;$

  $l(j) \leftarrow p]$

FIGURE 17-6

link of the head of the list, $l(1)$, points to the smallest key yet found.

Another sort procedure is the bubble sort. In each pass of the bubble sort, the record with the largest key is bubbled up to the top of those records remaining to be sorted (see Fig. 17-8). Note that the original position of the records in Fig. 17-8 has record 16 on top so that the record with the largest key will bubble up to position 16, the record with the second largest key will bubble up to position 15, etc. A bubble-sort program in TL is provided in Fig.

Bubble sort

$$j=1$$
(Entries in table are links)

POSITION		16	15	14	13	12	11	10	9	8	7	6	5	4	3	2	FINAL
1	0	17		14		12	11										11
2	445															5	5
3	353														12		12
4	112													7			7
5	494												14				14
6	956											0					0
7	285										12				3		3
8	106									12	7			4			4
9	66								12	8							8
10	441							14					5			2	2
11	55						12		9								9
12	353					14		10									10
13	625				15												15
14	569			17													17
15	790			0								6					6
16	615		0	15	13												13
17	579	0	16														16

FIGURE 17-7
An example of list-insertion sorting.

POSI-TION	ORIG-INAL	t=									FINAL
		15	14	13	12	5	4	3	2	1	
16	579	956									956
15	615	579	790								790
14	790	615	579	625							625
13	569	790	615	579	615						615
12	625	569	625	615	579						579
11	353	625	569								569
10	55	353	494								494
9	441	55	353	445							445
8	66	441	55	353	441						441
7	106	66	441	55	353						353
6	285	106	66	441	55	353					353
5	956	285	106	66	353	55	285				285
4	494		285	106	66	285	55	112			112
3	112	445		285	106	66	112	55	106		106
2	353	112	353		285	106	66	106	55	66	66
1	445	353	112				106	66		55	55

FIGURE 17-8
An example of bubble sorting.

17-9. The inner loop of the bubble-sort procedure provides a mechanism for making a single pass through the file and moving the largest value to the top of the list. This inner loop could be required $n-1$ times, but usually will not have to be executed that many times. Consider a table with only records 1 and 2 out of order, that is, $r(9)=9$, $r(8)=8$, $r(7)=7$, . . . , $r(2)=1$, $r(1)=2$.

"Bubble sort";

    bound ← *n*;   *bound* is the limit on each pass.

Loop:

    t ← 0;

    for *j* ← 1 **thru** *bound* − 1   Each pass through this iteration bubbles the record with the largest remaining key to *bound*.

      [**if** $k(j) > k(j+1)$

        then

          [$x ← r(j)$;   This is the standard exchange sequence between adjacent records with *x* as the additional storage. *t* is the flag used to indicate whether an exchange has occurred on this pass and where it took place.

        $r(j) ← r(j+1)$;

        $r(j+1) ← x$;

        $t ← j$]];

    if $t = 0$

    then done

    else

      [*bound* ← *t*;

      to *Loop*];   FIGURE 17-9

The table will be ordered after the first pass, but in its simplest form the procedure would continue to make $n-2$ more passes. A solution to this problem is presented in the procedure in Fig. 17-9. A flag *t* is used to keep track of whether any interchanges were made on a pass through the list and where the last interchange was made. If no interchanges were made, the list is sorted. If interchanges were made, the bound on the next pass need not exceed the position of the last interchange. So this version of the procedure requires at most one pass on which no interchanges are made.

    Like most sorting procedures, bubble sort has a perverse case. Consider a table which is in order except for the record in the largest position, that is, $r(9) = 1$, $r(8) = 9$, $r(7) = 8$, . . . , $r(1) = 2$. The bubble-sort procedure of Fig. 17-9 will require eight passes to order the list. But if the procedure were inverted so it bubbled the smallest record down (instead of the largest record up), the table would be sorted in one pass. Iverson (1962, pp. 218–219) recommends that the bubble-sort procedure alternate between upward and downward passes. Knuth (1973, pp. 110–111) refers to this as the *cocktail-shaker sort*.

Selection sorting is perhaps the most straightforward sorting technique. The procedure consists of finding the largest key, placing the record containing this key in position *n* of an auxiliary file, finding the largest key in the remaining $n-1$ records, placing the record with this key in position $n-1$, etc. When space is at a premium (e.g., in working with large files), the selection-sort pro-

Selection sort

"Straight selection sort";

for $j \leftarrow n$ **thru** 2 **by** -1 — Starting at bottom of list, consider the key of each record in turn.

[largest $\leftarrow k(j)$; index $\leftarrow j$;

for $i \leftarrow j-1$ **thru** 1 **by** -1 — This iteration finds the record with the largest key in the list.

[**if** $k(i) >$ largest

then

[largest $\leftarrow k(i)$;

index $\leftarrow i$]];

$k(index) \leftarrow k(j)$; — After each pass through the list is completed, the record with the largest key is swapped with the jth record.

FIGURE 17-10 $\qquad$ $k(j) \leftarrow$ largest]

POSI-TION	ORIG-INAL	16	15	14	13	12	11	10	9	8	7	6	5	4	3	2	FINAL
1	445								441	66					55		55
2	353											285	106		55	66	66
3	112													55	106		106
4	494							55						112			112
5	956	579				569	353			106			285				285
6	285											353					353
7	106										353						353
8	66									441							441
9	441								445								445
10	55							494									494
11	353						569										569
12	625			615	569	579											579
13	569				615												615
14	790		615	625													625
15	615		790														790
16	579	956															956

$j=$ (column header spanning 16 through 2)

FIGURE 17-11
An example of straight-selection sorting.

cedure can be modified to interchange the record with the largest key with the record in position n, the second largest record with the record in position $n-1$, etc. The interchange variation of the selection-sort procedure is presented in Fig. 17-10. The reader may recall this procedure from exercise 3 of Chap. 7. An example of selection sorting on the same 16-record file used in previous examples is presented in Fig. 17-11. Only those records which are moved are indicated.

Two-way merge — If a file is already sorted, a new item can be merged (inserted) into the file so as to retain the sort order. A common problem is to develop a common sorted list from two files which are in sort order. For example, the registrar has a sorted file of returning students and a sorted file of incoming students, and he desires a sorted file of all students. A TL procedure for merging these two lists is presented in Fig. 17-12. The merge procedure can be visualized with two lines of children. Each line is sorted by height with the shortest first. The goal is to merge the two lines into one combined line in order by height. Compare child 1 in line 1 with child 1 in line 2. Place the smallest at the head of line 3. Get child 2 from the line which had the smallest child and compare again . . . .

"Two-way merge";   Merge the list of x's and the list of y's into a list of z's.

     $i \leftarrow 1; j \leftarrow 1; k \leftarrow 1;$

Compare:

     if $x(i) \leqslant y(j)$

         then

             $[z(k) \leftarrow x(i);$ x is smaller, so add the x to the list of z's.

             $k \leftarrow k+1;$

             $i \leftarrow i+1;$

             if $i \leqslant m$

             then [**to** *Compare*]   If there are x's left, continue the procedure.

               else

                  [**for** $j \leftarrow j$ **thru** n If not, add the rest of the y's to the z's.

                     $[z(i+j-1) \leftarrow y(j)];$

                done]]

         else

             $[z(k) \leftarrow y(j);$ y is smaller, so add the y to the list of z's.

             $k \leftarrow k+1;$

             $j \leftarrow j+1;$

             if $j \leqslant n$

               then [**to** *Compare*]   If there are y's left, continue the procedure.

               else

                  [**for** $i \leftarrow i$ **thru** m If not, add the rest of the x's to the z's.

                     $[z(i+j-1) \leftarrow x(i)];$

                done]]   FIGURE 17-12

     The merge procedure can also be used to sort an unordered list of records. Order all pairs, i.e., record 1 and record 2, record 3 and record 4, etc. Then merge pairs into quads, and so on until the list is completely ordered.

     One problem with the merge procedure is that it requires an output file as large as both input files combined. Again linked lists can be applied to reduce the amount of space required. If both original files are considered part of one larger file, the merge procedure has only to rearrange links to develop the combined file.

Evaluation of sorting methods

A rough evaluation of the four sorting methods (straight insertion, list insertion, bubble, and straight selection) for which examples were provided can be made by determining the number of comparisons and assignments required to sort the 16-record file by each method. The numbers in Fig. 17-13 were obtained by augmenting each procedure with four counters—key comparisons, key assignments, overhead comparisons, overhead assignments. Each time one of these actions was taken, the appropriate counter was increased by one. *Key comparisons* refer to tests made on keys. *Key assignments* refer to assignment statements where either the left-hand or right-hand side was a key. *Overhead comparisons* refer to tests made on variables which were not keys and *overhead assignments* refer to assignment statements not including keys. Entering a **for** statement costs one assignment; executing the closing bracket of the enclosed statement(s) costs one assignment and one comparison.

FIGURE 17-13
Evalution of four sorting methods on a randomly selected 16-record file.

SORTING METHODS	KEY COMPARISONS	KEY ASSIGNMENTS	OVERHEAD COMPARISONS	OVERHEAD ASSIGNMENTS
Straight insertion	57	77	62	78
List insertion	59	—	62	187
Bubble	75	141	85	152
Straight selection	120	69	135	190

This four-way classification attempts to abstract from the idiosyncrasies of particular languages and particular machines. The distinction between operations on keys and operations on other variables should permit some adjustments in estimates to be made for the size of keys. (Remember in all of these comparisons, the record consists only of the one-word key.)

The insertion-sorting methods appear to be preferable to both the bubble sort and the selection sort. The bubble sort moves too much information around. This conclusion can be verified by a casual comparison of Figs. 17-5, 17-7, 17-8, and 17-11. Since only those records which were moved are rewritten in each column of the tables, the density of each table gives an indication of the amount of data shuffling. While the selection sort makes only necessary record interchanges, it makes the maximum number of comparisons because it does not take advantage of any order which may exist in the file before sorting begins. In fact the number of key comparisons may easily be calculated. In a 16-record file, it is

$$15 + 14 + 13 + \cdots + 1 = (16 * 15)/2 = 120$$

In an n-record file, it is

$$n + (n-1) + (n-2) + \cdots + 1 = (n * (n+1))/2$$

Basing the entire evaluation of sorting methods on the basis of one 16-record file might be a bit dangerous. Maybe the sample file is atypical for one of the sorting methods. So nine more 16-record files were generated (with the same procedure

SORTING METHOD	KEY		OVERHEAD	
	COMPAR-ISONS	ASSIGN-MENTS	COMPAR-ISONS	ASSIGN-MENTS
Straight insertion	71.5	89	74	90
List insertion	71	0	74	211
Bubble	108.7	177	121.9	207.3
Straight selection	120	69.3	135	190.3

FIGURE 17-14
Evaluation of four sorting methods on 10 randomly selected 16-record files.

used to generate the first file). The average results on all 10 files are presented in Fig. 17-14. The results given there indicate that straight insertion and bubble sort now look a bit worse, but insertion is still the best method.

In Fig. 17-15 additional data are presented on two files used as examples by Knuth (1973). The K-16 file consists of 16 three-digit records. The K-1000 file consists of 1,000 full-word records. The additional data are consistent with our previous observations. A straight sum of operations for K-1000 gives about 1 million for each of the insertion methods; 2 million for bubble; and $1\frac{1}{2}$ million for straight selection. So roughly speaking, insertion is about n^2, bubble is $2 * n^2$, and selection is $1.5 * n^2$ for the 1,000-record file. These approximations are a bit low for the 10 samples of the 16-record files.

SORTING METHOD	KEY		OVERHEAD	
	COMPAR-ISONS	ASSIGN-MENTS	COMPAR-ISONS	ASSIGN-MENTS
Straight insertion				
16×1	57	77	62	78
16×10	71.5	89	74	90
K-16	54	71	56	72
K-1000	250,267	251,271	250,272	251,272
List insertion				
16×1	59	0	62	187
16×10	71	0	74	211
K-16	53	0	56	175
K-1000	250,267	—	250,272	504,543
Bubble				
16×1	75	141	85	152
16×10	108.7	177	121.9	207.3
K-16	75	123	84	143
K-1000	494,479	747,819	499,456	750,683
Straight selection				
16×1	120	69	135	190
16×10	120	69.3	135	190.3
K-16	120	69	135	190
K-1000	499,500	8,509	500,499	508,010

FIGURE 17-15
Evaluation of four sorting methods on four sets of data.

When records are large, the records themselves should usually not be moved, but pointers or links should be moved. So while list insertion looks about the same in cost as straight insertion in Fig. 17-15, the cost of sorting a file of multiword records would be much higher for straight insertion than for list insertion.

Two suggestions

The sorting methods presented here are the fundamental techniques which are available. Many refinements have been developed to these techniques, and these refinements can reduce sorting costs significantly. So, before writing or using any sorting programs for large files or for repeated applications, the programmer should consult Knuth (1973) and the current literature.

SEARCHING ORDERED FILES
Binary search

Once a file is ordered, the search procedure can take advantage of the order to guide the search. The general strategy for searching ordered files is the scientific trial-and-error strategy described in Chap. 9. A widely used procedure, binary search, is similar to the procedure commonly used for searching dictionaries and telephone books.

The fundamental principle of the binary search procedure is to determine which half of the unsearched file or subfile could contain the target. In a file of eight records, the first question would determine whether the target was in the first half or the second half of the file, the second question would determine which quarter, and the third question would determine whether the target was in the file or not. An idealized binary search procedure is represented in Fig. 17-16 in a flowchart for determining the value of a 3-bit key.

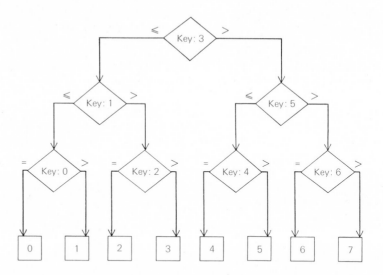

FIGURE 17-16
Flowchart for decoding 3-bit key.

A TL procedure for binary search is given in Fig. 17-17. Several points about the procedure are worth noting. To simplify the procedure, an initial set of tests designed to determine whether the target is within the range of the file, i.e., not less than the smallest key and not greater than the largest key, have been omitted. After determining that the target is within the range of values of the file, the next step is the computation of the midpoint of the file (or subfile) by calculating the midpoint of the range of search. The target is compared to the key at the midpoint. If the key is the target, the search is over. If the key is larger (smaller) than the target, the search is restricted to the upper (lower) half of the file by adjusting the value of the lower (upper) limit of search. The central part of the procedure is repeated until it terminates successfully when a key matching the target is found or it terminates unsuccessfully (i.e., target not in file) when the limits of search cross over.

"Binary search";	l is lower limit. u is upper limit.
$l \leftarrow 1; u \leftarrow n;$	
Midpoint:	
if $u < l$ **then** [**done**];	Check if *key* is in the table.
$i \leftarrow \textbf{int}((l+u)/2);$	Compute new midpoint.
if $key < k(i)$	If *key* is less than the key at the midpoint, search the lower half of the table, i.e., from l to $i-1$.
then	
$[u \leftarrow i-1;$	
to *Midpoint*];	
if $key > k(i)$	
then	If *key* is greater than the key at the midpoint, search the upper half of the table, i.e., from $i+1$ to u.
$[l \leftarrow i+1;$	
to *Midpoint*];	
[**if** $key = k(i)$	
then [**done**]	If $key = k(i)$, key is found.
else to *Error*]	FIGURE 17-17

The paths taken by the binary search procedure, i.e., the sequence of keys tested, can be represented as a tree in which the nodes are the indices (subscripts, row numbers) of the keys tested (see Fig. 17-18). Figure 17-19 contains the values of *l, u,* and *i* which are generated in searching for $k(1)$, $k(10)$, and $k(16)$ in a 16-record file. An examination of Fig. 17-18 can provide es-

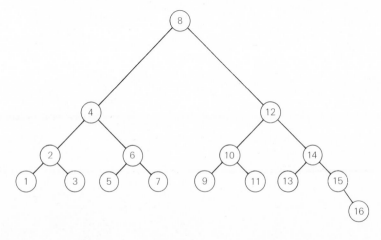

FIGURE 17-18
A tree representation of the binary search procedure.

k(1)			k(10)			k(16)		
l	*u*	*i*	*l*	*u*	*i*	*l*	*u*	*i*
1	16	8	1	16	8	1	16	8
1	7	4	9	16	12	9	16	12
1	3	2	9	11	10	13	16	14
1	1	1				15	16	15
						16	16	16

FIGURE 17-19
Some binary search examples.

timates of the average and maximum number of keys which have to be examined for keys in the table and keys not in the table.

If the target is $k(8)$, only one key need be examined. If the target is $k(4)$ or $k(12)$, only two keys need be examined. Continuing in this fashion, we can calculate the average number of keys to be examined as the total number of keys examined divided by the number of keys sought. For a 16-record file, the total number of keys examined is

$$(1 * 1) + (2 * 2) + (4 * 3) + (8 * 4) + (1 * 5) = 54$$

The average is $54/16 = 3\ 6/16$. From Fig. 17-18, we can see that the maximum is 5. For files which have $n = 2^k$ records, the

```
"Binary search with table";
for j ← 1 thru int(log(n)) + 2                    Generate the table.
    [delta(j) ← int((n + 2 ↑ (j−1))/2 ↑ j)]
i ← delta(1); j ← 2;                              The search procedure.
Compare:
        if key < k(i)                             If the key is less than the midpoint, check to see if there is anything left in the table.
        then
            [if delta(j) = 0
            then [done]
            else                                  If there is, compute midpoint of lower half and repeat.
                [i ← i − delta(j);
                j ← j + 1;
                to Compare]];
        if key > k(i)                             If the key is greater than...
        then
            [if delta(j) = 0
            then [done]
            else
                [i ← i + delta(j);
                j ← j + 1;
                to Compare]];
        [if key = k(i)
        then [done]
        else to Error]
```

FIGURE 17-20

j	delta(j)
1	8
2	4
3	2
4	1
5	1
6	0

FIGURE 17-21
A table for binary search.

average number of key comparisons will approach $\log_2 (n-1)$ and will not exceed $\log_2 (n+1)$.

A variation on the binary search procedure makes use of an associated table to direct the search. The table is a substitute for that part of the procedure which calculates the next key to be tested (see Figs. 17-20 and 17-21).

Binary tree searching

Binary search procedures as discussed in the preceding section are optimal procedures under three conditions: (1) the records are ordered, (2) the expected number of searches per key is the same, and (3) the file is stable, i.e., records will not be added or deleted. If records are added or deleted, the entire file will have to be re-sorted with a corresponding increase in the total cost of retrieval.

The symbol table problem discussed in Chap. 14 is just such a situation in which the table is continuously updated. Every time a new symbol is encountered in the location field, a new entry must be made in the table. Since the symbol table need not be searched while it is being collected in a two-pass translation, it is possible, as was indicated in Chap. 14, to collect the symbol table information in the first pass and sort it before the second pass. The tree structure proposed in Chap. 14 to handle the symbol table problem utilizes nodes with right and left links. The tree begins with the first symbol. All symbols to the left precede the first symbol in a lexicographical ordering, and all symbols to the right follow the first symbol in a lexicographical ordering. As was seen in Chap. 14, such a structure keeps the symbols ordered and permits easy insertion. This tree structure also provides an efficient search method provided the symbols are entered in a reasonably random fashion, i.e., the tree remains reasonably well balanced. In the worst cases, e.g., each symbol is less than its predecessor, the search will degenerate to sequential search on an ordered list.

DIRECT SEARCH
The key as an address

In the preceding sections of this chapter two kinds of files have been considered: (1) files whose records were *not* ordered on the basis of the relevant key and (2) files whose records were ordered on the basis of the relevant key. In the simplest cases, the average number of queries to find a target in the unordered file is about $n/2$. The comparable number for the ordered file is $\log_2 n$. But may it not be possible to locate a record directly with a single query?

If the key can be used as an address (an actual address in assembly language programming or a table index in higher-level languages), then the record can be located directly at the address. This type of search procedure is a direct computation strategy. It requires that the key itself be an address and that the table not be too sparse. For example, in a file of 1,000 students, if each student were identified by a nine-digit social security number, it would be impractical to use a social security number directly as an index into the file. But if each student had a unique three- or four-digit identification number, this number might be a good index.

Key transformations

Because it is often impractical to use the key itself as an address or index, techniques have been developed to transform the key into a number within the appropriate range. For example, in the case of the student file with social security numbers as keys, an alternative to creating a new three- or four-digit identification number would be to use the last three or four digits of the social security number as an address. While this would be convenient, it could cause some problems: (1) the last three or four digits would not necessarily be unique, i.e., more than one student might have the same key; and (2) there might be some patterns in the last few digits which might affect the search process.

This idea of using the last digits of the social security number as an address (or table index) is a simple example of a widely used, more general technique of transforming keys and targets directly into addresses. There are two major aspects to the technique: (1) the selection of an appropriate transformation function (transforming a key is usually referred to by the more descriptive term *hashing*), and (2) a procedure for resolving conflicts. If two keys hash, i.e., transform, to the same address, the second key and its associated record have to be stored (and searched for) somewhere else.

The simplest hashing function is the key modulo the table size, e.g., the last three digits of the social security number in the example we have been using. While such a function might be sufficient for some cases, the presence of patterns in the last three digits might cause more conflicts than would result from the choice of another function.

Knuth (1973, pp. 508–509) recommends using the mod function for a hashing function,

$$H(k) = k \bmod m,$$

but selecting the modulus m to be a prime number such that

$$r \neq \pm a \ (\bmod \ m),$$

where r is the radix of the character set (e.g., 64, 256); and k and a are small numbers.

Acceptable values of m are, therefore, any primes except those for which $r = \pm a \ (\bmod \ m)$ for k and a both small. Figure 17-22 contains a list of primes less than 2,000 which meet the conditions that $r = 256$, $a < 11$, and $k = 1,2,3,4,5$. So for $r = 256$, any other prime less than 2,000 would be an acceptable value of m. Of course $H(k)$ should not generate values larger than the

2, 3, 5, 7, 11, 13, 17, 19, 23, 29, 31, 37, 41, 43, 47, 67, 71, 79, 83, 89, 101, 127, 151, 163, 167, 173, 191, 223, 233, 241, 251, 257, 311, 331, 337, 683, 809, 919, 1,039, 1,103, 1,597

FIGURE 17-22
Values of m under 2,000 for which 256^k (mod m) < 11 for k = 1, 2, 3, 4, 5.

table size. As with the use of random-number generators (see Chap. 19), the programmer should check the hashing function selected on the particular data base and particular computer being used to make sure that the hashing function is performing as expected.

Collisions can best be resolved by prevention, i.e., the selection of a good hashing function. But even with the best hashing function, some collisions will occur. One popular collision-resolution procedure is called *chaining*. Each entry in the hash table serves as the head of a linked list. The lists can be kept ordered if desired. This procedure for handling collisions is a straightforward application of the linked-list techniques previously used.

Another simple collision-resolution procedure cycles through the table in an orderly fashion starting at the point computed by the hashing function looking for the key or an empty space. If the key is found first, fine. If an empty space is found first, the key and associated material are inserted. A TL procedure for collision resolution using this method is presented in Fig. 17-23 and an example is presented in Fig. 17-24. This method is called *collision resolution by open addressing*.

ASSIGNMENT OF
HASH CODES
TO KEYS

HASH TABLE

KEY	H(k)		ROW	KEY
Aleph	5		0	Gimel
Bet	1		1	Bet
Gimel	0		2	Hay
Daled	4		3	Vov
Hay	2		4	Daled
Vov	3		5	Aleph
Zion	2		6	
Chet	3		7	
			8	
			9	Chet
			10	Zion

FIGURE 17-24
A hash coding example using open addressing.

"Collision resolution by open addressing";

       $i \leftarrow H(key)$ Compute the hash value of the key.

   Compare:

     if *table* (i) = *empty*   If *i*th slot in the *table* is empty and the *table* is full, done.

      [**then**   *m* is table size.

         if $n = m - 1$

           then [**done**]

         else   If the *table* is not full, place the key in the slot and stop.

            [$n \leftarrow n + 1$;

             table (i) ← *occupied*;

             $k(i) \leftarrow key$;

             done]]

      else

        [**if** $k(i) = key$ If the *i*th slot is occupied check to see if it is occupied by *key*.

        then [**done**]

        else   If it is not occupied by *key*, then prepare to check preceding slot.

          [$i \leftarrow i - 1$;   If run off top of table, start over again at bottom.

         if $i < 0$

           then [$i \leftarrow i + m$];

        to *Compare*];

FIGURE 17-23   **229**

1 Modify the merge procedure in Fig. 17-12 so it can be used to sort a list utilizing the technique suggested on p. 221.

2 Modify the merge procedure to operate on a linked list and eliminate the need for an auxiliary list.

3 Instrument (i.e., insert appropriate counters in) the four basic sorting programs, generate 16-item lists of numbers, and sort the lists using the instrumented programs. How do the results obtained compare to the results presented in Figs. 17-13 and 17-14? Are the results significantly different (see p. 257)?

4 In Chap. 14, two schemes were suggested for handling a symbol table in a translator. Design a scheme for using a hashing technique for the symbol table. Describe the hashing scheme for the symbol table in a few paragraphs, not more than two pages.

5 Study the write-up of the in-core sort package in the program library of your computer center. What is the basic sort technique used? How well is it described? Run the program on a small data file and provide some measure of the cost of running the sort package.

6 Develop a "cocktail-shaker" sort by modifying the bubble-sort procedure given in Fig. 17-9 to alternate direction after each pass.

7 Convert one of the sort procedures provided in this chapter into a library routine. The program should be written as a closed subroutine. What information must the calling program provide to the subroutine? What are the limitations of the subroutine? Can you advise users on estimation of costs? Provide an outline of the write-up which prospective users would require.

8 List some of the considerations which have to be made in developing a sorting procedure for a file which cannot be contained in core or primary memory.

9 Write a program to simulate a mechanical punched card sorter. What problems are involved with such a program? In what kinds of situations would such a procedure be advantageous?

10 Many computing experts consider conventional computing systems to be less than optimal systems for searching and sorting tasks. Do you agree? What changes might be made in computer architecture to improve the ability of computing systems on these two tasks?

11 Write a procedure for finding the median of a list of numbers. How many comparisons are required? Mathematically inclined students should refer to Knuth, D., *The Art of Programming,* vol. 3, pp. 216–220. Can the process be accelerated (or done more economically) on an interactive system? How (cf., pp. 117–118 above)?

REFERENCES   Brooks. Frederick P., Jr., and Kenneth E. Iverson: *Automatic Data Processing,* 2d ed., Wiley, New York, 1969.

Iverson, Kenneth E.: *A Programming Language,* Wiley, New York, 1962.

Knuth, Donald: *The Art of Programming,* vol. 3, *Searching and Sorting,* Addison-Wesley, Reading, Mass., 1973.

Martin, William A.: Sorting, *Computing Surveys,* **3:**147–174 (1971).

Price, C. E.: Table Lookup Techniques, *Computing Surveys,* **3:**49–65 (1971).

NUMERICAL METHODS

Historically, computing machines have been very useful in finding the zeros of functions and in solving systems of linear equations. Both of these problems occur frequently as parts of problem solutions in science and engineering. Several procedures for solving these two problems are presented, discussed, and evaluated here.

FINDING THE REAL ZEROS OF FUNCTIONS

The discussion of table or file searching in Chap. 17 can be extended to the search of continuous functions. A continuous function can be approximated as a two-column table, one column containing the values of the argument and the other column containing the corresponding values of the functions (see Fig. 18-1). While such a tabular representation suggests the possible application of table search techniques to the problem of searching continuous functions, there is no need to create a table of all values if, given an x, the function $f(x)$ can be evaluated directly. Furthermore, the values of x are often the set of real numbers, and it is not possible to construct a table of function values for all the real numbers, and it is unnecessary when only a small portion of the table is relevant.

For present purposes, the discussion of searching continuous functions is confined to finding the real zeros of functions, that is, the real x's for which $f(x)$ is zero.

x	$F(x)$
0	0
1	1
2	4
3	9
4	16
5	25
6	36
...	...

FIGURE 18-1
A partial table of squares of integers.

Binary search

The binary search procedure described in Chap. 17 can be readily extended to this purpose. The file or table is replaced with a definition of the function $f(x)$. The limits of search are best obtained from looking at a rough graph of the function or by searching the function linearly with a large interval. The only constraint on the limits of search is that the function changes signs in the interval between lower limit l and upper limit u, that is, $f(l) * f(u) < 0$.

The trial value x is the midpoint of the interval. If $f(l) * f(x) < 0$, then the function changes signs between l and x; and x becomes the new upper limit of the interval. If $f(l) * f(x) > 0$, then $f(l)$ and $f(x)$ are of the same sign; and x becomes the new

"Binary search for real zeros";

      read $l, u;$ This procedure assumes the function $f(x)$ is available. l and u are the initial limits of search.

    $fl \leftarrow F(l); fu \leftarrow F(u);$

    if $fl * fu < 0$ Check to make sure fl and fu are of opposite sign.

        then [**to** *Midpoint*]

        else [**done;** "error"];

Midpoint:

      $x \leftarrow (l+u)/2; fx \leftarrow F(x); z \leftarrow fl * fx;$ Compute the midpoint, the value of the function at the midpoint, and the product of the values of the function at l and x.

      if $z < 0$ If product is negative, search between l and x.

        then [$u \leftarrow x; fu \leftarrow fx;$ **to** *Midpoint*];

      if $z > 0$ If product is positive, search between x and u.

        then [$l \leftarrow x; fl \leftarrow fx;$ **to** *Midpoint*];

      if $z = 0$ If product is zero, $F(x)$ must be zero.

        then [**done;** "x is zero of F"];

FIGURE 18-2

lower limit of the interval. If $f(l) * f(x) = 0$, then $f(x) = 0$; and x is a zero.

    For reasons discussed in Chaps. 11 and 12, it is unlikely that $f(x)$ will be exactly zero even though it may come very close. So the procedure of Fig. 18-2 should be modified to provide an alternative test for termination. An intuitively desirable stopping rule would be that $-e < f(x) < +e$ or $|f(u) - f(l)| < e$, for some small e. However, if there is a discontinuity in the function, i.e., as u and l approach each other $f(u)$ and $f(l)$ move away from each other, this stopping rule would have difficulties. A second possible stopping rule would be $u - l < e$. When u and l get sufficiently close, stop searching. If u and l are large, the sparseness of floating-point representations for large numbers must be considered when setting e. This problem can be corrected by using $(u - l)/u < e$, where the difference is relativized with the divisor. But the vagaries of number representation can strike even here; for example, consider the case in which u is close to zero. Hamming (1971, p. 41) recommends stopping the procedure after 10 or 20 iterations as the simplest and safest rule.

Linear iteration

The roots of the equation $f(x) = 0$ may be found by algebraically transforming the equation into the form $g(x) = x$, evaluating $g(x)$ with a trial value of x to obtain a new trial value of x, using the new trial value of x to obtain another trial value, and so forth. This process can be represented by a function $y = g(x)$ and a straight line $y = x$ [see Fig. 18-3(a)].

    Consider the equation

$$x^2 - 5x + 4 = 0$$

This can be rearranged into the form

$$x = \frac{x^2 + 4}{5}$$

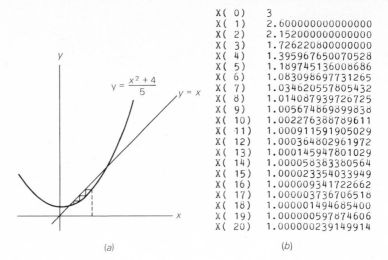

```
X( 0)    3
X( 1)    2.600000000000000
X( 2)    2.152000000000000
X( 3)    1.726220800000000
X( 4)    1.395967650070528
X( 5)    1.189745136008686
X( 6)    1.083098697731265
X( 7)    1.034620557805432
X( 8)    1.014087939726725
X( 9)    1.005674869899838
X( 10)   1.002276388789611
X( 11)   1.000911591905029
X( 12)   1.000364802961972
X( 13)   1.000145947801029
X( 14)   1.000058383380564
X( 15)   1.000023354033949
X( 16)   1.000009341722662
X( 17)   1.000003736706518
X( 18)   1.000001494685400
X( 19)   1.000000597874606
X( 20)   1.000000239149914
```

FIGURE 18-3
(a) **Graph of** $y=(x^2+4)/5$ **and** $y=x$;
(b) **successive values of** x **obtained with linear-iteration method for** $y=(x^2+4)/5$.

(a)

(b)

and this latter function is plotted in Fig. 18-3(a) as

$$y = \frac{x^2 + 4}{5}$$

along with the straight line $y = x$. As an example, if the initial value chosen for x, (x_0), is 3, then $g(x) = 13/5 = x_1$. For $x_1 = 13/5$, $g(x_1) \cong 2$. The results of continuing this process are given in Fig. 18-3(b).

A procedure for linear iteration is quite simple, a loop computing $g(x)$ with a stopping criterion for the number of iterations and for the proximity of successive values of x.

The two major considerations in using linear iteration are whether the process will converge to the root and the speed of convergence. The behavior of the process depends on the derivative $g'(x)$ of the function $g(x)$ when evaluated at x_0; Stark (1970, pp. 74–79) discusses the four possible cases:

1 When $g'(x)$ is between 0 and 1, the process converges monotonically from one side.
2 When $g'(x)$ is between -1 and 0, the process converges in an inward spiral around the root.
3 When $g'(x)$ is greater than 1, the process diverges monotonically. Consider what would happen if x was 10 in Fig. 18-3(a).
4 When $g'(x)$ is less than -1, the process diverges in an outward spiral around the root.

This process is not really recommended for root finding. It is presented so that it can be compared with better root-finding procedures and because it is the underlying rationale in the iterative procedure for solving systems of linear equations.

False position

While the linear-iteration method generates the next trial value of x from the line $y = x$, the false-position method generates the trial value of x by drawing a line from $(l, f(l))$ to $(u, f(u))$ and taking as the new value of x the intersection of that line with the x axis. The method is represented graphically in Fig. 18-4.

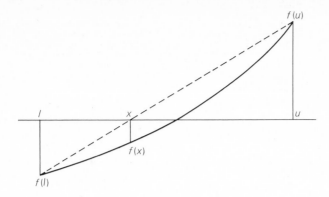

FIGURE 18-4
A graphic representation of the
false-position method.

The slope of this line (the dashed line in Fig. 18-4) is

$$m = \frac{f(u) - f(l)}{u - l} \qquad (1)$$

Another measure of the slope can be taken from the point $(x,0)$ (see Fig. 18-4)

$$m = \frac{f(u) - 0}{u - x} \qquad (2)$$

Solving Eq. (2) for x yields

$$x = u - \frac{f(u)}{m} \qquad (3)$$

Substituting the value of m from Eq. (1) into Eq. (3) and simplifying yields

$$x = \frac{l * f(u) - u * f(l)}{f(u) - f(l)} \qquad (4)$$

"False position search for real zeros";

    read $l, u;$ This procedure assumes $F(x)$ is available.

    $fl \leftarrow F(l);\ fu \leftarrow F(u);$

    if $fl * fu < 0$

        then [**to** *Newpoint*]

        else [**done;** "error"];

Newpoint:

        $x \leftarrow (l * fu - u * fl)/(fu - fl);$ This is the only change from the binary search procedure, i.e., the method of computing the trial value.

        $fx \leftarrow F(x);\ z \leftarrow fl * fx;$

        if $z < 0$

            then [$u \leftarrow x;\ fu \leftarrow fx;$ **to** *Newpoint*];

        if $z > 0$

            then [$l \leftarrow x;\ fl \leftarrow fx;$ **to** *Newpoint*];

        if $z = 0$

            then [**done;** "x is zero of F"];

FIGURE 18-5   **235**

where x is the next trial value of x generated by the false-position method, and is then taken as the new l or u, as appropriate. A TL procedure for the false-position method is given in Fig. 18-5. Note that the false-position procedure is identical to the binary search procedure (Fig. 18-2) except for the method of calculating the trial value of x.

The number of iterations is not a practical stopping rule for the false-position method because of the possibly relatively slow convergence of the method (see Fig. 18-6). One of the other stopping rules must be used. Because it tends to approach from one side and tends to converge slowly, the false-position method is generally inferior to the binary search method.

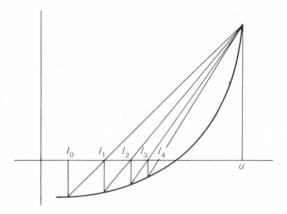

FIGURE 18-6
A slow convergence example with the false-position method.

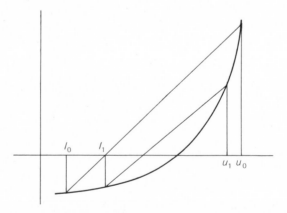

FIGURE 18-7
An example of the modified false-position method.

Hamming (1971, p. 47) suggests modifying the false-position method to improve its convergence by halving $f(l)$ when $f(u)$ is reset and halving $f(u)$ when $f(l)$ is reset (see Fig. 18-7). The two required changes are indicated in Fig. 18-8. Hamming says that this revised false-position method "is usually the most effective *simple* method to use so far as speed is concerned."

Newton-Raphson

While the false-position method approximates a curve with a secant, the Newton-Raphson method approximates the curve with a tangent (see Fig. 18-9).

. . .

if $z < 0$
    then $[u \leftarrow x; fu \leftarrow fx; fl \leftarrow fl/2;$ **to** *Newpoint*$];$
if $z > 0$
    then $[l \leftarrow x; fl \leftarrow fx; fu \leftarrow fu/2;$ **to** *Newpoint*$];$
. . .

FIGURE 18-8

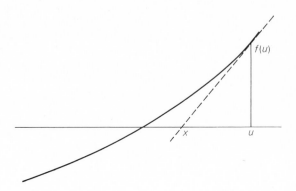

FIGURE 18-9
A graphic representation of the Newton-Raphson method.

The slope of the tangent at u is

$$m = \frac{f(u) - 0}{u - x} \tag{1}$$

Solving Eq. (1) for x gives

$$x = u - \frac{f(u)}{m} \tag{2}$$

These equations are the same as Eqs. (2) and (3) in the derivation for the false-position method. The slope of the tangent at u, that is, m, is equal to the value of $f'(u)$, so the new trial value for x is given by

$$x = u - \frac{f(u)}{f'(u)} \tag{3}$$

A TL procedure for the Newton-Raphson method is given in Fig. 18-10.

"Newton-Raphson search for real zeros";

    read $u; fu \leftarrow F(u);$
                                This procedure assumes that functions $F(x)$ and *F prime* (x) are available.

Newpoint:

    $x \leftarrow u - fu/Fprime\,(u);$ Compute new trial value.

    $fx \leftarrow F(x);$

    if $fx \neq 0$

      then $[u \leftarrow x; fu \leftarrow fx;$ **to** *Newpoint*$];$

    if $fx = 0$

      then $[$**done**; "x is zero of F"$];$

FIGURE 18-10

Newton's method has the advantage of possible fast convergence. In the general case, it has two major potential disadvantages: requiring the derivative of the function and being sensitive to the initial value of u. Obtaining the derivative may be impossible, difficult, or expensive. A poor choice of initial values may cause the method to diverge or converge on another root (Conte, 1965, p. 34).

When the function is a polynomial, the derivative is easily obtained, but the difficulties which can be caused by a poor choice of initial values and other potential difficulties can be easily seen. Three of the several cases which Conte (pp. 55–58) discusses are presented below.

1 When the value of the derivative is small near the zero of the polynomial, convergence will be slower and accuracy will be a

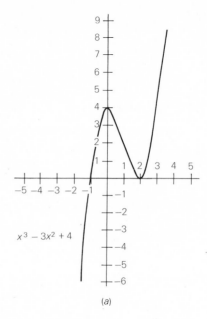

$x^3 - 3x^2 + 4$

(a)

Iteration	x	F(x)	F'(x)	F(x)/F'(x)
1	1.50000	0.625000000000000	−2.2500000000	−0.2777777778
2	1.77778	0.137174211248286	−1.1851851852	−0.1157407407
3	1.89352	0.032807598085912	−0.6048739712	−0.0542387334
4	1.94776	0.008045327791042	−0.3052685741	−0.0263549165
5	1.97411	0.001993189958784	−0.1533164496	−0.0130004964
6	1.98711	0.000496109842473	−0.0768257602	−0.0064575976
7	1.99357	0.000123758757285	−0.0384544003	−0.0032183250
8	1.99679	0.000030906390985	−0.0192375355	−0.0016065671
9	1.99840	0.000007722453327	−0.0096213460	−0.0008026375
10	1.99920	0.000001930096390	−0.0048113169	−0.0004011576
11	1.99960	0.000000482459549	−0.0024058193	−0.0002005386
12	1.99980	0.000000120606823	−0.0012029499	−0.0001002592
13	1.99990	0.000000030150698	−0.0006014850	−0.0000501271
14	1.99995	0.000000007537549	−0.0003007450	−0.0000250629
15	1.99997	0.000000001884372	−0.0001503731	−0.0000125313
16	1.99999	0.000000000471091	−0.0000751867	−0.0000062656
17	1.99999	0.000000000117772	−0.0000375933	−0.0000031328
18	2.00000	0.000000000029443	−0.0000187967	−0.0000015664
19	2.00000	0.000000000007361	−0.0000093983	−0.0000007832
20	2.00000	0.000000000001841	−0.0000046991	−0.0000003917
21	2.00000	0.000000000000460	−0.0000023490	−0.0000001960
22	2.00000	0.000000000000115	−0.0000011732	−0.0000000982

(b)

FIGURE 18-11
Newton-Raphson example 1.

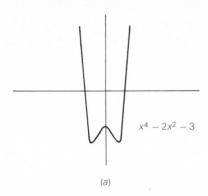

$$x^4 - 2x^2 - 3$$

(a)

Iteration	I x	II x	III x	IV x
1	2.000000	0.500000	-0.400000	-1.500000
2	1.791667	-1.791667	2.051190	-1.825000
3	1.735829	-1.735829	1.812273	-1.740843
4	1.732067	-1.732067	1.738709	-1.732139
5	1.732051	-1.732051	1.732102	-1.732051
6			1.732051	-1.732051

(b)

FIGURE 18-12
Newton-Raphson example 2.

problem. Consider the polynomial

$$x^3 - 3x^2 + 4$$

which is plotted in Fig. 18-11(a). The results obtained using double-precision floating-point arithmetic on the Xerox SIGMA 7 are presented in Fig. 18-11(b).

2 An initial value which may intuitively appear to be close to one zero of the polynomial may converge on another. Consider the polynomial

$$x^4 - 2x^2 - 3$$

which is plotted in Fig. 18-12(a). The results obtained for four different initial values appear in Fig. 18-12(b).

3 A poor choice of an initial value for u may cause the process to diverge. Conte offers the example

$$x^3 - x - 1$$

which is plotted in Fig. 18-13(a). The results obtained for the initial value of $u = 0$ appear in Fig. 18-13(b). The first few values of x are oscillating about the local maximum, $x = (-1/3)\sqrt{3}$, and Conte cites this as an example of failure to converge. However, if the process is permitted to run to 22 iterations, it does in fact converge. Conte's conclusions were based on using the program on a machine with a 36-bit word size while Fig. 18-13(c) was obtained using effectively a 64-bit word size, i.e., double-precision floating-point arithmetic on a 32-bit word.

Summary

Binary search and the modified false-position method are relatively sure and safe root-finding techniques and can be used by themselves or as preliminary methods for finding starting points for the Newton-Raphson technique. When the derivative is easily obtained and when the function is sufficiently well understood to avoid the problems of this method, the Newton-Raphson tech-

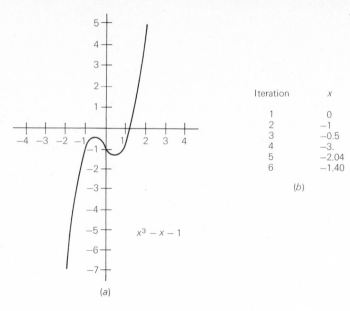

Iteration	x
1	0
2	−1
3	−0.5
4	−3.
5	−2.04
6	−1.40

(b)

Iteration	x	F(x)	F'(x)	F(x)/F'(x)
1	0.000000	−1.000000	−1.000000	1.000000
2	−1.000000	−1.000000	2.000000	−0.500000
3	−0.500000	−0.625000	−0.250000	2.500000
4	−3.000000	−25.000000	26.000000	−0.961538
5	−2.038462	−7.432010	11.465976	−0.648179
6	−1.390282	−2.296973	4.798653	−0.478670
7	−0.911612	−0.845971	1.493109	−0.566583
8	−0.345028	−0.696045	−0.642866	1.082722
9	−1.427751	−2.482679	5.115416	−0.485333
10	−0.942418	−0.894592	1.664455	−0.537469
11	−0.404949	−0.661456	−0.508048	1.301955
12	−1.706905	−4.266202	7.740570	−0.551148
13	−1.155756	−1.388072	3.007318	−0.461565
14	−0.694192	−0.640341	0.445707	−1.436686
15	0.742494	−1.333159	0.653893	−2.038802
16	2.781296	17.733717	22.206821	0.798571
17	1.982725	4.811763	10.793598	0.445798
18	1.536927	1.093519	6.086437	0.179665
19	1.357262	0.143034	4.526484	0.031599
20	1.325663	0.004034	4.272148	0.000944
21	1.324719	0.000004	4.264640	0.000001
22	1.324718	0.000000	4.264633	0.000000

(c)

FIGURE 18-13
Newton-Raphson example 3.

nique can converge more quickly than either binary search or modified false position. Since most modern medium- to large-scale computers come equipped with double-precision floating-point hardware, double-precision operations should be used routinely to reduce the frequency of cases in which roundoff errors do cause problems.

SOLUTION OF SIMULTANEOUS LINEAR EQUATIONS

This section is concerned with solutions to systems of equations of the general form of Fig. 18-14. Except for certain degenerate cases, there is a set of values for the x's which satisfies the system of equations. Two solution methods are presented: the method of elimination and the iterative method.

$$a(1,1) * x(1) + a(1,2) * x(2) + \cdots + a(1,n) * x(n) = b(1)$$
$$a(2,1) * x(1) + a(2,2) * x(2) + \cdots + a(2,n) * x(n) = b(2)$$
$$a(3,1) * x(1) + a(3,2) * x(2) + \cdots + a(3,n) * x(n) = b(3)$$
$$\cdots\cdots\cdots\cdots\cdots\cdots\cdots\cdots\cdots\cdots\cdots\cdots\cdots\cdots\cdots\cdots\cdots$$
$$a(n,1) * x(1) + a(n,2) * x(2) + \cdots + a(n,n) * x(n) = b(n)$$

FIGURE 18-14
General form of a system of simultaneous linear equations.

The method of elimination uses conventional algebraic manipulation (i.e., multiplying or dividing both sides of an equation by a constant, and adding or subtracting equations) to convert the general form of the system (Fig. 18-14) to a triangularized form (Fig. 18-15). (Note that except for the first row, the coefficients (a's) in the triangularized form will not be the same as those in the original form.) Then the value of $x(n)$ can be determined by dividing $b(n)$ by $a(n,n)$ and the value of $x(n-1)$ can be determined by substituting the value of $x(n)$ and doing straightforward algebraic simplification.

The method of elimination

$$a(1,1) * x(1) + a(1,2) * x(2) + a(1,3) * x(3) + \cdots + a(1,n) * x(n) = b(1)$$
$$0 \quad + a(2,2) * x(2) + a(2,3) * x(3) + \cdots + a(2,n) * x(n) = b(2)$$
$$0 \quad + \quad 0 \quad + a(3,3) * x(3) + \cdots + a(3,n) * x(n) = b(3)$$
$$\cdots\cdots\cdots\cdots\cdots\cdots\cdots\cdots\cdots\cdots\cdots\cdots\cdots\cdots\cdots\cdots\cdots$$
$$0 \quad + \quad 0 \quad + \quad 0 \quad + \cdots + a(n,n) * x(n) = b(n)$$

FIGURE 18-15
A triangularized form of a system of simultaneous linear equations.

One word of warning before proceeding. Because the rules of algebra do not really hold in computer arithmetic (see Chap. 12), arithmetic operations on numbers can and will introduce errors.

Consider the system of equations in Fig. 18-16(a). Instead of working with the full set of equations in the standard algebraic notation, it is usually more convenient to work with a 3×3 array of coefficients (the a's) and a 3×1 array of constants (the b's). The two arrays are typically concatenated into a 3×4 array [see Fig. 18-16(b)].

An example

a
$$2 * x(1) + 4 * x(2) + 6 * x(3) = 2$$
$$3 * x(1) + 9 * x(2) + 6 * x(3) = 18$$
$$4 * x(1) + 16 * x(2) + 20 * x(3) = 12$$

b

2	4	6	2
3	9	6	18
4	16	20	12

c

2	4	6	2
0	3	-3	15
0	8	8	8

d

2	4	6	2
0	3	-3	15
0	0	16	-32

e
$$x(3) = -32/16 = -2$$
$$x(2) = (15 - (-3 * -2))/3 = 3$$
$$x(1) = (2 - (6 * -2) - (4 * 3))/2 = 1$$

FIGURE 18-16
An example system of linear equations solved by the elimination method.

To eliminate the coefficient of $x(1)$ in Eq. (2), multiply Eq. (1) by 3 [the coefficient of $x(1)$ in Eq. (2)], divide the result by 2, and subtract each term in the result from Eq. (2). The result is in row 2 of Fig. 18-16(c).

To eliminate the coefficient of $x(1)$ in Eq. (3), multiply Eq. (1) by 4, divide by 2, and subtract each term in the result from Eq. (3). The result is in row 3 of Fig. 18-16(c).

To eliminate the coefficient of $x(2)$ in Eq. (3), multiply Eq. (2) [in Fig. 18-16(c)] by 8, divide it by 3, and subtract each term in the result from Eq. (3). The result is in row 3 of Fig. 18-16(d).

The back substitution and simplification required to obtain the values for the x's are shown in Fig. 18-16(e).

A procedure for the elimination method

The procedure for the elimination method (see Fig. 18-17) can be generalized from the preceding example. The data are represented in an augmented array of n rows and $n + 1$ columns.

"Elimination method";	Triangularize.
for $r \leftarrow 1$ **to** $n-1$	For all rows but last.
[**for** $r1 \leftarrow r+1$ **to** n	For all following rows.
[**for** $c \leftarrow n+1$ **to** r **by** -1	For all necessary columns.
$[a(r1, c) \leftarrow a(r1,c) - (a(r, c) * a(r1, r))/a(r,r)]]]$;	Compute the new value of the coefficient.
	Back substitution.
for $r \leftarrow n$ **to** 1 **by** -1	For all rows starting from the last.
$[x(r) \leftarrow a(r, n+1)$;	Start with the constant terms.
for $c \leftarrow r+1$ **to** n	For all columns greater than r.
$[x(r) \leftarrow x(r) - x(c) * a(r, c)]$;	Subtract the coefficient times the value of x.
$x(r) \leftarrow x(r)/a(r, r)]$;	Divide by coefficient of $x(r)$.

FIGURE 18-17

Row r is used to eliminate coefficient $a(r1,r)$ for $r1 = r+1$ to n, by subtracting $(a(r,c) * a(r1,r))/a(r,r)$ from each coefficient in each of these rows, i.e., from $a(r1,c)$. This fundamental operation is done for each column in each row after row r. Note that the column loop is done from $n+1$ to r by -1 to preserve the value of $a(r1,r)$. An alternative would have been to save the value of $a(r1,r)$ in a temporary variable.

After the array is triangularized, the back substitution is performed. Each $x(r)$ is initialized to $a(r,n+1)$, then the products $x(r+1) * a(r,r+1)$, $x(r+2) * a(r,r+2)$, etc., are subtracted, then the result is divided by $a(r,r)$:

$$x(r) \leftarrow (a(r,n+1) - a(r,r+1) * x(r+1) -$$
$$a(r,r+2) * x(r+2) - \cdots - a(r,n) * x(n))/a(r,r)$$

Improving the elimination method

Examination of the example and the procedure reveals the critical nature of the coefficients on the diagonal, that is, $a(1,1)$, $a(2,2)$, . . . ,$a(n,n)$. These are also called *pivotal elements* or *pivots*. Since the pivots are the divisors in the triangularization process, relatively small diagonal elements will produce large values of a's in the triangularized array and an increase in errors. The accuracy of the elimination method is improved by having relatively large pivots. Often the pivots can be made larger by rearranging the rows of the array. This technique is called *pivotal condensation*. The rows of the array are the equations of the system, and rearranging the equations will not disturb the solution of the system except for any increases in accuracy which may be obtained.

Pivotal condensation, the rearrangement of rows to obtain the largest pivots in each column, is demonstrated in Fig. 18-18. The previous example is reproduced in Fig. 18-18(a). The largest value in column 1 is in row 3, so rows 3 and 1 are interchanged [see Fig. 18-18(b)]. Row 1 is then used to eliminate the coefficients of x(1) in rows 2 and 3 [see Fig. 18-18(c)]. The largest value in column 2 from rows 2 and beyond is in row 3 [see Fig. 18-18(c)], and so rows 3 and 2 are interchanged [the result is shown in Fig. 18-18(d)]. Row 2 is then used to eliminate the coefficient of x(2) in row 3, and the triangularized matrix is shown in Fig. 18-18(e). The back substitution required to derive the values of x(3), x(2), and x(1) is shown in Fig. 18-18(f).

The example revisited

a	2	4	6	2
	3	9	6	18
	4	16	20	12
b	4	16	20	12
	3	9	6	18
	2	4	6	2
c	4	16	20	12
	0	−3	−9	9
	0	−4	−4	−4
d	4	16	20	12
	0	−4	−4	−4
	0	−3	−9	9
e	4	16	20	12
	0	−4	−4	−4
	0	0	−6	12

f
x(3)=12/−6=−2
x(2)=(−4−(−4*−2))/−4=3
x(1)=(12−(20*−2)−(16*3))/4=1

FIGURE 18-18
An example system of linear equations solved by the elimination method with pivoting.

The procedure for the elimination method with pivotal condensation (Fig. 18-19) is a straightforward extension of the procedure given in Fig. 18-17. Before eliminating the coefficients in column r in rows r + 1 to n, the procedure finds the largest coefficient in column r in rows r to n. If that coefficient is not in row r, that row and row r are exchanged. The rest of the procedure is the same as that in Fig. 18-17 and is not reproduced.

A procedure for pivotal condensation

"Elimination method with pivotal condensation";

for $r \leftarrow 1$ to $n-1$ Condense pivots and triangularize. For all rows but last.

     [$max \leftarrow$ **abs**$(a(r, r))$; $maxi \leftarrow r$;   This part of the procedure finds the largest coefficient in column r for all rows.

     for $r2 \leftarrow r+1$ to n

      [if **abs**$(a(r2, r)) > max$

        then [$max \leftarrow$ **abs**$(a(r2, r))$;

           $maxi \leftarrow r2$]];

    if $maxi \neq r$ If the coefficient in row r is not the largest one, swap the rows.

     then

       [for $r2 \leftarrow 1$ to $n+1$

       [$t \leftarrow a(r, r2)$;

       $a(r, r2) \leftarrow a(maxi, r2)$;

       $a(maxi, r2) \leftarrow t$]];

     [for $r1 \leftarrow r+1$ to n Continue with the elimination method program (Fig. 18-17).

      [for ...

FIGURE 18-19

Conte (1965, p. 160) presents a small example to illustrate the advantages of pivotal condensation. The original array is reproduced in Fig. 18-20(a) and the answers obtained using the elimination method and single-precision floating point with four-decimal-digit accuracy in the fraction are reproduced in Fig. 18-20(b). Quite a difference from the true values of $x(1) = 1.0$ and $x(2) = .25$. With the array rearranged to use the larger value in column 1 as the pivot [Fig. 18-20(c)] the answers are correct to four places [Fig. 18-20(d)]. Again the advantages of double-precision arithmetic can be seen in this example. Solving the system in Fig. 18-20(a) with double precision yields the answers in Fig. 18-20(b') showing errors in the fifteenth and sixteenth digits. Solving the rearranged system [Fig. 18-20(c)] with double precision yields answers correct to 16 places [Fig. 18-20(d')].

a	.2420 * 10↑−3	.6004 * 10↑−2	.1743 * 10↑−2
	.4000 * 10↑0	.9824 * 10↑1	.2856 * 10↑1
b	$x(1) = 1.021$	$x(2) = 0.2475$	
c	.4000 * 10↑0	.9824 * 10↑1	.2856 * 10↑1
	.2420 * 10↑−3	.6004 * 10↑−2	.1743 * 10↑−2
d	$x(1) = 1.000$	$x(2) = .2500$	
b'	$x(1) = 1.000000000000014$	$x(2) = .2499999999999994$	
d'	$x(1) = 1.000000000000000$	$x(2) = .2500000000000000$	

FIGURE 18-20
An example illustrating the advantages of pivotal condensation after Conte (1965, p. 160).

The iterative method

The linear-iteration method of root finding is the basis for the iterative method of solving a system of linear equations. The equation system of Fig. 18-14 is rewritten in the form of Fig.

$$x(1)=(b(1) \qquad\qquad -a(1,2)*x(2)-a(1,3)*x(3)-\cdots-a(1,n)*x(n))/a(1,1)$$
$$x(2)=(b(2)-a(2,1)*x(1) \qquad\qquad -a(2,3)*x(3)-\cdots-a(2,n)*x(n))/a(2,2)$$
$$x(3)=(b(3)-a(3,1)*x(1)-a(3,2)*x(2) \qquad\qquad -\cdots-a(3,n)*x(n))/a(3,3)$$

....

$$x(n)=(b(n)-a(n,1)*x(1)-a(n,2)*x(2)-a(n,3)*x(3)-\cdots \qquad\qquad /a(n,n)$$

FIGURE 18-21
A system of simultaneous linear equations arranged for iterative solution.

18-21. The process begins with the selection of an initial set of trial values for the x's, substituting this initial set of trial values into the equation system to generate another set of x's, substituting this set of x's into the system yields another set, and the process is repeated until the desired accuracy is achieved. Accuracy is usually measured in terms of relative distance of successive sets of x's, but this is not a foolproof measure.

A TL procedure for the iteration method is given in Fig. 18-22. Note the loop which limits the number of iterations. The evaluation of each equation is done similarly to back substitution in the elimination method. The stopping criteria are the number of iterations and the maximum of the relative discrepancies between successive values of x. If the number of iterations will be large, the procedure might be modified to print only every nth iteration.

"Iteration method";

Assume that x's are initialized, a's read in, and *tolerance* set.

Loop:

    maxdiff ← 0;   *maxdiff* initialized.

    for r ← 1 **to** n For all rows.

        [*old* ← $x(r)$;   Save old x.

        $x(r)$ ← $a(r, n+1)$;   Start with constant term.

          [**for** c ← 1 **to** n For all columns except

            [**if** $c \neq r$ column r.

            then

               [$x(r)$ ← $x(r)-x(c)*a(r, c)$]];   Calculate.

        $x(r)$ ← $x(r)/a(r, r)$;   Divide by coefficient of $x(r)$.

        diff ← **abs**($(old-x(r))/x(r)$);   Calculate difference between successive values of $x(r)$.

        if *diff* > *maxdiff*   Reset *maxdiff* if necessary.

          then [*maxdiff* ← *diff*]];

      if *maxdiff* > *tolerance*   Decision to continue or stop.

      then [**to** *Loop*]

      else [**done**];

FIGURE 18-22

Conte (1965, pp. 195–198) provides an example problem for the iterative method (see Fig. 18–23). In using Conte's examples earlier in this chapter, double-precision floating-point arithmetic has shown advantages over the single-precision floating point used by Conte to solve his example problems. But in this iterative method example, double-precision arithmetic

	1	2	3	4	5	6	7	8	9	10	11	12	13	14	15	16	17	18	19	20	21
1	2	−1																			1
2	−1	2	−1																		0
3		−1	2	−1																	0
4																					
5																					
6						...															
7							...														
8								...													
9									...												
10										...											
11											...										
12																					
13																					
14																					
15																					
16																					
17																					
18																					
19																					
20																			−1	2	1

FIGURE 18-23
Conte's example problem for the iteration method.

showed no advantage at all. Both arithmetic methods required the same number of iterations, 458, to reach the convergence criterion. The iterative method is quite insensitive to roundoff errors, hence, the reduction in roundoff errors provided by double-precision arithmetic does not help in this case (see Fig. 18-24).

The convergence conditions of the iteration method are understood but are not easily verified on the basis of inspection of the array. Pennington (1970) provides an interesting discussion

		x(10)	
ITERATION	*MAXDIFF*	*CONTE*	*DOUBLE PRECISION*
50	$0.16299034 * 10\uparrow-1$	0.58128624	0.5812863175496489
99	$0.36804064 * 10\uparrow-2$	0.86056850	0.8605686722751934
100	$0.35857904 * 10\uparrow-2$	0.86366542	0.8636655926734746
101	$0.34939157 * 10\uparrow-2$	0.86669358	0.8666937498321620
199	$0.34009875 * 10\uparrow-3$	0.98525032	0.9852505233398973
200	$0.33243365 * 10\uparrow-3$	0.98557796	0.9855781622323502
201	$0.32494229 * 10\uparrow-3$	0.98589832	0.9858985230898908
273	$0.63746723 * 10\uparrow-4$	0.99720190	0.9972021001806310
350	$0.11278326 * 10\uparrow-4$	0.99950363	0.9995038423719605
400	$0.36662780 * 10\uparrow-5$	0.99983843	0.9998386312792958
457	$0.10207755 * 10\uparrow-5$	0.99995495	0.9999551536610465
458	$0.99097087 * 10\uparrow-6$	0.99995594	0.9999561498595517

FIGURE 18-24
Single-precision and double-precision results on Conte's problem.

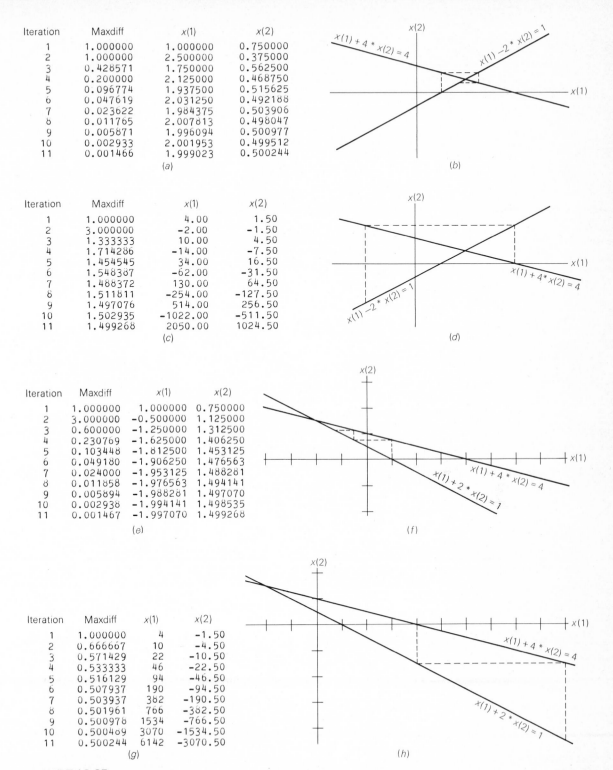

Iteration	Maxdiff	x(1)	x(2)
1	1.000000	1.000000	0.750000
2	1.000000	2.500000	0.375000
3	0.428571	1.750000	0.562500
4	0.200000	2.125000	0.468750
5	0.096774	1.937500	0.515625
6	0.047619	2.031250	0.492188
7	0.023622	1.984375	0.503906
8	0.011765	2.007813	0.498047
9	0.005871	1.996094	0.500977
10	0.002933	2.001953	0.499512
11	0.001466	1.999023	0.500244

(a)

(b)

Iteration	Maxdiff	x(1)	x(2)
1	1.000000	4.00	1.50
2	3.000000	-2.00	-1.50
3	1.333333	10.00	4.50
4	1.714286	-14.00	-7.50
5	1.454545	34.00	16.50
6	1.548387	-62.00	-31.50
7	1.488372	130.00	64.50
8	1.511811	-254.00	-127.50
9	1.497076	514.00	256.50
10	1.502935	-1022.00	-511.50
11	1.499268	2050.00	1024.50

(c)

(d)

Iteration	Maxdiff	x(1)	x(2)
1	1.000000	1.000000	0.750000
2	3.000000	-0.500000	1.125000
3	0.600000	-1.250000	1.312500
4	0.230769	-1.625000	1.406250
5	0.103448	-1.812500	1.453125
6	0.049180	-1.906250	1.476563
7	0.024000	-1.953125	1.488281
8	0.011858	-1.976563	1.494141
9	0.005894	-1.988281	1.497070
10	0.002938	-1.994141	1.498535
11	0.001467	-1.997070	1.499268

(e)

(f)

Iteration	Maxdiff	x(1)	x(2)
1	1.000000	4	-1.50
2	0.666667	10	-4.50
3	0.571429	22	-10.50
4	0.533333	46	-22.50
5	0.516129	94	-46.50
6	0.507937	190	-94.50
7	0.503937	382	-190.50
8	0.501961	766	-382.50
9	0.500978	1534	-766.50
10	0.500469	3070	-1534.50
11	0.500244	6142	-3070.50

(g)

(h)

FIGURE 18-25

of convergence for the two-equation system. Consider the two-equation system

$$x(1)-2*x(2)=1$$
$$x(1)+4*x(2)=4$$

The path of the iterative method is represented in Fig. 18-25(b). The initial values are $x(1) = x(2) = 0$. The successive values of the x's are given in Fig. 18-25(a) and graphed in Fig. 18-25(b). If the order of computation of the equations is interchanged to yield the system

$$x(1)+4*x(2)=4$$
$$x(1)-2*x(2)=1$$

the iteration process will diverge in an outward spiral as shown in Fig. 18-25(c) and (d).

If the slopes of both equations have the same sign, the iteration process will converge or diverge without spiraling. The system

$$x(1)+2*x(2)=1$$
$$x(1)+4*x(2)=4$$

is plotted in Fig. 18-25(f). The x values are tabled in Fig. 18-25(e). The system

$$x(1)+4*x(2)=4$$
$$x(1)+2*x(2)=1$$

is tabled and plotted in Fig. 18-25(g) and (h).

The convergence problems cannot be illustrated as easily for larger systems. A sufficient condition for convergence is

$$|a(r,r)| > \sum_{c=1}^{n} |a(r,c)| \text{ for all } r, c \neq r$$

or

$$|a(r,r)| > \sum_{r=1}^{n} |a(r,c)| \text{ for all } c, r \neq c$$

The absolute value of the diagonal element must be greater than the sum of the absolute values of all the row elements or column elements. So pivotal condensation can sometimes be helpful in achieving convergence in the iterative method. However, this condition is sufficient but not necessary, and the iterative method will also converge on systems which do not satisfy this condition.

Ill-conditioned systems

When relatively small changes in the values of coefficients or constant terms cause relatively large changes in the solution, the system of linear equations is said to be ill-conditioned. This ill-conditioning can result from the physical situation underlying (being represented by) the problem, the mathematical representation of that situation, the constant terms, and/or pivotal condensation (Hamming, 1971, pp. 117–123). One or more of these causes can result in what Hamming calls "almost linear dependency." Two equations are linear dependent if the equations differ from each other only by a multiplicative constant, in which case the elimination step of subtracting one from another would result in all coefficients becoming zero.

One test for ill-conditioning is to perturb the coefficients and constants slightly, resolve the system, and compare the answers. Since ill-conditioned systems are particularly prone to the loss of numerical accuracy, the user should treat the solution with special care.

Choice of solution methods

Either of the above solution methods for systems of linear equations can involve a large number of arithmetic operations, so consideration must be given to choices which will reduce the number of operations and, perhaps more important, the propagation of errors resulting from these operations. Conte (1965, p. 202) recommends use of the elimination method for small, dense systems and the iterative method for large ($n > 100$), sparse systems (many zero coefficients). While double precision can be helpful in some cases, it is not of any real value in the iterative method, nor will it help in cases of ill-conditioning.

EXERCISES

1 Finding the root(s) of a polynomial usually involves repeated evaluation of the polynomial. Thus, a root-finding program will have a step or steps equivalent to

$$Y \leftarrow X \uparrow 3 - 5.67 * X \uparrow 2 - 18.67 * X + 80 \qquad \textbf{(1)}$$

While this is a perfectly valid statement, there is a more efficient procedure. First, we factor X out of the first three terms of Eq. (1) and rewrite it as Eq. (2).

$$Y \leftarrow (X \uparrow 2 + 5.67 * X - 18.67) * X + 80 \qquad \textbf{(2)}$$

Next, factor X out of the first two terms:

$$Y \leftarrow ((X + 5.67) * X - 18.67) * X + 80 \qquad \textbf{(3)}$$

This method of representing the polynomial is called the *nesting method*.

Write a TL procedure to evaluate a polynomial using the nesting method of representation. What are the advantages of the nesting method over the straightforward approach? Compare the number of arithmetic operations involved with each method, treating exponentiation as repeated multiplication. What about roundoff errors?

2 Write a procedure to find square roots using the Newton-Raphson method (cf., exercise 3 in Chap. 9).

3 Write a procedure combining the binary search method and the Newton-Raphson method as suggested on p. 239.

4 Expand the nesting method for polynomial evaluation to include the calculation of the value of the derivative of the polynomial.

5 What would happen to either the elimination method or the iterative method for solving systems of linear equations if one of the coefficients on the diagonal were zero? How can the zero coefficient be eliminated? What if the zero coefficient cannot be eliminated?

6 The pivotal condensation technique used in this chapter reorders the rows. The pivots might be made even larger by moving columns too. Hamming (1971, p. 110) suggests that complete pivoting is not worth the extra effort involved. Comment.

7 In the Gauss-Jordan method for solving simultaneous linear equation systems all nondiagonal coefficients are reduced to zero, thereby eliminating the need for back substitution. Compare the amount of calculation involved in Gauss-Jordan and back substitution.

8 Solve the following two simultaneous linear equation systems

$$x(1) + 5 * x(2) = -17$$
$$1.5 * x(1) + 7.501 * x(2) = -25.503$$

$$x(1) + 5 * x(2) = -17$$
$$1.5 * x(1) + 7.501 * x(2) = -25.50$$

9 Use the elimination method for solving simultaneous linear equation systems as a subroutine in a procedure to check for ill-conditioned systems.

REFERENCES

Conte, S. D.: *Elementary Numerical Analysis: An Algorithmic Approach,* McGraw-Hill, New York, 1965.

Hamming, Richard W.: *Introduction to Applied Numerical Analysis,* McGraw-Hill, New York, 1971.

Pennington, Ralph H.: *Introductory Computer Methods and Numerical Analysis,* 2d ed., Macmillan, New York, 1970.

Stark, Peter A.: *Introduction to Numerical Methods,* Macmillan, New York, 1970.

SIMULATION AND RANDOM NUMBERS

Much, if not most, of scientific study and research consists of the development and study of models of "real world" processes. The "real world" situation can often be represented by the over-simplified schema of Fig. 19-1(*a*). To study the real world processes, the researcher uses the analogous model schema represented in Fig. 19-1(*b*).

MODELS AND THEIR REPRESENTATION
Models and the study of the real world

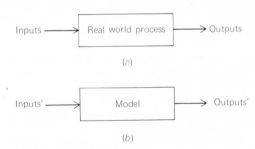

(*a*)

(*b*)

FIGURE 19-1
Paradigms for scientific study. (*a*) **Real world paradigm;** (*b*) **model paradigm.**

The researcher tries to develop a model whose behavior (outputs) is a close match to the behavior of the real world process (outputs') for comparable input stimuli. If the behavior of the model matches the behavior of the real world process, then the model can be used to predict the behavior of the real world process. For example, models of the economy can be used to predict the impact of taxes on inflation, and models of highway systems can be used to predict the impact of changes in road networks, speed limits, and size of vehicles.

How can anyone be sure that the predictions of a model are correct? Or, to put it another way, that the model is an adequate representation of the real world process? In a fundamental sense, the situation is no different than the problem of determining how you can trust a person. The researcher develops confidence in a model as the model demonstrates its ability to predict the behavior of the corresponding real world process. If a model of the economy makes correct predictions of gross national product for several years in a row, the researcher begins to believe that the model is trustworthy, i.e., a good representation of those aspects of the economy necessary to predict gross national product, and the researcher has greater confidence in the model's next prediction.

Representation of models

The model itself is a procedure, indistinguishable from and identical to the procedures which have been described in this book. While most of this book has been concerned with the development of procedures and their representation in the form of computer programs, procedures (models) can be represented in at least three other forms.

One form of representation is natural language. A prose description of a model is a perfectly good representation which is often easily communicated to others. But the imprecision of natural language and the lack of good techniques for analyzing the implications of a set of natural language statements (see Chap. 1) suggest that one of the following representations might be more useful.

A second form of representation is physical. It is often possible and useful to build a physical representation of a model and study the model by experimenting with the physical representation. The Forest Service studies forest fires and fire fighting on sand table models; the Corps of Engineers studies San Francisco Bay with a hydraulic model of the Bay; Prof. Abba Lerner used a model consisting of interconnected glass tubes filled with colored water to study the economy. Physical models are infrequently used because they are generally relatively inflexible representations, and the construction of physical models often requires considerable specialized talent and expense.

Symbolic representations of models are probably the most popular form of representation. Some of the symbolic representations are amenable to mathematical analysis; and so methods of analysis (often corresponding to the direct computation strategy of Chap. 8 or the numerical methods of Chap. 18) are used where possible to determine the behavior of these models. Mathematical analysis is usually a general and inexpensive analytic technique. It often has the virtue of being algorithmic in nature and, therefore, guarantees a solution.

A flexible and useful representation for models is a computer program. While techniques for the logical analysis of programs are just developing, the computer itself can be used to determine the behavior of models represented as programs. The real world process is simulated by running the program representation of the model. This technique is often called *computer simulation.*

Three simulations have been introduced in earlier chapters. In Chap. 8 two examples were used to introduce simulation as a problem-solving strategy: a program to simulate the movement of a billiard ball was developed and a program representing the birth and death processes specified in the Game of Life was constructed. In Chap. 13 a program representing the example computer was developed to enable the simulation of this tutorial computer's behavior on a real computer.

No model can be an exact replica in every detail of the real world process. We never completely understand the real world process, and so are limited to making inferences about its internal structure on the basis of experiments conducted by man or nature. In addition, in most cases it is impractical to construct exact replicas. We may operate a lunar rover in a simulated moon atmosphere, but we do not pretend to replicate the moon environment in all of its detail. Models are abstracts of reality; the trick is to capture the relevant aspects of reality in the model and ignore those aspects which are irrelevant for the problems under study. The catch is that the question of which aspects are relevant or irrelevant is often a part of the problems being studied.

In general, less elaboration is preferred to more in model construction. The simplest explanation consistent with the phenomenon being explained is preferred. This preference is sometimes referred to as the principle of Ockham's Razor.

However, the developer of models must be careful not to overdo simplicity. While simple models may be consistent with the data in a stable environment, only a more complex model may be able to predict behavior in a changed environment.

While this is not the appropriate place for a lengthy discussion of simple versus complex models, the reader should realize that the construction of models is an art, better known as the practice of science. Often the best question to ask is not whether model A is better than model B, but how can any model be improved so that it will predict better.

For present purposes we divide the processes that can take place in the world, and the outcomes that result from them, into two classes—deterministic and stochastic. Deterministic processes contain no random elements; they follow strictly determined rules, and their outcomes can be predicted. So we say that the sun will rise tomorrow; that if we dial a telephone number we will in fact get the number; that if we devise and test a procedure for doing binary search, it will work the next time we use it. The three simulations presented in previous chapters are simulations of deterministic processes. While some processes are difficult to represent, and sometimes it is difficult to keep track of the passage of time in a simulation (if that is important), no new programming concepts are required to simulate deterministic processes. (Of course, underlying what we choose to regard as a deterministic process may be randomness as in the behavior of the molecules making up the billiard ball. But for the purposes of our interests, the process can be viewed as deterministic.)

Because stochastic processes (sometimes called *probabilistic processes*) involve random elements, the exact outcome of these processes cannot necessarily be predicted with great confidence even when we can specify the set of possible events and can predict the frequency of their occurrence. Common examples of such processes often involve games of chance. Coin tossing is a stochastic process. While either a head or a tail may occur, and for a fair coin each event will occur about half of the time, one cannot predict with certainty which event will occur on any particular toss. Rolling dice is a similar process. And many aspects of genetics, of the behavior of atoms, and of the behavior of animals and human beings can be approximated by stochastic processes. (Of course, underlying what we choose to regard as a stochastic process may be a set of deterministic rules that we do not understand or that are too detailed to be represented, but for the purpose of our interests, the process can be viewed as stochastic.)

The game "Monopoly" is a familiar attempt to represent the real world in a board game. The occurrence of events in the real world depends on many factors; and some believe that a stochastic process can represent the real world process that generates these events. "Monopoly" replaces the stochastic process "real world" with another stochastic process "rolling dice." Most of the actions in playing "Monopoly" are deterministic, but to completely represent "Monopoly" with a computer program one would have to develop a procedure to simulate the throwing of dice. Similarly, to represent any stochastic process, one would have to develop a procedure to simulate that process. The major difference in developing programs for deterministic and stochastic simulations is the need to include in the latter a procedure for generating a sequence of random events. The major difference in using the results of deterministic and stochastic simulations is in determining what meaning to give in the latter to particular simulation outcomes, dependent as they are on random events.

RANDOM NUMBERS
A sequence of random events

A good synonym for random is patternless. A sequence of events is random if it does not exhibit any patterns or regularities that can be used to predict successive events in the sequence.

In operational terms, a sequence of events is judged to be random if the sequence can pass certain tests. One set of tests examines the frequency of each event in the sequence. The observed frequency of each event in the sequence is compared to the expected frequency for that event. For example, in a uniform distribution, each event is equally likely; so if the sequence is supposed to be a uniform distribution of the digits 0–9, then each of these digits should occur about as frequently as every other digit. The exact meaning of "about" in this context is usually resolved by using a statistical test to measure the "goodness of fit" of the expected frequencies and the observed frequencies. The frequency test is a necessary condition for randomness, but it is not a sufficient condition. The sequence of decimal digits 01234567890123456789 . . . satisfies the frequency test for a uniform distribution of digits 0–9, i.e., all digits are equally likely, but it clearly has a pattern, namely $digit(t) = (digit(t-1)+1)$ (modulo 10). Thus a sequence being tested for patterns should also be tested for relations between successive events in the sequence. There are some problems in selecting which relations to test for. Since different applications may be sensitive to different sequential relations, each user of purportedly random sequences should devise tests appropriate to his own application.

In the early part of this century, random sequences were obtained by using devices employed in games of chance, e.g., decks of cards, dice, urns of balls. The slowness of these procedures and reservations about their ability to generate random sequences led to the development of tables of random digits. Early tables were generated from census reports; later tables were developed using special machinery to record the outcomes of random physical phenomena. The desire to use random sequences in computer programs resulted in a shift of emphasis from tables to procedures for generating random sequences. Because of their size, the tables were quite impractical for use with computers.

The most frequently used algorithm for generating random sequences is of the form:

$$x(j) \leftarrow [a * x(j-1)+c] \ (\text{mod } m)$$

To use this algorithm, select three positive integers, $x(0)$, a, and c. Then $x(1)$ is obtained from the expression given above. $x(2)$ is generated in the same manner from $x(1)$, and so forth. Thus, if $x(0)$ were 1, a were 3141592621, and c were 2113248654051871, $x(1)$ would be 2113251795644492. The x's are usually divided by m to create random fractions between 0 and 1.

Now it is obvious that neither this nor any other algorithm can generate a random sequence, for $x(j)$ will be related to $x(j-1)$ by precisely the relationship defined by the algorithm. Hence, the qualification of random-number generators by the prefix "pseudo." But with appropriate values of a, c, and m, this procedure generates a sequence of numbers which will pass the standard tests for randomness.

While the casual requirements of most computer users for random numbers are adequately met by the random-number-generating functions provided in higher-level programming languages or subroutine libraries, some users may have to develop their own random-number generators if the standard ones are inappropriate for a particular problem.

Knuth (1969, pp. 1–160) presents an encyclopedic review of random-number generation and testing. To give the reader some feeling for the problem, we reproduce in Fig. 19-2 Knuth's summary (pp. 155–156) of the six "rules" to use in developing a random-number generator. The parenthetical references to sections in Fig. 19-2 are references to particular sections in Knuth's book. In paragraph v the number in brackets is the value referred to.

This information is presented in the spirit of consumer protection. Much has been written about the generation of random numbers with computers. Some things are known; many old

The detailed investigations in this chapter suggest that the following procedure gives the "nicest" and "simplest" random-number generator: At the beginning of the program, set an integer variable X to some value X_0. This variable X is to be used only for the purpose of random-number generation. Whenever a new random number is required by the program, set

$$X \leftarrow (aX+c) \bmod m \tag{1}$$

and use the new value of X as the random value. It is necessary to choose X_0, a, c, and m properly, and to use the random numbers wisely, according to the following principles:

i) The number X_0 may be chosen arbitrarily. If the program is run several times and a different source of random numbers is desired each time, set X_0 to the last value attained by X on the preceding run; or (if more convenient) set X_0 to the current date and time.

ii) The number m should be large. It may conveniently be taken as the computer's word size, since this makes the computation of $(aX+c)$ mod m quite efficient. Section 3.2.1.1 discusses the choice of m in more detail. The computation of $(aX+c)$ mod m must be done *exactly*, with no roundoff error.

iii) If m is a power of 2 (i.e., if a binary computer is being used), pick a so that a mod $8 = 5$. If m is a power of 10 (i.e., if a decimal computer is being used), choose a so that a mod $200 = 21$. This choice of a together with the choice of c given below ensures that the random-number generator will produce all m different possible values of X before it starts to repeat (see Section 3.2.1.2) and ensures high "potency" (see Section 3.2.1.3).

iv) The multiplier a should be larger than $\sqrt{m}$, preferably larger than $m/100$, but smaller than $m - \sqrt{m}$. The digits in the binary or decimal representation of a should *not* have a simple, regular pattern; for example, see Section 3.2.1.3 and exercise 3.2.1.3–8. The best policy is to take some haphazard constant to be the multiplier, such as

$$a = 3141592621 \tag{2}$$

(which satisfies both of the conditions in (iii)). These considerations will almost always give a reasonably good multiplier; but if the random-number generator is to be used extensively, the multiplier a should also be chosen so that it passes the "spectral test" (Section 3.3.4).

v) The constant c should be an odd number (when m is a power of 2) and also not a multiple of 5 (when m is a power of 10). It is preferable to choose c so that c/m has approximately the value given in Section 3.3.3, Eq. (41).

[0.21132 48654 05187 1]

vi) The least significant (right-hand) digits of X are not very random, so decisions based on the number X should always be primarily influenced by the most significant digits. It is generally best to think of X as a random fraction X/m between 0 and 1, that is, to visualize X with a decimal point at its left, than to regard X as a random integer between 0 and $m - 1$. To compute a random integer between 0 and $k - 1$, one should multiply by k and truncate the result (see the beginning of Section 3.4.2).

FIGURE 19-2
Knuth's six principles for random-number generators.

wives' tales are still around. We urge the reader who makes extensive use of random-number generators to beware. Random-number generators, including those provided with higher-level languages, sometimes behave in unexpected manners. Before making any really important computation, such as simulating a moon shot or a stock market strategy, the user is well-advised to test the statistical properties of the random-number generator in his own simulation situation.

As we indicated above, two characteristics of uniformly distributed random sequences of numbers are (1) that each number occurs about as often as every other number and (2) that numbers are not simply related to earlier numbers in the sequence.

The first characteristic, equal frequency, can be examined by counting the frequency of each number or more commonly each class of numbers. If the numbers generated by the random-number function are divided into 10 classes on the basis of magnitude, a sequence of 1,000 numbers might yield the results indicated in Fig. 19-3. Are the frequencies in each of the cells in Fig. 19-3 sufficiently close to the expected values of 100 to enable us to say that the sequence is random?

This question is usually rephrased by statisticians in the following form: What is the probability (likelihood) that a sample with these frequencies in the 10 classes could be drawn from a population with a uniform distribution, i.e., equal frequencies in each of the 10 classes? In more concrete terms, consider an urn with a very large number of balls each having a number between 0 and 1. Stir the balls well, draw a ball out of the urn, look at the number, add one to the frequency count in the appropriate class, replace the ball in the urn, and repeat. After drawing 1,000 balls, start a new frequency table. Continue until you have drawn many samples of 1,000. What is the possibility that the frequencies in Fig. 19-3 could be generated in such a fashion?

Testing sequences of numbers for randomness

$f(j)$

Range	0–.1	.1–.2	.2–.3	.3–.4	.4–.5	.5–.6	.6–.7	.7–.8	.8–.9	.9–1.0	Σ
Frequency	104	92	83	91	109	87	93	115	113	113	1,000

FIGURE 19-3
Frequency of random fractions in 10 classes.

This question is usually answered by computing some statistic (function) of the observed sample and determining the probability that a sample with that statistic could have been randomly drawn from a population with equal frequencies. A statistic commonly used for this purpose is the sum of the squares of the differences between the actual frequencies and the expected frequencies divided by the expected frequencies. Where the expected frequencies are 100, the formula for this statistic, which we shall call $c(1)$, is

$$c(1) = \tfrac{1}{100} \sum_{j=1}^{10} (f(j) - 100)^2$$

where $f(j)$ is the frequency in each cell. $c(1)$ is used because it is a good intuitive measure of goodness of fit and because it has the same distribution as χ^2 and the distribution of χ^2 is known (tables of χ^2 are given in most statistics texts). The $c(1)$ of the data in Fig. 19-3 is distributed as χ^2 with 9 degrees of freedom. Degrees of freedom is a parameter of the χ^2 distribution. In this case if the total of the frequencies is fixed at 1,000, nine of the frequencies are free to vary and the tenth is just 1,000 less the sum of the other nine.

By using a table of the χ^2 distribution, we can determine that if $c(1)$ has a value > 16.9, it is unlikely (probability$=.05$) that the sequence is random, i.e., that it was drawn from a population having equal frequencies in each class.

One test of the second characteristic (absence of simple sequential relations) can be conducted by counting the frequencies of consecutive pairs of numbers. Thus if the x's are again divided into 10 classes, successive but not overlapping pairs, $x(j)$ and $x(j + 1)$, $x(j + 2)$ and $x(j + 3)$, etc., can be divided into 100 classes as in Fig. 19-4. A sequence of 2,000 numbers will yield 1,000 nonoverlapping pairs. The expected value in each one of these cells in Fig. 19-4 is 10. Whether the frequencies in any given table of this type are sufficiently close to their expected value to enable us to say that the sequence is random is usually answered by computing

$$c(2) = \tfrac{1}{10} \sum_{j,k=1}^{10} (f(j,k) - 10)^2$$

$c(2)$ is distributed as χ^2 with a number of degrees of freedom equal to one less than the number of categories. In the case discussed here, there would be 99 degrees of freedom. If $c(2)$ is > 123, it is unlikely (probability $= .05$) that the sequence is random, i.e., that it was drawn from a population having equal frequencies of pairs.

$f(j,k)$

$x(j)$ \ $x(j+1)$	0–.1	.1–.2	.2–.3	.3–.4	.4–.5	.5–.6	.6–.7	.7–.8	.8–.9	.9–1.0	Σ
0–.1	14	7	9	13	12	8	10	5	18	9	105
.1–.2	8	4	8	11	8	4	10	14	12	13	92
.2–.3	7	12	4	4	11	11	8	7	8	11	83
.3–.4	8	6	9	10	11	12	10	8	6	11	91
.4–.5	13	9	10	11	16	10	7	10	9	14	109
.5–.6	8	13	4	7	11	10	5	11	10	8	87
.6–.7	13	8	9	8	5	5	12	13	10	9	92
.7–.8	9	6	14	7	10	10	11	21	14	13	115
.8–.9	14	13	7	8	9	7	11	15	15	14	113
.9–1.0	10	14	9	12	16	10	9	11	11	11	113
Σ	104	92	83	91	109	87	93	115	113	113	1000

FIGURE 19-4
Frequency of successive pairs of random fractions.

In using the χ^2 statistic, there are two things to remember: the frequency in each cell should be greater than 5 and preferably greater than 10, and the frequencies should be independent—the reason for using nonoverlapping pairs in computing $c(2)$.

For a comprehensive discussion of tests of random-number generators, the reader is referred to Knuth (1969, pp. 34–99).

The dice game of craps has the following rules. The player rolls two dice.

- a If the player rolls 7 or 11, he wins.
- b If the player rolls 2, 3, or 12 on the first roll, he loses.
- c If the player rolls any other combination on the first roll, the number becomes his "point." He continues rolling until either he again rolls his point, in which case he wins, or he first rolls 7, in which case he loses.

(See also exercise 9, Chap. 9.)

Aside from considerations of betting strategy, the critical part of a simulation of the game of craps is the simulation of the roll of the dice. The simulator can most likely ignore such aspects as the dice cup (if one is used), blowing on the hands, and other activities like the chants of the roller, and safely assume that rolling a pair of dice is a random process in which each die will show each of its six sides, i.e., the numbers 1, 2, 3, 4, 5, 6, with approximately equal frequency over some reasonable number of rolls.

So the simulation requires a process which will generate the numbers 1, 2, 3, 4, 5, and 6 with equal probability. Most higher-level languages provide a random-number generator which will generate random fractions uniformly distributed between 0 and 1. These fractions can be translated into the integers 1–6 by the following statement

$$d1 \leftarrow \textbf{int}(6 * \textbf{rnd} + 1)$$

where **rnd** is the function which generates random fractions.

The roll of the second die can be represented by a similar statement

$$d2 \leftarrow \textbf{int}(6 * \textbf{rnd} + 1)$$

Note that each time **rnd** is executed it provides a "different" fraction. Using these two statements to simulate the roll of the dice, the program to play craps follows directly (see Fig. 19-5).

A stat-rat

In this example, the real world process being studied is a rat in a T maze. The situation is represented schematically in Fig. 19-6. (See also exercises 10 and 11 of Chap. 10.) Psychologists design experiments to explore the behavior of rats in the T-maze environment. The rat is deprived of food, placed at the "start" point in the maze, and permitted to run, presumably in search of food. If the food is always placed at the end of the right arm of the maze, the rat learns to turn right at the decision point. If the food is placed in the left arm, the rat learns to turn left. What happens if

"Craps procedure";

Start:

    sum ← *Roll;*   First roll.

    if *sum* = 7 **or** *sum* = 11

      then to *Win;*

    if *sum* = 2 **or** *sum* = 3 **or** *sum* = 12

      then to *Lose;*

Point: Second and succeeding rolls.

    rl ← *Roll;*

    if *sum* = *rl*

      then to *Win;*

    if *sum* = 7

      then to *Lose;*

    to *Point;*

Win:

    "Adjust bets"; **to** *Start;*   This is place to make adjustments to
                                    stake and place new bets.

Lose:

    "Adjust bets"; **to** *Start;*

Roll: Roll dice procedure.

    [*d1* ← **int**(6 * **rnd** + 1);

    d2 ← **int**(6 * **rnd** + 1);

FIGURE 19-5   **return** (*d1* + *d2*)];

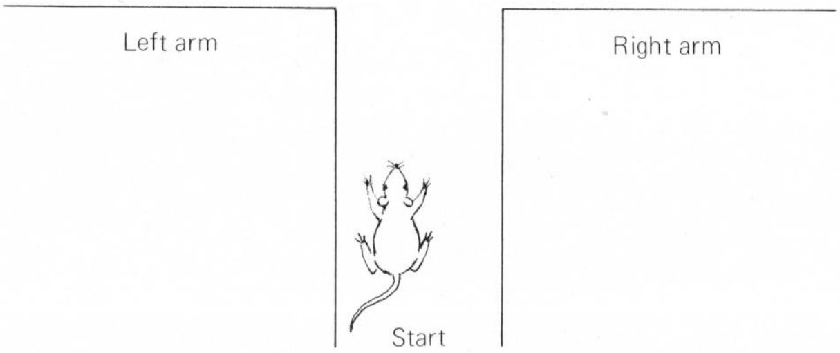

FIGURE 19-6
Schematic representation of a rat in a T maze.

sometimes the food is placed on the left and sometimes the food is placed on the right? To answer this question, we need a model of rat behavior.

    The following simple stat-rat (short for "statistical rat") model is consistent with some aspects of the observed behavior of rats (and people) in the situation where food (or some other reward) is sometimes placed on the left and sometimes placed on the right:

If food was in the right-hand arm of the maze on trial $t-1$, the probability $p(t)$ that stat-rat will go right on trial t is $a * p(t-1)+(1-a)$. If food was on the left on trial $t-1$, the probability $p(t)$ that stat-rat will go right is $a * p(t-1)$.

The model can be summarized in two conditional statements:

If food in right arm on trial $t-1$,
$$p(t) \leftarrow a * p(t-1)+(1-a)$$
If food in left arm on trial $t-1$,
$$p(t) \leftarrow a * p(t-1)$$

$p(t)$ is the probability of the rat turning right at the choice point on trial t; a is a parameter between 0 and 1. For many purposes, assigning a value of approximately .9 to a will be satisfactory.

The stat-rat with $a = .9$ is a simple-minded creature whose probability of turning right increases when food has been on the right and decreases when food shows up on the left. If $p(1)$ is .5 and food is placed on the right in trial 1, then $p(2) = .45 + .1 = .55$. If on trial 2, food is placed on the left, $p(3) = .495$. The more often food is placed on one side the less the impact of the placement.

All of this information must be incorporated into the simulation program. The simulation program has two parts: The "experimenter" makes decisions about food placement and keeps records of the stat-rat's behavior. The stat-rat behaves according to the model described above. A TL version of the simulation program is presented in Fig. 19-7.

"Stat-rat procedure";

$t \leftarrow 1$; $p(t) \leftarrow .5$; *Experimenter;*   Trial 1 is treated separately because there is not any preceding event.

for $t \leftarrow 2$ **to** 100   This iteration statement controls the number of trials in the experiment.

  [**if** $e(t-1)=$"right"   Test on last event.

    then

      [$p(t) \leftarrow a * p(t-1)+(1-a)$]   Adjust $p(t)$ if "right."

    else

      [$p(t) \leftarrow a * p(t-1)$];   Adjust $p(t)$ if "left."

    Experimenter];   Determine the event.

done;

Experimenter:

  [**if rnd** $> .5$

    then [$e(t) \leftarrow$"right"]

    else [$e(t) \leftarrow$"left"]];

FIGURE 19-7

Although this example is quite simple, it contains all elements of most stochastic simulations. The loop on t is the clock. The statements included in the brackets define what happens in one clock tick (cycle or trial). The stat-rat's propensity to turn right is modified as a result of the food placement on the previous trial. Then the experimenter places the food on the basis of "flipping a fair coin." While the random-number generator could be used in conjunction with $p(t)$ to simulate the actual turn decision, the actual behavior of the stat-rat, right turn or left turn, need not really be simulated because that behavior does not affect any other part of the simulation, that is, $p(t)$ does not depend on the actual behavior on previous trials, only on $p(t-1)$. Records of probability of turning and of food placement are kept in the p and e arrays, but the program could be augmented to record additional data.

Testing the simulation model

In deterministic simulations the model can be checked by directly comparing the behavior of the model to the behavior of the real world process. Where does the billiard ball go when it is hit with a certain force in a certain direction from a certain initial position? And where does the model say it will go? Where the model is not a model of a real world process but rather a model of some idealized process, the program's behavior can be compared to the results obtained by hand simulation (following the rules of the model without the aid of the computer).

Testing stochastic simulations is more difficult. Because of the nature of stochastic processes, the exact outcomes cannot be predicted. One alternative is to compare certain summary statistics, e.g., the average value of p for the stat-rat on trials 75–100 with the average number of right turns made by rats over trials 75–100. The stat-rat is obviously a typical or average rat, and so it is appropriate to compare its behavior to the average behavior of many (how many?) rats. But the behavior of the stat-rat is a function of the sequence of food placements. Perhaps the stat-rat should be run on several different sequences of food placements to determine how it reacts to classes of food placement sequences. The parameter "a" or other aspects of the model might be changed to try to improve the match between "real" behavior and "model" behavior.

Testing models where the behavior of the model is a function of the previous behavior of the model [as in the stat-rat where $p(t)$ is a function of $p(t-1)$] complicates matters. The predictions of the model for trial-by-trial behavior are not independent and, therefore, any comparisons of "real" behavior and "model" behavior on sequences of trials are not independent comparisons. Where practicable, it is better to set the model back on the track [e.g., substitute the percentage of rats which turn right on trial t in this experiment for the model's estimate of $p(t)$ to avoid the accumulation of errors]. The problem created by an accumulation of errors which could result from not setting the model back on the track is similar to the problems of accumulation of roundoff errors.

Summary

The representation of a model as a computer program and the use of the computer to determine the implications of the model has opened up new vistas for the model builder. A program is a very flexible medium for representing a model, and the computer is a powerful tool for exploring the behavior of the model.

But the use of programs and computers does not solve all of the model builder's problems. The model builder is still faced with three basic problems.

1 *The development of the basic ideas of the model.* The program is only a form of representation. The model builder has to determine what is to be represented and how. The program as a medium provides great flexibility. It gives the model builder a magnificent palette, but he or she must still decide on the basic concepts of the model and how they are to be represented.

2 *The refinement of the ideas.* Getting the bugs out of a model is like getting the bugs out of a program. However, in debugging programs the programmer usually has a correct algorithm he is trying to represent. The debugging of a model is really an effort in the development or improvement of the algorithm.

3 *The testing of the model.* The behavior of the model is compared to the behavior of the real world process during the development of the model. And the model builder has to be able to make comparisons which will contribute to the improvement of the model. After the development stage, the model is tested on other data. The testing begins with the determination of the goodness-of-fit of the behavior of the model to the behavior of the real world process. Since there is no absolute criterion for goodness-of-fit, the goodness-of-fit measures of several alternative models are compared. One of the alternative models is usually some simplistic random process.

EXERCISES

1 Describe a real world process and a model of that process. List the inputs and the outputs for both the process and the model. What aspects of the process are left out of the model? How was the model developed? How was it or could it be tested?

2 Test one of the random-number generators in the computing system available to you by computing the frequency of occurrence of each of the leftmost digits in the first 1,000 random fractions generated, i.e., develop a table comparable to Fig. 19-3. Develop a table comparable to Fig. 19-4 to check for sequential patterns. Compute $c(1)$ and $c(2)$ and determine the probability of those values by consulting a table of values of χ^2. What other tests could be used to check the random-number generator?

3 Some random-number generators permit the programmer to provide an arbitrary value for $x(0)$ on the basis of the time of day in order to be able to generate different sequences of random numbers. If a random-number generator has neither of these capabilities, that is, $x(0)$ is the same every time the **rnd** is initialized, how could you generate different sequences of random numbers?

4 Use a conventional random-number generator which generates a uniform distribution (every number equally likely) to

generate a nonuniform distribution, e.g.,

NUMBER	PROBABILITY
1	1/55
2	2/55
3	3/55
. . .	. . .
10	10/55

5 Why cannot the craps simulation be modified to generate a number between 1 and 12 with the expression **int**(12 * **rnd** + 1) rather than use **int**(6 * **rnd** + 1) twice? How would you simulate the role of two dice with one random number?

6 In generating sequences of food placements for the stat-rat experiment, some psychologists prefer to have x right-hand placements in every block of 10 rather than $x * 10$ percent right-hand placements in a series of 100 placements. Program an event generator to make 7 right-hand placements out of every 10 events.

7 Write a program to simulate the dealing of a deck of cards. What is the least number of random fractions you have to generate to deal 52 cards?

8 Run a two-choice experiment—rats in a T maze or people predicting a sequence of binary symbols. How well does the stat-rat model predict the data? How could you change the model to improve the fit?

9 Modify the craps program to check for biases in the dice.

REFERENCES

Dutton, John M., and William H. Starbuck (eds.): *Computer Simulation of Human Behavior,* Wiley, New York, 1971.

Emshoff, J. R., and Roger L. Sisson: *Design and Use of Computer Simulation Models,* Macmillan, New York, 1970.

Forester, Jay W.: *Industrial Dynamics,* MIT Press, Cambridge, Mass., and Wiley, New York, 1961.

Knuth, Donald: *The Art of Computer Programming,* vol. 2, *Seminumerical Algorithms,* Addison-Wesley, Reading, Mass., 1969.

Martin, Francis F.: *Computer Modeling and Simulation,* Wiley, New York, 1968.

Naylor, Thomas H., J. L. Balintfy, D. S. Burdick, and Chu Kong: *Computer Simulation Techniques,* Wiley, New York, 1966.

Tocher, K. D.: *The Art of Simulation,* English Universities Press, London, 1961.

APPENDIXES

SUMMARY OF TL

† May be of form: ⟨string⟩ **@** (⟨number⟩)
     or: ⟨string⟩ **@** (⟨number⟩, ⟨number⟩)
†† Of equal precedence.

Expressions may be enclosed in parentheses. ( ) **45**

TRANSLITERATIONS OF EXAMPLE PROGRAMS

In this appendix, we present transliterations into several common programming languages of a number of the program segments given in Chaps. 5 to 7. All transliterations are into a specific implemented version of the language in question and have been debugged and run on the specified system. Please read these transliterations with the following considerations in mind.

1 We have tried to make the transliterations simple and straight-forward, and in so doing have not taken full advantage of the special features and characteristic programming styles of each language. In some cases, the example programs could not be transliterated in a reasonable manner because of the nature of the target language, and in such cases we have discussed the relevant restrictions.

2 These examples were not intended as complete programs, but rather were introduced to illustrate specific points in the text. For example, they typically do not include such checks on the acceptability of input data as tests for zero value or for end-of-file on input. Also, the examples themselves do not include all of the "setup" statements necessary to translate and execute them in actual implementations, such as END statements in FORTRAN or the statements necessary to call and print out values from those examples which are subprocedures.

3 Many of the target languages as formally defined contain no provision for handling strings or for input-output. Thus, what is presented in the transliteration incorporates the "local conventions" of a specific implementation. This specificity is a necessary part of ensuring by execution that the transliterations are correct.

We believe that these examples provide a sufficient foundation from which the reader can produce his own translations of other programs in the text, and from which he can develop for his own use the special features and style appropriate to the target language.

B.1 TL TO ALGOL Following are transliterations of example programs into ALGOL-60 as implemented on the PDP-10. (Reference document:

Decsystem10 ALGOL Programmer's Reference Manual, DEC-10-KAZB-D, Digital Equipment Corporation, 1972.)

"Reverse a word";

"This program reads in a word and writes out that word spelled backwards";

```
read word;
    rev ← "";
    until word = ""
    [rev ← word @ (1,1) & rev; word ← word @ (2)];
    write rev;
```

CHAPTER 5, EXAMPLE 1

```
BEGIN
    COMMENT REVERSE A WORD;
    COMMENT THIS PROGRAM READS IN A WORD AND
                    WRITES OUT THAT WORD SPELLED BACKWARDS;
    STRING WORD,REV; INTEGER I,L;
    READ(WORD);
    REV: = COPY(WORD);
    L: = LENGTH(WORD);
    FOR I: = L,I − 1 WHILE I > Ø DO
            REV.[L + 1 − I]: = WORD.[I];
    WRITE(REV);
END;
```

"Find greatest common divisor";

"This program reads in two numbers, *a* and *b*, and writes out their greatest common divisor found using Euclid's algorithm. The program uses the function **int**, which returns as its value the largest integer not greater than its input. The program assumes that the two numbers read in are positive integers. The program uses variable z as the remainder on division";

```
    read a,b;
    if a < b then to Bigb else to Biga;
Biga:
    z ← a − b * int(a/b);
    if z = 0 then write b else [a ← z; to Bigb]; done;
Bigb:
    z ← b − a * int(b/a);
    if z = 0 then write a else [b ← z; to Biga]; done;
```

CHAPTER 5, EXAMPLE 2

```
BEGIN
    COMMENT FIND GREATEST COMMON DIVISOR;
    COMMENT THIS PROGRAM READS IN TWO NUMBERS . . . ;
    INTEGER A,B,Z;
    READ(A,B);
    IF A < B THEN GOTO BIGB ELSE GOTO BIGA;
    BIGA: Z: = A − B * ENTIER(A/B);
            IF Z = Ø THEN PRINT(B)
                    ELSE BEGIN A: = Z;
                                GOTO BIGB
                        END;
            GOTO DONE;
    BIGB: Z: = B − A * ENTIER(B/A);
            IF Z = Ø THEN PRINT(A)
                    ELSE BEGIN B: = Z;
                                GOTO BIGA
                        END;
            GOTO DONE;
    DONE: COMMENT END OF PROGRAM;
END;
```

Figure 6-1 is identical to Chapter 5, Example 2 except for the first comment.

"Greatest common divisor − version 2";

```
    read a,b;
    if a < b
        then [z ← a; a ← b; b ← z];
Loop:
    z ← a − b * int(a/b);
    if z = 0
        then write b
        else [a ← b; b ← z; to Loop];
    done;
```

FIGURE 6-2

```
BEGIN
    COMMENT GREATEST COMMON DIVISOR − 2;
    INTEGER A,B,Z;
    READ(A,B);
    IF A < B THEN BEGIN Z: = A;A: = B;B: = Z END;
    LOOP: Z: = A − B * ENTIER(A/B);
            IF Z = Ø THEN PRINT(B)
                    ELSE BEGIN A: = B;B: = Z;GOTO LOOP END;
END;
```

269

"Greatest common divisor—version 3";

```
    read a,b;
    z←a;
    if a<b
      then [a←b; b←z];
    until z=0
      [z←a−b * int(a/b);
       a←b; b←z];
    write a;
```

FIGURE 6-4

```
BEGIN
  COMMENT GREATEST COMMON DIVISOR−3;
  INTEGER A,B,Z;
  READ(A,B);
  Z:=A;
  IF A<B THEN BEGIN A:=B;B:=Z END;
  FOR Z:=A−B * ENTIER(A/B) WHILE Z>∅ DO
                       BEGIN A:=B;B:=Z END;
  PRINT(B);
END;
```

"Reverse a word—version 2";

```
    read word;
    rev←"";
    for i←1 thru #word
      [rev←word @ (i,1) & rev];
    write rev;
```

FIGURE 6-5

```
BEGIN
  COMMENT REVERSE A WORD−VERSION 2;
  STRING WORD,REV; INTEGER I,L;
  READ(WORD);
  REV:=COPY(WORD);
  L:=LENGTH(WORD);
  FOR I:=1 UNTIL L DO
      REV.[L+1−I]:=WORD.[I];
  WRITE(REV);
END;
```

"Greatest common divisor—version 4";

Gcd(a,b):

```
    [local z; z←a;
    if a<b
      then [a←b; b←z];
    until z=0
      [z←a−b * int(a/b);
       a←b; b←z];
    return a]
```

FIGURE 6-6

```
COMMENT GREATEST COMMON DIVISOR−VERSION 4;
INTEGER PROCEDURE GCD(A,B);
  VALUE A,B; INTEGER A,B;
  BEGIN INTEGER Z; Z:=A;
        IF A<B THEN BEGIN A:=B;B:=Z END;
        FOR Z:=A−B * ENTIER(A/B) WHILE Z>∅ DO
                         BEGIN A:=B;B:=Z END;
        GCD:=B;
  END;
```

"Reverse a word—version 3";

Reverse(word):

```
    [local rev; rev←"";
    until word=""
      [rev←word @ (1,1) & rev;
       word←word @ (2)];
    return rev]
```

FIGURE 6-7

```
COMMENT REVERSE A WORD−VERSION 3;
STRING PROCEDURE REVERSE(WORD);
  STRING WORD;
  BEGIN STRING REV; INTEGER I,L;
        REV:=COPY(WORD);
        L:=LENGTH(WORD);
        FOR I:=L,I−1 WHILE I>∅ DO
            REV.[L+1−I]:=WORD.[I];
        REVERSE:=COPY(REV);
  END;
```

"Greatest common divisor—version 5";

Gcd(a,b):

    [**if** $a < b$

      then [**return** Gcd(b,a)]

      else

        [$a \leftarrow a - b *$ **int**(a/b);

        if $a = 0$

          then return b

          else return Gcd(b,a)]]

```
COMMENT GREATEST COMMON DIVISOR—VERSION 5;
INTEGER PROCEDURE GCD(A,B);
   VALUE A,B; INTEGER A,B;
   BEGIN IF A < B THEN GCD:=GCD(B,A)
              ELSE BEGIN A:=A−B * ENTIER(A/B);
                        IF A=Ø THEN GCD:=B
                                ELSE GCD:=GCD(B,A)
              END;
   END;
```

FIGURE 6-8

The nature of string concatenation in DECsystem10 ALGOL is such that Fig. 6-9 is not easily transliterated into that implementation. Therefore, Fig. 6-9 is omitted from the appendix.

"Greatest common divisor—version 6";

Gcd(a,b):

    [**local** z;

    $z \leftarrow$ **mod** (**max**(a,b), **min**(a,b));

    if $z = 0$

      then return min(a,b)

      else return Gcd(**min**(a,b),z)]

```
COMMENT GREATEST COMMON DIVISOR—VERSION 6;
INTEGER PROCEDURE GCD(A,B);
   VALUE A,B; INTEGER A,B;
   BEGIN INTEGER Z;
        Z:=IMAX(A,B) REM IMIN(A,B);
        IF Z=Ø THEN GCD:=IMIN(A,B)
               ELSE GCD:=GCD(IMIN(A,B),Z);
   END;
```

FIGURE 6-11

"Add the first n integers—version 1";

    $sum \leftarrow 0$; $integer \leftarrow 0$;

Loop:

    if $integer \geq n$

      then write sum

      else

        [$integer \leftarrow integer + 1$;

        $sum \leftarrow sum + integer$;

        to Loop];

```
BEGIN
   COMMENT ADD THE FIRST N INTEGERS—VERSION 1;
   INTEGER SUM,INT;
   SUM:=INT:=Ø;
   LOOP: IF INT >=N THEN PRINT(SUM)
                    ELSE BEGIN INT:=INT+1;
                              SUM:=SUM+INT;
                              GOTO LOOP
                         END;
END;
```

(a)

"Add the first n integers—version 2";

    $sum \leftarrow 0$;

    for $integer \leftarrow 1$ **thru** n

      $sum \leftarrow sum + integer$;

    write sum;

```
BEGIN
   COMMENT ADD THE FIRST N INTEGERS—VERSION 2;
   INTEGER SUM,INT;
   SUM:=Ø;
   FOR INT:=1 UNTIL N DO SUM:=SUM+INT;
   PRINT(SUM);
END;
```

(b)

FIGURE 7-2

Note that both of the above program segments assume that a value for N has been assigned.

"Find the earliest and latest words";

$e \leftarrow w(1); l \leftarrow w(1); j \leftarrow 2$

Loop:

  if $j > n$

    then write e, "through", l

    else

      [**if** $w(j) < e$

        then $e \leftarrow w(j)$;

      if $w(j) > l$

        then $l \leftarrow w(j)$;

      $j \leftarrow j+1$;

      to *Loop*];

```
BEGIN
  COMMENT FIND THE EARLIEST AND LATEST WORDS;
  INTEGER E,L;
  E:=L:=W[1];J:=2;
  LOOP: IF J>N THEN BEGIN PRINT(E);PRINT(L) END
              ELSE BEGIN IF W[J]<E THEN E:=W[J];
                         IF W[J]>L THEN L:=W[J];
                         J:=J+1; GOTO LOOP
              END
END;
```

FIGURE 7-6

Note that this program segment assumes values for the array W
and for N are already assigned.

"Read in and total questionnaire data";

for $i \leftarrow 1$ **thru** 20

  for $j \leftarrow 1$ **thru** 10

    $count\ (i,j) \leftarrow 0$;

for $j \leftarrow 1$ **thru** 10

  for $k \leftarrow 1$ **thru** 31

    for $i \leftarrow 1$ **thru** 20

      [**read** *mark*;

      $count\ (i,j) \leftarrow count\ (i,j)$

           $+ mark$];

```
COMMENT READ IN AND TOTAL QUESTIONNAIRE DATA;
INTEGER ARRAY COUNT[1:2Ø,1:1Ø];INTEGER I,J,K,MARK;
REAL AVE;
FOR I:=1 UNTIL 2Ø DO
  FOR J:=1 UNTIL 1Ø DO
    COUNT[I,J]:=Ø;
FOR J:=1 UNTIL 1Ø DO
  FOR K:=1 UNTIL 31 DO
    FOR I:=1 UNTIL 2Ø DO
      BEGIN READ(MARK);COUNT[I,J]:=COUNT[I,J]+MARK;
      END;
```

FIGURE 7-9

"Compute average count";

for $i \leftarrow 1$ **thru** 20

  [$ave \leftarrow 0$;

  for $j \leftarrow 1$ **thru** 10

    $ave \leftarrow ave + count\ (i,j)$;

  write "for item", i, "ave=", $ave/10$];

```
COMMENT COMPUTE AVERAGE COUNT;
FOR I:=1 UNTIL 2Ø DO
  BEGIN AVE:=Ø;
        FOR J:=1 UNTIL 1Ø DO AVE:=AVE+COUNT[I,J];
        AVE:=AVE/1Ø;
        PRINT(I);PRINT(AVE)
  END;
```

FIGURE 7-10

Following are transliterations of example programs into Xerox APL as implemented on the SIGMA 6/7/9 computers. (Reference document: *Xerox APL Language and Operations Reference Manual*, 90 19 31B, Xerox Corporation, 1973.)

"Reverse a word";

"This program reads in a word and writes out that word spelled backwards";

   read *word;*

   rev ← "";

   until *word* = ""

      [*rev* ← *word* **@** (1,1) **&** *rev; word* ← *word* **@** (2)];

   write *rev;*

```
[1]    ⍝ REVERSE A WORD
[2]    ⍝ THIS PROGRAM READS IN A WORD AND
[3]    ⍝ WRITES OUT THAT WORD SPELLED BACKWARDS
[4]    WORD ← ⎕
[5]    REV ← "
[6]    LOOP: → (0 = ρWORD)/END
[7]    REV ← WORD[1],REV
[8]    WORD ← 1 ↓ WORD
[9]    → LOOP
[10]   END:REV
```

Since the APL language contains a number of powerful operators for processing sequences of data items, programs can often be written in a much more compact form in APL than in most other languages. We shall present straightforward transliterations for most of the examples in this appendix, thus not using these more powerful features. But it would be remiss not to point out that the above program segment could be replaced by the following APL program:

```
[1]    ⌽⎕
```

CHAPTER 5, EXAMPLE 1

"Find greatest common divisor";

"This program reads in two numbers, *a* and *b*, and writes out their greatest common divisor found using Euclid's algorithm. The program uses the function **int**, which returns as its value the largest integer not greater than its input. The program assumes that the two numbers read in are positive integers. The program uses variable *z* as the remainder on division";

   read *a,b;*

   if *a* < *b* **then to** *Bigb* **else to** *Biga;*

Biga:

   z ← *a* − *b* * **int**(*a/b*);

   if *z* = 0 **then write** *b* **else** [*a* ← *z;* **to** *Bigb*]; **done;**

Bigb:

   z ← *b* − *a* * **int**(*b/a*);

   if *z* = 0 **then write** *a* **else** [*b* ← *z;* **to** *Biga*]; **done;**

CHAPTER 5, EXAMPLE 2

Figure 6-1 is identical to Chapter 5, Example 2 except for the first comment.

```
[1]    ⍝ FIND GREATEST COMMON DIVISOR
[2]    ⍝ THIS PROGRAM READS IN TWO NUMBERS . . .
[3]    A ← ⎕
[4]    B ← ⎕
[5]    → (A < B)/BIGB
[6]    BIGA:Z ← B | A
[7]    → (Z = 0)/WRITEB
[8]    A ← Z
[9]    BIGB:Z ← A | B
[10]   → (Z = 0)/WRITEA
[11]   B ← Z
[12]   → BIGA
[13]   WRITEB:B
[14]   → 0
[15]   WRITEA:A
[16]   → 0
```

"Greatest common divisor—version 2";

```
    read a,b;
    if a < b
        then [z←a; a←b; b←z];
Loop:
    z←a−b * int(a/b);
    if z=0
        then write b
        else [a←b; b←z; to Loop];
    done;
```

```
[1]     ⍺ GREATEST COMMON DIVISOR—VERSION 2
[2]     A←□
[3]     B←□
[4]     →(A ≥ B)/LOOP
[5]     Z←A
[6]     A←B
[7]     B←Z
[8]     LOOP:Z←B|A
[9]     →(Z=0)/WRITEB
[10]    A←B
[11]    B←Z
[12]    →LOOP
[13]    WRITEB:B
```

FIGURE 6-2

"Greatest common divisor—version 3";

```
    read a,b;
    z←a;
    if a < b
        then [a←b; b←z];
    until z=0
        [z←a−b * int(a/b);
         a←b; b←z];
    write a;
```

```
[1]     ⍺ GREATEST COMMON DIVISOR—VERSION 3
[2]     A←□
[3]     B←□
[4]     Z←A
[5]     →(A ≥ B)/NEXT
[6]     A←B
[7]     B←Z
[8]     NEXT:→(Z=0)/WRITEA
[9]     Z←B|A
[10]    A←B
[11]    B←Z
[12]    →NEXT
[13]    WRITEA:A
```

FIGURE 6-4

"Reverse a word—version 2";

```
    read word;
    rev←"";
    for i←1 thru #word
        [rev←word @ (i,1) & rev];
        write rev;
```

```
[1]     ⍺ REVERSE A WORD—VERSION 2
[2]     WORD←⍞
[3]     REV←"
[4]     I→1
[5]     L←ρWORD
[6]     FOR:→(I > L)/WRITEREV
[7]     REV←(⁻1 ↑ I ↑ WORD),REV
[8]     I←I+1
[9]     →FOR
[10]    WRITEREV:REV
```

FIGURE 6-5

"Greatest common divisor—version 4";
Gcd(a,b):

```
    [local z; z←a;
     if a < b
        then [a←b; b←z];
     until z=0
        [z←a−b * int(a/b);
         a←b; b←z]
     return a]
```

```
[1]     ⍺ GREATEST COMMON DIVISOR—VERSION 4
[2]     Z←A
[3]     →(A ≥ B)/UNTIL
[4]     A←B
[5]     B←Z
[6]     UNTIL:→(Z=0)/0
[7]     Z←B|A
[8]     A←B
[9]     B←Z
[10]    →UNTIL
```

FIGURE 6-6

"Reverse a word—version 3";

Reverse(word):

   [**local** rev; rev ← "";

   until word = ""

     [rev ← word **@** (1,1) **&** rev;

     word ← word **@** (2)];

     return rev]

FIGURE 6-7

```
       ∩ REVERSE A WORD—VERSION 3
[2]    REV ← "
[3]    UNTIL: → (0 = ρWORD)/0
[4]    REV ← WORD[1],REV
[5]    WORD ← 1 ↓ WORD
[6]    → UNTIL
```

"Greatest common divisor—version 5";

Gcd(a,b):

   [**if** a < b

     then [**return** Gcd(b,a)]

     else

       [a ← a − b * **int**(a/b);

      if a = 0

        then return b

        else return Gcd(b,a)]]

FIGURE 6-8

```
       ▽ B ← A GCD B
[1]    ∩ GREATEST COMMON DIVISOR—VERSION 5
[2]    → (A < B)/GCDBA
[3]    A ← B|A
[4]    → (A = 0)/0
[5]    GCDBA:B ← B GCD A
       ▽
```

"Reverse a word—version 4";

Reverse(word):

   [**if** word = ""

     then return ""

     else return Reverse(word **@** (2)) **&** word **@** (1,1)]

FIGURE 6-9

```
       ▽ REV ← REVERSE WORD
[1]    ∩ REVERSE A WORD—VERSION 4
[2]    → (0 = ρWORD)/ρREV ← "
[3]    REV ← (REVERSE 1 ↓ WORD),1 ↑ WORD
       ▽
```

"Greatest common divisor—version 6";

Gcd(a,b):

   [**local** z;

   z ← **mod** (**max**(a,b), **min**(a,b));

   if z = 0

     then return min(a,b)

     else return Gcd(min(a,b),z)]

FIGURE 6-11

```
       ▽ R ← A GCD B;Z
[1]    ∩ GREATEST COMMON DIVISOR—VERSION 6
[2]    Z ← (A⌊B)|A⌈B
[3]    → (Z = 0)/0 × R ← A⌊B
[4]    R ← Z GCD A⌊B
       ▽
```

In the examples from Chap. 7, we shall make use of some of the more powerful APL operators rather than just doing a straight-forward transliteration from TL.

"Add the first *n* integers—version 1";

    sum ← 0; integer ← 0;

Loop:

    if *integer* ≥ *n*

        then write *sum*

        else

        [*integer* ← *integer* + 1;

        sum ← *sum* + *integer*;

        to *Loop*];

              (*a*)

FIGURE 7-2

"Add the first *n* integers—version 2";

    sum ← 0;

    for *integer* ← 1 **thru** *n*

      sum ← *sum* + *integer*;

    write *sum*;

         (*b*)

[1] ⍝ *ADD THE FIRST N INTEGERS*
[2] +/ιN

"Find the earliest and latest words";

    e ← *w*(1); *l* ← *w*(1); *j* ← 2

Loop:

    if *j* > *n*

      then write *e*, "through", *l*

      else

        [**if** *w*(*j*) < *e*

          then *e* ← *w*(*j*);

        if *w*(*j*) > *l*

          then *l* ← *w*(*j*);

        j ← *j* + 1;

        to *Loop*];

FIGURE 7-6

[1] ⍝ *FIND THE EARLIEST AND LATEST WORDS*
[2] *RANK* ← ⍋*W*
[3] *W*[1 ↑ *RANK*];' *THROUGH* ';*W*[⁻1 ↑ *RANK*]

"Read in and total questionnaire data";

for *i* ← 1 **thru** 20

    for *j* ← 1 **thru** 10

    count (*i,j*) ← 0;

for *j* ← 1 **thru** 10

  for *k* ← 1 **thru** 31

  for *i* ← 1 **thru** 20

    [**read** *mark*;

    count (*i,j*) ← *count* (*i,j*)

        + *mark*];

FIGURE 7-9

[1] ⍝ *READ IN AND TOTAL QUESTIONNAIRE DATA*
[2] *COUNT* ← +/[2]10 31 20ρ⎕

"Compute average count";

for *i* ← 1 **thru** 20

  [*ave* ← 0;

  for *j* ← 1 **thru** 10

    ave ← *ave* + *count* (*i,j*);

  write "for item", *i*, "ave =", *ave*/10];

FIGURE 7-10

[1] ⍝ *COMPUTE AVERAGE COUNT*
[2] *AVE* ← +/[1]*COUNT*
[3] '*FOR ITEM* ';ι20
[4] '*AVE*   =';*AVE* ÷ 10

Following are transliterations of example programs into Xerox Data Systems UTS BASIC. (Reference document: *Xerox BASIC: Language and Operations Reference Manual,* 90 15 46D, Xerox Data Systems, 1971.) In those cases where Digital Equipment Corporation PDP11 BASIC-Plus differs from UTS BASIC, transliterations into BASIC-Plus are also given. [Reference document: *PDP-11 Resource Time-Sharing System (RST-11) User's Guide, BASIC-PLUS Programming Language,* PL-11-71-01-01-A-D, Digital Equipment Corporation, 1972.]

"Reverse a word";

"This program reads in a word and writes out that word spelled backwards";

```
    read word;
    rev ← "";
    until word = ""
        [rev ← word @ (1,1) & rev; word ← word @ (2)];
    write rev;
```

```
10     REM REVERSE A WORD
20     REM THIS PROGRAM READS IN A WORD AND WRITES OUT
30     REM THAT WORD SPELLED BACKWARDS
40     INPUT $W
50     $R = "
60     IF $W = " THEN 100
70     $R = $W(:1,1) + $R
80     $W = $W(:2)
90     GOTO 60
100    PRINT $R
```

In PDP11 BASIC-Plus this program would be:

```
10     REM REVERSE A WORD
20     REM THIS PROGRAM READS IN A WORD AND WRITES
30     REM OUT THAT WORD SPELLED BACKWARDS
40     INPUT W$
50     R$ = ""
60     IF W$ = "" THEN 100
70     R$ = LEFT(W$,1) + R$
80     W$ = RIGHT(W$,2)
90     GO TO 60
100    PRINT R$
```

CHAPTER 5, EXAMPLE 1

"Find greatest common divisor";

"This program reads in two numbers, a and b, and writes out their greatest common divisor found using Euclid's algorithm. The program uses the function **int**, which returns as its value the largest integer not greater than its input. The program assumes that the two numbers read in are positive integers. The program uses variable z as the remainder on division";

```
    read a,b;
    if a < b then to Bigb else to Biga;

Biga:
    z ← a − b * int(a/b);
    if z = 0 then write b else [a ← z; to Bigb]; done;

Bigb:
    z ← b − a * int(b/a);
    if z = 0 then write a else [b ← z; to Biga]; done;
```

```
10     REM FIND GREATEST COMMON DIVISOR
20     REM THIS PROGRAM READS IN TWO NUMBERS...
60     INPUT A,B
70     IF A < B THEN 140
80     Z = A − B * INT(A/B)
90     IF Z = 0 THEN 120
100    A = Z
110    GO TO 140
120    PRINT B
130    STOP
140    Z = B − A * INT(B/A)
150    IF Z = 0 THEN 180
160    B = Z
170    GO TO 80
180    PRINT A
```

CHAPTER 5, EXAMPLE 2

Figure 6-1 is identical to Chapter 5, Example 2 except for the first comment.

"Greatest common divisor—version 2";

```
    read a,b;
    if a < b
        then [z ← a; a ← b; b ← z];
Loop:
    z ← a − b * int(a/b);
    if z = 0
        then write b
        else [a ← b; b ← z; to Loop];
    done;
```

```
5    REM GREATEST COMMON DIVISOR—VERSION 2
10   INPUT A,B
20   IF A>=B THEN 60
30   Z=A
40   A=B
50   B=Z
60   Z=A−B * INT(A/B)
70   IF Z=Ø THEN 11Ø
80   A=B
90   B=Z
100  GO TO 6Ø
110  PRINT B
```

FIGURE 6-3

"Greatest common divisor—version 3";

```
    read a,b;
    z ← a;
    if a < b
        then [a ← b; b ← z];
    until z = 0
        [z ← a − b * int(a/b);
        a ← b; b ← z];
    write a;
```

```
1Ø   REM GREATEST COMMON DIVISOR—VERSION 3
2Ø   INPUT A,B
3Ø   Z=A
4Ø   IF A>=B THEN 7Ø
5Ø   A=B
6Ø   B=Z
7Ø   IF Z=Ø THEN 12Ø
8Ø   Z=A−B * INT(A/B)
9Ø   A=B
1ØØ  B=Z
11Ø  GO TO 7Ø
12Ø  PRINT A
```

FIGURE 6-4

(Both the BASIC programs in Figs. 6-3 and 6-4 can be shortened without changing their effect. Do you see how?)

"Reverse a word—version 2";

```
    read word;
    rev ← "";
    for i ← 1 thru #word
        [rev ← word @ (i,1) & rev];
    write rev;
```

```
1Ø   REM REVERSE A WORD—VERSION 2
2Ø   INPUT $W
3Ø   $R="
4Ø   L=LEN($W)
5Ø   FOR I=1 TO L
6Ø   $R=$W(:I,1)+$R
7Ø   NEXT I
8Ø   PRINT $R
```

In BASIC-Plus, this program would be:

```
10   REM REVERSE A WORD—VERSION 2
20   INPUT W$
30   R$="
40   FOR I=1 TO LEN(W$)
50   R$=MID(W$,I,1)+R$
60   NEXT I
70   PRINT R$
```

FIGURE 6-5

The BASIC language allows definition of simple "one line" functions. Also, a simple form of block evocation can be achieved using the GOSUB statement and ending the block with a RETURN statement. However, BASIC has no concept of multiple arguments, local variables, or returning a value from a multi-statement function. Therefore, Figs. 6-6 to 6-9 and 6-11 cannot be translated directly into BASIC.

However, in order to illustrate the use of GOSUB, RETURN, we include the following version of Fig. 6-6. Note that A, B, and Z are common to all parts of the BASIC program which includes this segment; there are no local variables or arguments. The subroutine would be evoked by assigning values to A and B and then executing GOSUB 200, and the evoking program would expect the subroutine to assign the value of the g.c.d. to variable A.

```
"Greatest common divisor—version 4";      200   REM GREATEST COMMON DIVISOR—VERSION 4
Gcd(a,b):                                  210   Z=A
                                           220   IF  A>=B THEN 250
    [local z; z←a;                         230   A=B
                                           240   B=Z
    if a<b                                 250   IF Z=0 THEN 280
      then [a←b; b←z];                     260   Z=A−B * INT(A/B)
    until z=0                              270   GO TO 230
      [z←a−b * int(a/b);                   280   RETURN
      a←b; b←z];

    return a]
```

FIGURE 6-6

The above comments do not hold for BASIC-Plus, which allows both multiple-line function definitions and recursive functions. Transliterations into BASIC-Plus of Figs. 6-6 to 6-9 and 6-11 follow.

```
200   REM GREATEST COMMON DIVISOR—VERSION 4
210   DEF FNG(A,B)
220   Z=A
230   IF A>=B THEN 250
240   A=B: B=Z
250   IF Z=0 THEN 280
260   Z=A−B * INT(A/B)
270   GO TO 240
280   FNG=A
290   FNEND
```

FIGURE 6-6 (continued)

```
"Reverse a word—version 3";        300   REM REVERSE A WORD—VERSION 3
  Reverse(word):                   310   DEF FNR$(W$)
                                   320   R$=""
    [local rev; rev←"";            330   IF W$="" THEN 370
    until word=""                  340   R$=LEFT(W$,1)+R$
      [rev←word @ (1,1) & rev;     350   W$=RIGHT(W$,2)
      word←word @ (2)];            360   GO TO 330
    return rev]                    370   FNR$=R$
                                   380   FNEND
```

FIGURE 6-7

"Greatest common divisor—version 5";

Gcd(a,b):

    [**if** a < b

        then [**return** Gcd(b,a)]

        else

            [a ← a − b * **int**(a/b);

            if a = 0

                then return b

                else return Gcd(b,a)]]

FIGURE 6-8

```
200   REM GREATEST COMMON DIVISOR—VERSION 5
210   DEF FNG(A,B)
220   IF A<=B THEN 260
230   A=A−B * INT(A/B)
250   IF A=0 THEN FNG=B ELSE 260
255   GO TO 270
260   FNG=FNG(B,A)
270   FNEND
```

"Reverse a word—version 4";

Reverse(word):

    [**if** word = ""

        then return ""

        else return Reverse(word **@** (2)) **&** word **@** (1,1)]

FIGURE 6-9

```
300   REM REVERSE A WORD—VERSION 4
310   DEF FNR$(W$)
320   IF W$="" THEN FNR$="" ELSE FNR$=FNR$(RIGHT(W$,2))+
                                              LEFT(W$,1)
330   FNEND
```

"Greatest common divisor—version 6";

Gcd(a,b):

    [**local** z;

    z ← **mod** (**max**(a,b), **min**(a,b));

    if z = 0

        then return **min**(a,b)

        else return Gcd(**min**(a,b),z)]

FIGURE 6-11

```
200   REM GREATEST COMMON DIVISOR—VERSION 6
210   DEF FNG(A,B)
220   Z=FNM(FNX(A,B),FNN(A,B))
230   IF Z=0 THEN FNG=FNN(A,B) ELSE FNG=FNG(FNN(A,B),Z)
240   FNEND
250   REM MOD FUNCTION
260   DEF FNM(A,B)
270   FNM=A−B * INT(A/B)
280   FNEND
290   REM MAX FUNCTION
300   DEF FNX(A,B)
310   IF A<B THEN FNX=B ELSE FNX=A
320   FNEND
330   REM MIN FUNCTION
340   DEF FNN(A,B)
350   IF A>B THEN FNN=B ELSE FNN=A
360   FNEND
```

"Add the first n integers—version 1";

        sum ← 0; integer ← 0;

Loop:

    if integer ≥ n

        then write sum

        else

            [integer ← integer + 1;

            sum ← sum + integer;

            to Loop];

```
5    REM ADD THE FIRST N INTEGERS—VERSION 1
10   S, I=Ø
20   IF I>=N THEN 6Ø
3Ø   I=I+1
4Ø   S=S+I
5Ø   GO TO 2Ø
6Ø   PRINT S
```

(a)

"Add the first *n* integers—version 2";

```
sum ← 0;
for integer ← 1 thru n
    sum ← sum + integer;
write sum;
```

```
5   REM ADD THE FIRST N INTEGERS—VERSION 2
10  S=Ø
60  FOR I=1 TO N
30  S=S+I
40  NEXT I
50  PRINT S
```

(b)

FIGURE 7-2

Note that both (a) and (b) assume that a value for N has been assigned.

"Find the earliest and latest words";

```
e ← w(1); l ← w(1); j ← 2

Loop:
    if j > n
        then write e, "through", l
    else
        [if w(j) < e
            then e ← w(j);
        if w(j) > l
            then l ← w(j);
        j ← j + 1;
        to Loop];
```

```
5    REM FIND THE EARLIEST AND LATEST WORDS
10   E,L=W(1)
20   J=2
30   IF J>N THEN 12Ø
40   IF W(J)<E THEN 8Ø
50   IF W(J)>L THEN 1ØØ
60   J=J+1
70   GO TO 3Ø
80   E=W(J)
90   GO TO 5Ø
100  L=W(J)
110  GO TO 6Ø
120  PRINT E;"THROUGH";L
```

FIGURE 7-6

While some versions of BASIC (such as UTS BASIC and BASIC-Plus) provide default dimensions for arrays, others require a dimension statement in all cases.

Following is an alternative version of this program in BASIC-Plus.

```
5   REM FIND THE EARLIEST AND LATEST WORD
10  E,L=W(1)
20  FOR J=2 TO N
30  IF W(J)<E THEN E=W(J)
40  IF W(J)>L THEN L=W(J)
50  NEXT J
60  PRINT E; "THROUGH";L
```

FIGURE 7-6 (continued)

"Read in and total questionnaire data";

for *i* ← 1 **thru** 20
  for *j* ← 1 **thru** 10
    count (*i,j*) ← 0;

for *j* ← 1 **thru** 10
  for *k* ← 1 **thru** 31
    for *i* ← 1 **thru** 20
      [**read** *mark*;
      count (*i,j*) ← *count* (*i,j*)
                + *mark*];

FIGURE 7-9

```
 10   REM READ IN AND TOTAL QUESTIONNAIRE DATA
 15   DIM C(20,10)
 20   FOR I=1 TO 20
 30   FOR J=1 TO 10
 40   C(I,J)=0
 50   NEXT J
 60   NEXT I
 70   FOR J=1 TO 10
 80   FOR K=1 TO 31
 90   FOR I=1 TO 20
100   INPUT M
110   C(I,J)=C(I,J)+M
120   NEXT I
130   NEXT K
140   NEXT J
```

"Compute average count";

for *i* ← 1 **thru** 20
  [*ave* ← 0;
  for *j* ← 1 **thru** 10
    ave ← *ave* + *count* (*i,j*);
  write "for item", *i*, "ave =", *ave*/10];

FIGURE 7-10

```
500   REM COMPUTE AVERAGE COUNT
510   FOR I=1 TO 20
520   A=0
530   FOR J=1 TO 10
540   A=A+C(I,J)
550   NEXT J
560   PRINT "FOR ITEM";I;"AVE=";  A/10
570   NEXT I
```

B.4 TL TO FORTRAN

Following are transliterations of example programs into FORTRAN IV as implemented on the PDP-10. (Reference document: *Decsystem10 FORTRAN IV Programmer's Reference Manual*, DEC-10-AFDO-D, Digital Equipment Corporation, 1972.)

"Reverse a word";

"This program reads in a word and writes out that word spelled backwards";
  read *word*;
  rev ← "";
  until *word* = ""
    [*rev* ← *word* @ (1,1) & *rev*; *word* ← *word* @ (2)];
  write *rev*;

CHAPTER 5, EXAMPLE 1

```
C     REVERSE A WORD
C     THIS PROGRAM READS IN A WORD AND WRITES
C     OUT THAT WORD SPELLED BACKWARDS
      INTEGER  WORD(10),REV(10),LENGTH,BLANK
      DATA BLANK/1H /
      READ (5,1) (WORD(I),I=1,10)
1     FORMAT (10A1)
      LENGTH=10
5     IF (WORD(LENGTH).NE.BLANK) GO TO 10
      REV(LENGTH)=BLANK
      LENGTH=LENGTH-1
      IF(LENGTH.EQ.0) GO TO 20
      GO TO 5
10    I=1
15    REV(LENGTH+1-I)=WORD(I)
      I=I+1
      IF (I.LE.LENGTH) GO TO 15
20    WRITE (6,2) (REV(I),I=1,10)
2     FORMAT (1H 10A1)
      STOP
```

In FORTRAN string processing is most easily accomplished by unpacking the string into a sequence of individual elements (a one-dimensional array), one character per element. We have taken that approach in the above example, and in Figs. 6-5 and 6-7. Thus, while these program segments are not direct transliterations from TL, they do illustrate one simple approach to string processing in FORTRAN.

"Find greatest common divisor";

"This program reads in two numbers, a and b, and writes out their greatest common divisor found using Euclid's algorithm. The program uses the function **int,** which returns as its value the largest integer not greater than its input. The program assumes that the two numbers read in are positive integers. The program uses variable z as the remainder on division";

> **read** a,b;
> **if** a < b **then to** Bigb **else to** Biga;

Biga:

> z ← a − b * **int**(a/b);
> **if** z=0 **then write** b **else** [a ← z; **to** Bigb]; **done;**

Bigb:

> z ← b − a * **int**(b/a);
> **if** z=0 **then write** a **else** [b ← z; **to** Biga]; **done;**

CHAPTER 5, EXAMPLE 2
Figure 6-1 is identical to Chapter 5, Example 2 except for the first comment.

```
C     FIND THE GREATEST COMMON DIVISOR
C     THIS PROGRAM READS IN TWO NUMBERS . . .
      INTEGER A,B,Z
      READ (5,1) A,B
1     FORMAT (2I5)
      IF (A.LT.B) GO TO 20
30    Z=A−B*(A/B)
      IF (Z.EQ.Ø) GO TO 40
      A=Z
20    Z=B−A*(B/A)
      IF (Z.EQ.Ø) GO TO 50
      B=Z
      GO TO 30
40    WRITE (6,2) B
2     FORMAT (I5)
      STOP
50    WRITE (6,2) A
      STOP
```

"Greatest common divisor — version 2";

> **read** a,b;
> **if** a < b
>> **then** [z ← a; a ← b; b ← z];

Loop:

> z ← a − b * **int**(a/b);
> **if** z=0
>> **then write** b
>> **else** [a ← b; b ← z; **to** Loop];
> **done;**

```
C     GREATEST COMMON DIVISOR — VERSION 2
      INTEGER A,B,Z
      READ (5,1) A,B
1     FORMAT (2I5)
      IF (A.GE.B) GOTO 1Ø
      Z=A
      A=B
      B=Z
1Ø    Z=A−B*(A/B)
      IF (Z.EQ.Ø) GOTO 2Ø
      A=B
      B=Z
      GOTO 1Ø
2Ø    WRITE (6,2) B
2     FORMAT (I5)
      STOP
```

FIGURE 6-2

"Greatest common divisor—version 3";

    read a,b;

    z ← a;

    if a < b

      then [a ← b; b ← z];

    until z = 0

      [z ← a − b * **int**(a/b);

        a ← b; b ← z];

    write a;

FIGURE 6-4

```
C     GREATEST COMMON DIVISOR—VERSION 3
      INTEGER A,B,Z
      READ (5,1) A,B
1     FORMAT (2I5)
      Z=A
      IF (A.GE.B) GOTO 1Ø
      A=B
      B=Z
1Ø    IF (Z.EQ.Ø) GOTO 2Ø
      Z=A−B * (A/B)
      A=B
      B=Z
      GOTO 1Ø
2Ø    WRITE (6,2) A
2     FORMAT (I5)
      STOP
```

(Both of the above FORTRAN programs can be shortened without changing their effect. Do you see how?)

"Reverse a word—version 2";

    read word;

    rev ← "";

    for i ← 1 **thru** #word

      [rev ← word **@** (i,1) & rev];

    write rev;

FIGURE 6-5

```
C     REVERSE A WORD—VERSION 2
      INTEGER WORD(1Ø),REV(1Ø),LENGTH,BLANK
      DATA BLANK/1H /
      READ (5,1) (WORD(I),I=1,1Ø)
1     FORMAT (1ØA1)
      DO 1Ø I=1,1Ø
      LENGTH=11−I
      IF (WORD(LENGTH).NE.BLANK) GOTO 11
1Ø    REV(LENGTH)=BLANK
      GOTO 2Ø
11    DO 15 I=1,LENGTH
15    REV(LENGTH+1−I)=WORD(I)
2Ø    WRITE (6,2) (REV(I),I=1,1Ø)
2     FORMAT (1H 1ØA1)
      STOP
```

"Greatest common divisor—version 4";

Gcd(a,b):

    [**local** z; z ← a;

    if a < b

      then [a ← b; b ← z];

    until z = 0

      [z ← a − b * **int**(a/b);

        a ← b; b ← z];

    return a]

FIGURE 6-6

```
C     GREATEST COMMON DIVISOR—VERSION 4
      INTEGER FUNCTION GCD(A,B)
      INTEGER A,B,Z
      Z=A
      IF (A.GE.B) GOTO 1Ø
      A=B
      B=Z
1Ø    IF (Z.EQ.Ø) GOTO 2Ø
      Z=A−B * (A/B)
      A=B
      B=Z
      GOTO 1Ø
2Ø    GCD=A
      RETURN
```

"Reverse a word—version 3";

Reverse(word):

    [**local** rev; rev ← "";
    until word = ""
        [rev ← word @ (1,1) & rev;
        word ← word @ (2)];
    return rev]

FIGURE 6-7

```
C    REVERSE A WORD—VERSION 3
     SUBROUTINE REVERSE(WORD,REV)
     INTEGER WORD(1Ø),REV(1Ø),LENGTH,BLANK
     DATA BLANK/1H /
     LENGTH=1Ø
5    IF (WORD(LENGTH).NE.BLANK) GO TO 1Ø
     REV(LENGTH)=BLANK
     LENGTH=LENGTH−1
     IF(LENGTH.EQ.Ø) GO TO 2Ø
     GO TO 5
1Ø   I=1
15   REV(LENGTH+1−I)=WORD(I)
     I=I+1
     IF (I.LE.LENGTH) GO TO 15
2Ø   RETURN
```

The FORTRAN language includes no concept of recursive functions, and so there is no simple transliteration of Figs. 6-8, 6-9, and 6-11 into FORTRAN.

"Add the first n integers—version 1";
    sum ← 0; integer ← 0;

Loop:
    if integer ≥ n
        then write sum
        else
            [integer ← integer+1;
        sum ← sum+integer;
        to Loop];

(a)

```
C    ADD THE FIRST N INTEGERS—VERSION 1
     INTEGER SUM
     SUM=Ø
     INT=Ø
1Ø   IF (INT.GE.N) GOTO 6Ø
     INT=INT+1
     SUM=SUM+INT
     GOTO 1Ø
6Ø   WRITE (6,2) SUM
2    FORMAT (I5)
     STOP
```

"Add the first n integers—version 2";
    sum ← 0;
    for integer ← 1 **thru** n
        sum ← sum+integer;
    write sum;

(b)

```
C    ADD THE FIRST N INTEGERS—VERSION 2
     INTEGER SUM
     SUM=Ø
     DO 2Ø INT=1,N
2Ø   SUM=SUM+INT
     WRITE (6,2) SUM
2    FORMAT (I5)
     STOP
```

FIGURE 7-2
Note that both of the above program segments assume that a value for N has been assigned.

"Find the earliest and latest words";

$e \leftarrow w(1); \ l \leftarrow w(1); \ j \leftarrow 2$

Loop:

  if $j > n$

    then write e, "through", l

    else

      [**if** $w(j) < e$

        then $e \leftarrow w(j);$

      if $w(j) > l$

        then $l \leftarrow w(j);$

      $j \leftarrow j+1;$

      to *Loop*];

FIGURE 7-6

```
C    FIND THE EARLIEST AND LATEST WORDS
     REAL L
     DIMENSION W(10)
     N=10
     F=W(1)
     L=W(1)
     J=2
30   IF (J.GT.N) GOTO 40
     IF (W(J).LT.E) E=W(J)
     IF (W(J).GT.L) L=W(J)
     J=J+1
     GO TO 30
40   WRITE (6,2) E,L
2    FORMAT (I5,9H THROUGH 15)
     STOP
```

"Read in and total questionnaire data";

for $i \leftarrow 1$ **thru** 20

  for $j \leftarrow 1$ **thru** 10

    count $(i,j) \leftarrow 0;$

for $j \leftarrow 1$ **thru** 10

  for $k \leftarrow 1$ **thru** 31

    for $i \leftarrow 1$ **thru** 20

      [**read** *mark*;

      count $(i,j) \leftarrow count \ (i,j)$

               $+ mark];$

FIGURE 7-9

```
C    READ IN AND TOTAL QUESTIONNAIRE DATA
     INTEGER COUNT(20,10)
     DO 50 I=1,20
     DO 50 J=1,10
50   COUNT(I,J)=0
     DO 60 J=1,10
     DO 60 K=1,31
     DO 60 I=1,20
     READ (5,1) MARK
1    FORMAT (I1)
60   COUNT(I,J)=COUNT(I,J)+MARK
     STOP
```

"Compute average count";

for $i \leftarrow 1$ **thru** 20

  [$ave \leftarrow 0;$

    for $j \leftarrow 1$ **thru** 10

      $ave \leftarrow ave + count \ (i,j);$

    write "for item", i, "ave=", $ave/10$];

FIGURE 7-10

```
C    COMPUTE AVERAGE COUNT
     DO 150 I=1,20
        AVE=0
        DO 160 J=1,10
160        AVE=AVE+COUNT(I,J)
        AVE=AVE/10
150     WRITE (6,2) I,AVE
2    FORMAT (11H FOR ITEM# ,I2,7H  AVE= ,F5.1)
     STOP
```

B.5 TL TO PL/1

Following are transliterations of example programs into PL/1 (F), as run under OS/360, version 5.4. [Reference document: *IBM System/360 Operating System PL1(F) Language Reference Manual*, GC28-8201-3, IBM Corporation, 1970.]

"Reverse a word";

"This program reads in a word and writes out that word spelled backwards";

    read *word;*

    rev ← "";
    until *word*="" [*rev* ← *word* **@** (1,1) **&** *rev; word* ← *word* **@** (2)];
    write *rev;*

CHAPTER 5, EXAMPLE 1

```
/ * REVERSE A WORD,
     THIS PROGRAM READS IN A WORD AND
        WRITES OUT THAT WORD SPELLED BACKWARDS * /
START: PROCEDURE OPTIONS(MAIN);
        DECLARE (WORD,REV) CHARACTER(10) VARYING;
        GET LIST(WORD);
        REV=";
        DO WHILE (WORD  ¬=");
           REV=SUBSTR(WORD,1,1)‖REV;
           WORD=SUBSTR(WORD,2);
        END;
        PUT LIST(REV);
END START;
```

"Find greatest common divisor";

"This program reads in two numbers, *a* and *b*, and writes out their greatest common divisor found using Euclid's algorithm. The program uses the function **int**, which returns as its value the largest integer not greater than its input. The program assumes that the two numbers read in are positive integers. The program uses variable *z* as the remainder on division";

    read *a,b;*
    if *a* < *b* **then to** *Bigb* **else to** *Biga;*

Biga:
    z ← *a* − *b* * **int**(*a/b*);
    if *z*=0 **then write** *b* **else** [*a* ← *z;* **to** *Bigb*]; **done;**

Bigb:
    z ← *b* − *a* * **int**(*b/a*);
    if *z*=0 **then write** *a* **else** [*b* ← *z;* **to** *Biga*]; **done;**

CHAPTER 5, EXAMPLE 2
Figure 6-1 is identical to Chapter 5, Example 2 except for the first comment.

```
/ * FIND GREATEST COMMON DIVISOR
     THIS PROGRAM READS IN TWO NUMBERS . . . * /
START: PROCEDURE OPTIONS(MAIN);
        DECLARE (A,B) FIXED;
        GET LIST(A,B);
        IF  A < B THEN
                   BIGA: DO;  Z=MOD(A,B);
                        IF  Z=0 THEN PUT LIST(B);
                              ELSE DO; A=Z;
                                   GO TO BIGB;
                   END BIGA;
                   ELSE
                   BIGB: DO;  Z=MOD(B,A);
                        IF  Z=0 THEN PUT LIST(A);
                                ELSE DO;  B=Z;
                                   GO TO BIGA;
                   END BIGB;
END START;
```

"Greatest common divisor—version 2";

```
        read a,b;
        if a < b
            then [z ← a; a ← b; b ← z];
Loop:
        z ← a − b * int(a/b);
        if z = 0
            then write b
            else [a ← b; b ← z; to Loop];
        done;
```

FIGURE 6-2

```
/ * GREATEST COMMON DIVISOR—VERSION 2 * /
GCD:PROCEDURE OPTIONS(MAIN);
DECLARE(A,B,Z)FIXED;
GET LIST(A,B);
IF A < B THEN DO;Z=A;A=B;B=Z;END;
LOOP: Z=MOD(A,B);
IF Z=0 THEN PUT LIST(B);
        ELSE DO;A=B;B=Z;GO TO LOOP;END;
END GCD;
```

"Greatest common divisor—version 3";

```
        read a,b;
        z ← a;
        if a < b
            then [a ← b; b ← z];
        until z = 0
            [z ← a − b * int(a/b);
             a ← b; b ← z];
        write a;
```

FIGURE 6-4

```
/ * GREATEST COMMON DIVISOR—VERSION 3 * /
GCD: PROCEDURE OPTIONS(MAIN);
DECLARE(A,B,Z)FIXED;
GET LIST (A,B);
IF A < B THEN DO;Z=A;A=B;B=Z; END;
DO WHILE (Z¬=0);
        Z=MOD(A,B);
        A=B;B=Z;END;
PUT LIST(A);
END GCD;
```

"Reverse a word—version 2";

```
        read word;
        rev ← "";
        for i ← 1 thru #word
            [rev ← word @ (i,1) & rev];
        write rev;
```

FIGURE 6-5

```
/ * REVERSE A WORD—VERSION 2 * /
START:PROCEDURE OPTIONS(MAIN);
        DECLARE(WORD,REV)CHARACTER(10) VARYING,
            I FIXED;
        GET LIST(WORD); REV=";
        DO I=1 TO LENGTH(WORD);
        REV=SUBSTR(WORD,I,1)||REV;
        END;
        PUT LIST(REV);
END START;
```

"Greatest common divisor—version 4";

Gcd(a,b):

```
        [local z; z ← a;
        if a < b
            then [a ← b; b ← z];
        until z = 0
            [z ← a − b * int(a/b);
             a ← b; b ← z];
        return a]
```

FIGURE 6-6

```
/ * GREATEST COMMON DIVISOR—VERSION 4 * /
GCD:PROCEDURE(A,B);
        DECLARE(A,B,Z)FIXED;
        IF A < B THEN DO; Z=A;A=B;B=Z;END;
        DO WHILE(Z¬=0);
            Z=MOD(A,B);A=B;B=Z;END;
            RETURN(A);
END GCD;
```

"Reverse a word—version 3";

Reverse(word):

    [**local** *rev*; *rev* ← "";

    until *word* = ""

        [*rev* ← *word* @ (1,1) & *rev*;

        word ← *word* @ (2)];

    return *rev*]

FIGURE 6-7

```
/*REVERSE A WORD—VERSION 3*/
REVERSE:PROCEDURE(WORD) RETURNS (CHARACTER(10) VARYING);
        DECLARE(WORD,REV) CHARACTER(10)VARYING;
        REV='';
        DO WHILE(WORD¬='');
              REV=SUBSTR(WORD,1,1)||REV;
              WORD=SUBSTR(WORD,2);
        END;
        RETURN(REV);
END REVERSE;
```

"Greatest common divisor—version 5";

Gcd(a,b):

    [**if** *a* < *b*

    then [**return** *Gcd*(b,a)]

    else

        [*a* ← *a* − *b* * **int**(a/b);

        if *a* = 0

            then return *b*

            else return *Gcd*(b,a)]]

FIGURE 6-8

```
/ * GREATEST COMMON DIVISOR—VERSION 5 * /
GCD:PROCEDURE(A,B)RECURSIVE RETURNS(FIXED);
      DECLARE(A,B)FIXED;
      IF A < B THEN RETURN (GCD(B,A));
            ELSE DO; A=MOD(A,B);
                  IF A=0 THEN RETURN(B);
                        ELSE RETURN(GCD(B,A));
END GCD;
```

"Reverse a word—version 4";

Reverse(word):

    [**if** *word* = ""

    then return ""

    else return

        Reverse(word @ (2)) & *word* @ (1,1)]

FIGURE 6-9

```
/ * REVERSE A WORD—VERSION 4 * /
REVERSE:PROCEDURE(WORD)RECURSIVE RETURNS(CHARACTER(10) VARYING);
        DECLARE(WORD,REV)CHARACTER(10)VARYING;
        IF WORD=''
              THEN RETURN('');
              ELSE RETURN(REVERSE(SUBSTR(WORD,2))||SUBSTR(WORD,1,1));
END REVERSE;
```

"Greatest common divisor—version 6";

Gcd(a,b):

    [**local** *z*;

    z ← **mod** (**max**(a,b), **min**(a,b));

    if *z* = 0

        then return **min**(a,b)

        else return *Gcd*(**min**(a,b),z)]

FIGURE 6-11

```
/ * GREATEST COMMON DIVISOR—VERSION 6 * /
GCD:PROCEDURE(A,B)RECURSIVE;
      DECLARE(A,B,Z)FIXED;
      Z=MOD(MAX(A,B),MIN(A,B));
      IF Z=0 THEN RETURN(MIN(A,B));
            ELSE RETURN(GCD(MIN(A,B),Z));
END GCD;
```

"Add the first *n* integers—version 1";

    sum ←0; *integer* ←0;

Loop:
    if *integer* ≥ *n*
      then write *sum*
      else
        [*integer* ←*integer*+1;
        sum ←*sum*+*integer*;
        to *Loop*];

```
/ * ADD THE FIRST N INTEGERS — VERSION 1 * /
START: PROCEDURE;
            DECLARE (SUM,INTEGER) FIXED;
            SUM=0;  INTEGER=0;
            LOOP: IF INTEGER >=N
                THEN PUT LIST(SUM);
                ELSE DO; INTEGER=INTEGER+1;
                        SUM=SUM+INTEGER;
                        GO TO LOOP;
END START;
```

(*a*)

"Add the first *n* integers—version 2";

    sum ←0;
    for *integer* ←1 **thru** *n*
      sum ←*sum*+*integer*;
    write *sum;*

```
/ * ADD THE FIRST N INTEGERS — VERSION 2 * /
START:PROCEDURE;
            DECLARE(SUM,INTEGER) FIXED;
            SUM=0;
            DO INTEGER=1 TO N; SUM=SUM+INTEGER;END;
            PUT LIST(SUM);
END START;
```

(*b*)

FIGURE 7-2

"Find the earliest and latest words";

    e ←*w*(1); *l* ←*w*(1); *j* ←2

Loop:
    if *j* > *n*
      then write *e*, "through", *l*
      else
        [**if** *w*(*j*) < *e*
          then *e* ←*w*(*j*);
        if *w*(*j*) > *l*
          then *l* ←*w*(*j*);
        j ←*j*+1;
        to *Loop*];

```
/ * FIND THE EARLIEST AND LATEST WORDS * /
WORDS: PROCEDURE;
        E=W(1);L=W(1);J=2;
        LOOP: IF J>N THEN PUT LIST(E,'THROUGH',L);
                ELSE DO;
                        IF W(J)<E THEN E=W(J);
                        IF W(J)>L THEN L=W(J);
                        J=J+1;GO TO LOOP;
END WORDS;
```

FIGURE 7-6

"Read in and total questionnaire data";
for *i* ←1 **thru** 20
  for *j* ←1 **thru** 10
    count (*i,j*) ←0;

for *j* ←1 **thru** 10
  for *k* ←1 **thru** 31
    for *i* ←1 **thru** 20
      [**read** *mark;*
      count (*i,j*) ←*count* (*i,j*)
             + *mark*];

```
/ * READ IN AND TOTAL QUESTIONNAIRE DATA * /
READIN: PROCEDURE;
CLEAR: DO I=1 TO 20; DO J=1 TO 10;COUNT(I,J)=0;
            END CLEAR;
            DO J=1 TO 10; DO K=1 TO 31; DO I=1 TO 20;
            GET LIST(MARK); COUNT(I,J)=COUNT(I,J)+MARK;
END READIN;
```

FIGURE 7-9

"Compute average count";

for *i* ← 1 **thru** 20
   [*ave* ← 0;
   for *j* ← 1 **thru** 10
      ave ← *ave* + *count* (*i,j*);
   write "for item", *i,* "ave=", *ave*/10];

FIGURE 7-10

```
/ * COMPUTE AVERAGE COUNT * /
COMP: PROCEDURE;
        DO I=1 TO 20;
          AVE=0;
          DO J=1 TO 10;
                AVE=AVE+COUNT(I,J);
          END;
          PUT LIST('FOR ITEM',I,'AVE=',AVE/10);
END COMP;
```

POSTSCRIPT

The proper role of a postscript is to put in context that which has gone before. We can do that either by summarizing and elaborating on what has been said or by saying those things that we should have said but did not (or, more charitably, did not know how to). Let us try the latter.

In some strange but very real sense, there is a kind of magic in the air, a new power to manipulate symbols and draw logical conclusions at a speed and quantity far greater than ever known before. This power can be used as a "super-system," an amplifier of bureaucracy, or it can be used as a "hand tool" by many people living out their daily lives. Perhaps, if we are fortunate, it will be used as both.

Twenty years from now the computer (as a generally used device) will be almost twice as old as it is today. Twenty years from now almost everyone will be using a computer, in the sense that today almost everyone drives an automobile or flies on commercial airlines. Learning to communicate with the computer may have been very painful for you, but that pain was as nothing compared to the same undertaking in the primitive state of computing 20 years ago. And 20 years from now, there will be at least a similar increase in ease. Development of highly sophisticated packaged procedures and of specialized tools (hardware/software combinations) for specific jobs will make the power of computing many times more accessible to all.

Twenty years from now, perhaps every detail that you have learned will be outdated. Perhaps, also, if we have succeeded in what we tried to accomplish here, the basic ideas that you have learned will still be true. We hope so. For as Idries Shah so bluntly puts it in *Reflections:*

"To drown in treacle is just as unpleasant as to drown in mud.

"People today are in danger of drowning in information; but, because they have been taught that information is useful, they are more willing to drown than they need be.

"If they could handle information, they would not have to drown at all."

INDEX